BUSINESS MATHEMATICS
WITH STATISTICS

Dexter J Booth
John K Turner
University of Huddersfield

M&E
PITMAN
PUBLISHING

London · Hong Kong · Johannesburg · Melbourne · Singapore · Washington DC

PITMAN PUBLISHING
128 Long Acre, London WC2E 9AN
Tel: 0171 447 2000   Fax: 0171 240 5771

A Division of Pearson Professional Limited

First published in Great Britain 1996

© Pearson Professional Limited 1996

British Library Cataloguing in Publication Data
A CIP catalogue record for this book can be obtained from the British Library

ISBN 0 7121 0868 8

10 9 8 7 6 5 4 3 2 1

Typeset by Mathematical Composition Setters Ltd, Salisbury, Wiltshire
Printed and bound in Great Britain by Bell and Bain Ltd. Glasgow

The Publishers' policy is to use paper manufactured from sustainable forests.

BUSINESS MATHEMATICS
WITH STATISTICS

**Books are to be returned on or before
the last date below.**

CONTENTS

INTRODUCTION

In the commercial world, business problems are always posed as prose descriptions with a narrative that mixes objective fact with descriptive passages. This is the natural language of the business world where humans communicate their ideas within a commercial and financial context. The solutions to many of the problems posed in this manner can be found only through a quantitative assessment that can only be accessed via a mathematical framework. As a consequence, the student of business must develop abilities in three broad areas:

- The conversion of qualitative and quantitative descriptions into mathematical form
- The use of mathematics to discover consequences and to produce predictions
- The conversion of the mathematical consequences and predictions back into the less formal prose of the business world.

Any course in business mathematics should reflect this sequence of events and aim to assist the student in developing an acuity with each area.

In line with this philosophy, the general development of the material in the book will be problem driven with the mathematics introduced on a need to know basis. The only exception to this form of presentation will be in the first chapter where the elementary basics of arithmetic and algebra are displayed – albeit there, within a financial and commercial context as well.

Because the eventual aim of the reader is to pass an examination it is essential that the student have access to examination type questions. These are provided throughout the book where a full, descriptive solution is given. Additional such questions are included in the form of Exercises for the student to work through themselves, this time with solutions given at the end of the book.

Dexter J Booth
John K Turner
The University of Huddersfield 1996

1

VARIABLES, RELATIONSHIPS AND GRAPHS

When you have completed this chapter you will be able to:

- simplify and factorize algebraic expressions
- determine straight-line equations
- understand logarithms
- solve linear and quadratic equations
- solve sets of simultaneous equations
- reduce problems to linear form

In this chapter, the algebraic foundation is laid for many of the mathematical topics in this book.

1.1 FUNCTIONS, GRAPHS AND EQUATIONS

If x and y are two quantities, then y is said to be a **function of** x if there is a *relationship* between y and x, which ensures that the value of y can be determined for each value of x. Often this relationship takes the form of an equation. For example

$$y = 3x + 2$$

$$y = 2x^2 - 4x + 10$$

Graphs provide a useful way of visualising such relationships, i.e. functions, as the next example shows.

EXAMPLE 1.1.1

(a) Plot the graph of the function

$$y = 3x + 2$$

in the range $x = -2$ to 4.

(b) Plot the graph of the function

$$y = 210x - 3x^2$$

in the range $x = 0$ to 80.
   Hence, solve the equation

$$210x - 3x^2 = 75x$$

Solution 1.1.1(a)

To plot the graph, we produce a table of values as follows:

x	-2	-1	0	1	2	3	4
$y = 3x + 2$	-4	-1	2	5	8	11	14

For example, if $x = -2$, then $y = 3 \times (-2) + 2 = -6 + 2 = -4$.

You quickly realise that since x increases by the same amount each time, so does y. The graph is therefore a straight line, as shown in Figure 1.1.1.

Note: Since the graph is a straight line, you will appreciate that it is only necessary to plot two points, through which the line can be drawn. In fact, any equation of the form

$$y = ax + b \qquad a, b \text{ are constants}$$

has a straight line graph, and we will look at such equations in more detail later.

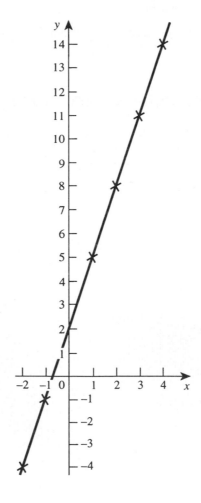

Figure 1.1.1

Solution 1.1.1(b)

This graph entails more work than the graph in (a), since the graph is a curve, rather than a line, because of the x^2 term of the equation. Again, we start with a table of values, and it is reasonable to initially use $x = 0$, 10, 20, etc.

x	0	10	20	30	40	50	60	70
$y = 210x - 3x^2$	0	1800	3000	3600	3600	3000	1800	0

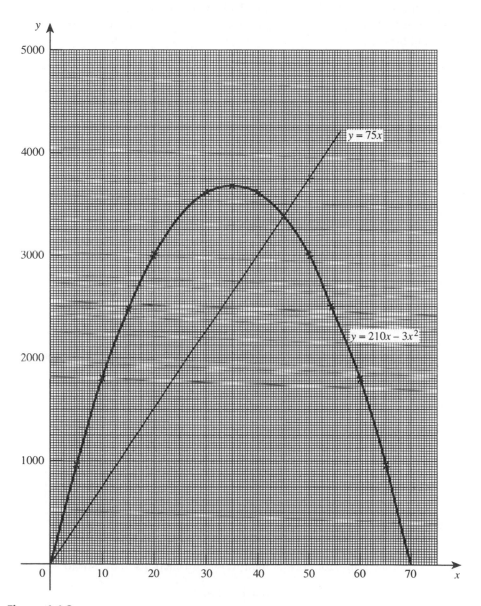

Figure 1.1.2

Care is needed in calculating the y values. For example, if $x = 20$

$$y = 210 \times 20 - 3 \times 20^2 = 4200 - 1200 = 3000 \qquad \text{(only the value of } x \text{ is squared)}$$

If the points calculated so far are plotted, as shown in Figure 1.1.2, then you can see that there are some difficulties in drawing a smooth curve. Between 0 and 10, 10 and 20, 50 and 60, 60 and 70, we would be guessing at the shape. Moreover, we are not certain where the maximum of the curve occurs, although it is obviously between 30 and 40, so we tabulate some extra points:

x	5	15	35	55	65
$y = 210x - 3x^2$	975	2475	3675	2475	975

Note: The vertical scale for the graph is chosen so that each small square is 25 units. This scale ensures that all the above points are easy to plot.

Finally, we need to solve the equation

$$210x - 3x^2 = 75x$$

We do so by plotting $y = 75x$ on the above graph. The graph is a straight line and if $x = 0$, $y = 0$, and if $x = 50$, $y = 3750$. The line intersects the curve at $x = 0$ and $x = 45$.

Conclusion: The equation has solutions 0 and 45.

EXERCISES 1.1

1 (a) Plot the graph of the function

$$y = 4x^2 - 12x + 16$$

in the range $x = -3$ to 4.
Hence, solve the equation

$$4x^2 - 12x + 16 = 7$$

(b) Plot the function

$$y = 180x - 2x^2$$

in the range $x = 0$ to 90.
By plotting another function on the same graph, solve the equation

$$180x - 2x^2 = 50x + 1400$$

2 Plot a separate graph for each of the following functions in the stated range:

(a) $y = 4x^3 - 2x + 4$ x in range -2 to 3
(b) $y = (x - 1)(2x + 3)$ x in range -5 to 4

1.2 STRAIGHT-LINE GRAPHS

When the function $y = 3x + 2$ was plotted in Example 1.1.1, a straight-line graph was obtained. In fact, we can show that any equation

$y = ax + b$ where a, b are constants

has a straight-line graph, and conversely any straight-line graph corresponds to an equation of this form.

Any straight line can be specified in one of two ways:

- we can specify *one* point on the line (normally the point at which the line cuts the y-axis) and the *slope* of the line.
- we can specify *two points* on the line

Figure 1.2.1 illustrates these two approaches.

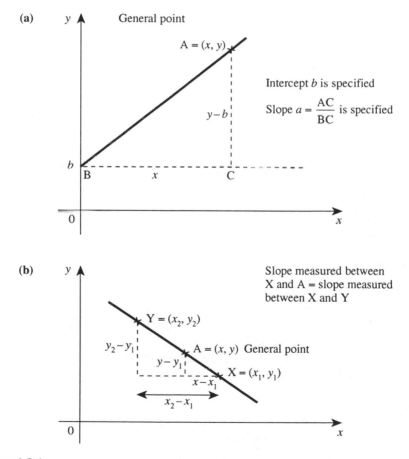

Figure 1.2.1

In graph (a), the *slope a* of the line and the *intercept b* of the line with the y-axis are specified, where

$$a = \frac{\text{increase in } y}{\text{increase in } x}$$ measured between any two points on the line – it is always the same

and *b* is the value of *y* at which the line cuts the *y*-axis. Using the general point A = (x, y) and the point B = $(0, b)$

$$a = \frac{\text{increase in } y}{\text{increase in } x} = \frac{y - b}{x - 0}$$

Therefore

$$y - b = ax$$

and we obtain

General equation of a straight-line with given slope and intercept

$$y = ax + b \qquad a = \textbf{slope}, \ b = \textbf{intercept} \qquad\qquad (1.2.1)$$

Such an equation is called a **linear equation**.

Look now at Figure (b) above, where X = (x_1, y_1) and Y = (x_2, y_2) are two given points on the line. If A = (x, y) is a general point on the line, then

Slope measured between X and A = Slope measured between X and Y

and therefore we obtain

General equation of the straight-line through two points (x_1, y_1) and (x_2, y_2)

$$\frac{y - y_1}{x - x_1} = \frac{y_2 - y_1}{x_2 - x_1} \qquad\qquad (1.2.2)$$

The next example illustrates the use of this general equation.

EXAMPLE 1.2.1

(a) Find the equation of the line passing through the points $(2, -7)$ and $(8, 2)$.
(b) The amount *x* units of a commodity purchased daily by consumers is dependent upon the selling price £*p*/unit, and it has been observed that 20 units are demanded daily at a price of £300/unit, whereas 30 units are demanded daily at a price of £250/unit. Assuming that the relationship between *p* and *x* is *linear*, find the equation for *p* in terms of *x*.

Solution 1.2.1(a)

These problems are direct exercises in using equation (1.2.2). It does not matter which point is (x_1, y_1) and which is (x_2, y_2). Let

$$x_1 = 2, \ y_1 = -7 \text{ and } x_2 = 8, \ y_2 = 2$$

Therefore, from equation (1.2.2)

$$\frac{y - (-7)}{x - 2} = \frac{2 - (-7)}{8 - 2}$$

$$\frac{y + 7}{x - 2} = \frac{9}{6}$$

$$6(y + 7) = 9(x - 2) \qquad \text{rearranging}$$
$$6y + 42 = 9x - 18 \qquad \text{expanding brackets}$$
$$6y = 9x - 60$$
$$y = 3x/2 - 10$$

Solution 1.2.1(b)

This is similar to (a), except that p now replaces y. Therefore, equation (1.2.2) becomes

$$\frac{p - p_1}{x - x_1} = \frac{p_2 - p_1}{x_2 - x_1}$$

Looking at the given pairs of values, let

$$x_1 = 20, \ p_1 = 300 \quad \text{and} \quad x_2 = 30, \ p_2 = 250$$

Therefore

$$\frac{p - 300}{x - 20} = \frac{250 - 300}{30 - 20} = \frac{-50}{10} = -5$$
$$p - 300 = -5(x - 20)$$
$$p = -5x + 100 + 300$$
$$p = 400 - 5x \tag{1.2.3}$$

Note: This price/demand relationship, based upon the assumption of linearity and the two pairs of price/demand values, could now be used to *forecast* the demand at *any* price. For example, if the price is £180/unit, then using equation (1.2.3)

$$180 = 400 - 5x$$
$$5x = 220$$
$$x = 44 \text{ units/day (forecasted demand)}$$

EXERCISES 1.2

With the exception of question 2 (a), assume that each line has the equation

$$y = ax + b$$

1 Find the equation of the line with

(a) intercept 20 on the y-axis and slope -3,

(b) intercept -5 on the y-axis and slope 4.

2 (a) The amount x units of a commodity purchased weekly by consumers is dependent upon the selling price £p/unit, and it is assumed that the relationship between p and x is linear.

Use eqn. 1.2.2 to find the equation relating p to x for each of the following sets of observed data:

(i)	p (£/unit)	150	60
	x (No. of units demanded weekly)	50	80
(ii)	p (£/unit)	135	90
	x (No. of units demanded weekly)	10	15

(b) For each of the following pairs of points, find the equation of the line passing through them:

(i) $(12, 6)$ and $(20, 18)$ (ii) $(4, -25)$ and $(8, -32)$

3 (a) Find the equation of the line which is parallel to the line

$$y = 3x - 20$$

and passes through the point $(2, 10)$.

(b) Find the equation of the line parallel to

$$y = 10 - 4x$$

which passes through the point $(-5, 2)$.

1.3 ALGEBRAIC EXPRESSIONS, INDICES AND LOGARITHMS

Each algebraic expression, such as

$$3x^3 + 2x - 3 \qquad 2a^2 - 4ab + b^3$$

is a **sum of terms**. Since the first expression above is

$$3x^3 + 2x + (-3)$$

the terms are $3x^3$, $2x$ and -3. The numbers 3, 2 and -3, respectively, are called the **coefficients** of the terms. The second expression is

$$2a^2 + (-4ab) + b^3$$

and so the terms are $2a^2$, $-4ab$ and b^3 (the last term is $1 \times b^3$), and have coefficients 2, -4 and 1, respectively. It is not actually necessary to rewrite the expression as a sum, provided that $-$ signs are included as part of the term. So

$$3a^2b^4 - 4abc - 6c^2$$

has terms $3a^2b^4$, $-4abc$, $-6c^2$.

Sometimes, expressions can be simplified by combining *like terms*. These are terms involving the same unknowns, in the same combination, but possibly different coefficients. They are combined by combining the coefficients. Therefore

$$4ab + 3a^2 - 6ab \qquad\qquad \text{becomes} \quad -2ab + 3a^2$$

$$2x^3y + 5x^3y - 8xy^2 - 4xy^2 \qquad \text{becomes} \quad 7x^3y - 12xy^2$$

Indices and index laws

Another way in which algebraic expressions can be simplified is by combining *powers* of the *same* unknown together. There are convenient rules for doing this. Consider, for example, the product

$$a^3 \times a^5$$

We know that this means

$$\underbrace{(a \times a \times a)}_{a^3} \times \underbrace{(a \times a \times a \times a \times a)}_{a^5} = \underbrace{a \times a \times a \times a \times a \times a \times a \times a}_{a^8}$$

and so the answer is $a^{3+5} = a^8$. The indices 3 and 5 are therefore *added when multiplying*. If we consider

$$a^5/a^3$$

then this is

$$\frac{a \times a \times a \times a \times a}{a \times a \times a} = \frac{a^5}{a^3}$$

which reduces to $a^{5-3} = a^2$. The indices are therefore *subtracted when dividing*. Finally, consider

$$(a^2)^3$$

This is

$$a^2 \times a^2 \times a^2 = a^4 \times a^2 = a^6 \qquad\qquad \text{powers are added when multiplying}$$

and so the indices 2 and 3 have been *multiplied* to get the final answer. These rules can be summarised thus:

Index laws

$$a^m a^n = a^{m+n}$$

$$\frac{a^m}{a^n} = a^{m-n} \qquad\qquad\qquad\qquad (1.3.1)$$

$$(a^m)^n = a^{mn}$$

So far we have considered positive, whole number powers. However, the following notations are also commonly used:

a^{-n} is used to denote $1/a^n$

$a^{1/n}$ is used to denote $\sqrt[n]{a}$ the nth root of a

$a^{m/n}$ is used to denote $(\sqrt[n]{a})^m$ think of this as $(a^{1/n})^m$

So, for example

$4^{-2} = 1/4^2 = 1/16$

$8^{1/3} = \sqrt[3]{8} = 2$

$64^{3/2} = (64^{1/2})^3 = (\sqrt[2]{64})^3 = 8^3 = 512$

The index laws (1.3.1) can be shown to be true for *all* indices. For example

$x^{2/3}x^{1/2} = x^{(2/3+1/2)} = x^{7/6}$

$x^{-3}x^8 = x^{-3+8} = x^5$ add indices when multiplying

Note: Any scientific calculator will have a key, usually denoted by x^y or y^x, which will calculate powers.

Removing brackets

Sometimes algebraic expressions involve brackets and it is useful to expand the brackets by multiplying out. Consider the expression

$2x^3(4x^2 - 2x + 8)$

When the bracket is removed, the quantity outside the bracket must be multiplied by *every* term inside the bracket. Thus, the expression becomes

$2x^3 \times 4x^2 - 2x^3 \times 2x + 2x^3 \times 8$

$= 8x^5 - 4x^4 + 16x^3$ multiply coefficients and add indices when multiplying

For the expression

$(2x^4 - 3x^2)(4x^3 - 2x)$

every term in the first bracket must be multiplied by every term in the second as shown. We therefore obtain

$2x^4 \times 4x^3 - 2x^4 \times 2x - 3x^2 \times 4x^3 + 3x^2 \times 2x$

$= 8x^7 - 4x^5 - 12x^5 + 6x^3$

$= 8x^7 - 16x^5 + 6x^3$ combine like terms

We conclude this section with a discussion of logarithms, which are themselves indices.

Logarithms

Logarithms occur when positive numbers are expressed as **powers** of some chosen positive number, called a **base number**. More specifically, given the positive base number b, the logarithm of any positive number N to the base b, denoted by $\log_b N$ is the power to which b has to be raised to equal N. Put another way

> **If $N = b^L$ then $L = \log_b N$**

For the purposes of illustration, consider the base 10 and the numbers 10000, 0.01, $\sqrt[3]{10}$. To find the logarithm to the base 10 of each of these numbers, it is necessary to express each number as a power of 10. Thus

$10000 = 10^4$ $\log_{10} 10000 = 4$ the power to which 10 must be raised to give 10000

$0.01 = 1/100 = 10^{-2}$ $\log_{10} 0.01 = -2$

$\sqrt[3]{10} = 10^{1/3}$ (by definition) $\log_{10} \sqrt[3]{10} = 1/3$

For the numbers considered, the logarithm can be determined without the need for a calculator. However, any scientific calculator will have a $\log_{10}$ key (usually denoted by **log**) which will calculate the log of any number. For example,

$\log_{10} 2.5 = 0.3979$ enter 2.5 and press the 'log' key

(How such a logarithm is calculated is by no means obvious, but we will not go into details here.) The answer can be checked by using the powers of 10 key (usually denoted by **10^x**). You will find that

$10^{0.3979} = 2.5$

(The way in which such a power, which is not fractional, is calculated is also by no means obvious.) As a further example, consider the base 8 and the numbers 512, 1/64, 16, say:

$512 = 8^3$ $\log_8 512 = 3$

$1/64 = 1/8^2 = 8^{-2}$ $\log_8 1/64 = -2$

$16 = 2^4 = (\sqrt[3]{8})^4 = 8^{4/3}$ $\log_8 16 = 4/3$

The last of these calculations is the trickiest. In order to express 16 as a power of 8, we have to observe that 2 provides the link between the two numbers, since 16 is an easy power of 2, and 2 is an easy root of the base 8.

Finally, we consider some laws for logarithms which will be useful later. We will not attempt to prove them.

Logarithm laws

$\log a^p = p \times \log a$ log of the power of a number = power × log

$\log ab = \log a + \log b$ log product = sum of logs   (1.3.2)

$\log a/b = \log a - \log b$ log quotient = difference of logs

As an illustration of the first law, consider $a = 100$ and $p = 4$. Then

$$\log_{10} a = 2 \qquad \text{since } 100 = 10^2$$

So

$$\log_{10} a^p = \log_{10}(10^2)^4 = \log_{10} 10^8 \qquad \text{last of the index laws (1.3.1)}$$

$$= 8 \qquad \text{definition of } \log_{10}$$

$$= 4 \times 2$$

$$= p \times \log_{10} a$$

The remaining two logarithm laws are demonstrated in the same way. They are both consequences of the index laws. The logarithm laws can be used to calculate some further logarithms, without using a calculator. For example

$$\log_8 128 = \log_8 (2 \times 64)$$

$$= \log_8 2 + \log_8 64 \qquad \text{second of the logarithm laws (1.3.2)}$$

$$= \log_8 8^{1/3} + \log_8 8^2$$

$$= 1/3 + 2 \qquad \text{definition of } \log_8$$

$$= 7/3$$

EXERCISES 1.3

1 Simplify the following

(a) $a^3 \times a^5$ (b) $\dfrac{a^{10}}{a^2}$ (c) $a^{-2} \times a^4$ (d) $\dfrac{b^2 \times b^3}{b^4}$

(e) $a^8 \times a^3 \times a^{-4}$ (f) $b^{3/2} \times b^{1/4} \times b^{3/4}$ (g) $\dfrac{a^{3/2}}{a}$ (h) $(b^3)^4$

(i) $(a^8)^{1/2}$ (j) $\dfrac{a^7}{a^3} \times a^6$ (k) $\left(\dfrac{a}{b}\right)^4 \times b^7$ (l) $\dfrac{(ab)^4 \times b^3}{a^2}$

2 Without using a calculator, determine

(a) $4^{1/2}$ (b) $4^{-3/2}$ (c) $8^{2/3}$ (d) $81^{-1/4}$ (e) $32^{0.6}$ (f) $16^{1/3} \times 16^{1/6}$

(g) $\dfrac{64^{3/4}}{64^{7/12}}$ (h) $(4^3)^{1/2}$ (i) $(6^{1/4})^{12}$ (j) $(\sqrt[3]{5})^2 \times (\sqrt[3]{5})^4$

3 Use a calculator to find the following:

(a) 2^6 (b) 1.2^{10} (c) $3^{1.5}$ (d) $9^{5.2}$

(e) $6^{-0.25}$ (f) 10^{-4} (g) $8^{1/5} \times 8^{3/10}$

4 Simplify the following algebraic expressions where possible, by collecting like terms:

(a) $3x + 2y - 4x + y^2 + 3$

(b) $10a - 3b + 4a - ab + 2$

(c) $2a - 8b + 6ab - 3b$

(d) $4b^2 - 3a + 2b^2 - 6a^2$

(e) $6b^3 - 2a^2 + 3ab - 2b^3 + 4a^3 - 4ab$

(f) $6x^2y - 10xy^2 + 4x^2 - 2y^2 + 3$

(g) $4a^2 + 2ab^3 - 8a^2 + 4a^3b - 6b^3a$

5 Expand the brackets and simplify the following expressions, where possible:

(a) $2(2x + 4y) + 4(5x + 2y)$

(b) $3(a - 2b + 4c) - 2(9a - 3b)$

(c) $4a(3c - 2b) - 2c(5b - 3a)$

(d) $x(x^2 - 3x + 8)$

(e) $2x^3(3x^2 - 5)$

(f) $ab^4(2ab^2 - 3a)$

(g) $a^2b^3(5ab + 2b)$

(h) $(2a - 3b)(4a + 6b)$

(i) $(6x + 3y)(8y + 6x - 5)$

(j) $(2x^2 - 3)(3x^4 + 2x^2)$

(k) $(3a^3 - 2b^4)(2a^2 + 3b^2)$

(l) $(2x^3 + 3x^2 - 2)(4y - 2xy + 3)$

6 Without using a calculator, determine the following:

(a) $\log_{10} 100$ (b) $\log_2 8$ (c) $\log_4 256$ (d) $\log_8 2$

(e) $\log_2 16$ (f) $\log_5 5$ (g) $\log_4 1/16$ (h) $\log_2 1/64$

(i) $\log_{36} 3 + \log_{36} 2$ (j) $\log_8 30 - \log_8 15$

(k) $2 \log_{10} 25 + 4 \log_{10} 2$ (l) $4 \log_5 10 - 2 \log_5 4$

1.4 FACTORIZATION

Whereas, in the previous section, we looked at bracket removal, the process of factorization involves inserting brackets. This is often useful when we wish to solve equations, as you will see in section 1.5. Consider, for example

$$4a^5b^3c - 8a^4b^2c + 12a^3b^5c$$

To factorize this expression, we look for *common factors*. First notice that 4 is a common factor and so the expression becomes

$$4(a^5b^3c - 2a^4b^2c + 3a^3b^5c)$$

where the coefficients in the bracket are obtained by *dividing* the original coefficients by 4.

Now observe that each term in the bracket contains some power of a. The common factor is a^3, where we choose the *smallest* power of a to ensure that the common factor *divides* each term. Dividing by this factor (and subtracting powers), we obtain

$$4a^3(a^{5-3}b^3c - 2a^{4-3}b^2c + 3b^5c)$$

$$4a^3(a^2b^3c - 2ab^2c + 3b^5c)$$

Similarly, b^2 and c are factors. So the expression becomes

$$4a^3b^2c(a^2b - 2a + 3b^3)$$

(You should check this factorization by removing the bracket and multiplying out.)

Consider the expression

$$8ab + 12ad - 4bc - 6cd$$

Since $4a$ is a common factor for the first two terms and $2c$ is a common factor for the last two terms, this can be written as

$$4a(2b + 3d) - 2c\,(2b + 3d)$$

Now the bracket is common to both terms and so this becomes

$$(2b + 3d)(4a - 2c)$$

Factorizing quadratics

Our concern in this section is the factorization of quadratic expressions, which are expressions in one unknown x, say, for which the only terms allowed are an x^2 term, an x term and a constant term. Such an expression therefore has the form

$$ax^2 + bx + c \qquad \text{(where } b \text{ or } c \text{ or both may be zero)}$$

If $c = 0$, then factorization is easy. For example

$$4x^2 + 12x = 4x(x + 3)$$

If $c \neq 0$, then such an expression can often (but not always) be factorized by expressing it as a product of two brackets. To understand the method, consider the multiplication

$$(x + 4)(x - 6) = x^2 + 4x - 6x - 24$$

$$= x^2 - 2x - 24$$

As you can see, the relationship between the two numbers 4 and -6 in the brackets and the right-hand side is as follows:

Sum of numbers $= 4 + (-6) = -2 =$ coefficient of x on right-hand side

Product of numbers $= 4 \times -6 = -24 =$ constant on right-hand side

Actually, only the second of these properties is true if the coefficient of x^2 is *not* one, but nonetheless we have a method of factorization, as the following example should make clear.

EXAMPLE 1.4.1

Factorize each of the quadratic functions:

(a) $x^2 - 7x + 10$ (b) $x^2 + 2x - 24$ (c) $8x^2 + 14x - 60$

Solution 1.4.1(a)

For the quadratic

$$x^2 - 7x + 10$$

We need to express this in the form $(x + ?)(x + ?)$. The coefficient of x^2 is *one*, and so we need to find two numbers with product $+10$ and sum -7. Since the product is positive, the two numbers must have the same sign, so they are either both positive or both negative. However, since the sum is negative, they must both be negative. We list the possibilities and check the sum in each case:

product = $+10$		sum	
-10	-1	-11	
-5	-2	-7	this is ok

Conclusion: The factorization is $(x - 5)(x - 2)$.

Note: You should check the answer by multiplying out the brackets.

Solution 1.4.1(b)

The coefficient of x^2 for the quadratic

$$x^2 + 2x - 24$$

is again one. So two numbers are required with product -24 and sum $+2$. Since the product is negative, they must have opposite signs. Since the sum is positive, the positive value must be numerically bigger than the negative value. Again, list the possibilities:

product = -24		sum	
$+24$	-1	$+23$	
$+8$	-3	$+5$	
$+6$	-4	$+2$	this is ok

Conclusion: The factorization is $(x + 6)(x - 4)$.

Solution 1.4.1(c)

First observe that

$$8x^2 + 14x - 60 = 2(4x^2 + 7x - 30)$$

and so the quadratic to be factorized is

$$4x^2 + 7x - 30$$

15

The x^2 term of this quadratic has coefficient 4. Therefore, the possible factorizations are

$$(4x + ?)(x + ?)$$

$$(2x + ?)(2x + ?)$$

The product of the two numbers is -30, so that the numbers have opposite sign, but we do not know the sum in this case, since the coefficient of x^2 is not one. However, we know that the final x term must be $+7x$.

$product = -30$		$Factorization$
-1	$+30$	The relatively large value of 30 rules this out, since the final answer must have $+7x$
$+30$	-1	same comment
-15	$+2$	$(4x - 15)(x + 2)$ no good
		$(4x + 2)(x - 15)$ $+7x$ is needed
		$(2x - 15)(2x + 2)$
$+15$	-2	$(4x + 15)(x - 2) = 4x^2 + 15x - 8x - 30$
		$\qquad\qquad\qquad = 4x^2 + 7x - 30$ ok

Conclusion: The factorization is $2(4x + 15)(x - 2)$.

EXERCISES 1.4

1   Factorize each of the following expressions:

(a) $20x - 5x^2$ (b) $6x^3 - 9x^5$

(c) $a^2b^3 - a^4b^2c$ (d) $ab^4c^3 + ab^2c^5$

(e) $8ab + 4bd - 12ac - 6cd$ (f) $12ab + 6bd^2 - 8ac^2 - 4c^2d^2$

2 Factorize each of the following quadratic functions:

(a) $x^2 + 2x - 3$ (b) $x^2 - 8x + 12$ (c) $x^2 + 11x + 24$

(d) $x^2 - 3x - 40$ (e) $x^2 - 8x + 7$

3 Factorize each of the following quadratic functions:

(a) $3x^2 + 12x + 12$ (b) $3x^2 - 14x + 8$ (c) $2x^2 + 3x - 2$

(d) $12x^2 - 22x - 20$ (e) $9x^2 + 13x + 4$ (f) $4x^2 - 4x + 1$

1.5   SOLVING EQUATIONS ALGEBRAICALLY

In section 1.1, we saw how equations can be solved graphically, by finding the points at which curves intersect. Here we look at the solution of certain commonly occurring types of equation in one variable. The solution usually involves rearranging the equation, and this is based upon **performing the same actions on both sides of the equation**. For example, the same quantity may be added to both sides of the equation or subtracted from both sides. Alternatively, each side may be multiplied by the same quantity or divided.

Linear equations

A linear equation in one unknown x, say, is one involving only constant terms and x terms. It is solved by rearranging the equation so that it has the form $ax = b$, where a, b are constants, in which case the solution is $x = b/a$. The next example should make this clear.

EXAMPLE 1.5.1

Solve the following equations

$\quad$ (a) $6x - 30 = 10 - 9x$ $\quad$ (b) $4x + 2(5x - 4) = 4 - 3(2x - 6)$

Solution 1.5.1(a)

Consider the equation

$$6x - 30 = 10 - 9x$$

It is necessary to collect both x terms on one side of the equation – we will choose the left side – and the constant terms on the other. The $6x$ term and the 10 term are therefore on the correct sides. The remaining terms are to be moved.

$\quad$ Since the x term on the right is *subtracted*, we add $9x$ to each side to cancel it out from the right-hand side. In other words, we perform the *opposite* operation. Therefore:

$$6x - 30 + 9x = 10 - 9x + 9x \qquad \text{adding } 9x \text{ to both sides}$$

$$15x - 30 = 10$$

Since the 30 term is *subtracted* on the left-hand side, 30 is added to each side to cancel it out:

$$15x - 30 + 30 = 10 + 30 \qquad \text{adding 30 to both sides}$$

$$15x = 40$$

$$x = 40/15 = 8/3 \qquad \text{dividing both sides by 15}$$

Note: As a useful check, when a term 'changes sides', it becomes the opposite of what it was. A term which was added is now subtracted, a term which was subtracted is now added, etc.

Solution 1.5.1(b)

Expanding the brackets

$$4x + 2(5x - 4) = 4 - 3(2x - 6)$$

becomes

$$4x + 10x - 8 = 4 - 6x + 18$$

$$14x - 8 = 22 - 6x$$

Rearranging in the same way as in (a)

$$14x - 8 + 6x = 22 \qquad \text{adding } 6x \text{ to both sides}$$

$$20x - 8 = 22$$

$$20x = 30 \qquad \text{adding } 8 \text{ to both sides}$$

$$x = 30/20 = 3/2 \qquad \text{dividing both sides by 20}$$

Quadratic equations

A quadratic equation in the unknown x, say, involves only constant, x and x^2 terms. The procedure for solving such an equation is as follows:

Step 1: Rearrange the equation so that one side is zero.
Step 2: Write the non-zero side in descending powers: x^2 term first, then the x term, then the constant term.
Step 3: To solve, factorize the non-zero side, if possible, or use the quadratic formula.

Quadratic formula

If the equation is written in the form

$$ax^2 + bx + c = 0$$

then

$$x = \frac{-b \pm \sqrt{(b^2 - 4ac)}}{2a} \qquad (1.5.1)$$

EXAMPLE 1.5.2

(a) Solve the equation

$$4 - 3x^2 = 8 - 13x$$

by using factorization and the quadratic formula.
(b) Solve the equation

$$5x^2 + x = 3x^2 - 2x - 40$$

by using the quadratic formula. State the answers to 2 decimal places.

Solution 1.5.2(a)
Consider the equation

$$4 - 3x^2 = 8 - 13x$$

The equation must first be rearranged so that one side is zero, and we will collect all the terms on the right-hand side. (It is slightly easier to collect terms on the side for which the x^2 term is positive.) Rearrangement is performed in the same way as in the previous example. Thus

$$4 = 8 - 13x + 3x^2 \qquad \text{adding } 3x^2 \text{ to both sides}$$

$$0 = 8 - 13x + 3x^2 - 4 \qquad \text{subtracting 4 from both sides}$$

$$0 = 4 - 13x + 3x^2$$

$$3x^2 - 13x + 4 = 0 \qquad \text{write in descending powers}$$

Using the factorization technique considered in the previous section:

$$(3x - 1)(x - 4) = 0$$

The equation can now be solved, since the only way that the product of the two brackets can be zero is if the expression in one of the brackets is zero. Therefore

either $\qquad 3x - 1 = 0 \qquad x = 1/3$

or $\qquad\qquad x - 4 = 0 \qquad x = 4$

In order to use the quadratic formula to calculate the values of x, the equation

$$3x^2 - 13x + 4 = 0$$

is compared with the general form

$$ax^2 + bx + c = 0$$

Comparing the x^2 terms, $a = 3$; comparing the x terms, $b = -13$ (the negative sign must be included in the value of b); and comparing the constants, $c = 4$. Therefore, using (1.5.1),

$$x = \frac{-b \pm \sqrt{(b^2 - 4ac)}}{2a}$$

$$= \frac{-(-13) \pm \sqrt{((-13)^2 - 4 \times 3 \times 4)}}{2 \times 3}$$

$$= \frac{13 \pm \sqrt{(169 - 48)}}{6}$$

$$= \frac{13 \pm \sqrt{121}}{6} = \frac{13 \pm 11}{6}$$

Either $\quad x = \dfrac{13 + 11}{6} = 4 \quad$ or $\quad x = \dfrac{13 - 11}{6} = 1/3$

the same values of x as before

Conclusion: The solutions are 4 and $1/3$.

Solution 1.5.2(b)

Rearranging the equation

$$5x^2 + x = 3x^2 - 2x + 40$$

we obtain

$$2x^2 + 3x - 40 = 0$$

Comparing this with

$$ax^2 + bx + c = 0$$

then $a = 2$, $b = 3$, $c = -40$. Notice the inclusion of the negative sign for c. The solution is

$$x = \frac{-3 \pm \sqrt{(3^2 - 4 \times 2 \times (-40))}}{2 \times 2}$$

$$= \frac{-3 \pm \sqrt{(9 + 320)}}{4} \qquad \text{(care is needed with signs here)}$$

$$= \frac{-3 \pm \sqrt{329}}{4} = \frac{-3 \pm 18.13836}{4}$$

therefore

$$x = -21.13836/4 = -5.28459 \quad \text{or} \quad x = 15.13836/4$$

Conclusion: $x = -5.28$ or $x = 3.78$ to 2 d.p.

Exponential equations

There is one other type of equation which will occur later. An exponential equation is one in which the unknown occurs in a *power* as in, for example,

$$2.5 = 4^x \tag{1.5.2}$$

This type of equation is solved by using the first property of logs in (1.3.2) which states that

$$\log a^p = p \log a \qquad \text{rewrite by moving } p \text{ to front of log}$$

This applies to logs to any base, but we will use base 10, and obtain the logs from a calculator. Applying the log function to both sides of equation (1.5.2)

$$\log_{10} 2.5 = \log_{10} 4^x$$

and using the above property

$$\log_{10} 2.5 = x \log_{10} 4$$

$$0.39794 = 0.60206x$$

$$x = 0.39794/0.60206 = 0.661 \text{ to 3 d.p.}$$

EXERCISES 1.5

1 Solve the equations

(a) $30x = 16x + 420$ (b) $5x - 3 = 9x + 5$

(c) $7x - 8 = 1.5x + 25$ (d) $4x - 5 + 5x = -3x + 4 + 6x$

(e) $2.5x - 4 + 4.7x = 2.2x - 6 + 3.7x$

2 Solve the equations

(a) $2(4x - 2) - 3(4 - 6x) = 2$ (b) $-3(2x - 4) = 5 + 2(x - 3)$

(c) $\dfrac{3x - 2}{2x + 1} = 2$ (d) $\dfrac{6x + 2}{x - 1} = -3$

3 (a) Solve each of the following equations by factorizing the left-hand side:

(i) $x^2 + 11x + 24 = 0$ (ii) $x^2 + 3x - 18 = 0$

(iii) $3x^2 + 4x - 15 = 0$

(b) Solve each of the following equations, by first rearranging to get a zero right-hand side, and then using factorization:

(i) $x^2 + 4x = 6x + 8$ (ii) $x^2 - 6x = 3x - 20$

(iii) $8x^2 - 2 = 2x^2 - 4x$

Use the quadratic formula to solve equations (i) and (iii).

(c) Use the quadratic formula to solve the equations below, by first rearranging the equation to get a zero right-hand side, if necessary. State all answers to two decimal places.

(i) $2x^2 - 12x + 9 = 0$ (ii) $4x^2 + 10x = 5$

(iii) $3x^2 + 8x = 2 - 2x^2$ (iv) $8x^2 + 2x - 3 = 2 - 2x$

4 Using logs to the base 10, and a calculator, solve each of the following equations for x:

(a) $3 = 4^x$ (b) $4 = (1.2)^x$ (c) $6.2 = (4.8)^x$

(d) $\dfrac{6^x}{2^x} = 4$ (e) $(2.5)^x = 2(1.5)^x$

1.6 SIMULTANEOUS LINEAR EQUATIONS

The problem considered here is that of finding the values of two or more unknowns which are known to satisfy two or more equations simultaneously. The equations considered are called *linear* because they involve only simple combinations of the unknowns, and do not involve products or quotients of unknowns, powers higher than one, roots, etc.

The basic approach is to add or subtract pairs of equations, in such a way that unknowns are eliminated. To ensure that an unknown is eliminated, it is often necessary to arrange for the unknown to have the same coefficient numerically in each equation. The secret of solving such equations is to be systematic – a problem with two equations in two unknowns is reduced to a problem with one equation in one unknown (which is easily solved); a problem with three equations in three unknowns is reduced to one with two equations in two unknowns, which is in turn reduced to one equation in one unknown, etc. The following example will illustrate the technique.

EXAMPLE 1.6.1

Solve each of the following sets of simultaneous equations:

(a) $2x + 6y = -3$

$3x - 4y = -11$

(b) $3x - 4y - 2z = 2$

$7x + 3y + 5z = -4$

$4x - 8y - 6z = 12$

Solution 1.6.1(a)

The equations are

$$2x + 6y = -3 \qquad (1)$$
$$3x - 4y = -11 \qquad (2)$$

As stated above, the aim is to reduce the problem to one equation in one unknown by adding or subtracting the equations, having first taken care to ensure that the unknown to be eliminated has the same coefficient numerically in each equation. On this occasion, neither of the two unknowns is the obvious candidate for elimination, since, for each unknown, neither coefficient is a multiple of the other. We will choose to eliminate x and **multiply each equation so that the coefficient of x is the same in each equation**. The coefficient of x in each equation is increased so that it equals the LCM (lowest common multiple) of 2 and 3, which is 6 (the smallest number divisible by both 2 and 3). Therefore:

$$6x + 18y = -9 \qquad 3 \times (1)$$
$$6x - 8y = -22 \qquad 2 \times (2)$$

$$26y = 13 \qquad \text{subtract } 3 \times (1) - 2 \times (2)$$
$$\text{since } x \text{ terms have the } same \ sign$$
$$y = 13/26 = 1/2$$

The value of y can now be substituted in either one of the two equations, say (1):

$$2x + (6 \times 1/2) = -3 \qquad 2x = -6 \qquad x = -3$$

Check Substitute the values of x and y into the other equation:

Left-hand side $= 3 \times (-3) - 4 \times 1/2 = -9 - 2 = -11$, as required

Conclusion: $x = -3$, $y = 1/2$

Solution 1.6.1(b)

The equations are

$$3x - 4y - 2z = 2 \qquad (1)$$

$$7x + 3y + 5z = -4 \qquad (2)$$

$$4x - 8y - 6z = 12 \qquad (3)$$

The basic procedure is as follows:

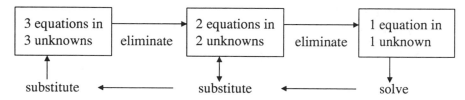

To decide which unknown to eliminate, look at the coefficients of the three unknowns. For x these are 3, 7 and 4, for y, -4, 3 and -8, and for z, -2, 5 and -6. The coefficients for x look awkward, but for each of y and z, one coefficient is a multiple of another, which makes things a little easier. We will choose to eliminate y.

What is important now is that we *systematically eliminate* y, by adding or subtracting the equations in pairs, in order to obtain two equations in x and z. As in **(a)**, we multiply each equation, if necessary, to ensure that the y terms cancel out.

Using equations (1) and (2)

$$3x - 4y - 2z = 2 \qquad (1)$$

$$7x + 3y + 5z = -4 \qquad (2)$$

the coefficients of y in the two equations are -4 and 3. The LCM of 3 and 4 is 12.

$$\begin{array}{ll} 9x - 12y - 6z = 6 & 3 \times (1) \\ 28x + 12y + 20z = -16 & 4 \times (2) \\ \hline 37x + 14z = -10 & \textit{add } 3 \times (1) + 4 \times (2), \qquad\qquad \text{eqn. (4)} \\ & \text{since } y \text{ terms have } \textit{opposite} \text{ signs} \end{array}$$

Next we use equations (1) and (3)

$$3x - 4y - 2z = 2 \qquad (1)$$

$$4x - 8y - 6z = 12 \qquad (3)$$

We could have used equations (2) and (3). However, it is easier to use equations (1) and (3), since the coefficient -8 of y in equation (3) is simply twice the coefficient -4 of y in equation (1).

$$6x - 8y - 4z = 4 \qquad 2 \times (1)$$
$$4x - 8y - 6z = 12 \qquad (3)$$

$$2x \quad\quad + 2z = -8 \qquad \textit{subtract } 2 \times (1) - (3), \qquad\qquad \text{eqn. (5)}$$
$$\text{since } y \text{ terms have the } \textit{same} \text{ sign}$$

We now have two equations in two unknowns:

$$37x + 14z = -10 \qquad (4)$$

$$2x + 2z = -8 \qquad (5)$$

and it is easiest to eliminate z:

$$37x + 14z = -10 \qquad (4)$$
$$14x + 14z = -56 \qquad 7 \times (5)$$

$$23x \quad\quad = 46 \qquad (4) - 7 \times (5)$$

Therefore

$$x = 46/23 = 2$$

To find z, we substitute into one of the two equations in two unknowns, either (4) or (5). Using (4)

$$(2 \times 2) + 2z = -8 \qquad 2z = -12 \qquad z = -6$$

Finally, substitute into one of the 3 equation in 3 unknowns, (1) or (2) or (3). Using (1)

$$(3 \times 2) - 4y - (2 \times -6) = 2 \qquad -4y = -16 \qquad y = 4$$

Check values in (2) or (3). Use (2), say:

$$\text{Left-hand side} = (7 \times 2) + (3 \times 4) + (5 \times -6) = -4 \text{ as required}$$

Conclusion: $x = 2$, $y = 4$, $z = -6$.

Fitting equations to data

Simultaneous equations can often be used to find the equation of a line or curve passing through a number of given points on a graph. It is possible to find the equation of a line passing through two points, as we saw in section 1.2. Given three points, not lying on a line, it is possible to find a quadratic function, of the form

$$y = ax^2 + bx + c$$

for which the curve passes through the given points. We will look at the example of a line, and leave you to look at quadratic functions as part of the exercises.

EXAMPLE 1.6.2

The amount x units of a commodity purchased daily by consumers is dependent upon the selling price £p/unit, and it has been observed that 20 units are demanded daily at a price of £300/unit, whereas 30 units are demanded daily at a price of £250/unit. Assuming that the relationship between p and x is *linear*, find the equation for p in terms of x.

Solution 1.6.2

(This is the problem considered in part (b) of Example 1.2.1. You should compare the approach here to that used earlier.)

Since the relationship between p and x is linear

$$p = ax + b \qquad \text{(straight-line relationship; } a, b \text{ are constants)}$$

To obtain two simultaneous equations in two unknowns, the given pairs of values are substituted for p and x.

Since $p = 300$ when $x = 20$

$$300 = 20a + b \qquad (1)$$

and since $p = 250$ when $x = 30$

$$250 = 30a + b \qquad (2)$$

These simultaneous equations are of a particularly simple type, since the coefficient of b in each is one. Therefore, b should be eliminated.

$(1) - (2)$ gives

$$300 = 20a + b$$
$$\underline{250 = 30a + b}$$
$$\underline{50 = -10a} \qquad a = 50/-10 = -5$$

Substituting for b in equation (1)

$$300 = 20 \times -5 + b \qquad b = 300 + 100 = 400$$

Check in equation (2):

$$\text{Left-hand side} = -5 \times 30 + 400 = 250, \text{ as required}$$

Substituting for a and b in the general equation

$$p = ax + b$$

the required conclusion is obtained.

Conclusion: $\quad p = 400 - 5x$

Note: For examples of fitting quadratic functions to data, see Exercise 5 onwards.

EXERCISES 1.6

1 Solve each of the following pairs of simultaneous equations:

(a) $x + 4y = 10$
     $3x - 8y = -50$

(b) $5b - 4a = 24$
     $2a + 6b = 56$

(c) $4x - 2y = 16$
     $3x - 5y = 19$

2 Solve each of the following sets of simultaneous equations:

(a) $x - 2y + 4z = 1$
     $3x - y + 2z = 3$
     $x + 2y - 3z = 2$

(b) $2x + 4y - 2z = 2$
     $4x - 3y + 4z = 8$
     $3x - 2y + 5z = -5$

(c) $-a + b = -3$
     $2a - 5b - 3c = 0$
     $a - 2b - 2c = 1$

3 (a) The amount x units of a commodity purchased weekly by consumers is dependent upon the selling price £p/unit, and it is assumed that the relationship between p and x is linear. Use simultaneous equations to find the equation relating p to x for each of the following sets of observed data:

(i) p (£/unit)	150	60
x (no. of units demanded weekly)	50	80
(ii) p (£/unit)	135	90
x (no. of units demanded weekly)	10	15

(b) For each of the following pairs of points, use simultaneous equations to find the equation of the line passing through them:

(i) (12, 6) and (20, 18)   (ii) (4, −25) and (8, −32)

4 Two production processes are available for producing a particular type of casting and, for each of these, the equation relating the total cost T to the quantity x produced is known to be *linear*. It has been found that the total cost of producing 20 units/week is £2200 when using process A and £1800 when using process B. For production of 50 units per week, the total costs are £2500 and £2400 for A and B, respectively.

(a) For each process, find an equation for T in terms of x.

(b) Determine the range of production quantities for which A is the cheaper process, and the range for which B is cheaper.

5 During the advertising campaign for a new product, the total sales was observed at different times, as the following table shows:

	5	10	15
t (time elapsed in weeks)	5	10	15
S (total number of units sold so far)	600	900	1400

It is assumed that the relationship between S and t has the quadratic form:

$$S = at^2 + bt + c \qquad (a, b, c \text{ are constants})$$

(a) Show that substituting $t = 5$, $S = 600$ leads to the equation

$$600 = 25a + 5b + c$$

and find two other equations by using the other observed data.

(b) By solving these three simultaneous equations, determine the equation for S in terms of t.

6 (a) The relationship between the total production cost £T for an item and the quantity x produced is thought to be quadratic, and so has the form.

$$T = ax^2 + bx + c \qquad (a, b, c \text{ are constants})$$

Using the observed data provided below, express T in terms of x.

x (no. of items produced)	10	20	50
T (total cost in £)	3450	4200	7050

(b) Repeat part (a) for the observed data:

x (no. of items produced)	5	10	30
T (total cost in £)	10840	11760	16240

7 For an item, the relationship between the quantity sold x units and the price p is known to be quadratic. Given the observed data

p (selling price in £/unit)	5	8	13
x (quantity sold)	332	254	44

determine the equation for x in terms of p.

1.7 REDUCTION TO LINEAR FORM

So far we have looked at variables for which there is a linear relationship. However, there are circumstances where a linear relationship still holds the key, even though the given variables are not related in this way. For such cases, the strategy is to reduce the problem to a linear one by *carefully choosing* the variables to be investigated.

EXAMPLE 1.7.1

The table below shows the observed monthly sales s (in hundreds of units) for a commodity at various prices £p/unit.

s (monthly sales in hundreds of units)	12.20	11.00	10.15	9.25	7.80	7.00
p (£/unit)	2	4	6	8	12	16

Show, graphically, that this set of data approximately satisfies a relationship of the form

$$s = a(\sqrt{p}) + b \qquad \text{(where } a, b \text{ are constants)} \qquad (1.7.1)$$

and determine *possible* values for a and b.

Solution 1.7.1

The problem is that curves are hard to recognise, whereas straight lines are easy and have a clear intercept and slope. However, an equation with a square root cannot have a straight-line graph. Remember that a graph of one quantity q against another r is a straight line provided that they are related by an equation of the form

$$q = ar + b \qquad \text{(where } a, b \text{ are constants)}$$

The answer, therefore, is to remove the square root by looking at the relationship between s and some other variable, rather than s and p. For this purpose a new variable x is introduced, where $x = \sqrt{p}$. Equation (1.7.1) now becomes

$$s = ax + b$$

Thus the graph of s plotted against x should be a straight line (approximately), if the original data is to approximately satisfy (1.7.1). It is therefore necessary to add an extra row to the original table as follows:

s	12.20	11.00	10.15	9.25	7.80	7.00
p	2	4	6	8	12	16
$x \ (=\sqrt{p})$	1.41	2.00	2.45	2.83	3.46	4.00

As Figure 1.7.1 shows, the points obtained by plotting s against x do approximately lie on a straight line, thus verifying the relationship (1.7.1) for the original

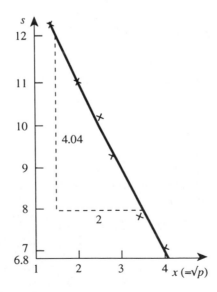

Figure 1.7.1 Graph of s against x

28

data. To find approximate values for a and b, a line of best fit can be drawn by eye, ensuring that points above and below the line balance out. This approach is not very scientific, and the equation of a line of best fit can actually be determined by using a technique called 'linear regression' – which is covered later. When drawing the line, it is useful to note that such a 'line of best fit' passes through the point with coordinates equal to the *averages* of the values of the two variables s and x. You should check that the average of the x values is 2.69 and the average of the s values is 9.57, and so the line passes through the point (2.69, 9.57).

Referring to Figure 1.7.1, the slope of the line gives a value of -2.02 for a. Using this and the point (2.69, 9.57) on the line, the value of 15.00 is obtained for b thus:

$$s = -2.02x + b$$

$$9.57 = -2.02 \times 2.69 + b \qquad b = 15.00$$

Finally

$$s = -2.02x + 15.00$$

$$= -2.02(\sqrt{p}) + 15.00$$

EXERCISES 1.7

1   The number of defective items, n, produced by a machine per day is thought to be related to the speed s (in thousands of revolutions per second) at which the machine is being operated by an equation of the form

$$n = as^2 + b \qquad \text{where } a, \ b \text{ are constants}$$

The following data have been observed:

n	20	50	100	170	260	370
s	2	4	6	8	10	12

By using reduction to linear form and plotting a suitable graph, show that the data is consistent with a relationship of the given form and determine the values of a and b, stating your answers to one decimal place.

2   The pairs of values of x and y below are thought to approximately satisfy an equation of the form $y = ax^3 + b$, where $a, \ b$ are constants.

x	0	1	2	3	4
y	1	1.5	2	6.5	14

By using reduction to linear form and plotting a suitable graph, show that the data is consistent with a relationship of the given form and determine approximate values of a and b, stating your answers to two decimal places.

3 The following table relates the residential value of land in the vicinity of a town to the distance of that land from the town centre:

Residential value £V of land	8100	4900	4000	3400	3200	3000	2800
Distance d (miles) of land from town centre	5	10	15	20	25	30	40

By using reduction to linear form and plotting a suitable graph, show that the data is consistent with a relationship of the form

$$V = \frac{a}{d} + b \qquad \text{where } a, b \text{ are constants}$$

Determine approximate values of a and b, stating your answers to the nearest whole number.

4 Consider the relationships below between variables y and x. In each case, state which variables should be plotted against each other, in order to obtain a straight-line graph.

(a) $y = ax^3 + b$

(b) $y = \frac{a}{x^2} + b$

(c) $y = \sqrt{(ax + b)}$

2

LINEAR PROGRAMMING

When you have completed this chapter you will be able to:

- represent constraints and objective functions algebraically
- plot the constraints and identify a feasible region
- plot and optimise an objective function
- investigate changes in resources and objectives

2.1 INTRODUCTION

Linear programming is the study of **optimisation under constraint**. By optimisation, we mean the maximisation of a quantity such as revenue or profit, or minimisation of a quantity such as cost. Whatever activity is undertaken by a company, there are always constraints. There may be limited staff available or limited equipment. Perhaps cost is an issue, and there is a budget which must not be exceeded, or even a worry about spending too little money and having the allocation cut for next year. There may be limited demand for a product, or a contract which requires that a minimum quantity of the product must be produced.

The aim is to look at a number of products, subject to a variety of constraints, and to optimise some target quantity – the **objective function**. Actually, since the approach is graphical, only *two* products will be considered, there being only two axes available to represent these. There is, however, a perfectly good numerical algorithm for handling three or more products and this will be the subject of the next chapter.

As an introduction, consider the small pottery which is run by Mr. and Mrs. Smith. They employ 4 members of staff and each works 45 hours per week. A range of large and small pots is produced, and they are seeking advice on how to maximise their profits. It takes $1\frac{1}{2}$ (staff) hours to produce each small pot, for which the profit is £20, and 3 hours for a large pot, for which profit is £25. The limited kiln facilities restrict the total output to a maximum of 80 pots per week.

The first step in maximising profits is to introduce unknowns for the quantities of pots produced. Let x and y be the quantities of small pots and large pots, respectively, produced weekly. To express the time constraint algebraically, it is necessary to compare the time actually required to produce the quantities x and y with the maximum time available. There are 4 staff, working a 45 hour week, and so 180 (staff) hours are available. Each small pot takes 1.5 hours to produce and so x of them require $1.5x$ hours. For y large pots, $3y$ hours are required. Therefore

$$1.5x + 3y \leqslant 180$$

Typically, a constraint is represented as an **inequality**, and this inequality is best understood graphically. To plot it, the inequality is first converted to an equation

$$1.5x + 3y = 180$$

Two points are required for the line, and the two extreme points obtained by substituting $x = 0$ (assuming that no small pots are produced) and $y = 0$ (assuming no large pots) are convenient. Thus

$$\begin{aligned} &\text{if } x = 0 & 3y = 180 & & y = 60 \\ &\text{if } y = 0 & 1.5x = 180 & & x = 120 \end{aligned}$$

Note that this is indeed a straight line, since the equation can be rearranged into the more traditional form $y = ax + b$ by writing

$$\begin{aligned} 3y &= 180 - 1.5x \\ y &= 60 - 0.5x \end{aligned}$$

However, rewriting in this way is not required for plotting the line.

The constraint is shown in Figure 2.1.1. Each point on the graph represents some combination of quantities of large and small pots, provided that only *non-negative* values of x and y are considered. However, not all these combinations are possible within the given time constraint. Consider, for example, 60 small pots and 40 large pots, corresponding to a point *outside* the line. Then

$$\text{Time required} = (1.5 \times 60) + (3 \times 40) = 210 \text{ hours}$$

and these quantities are not feasible.

For a point *inside* the line, the total time required is less than the time available. For example, if $x = 40$ and $y = 20$

$$\text{Time required} = (1.5 \times 40) + (3 \times 20) = 120 \text{ hours}$$

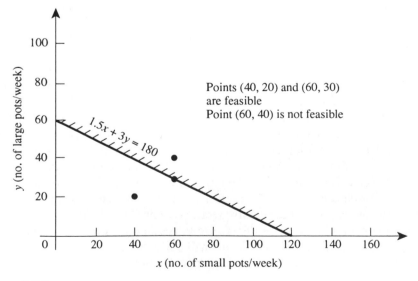

Points (40, 20) and (60, 30) are feasible
Point (60, 40) is not feasible

Figure 2.1.1

For a point on the line such as (60, 30), exactly the available 180 hours are used. To signify that points inside or on the line represent feasible quantities of pots, we shade the *outside* of the line, as shown.

Similar considerations apply to the kiln constraint which is stated as

$$x + y \leqslant 80 \qquad \text{(up to 80 pots in total can be produced weekly)}$$

Feasible points must therefore be inside or on this line as well as the time line, as the shading in Figure 2.1.2 shows.

It remains to maximise profit, and to do this a profit equation is required. Since the profit for a small pot is £20 and for a large pot £25

$$\text{Gross profit } G = 20x + 25y$$

This is called the *objective function*.

The problem now is to find the point in the feasible region for which G is greatest, and this is done by *choosing* a value for G and plotting a profit line, called an *iso-profit* line, at all points of which the profit is the same. A line which crosses the feasible region is preferable. It is convenient to have a value divisible by the profit margins 20 and 25, and so we choose $20 \times 25 = 500$. Thus

$$500 = 20x + 25y$$

if $x = 0$ $25y = 500$ $y = 20$
if $y = 0$ $20x = 500$ $x = 25$

This line is shown on the graph. If we chose a larger value for G, say $G = 1000$, then

$$1000 = 20x + 25y$$

if $x = 0$ $y = 40$
if $y = 0$ $x = 50$

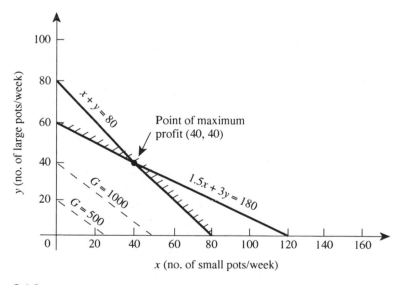

Point of maximum profit (40, 40)

Figure 2.1.2

33

This profit line is also plotted and, as you can see, it is parallel to the first line. In fact all profit lines are *parallel*. To see that this is true consider the objective function

$$G = 20x + 25y$$

Whatever the value of G, this can be rearranged as

$$25y = G - 20x$$
$$y = G/25 - 0.8x$$

The slope of the line is therefore always -0.8. Also, the intercept on the vertical axis is $G/25$, and this gets larger, that is the line moves outwards as G gets larger.

Rather than plot any more parallel profit lines, we put a straight edge along either one of the lines drawn, and move it out parallel to the *furthermost* point of the feasible region, which is (40, 40). Therefore, 40 of each type of pot should be produced. Finally,

$$G = 20x + 25y = (20 \times 40) + (25 \times 40) = £1800/\text{week}$$

is the maximum profit.

Note: There may be other constraints. For example, a *contract* to supply 20 small pots each week to a customer would be represented as $x \geqslant 20$. The feasible region would then be to the right of the vertical line $x = 20$.

The procedure for solving a linear programming problem is therefore as follows:

- **Stage 1**: Express the constraints and the objective function algebraically.
- **Stage 2**: Plot the constraints, and mark the feasible region.
- **Stage 3**: Plot the objective function and determine the optimum solution.

The next example will further illustrate this procedure.

EXAMPLE 2.1.1

The Warmline Company produces 2 types of quilt – the 'Florida' and the 'California'. Each quilt is filled with Fibron, a new synthetic fibre, and covered with a strong nylon fabric, and the table below shows the quantities of Fibron and Nylon fabric required to make one quilt of each type:

	Fibron (kgs)	Nylon Fabric (sq. metres)
Florida	3	5
California	6	8

The quilts are produced by hand and the time required is 3 man-hours per quilt for both Florida and California. The supply of Fibron is at most 2400 kgs per week and the supply of nylon fabric at most 4000 sq. metres per week. The maximum available production time is 1800 man-hours per week.

The profit on each Florida quilt is £30 and on each California quilt is £40. Demand for the California quilt is at most 300 per week.

Determine the number of each type of quilt which should be produced weekly to maximise profit, and state the maximum weekly profit.

Solution 2.1.1

Whilst we are not advocating that all the stages involved in the solution of a linear programming problem must be written out in detail, it is often useful to do so.

Stage 1: Formulating the problem algebraically The essential first step is to express the objective function (in this case, weekly profit), and the constraints, algebraically, and it is therefore necessary to introduce symbols for the quantities of quilts produced. Let

x = the number of Florida quilts produced weekly

y = the number of California quilts produced weekly

The equation for the objective function is straightforward. If G denotes the weekly profit (in £) then, multiplying the profit margins by the quantities x and y,

$G = 30x + 40y$ objective function

The constraints will be represented by inequalities and, for this particular problem, each constraint will have

an expression involving x and/or y on one side
and a *maximum figure* on the other   (2.2.1)

Note that the constraints on Fibron, nylon fabric, time, and on demand, are indeed all *maximum* limitations. However, the first three constraints involve resources and are different in character to the last. They involve both x and y, and are based upon resource requirements *per unit* as well as *total* availability. For this type of constraint, you may find it useful to draw up a table of the following form, showing unit resources required and the maximum availability of these:

Resource Requirements and Availability

	Florida (per quilt)	California (per quilt)	Maximum availability of resource
Fibron (kilograms)	3	6	2400
Nylon Fabric (sq. metres)	5	8	4000
Time (hours)	3	3	1800

Fibron constraint As stated in (2.2.1), only one side of the inequality for this constraint will involve x and y. For this side, we ask the question: 'How much Fibron is required to produce the quantities x and y of the quilts'? For this, we use the amounts of Fibron *per quilt* given in the first row of the table, and multiply these by the quantities x and y. So

x Florida quilts require $3x$ kilograms of Fibron

y California quilts require $6y$ kilograms of Fibron

Total Fibron actually required = $3x + 6y$ (one side of the inequality)

35

The other side of the inequality consists of the maximum figure of 2400 kilograms given for the availability of the resource. Therefore

$3x + 6y \leqslant 2400$

Nylon fabric constraint   The procedure is the same as before. Using the second row of the table:

Total nylon fabric required $= 5x + 8y$ (sq. metres)

Maximum amount of nylon fabric available $= 4000$ (sq. metres)

$5x + 8y \leqslant 4000$

Time constraint   Using the same approach

$3x + 3y \leqslant 1800$

Note: The units used (kilograms, sq. metres, hours) are different for each of these constraints. However, the constraints are independent, and all that matters is that the same units are used on *each side* of each inequality.

Demand for California Quilts   As pointed out earlier, the demand constraint is different in character to the others. It involves y only, and ensures that the number of California quilts produced weekly does not exceed the number which can be sold. Thus

$y \leqslant 300$

Additional constraints   It may come as a surprise that there are any additional constraints. However, it is implicit from the context of the problem that we are looking for *non-negative* answers for x and y, since these are the quantities of quilts produced. Thus, mathematically,

$x \geqslant 0, \ y \geqslant 0$

These constraints are important because they allow us to focus upon the positive quadrant of the graph, when seeking the optimum solution.

    Now that all the given information has been expressed algebraically, the final step for Stage 1 is to write down a summary, called a *linear program*.

Linear program

Maximise:	$G = 30x + 40y$	Objective function Weekly profit
subject to the constraints:	$3x + 6y \leqslant 2400$	Fibron
	$5x + 8y \leqslant 4000$	Nylon fabric
	$3x + 3y \leqslant 1800$	Time
	$y \leqslant 300$	Demand for California
	$x \geqslant 0, \quad y \geqslant 0$	Additional

A careful statement of the unknowns and a statement of the linear program are the essential ingredients of Stage 1. How much additional explanation is included is a matter for you to decide.

Stage 2: The next stage is to represent the constraints graphically, by converting each inequality to an equation and plotting the corresponding line, usually by substituting $x = 0$ and $y = 0$. Before attempting to decide the scales for the graph, it is sensible to look at the data to be plotted. The details are as follows:

$3x + 6y = 2400$ if $x = 0$, $y = 2400/6 = 400$
                         if $y = 0$, $x = 2400/3 = 800$

$5x + 8y = 4000$ if $x = 0$, $y = 4000/8 = 500$
                         if $y = 0$, $x = 4000/5 = 800$

$3x + 3y = 1800$ if $x = 0$, $y = 1800/3 = 600$
                         if $y = 0$, $x = 1800/3 = 600$

$y = 300$ this is a horizontal line cutting the y-axis at 300; x can take any value as far as this constraint is concerned

The graph is shown in Figure 2.1.3. The feasible region is indicated by shading the side of each line which is *invalid*, and this is determined by the corresponding *inequality*. Since the inequalities for the Fibron, Nylon fabric and time constraints are all ⩽, the points of the feasible region lie *on* or *inside* all these constraint lines. The demand inequality for California quilts is also ⩽, and so feasible points lie on or below this line. Notice that the nylon fabric line does not affect the feasible region – this is an example of a *redundant* constraint.

Stage 3: Finally, it is necessary to choose a profit value and plot an iso-profit line, preferably one which crosses the feasible region. This can then be

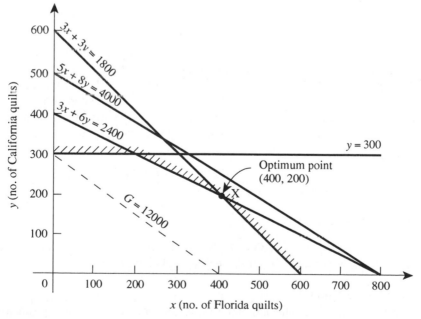

Figure 2.1.3

projected outwards to find the optimum point of the feasible region. The profit equation is

$$G = 30x + 40y$$

It is convenient to choose a value divisible by 30 and 40, and so we start with the value $30 \times 40 = 1200$. However, for this value, we obtain the line

$$1200 = 30x + 40y \qquad \text{where if } x = 0, y = 30 \text{ and if } y = 0, x = 40$$

and the scale of the graph is in hundreds. This is no problem, since we simply scale the value of G by 10 and plot

$$12000 = 30x + 40y \qquad \text{where if } x = 0, y = 300 \text{ and if } y = 0, x = 400$$

(This is the dotted line on Figure 2.1.3.) Finally, placing a straight edge along the profit line drawn, we project the line outwards to the *furthermost* point of the feasible region, and obtain the point (400, 200), point X on the graph Therefore, $x = 400$, $y = 200$ and, using the profit equation,

$$G = (30 \times 400) + (40 \times 200) = 20000$$

Conclusion: Warmline should produce 400 Florida quilts and 200 California quilts each week. The maximum profit is £20,000.

Post-optimal analysis The initial optimum solution to a linear programming problem is usually only the start. Once the solution has been considered, it will usually be desirable or necessary to consider changes in the amount of the resources used (in order to cut back on an expensive resource perhaps, or deal with a change in availability of a resource), or changes in the profit margins resulting from increased costs or changes in the market. The following are some typical questions:

- Does the solution lead to a *surplus* of any resource? If so, it will be possible to cut back on this resource, without reducing profits.
- If more of a particular resource can be made available, would profits increase? If so, how much extra of the resource would be desirable?
- If there were to be a change in one or more of the profit margins for the products, at what revised profit margin(s) will the production mix have to change?

The solution of the previous problem resulted in a surplus of nylon fabric. We will next illustrate the second of the questions above.

EXAMPLE 2.1.1 (continued)

If the weekly supply of Fibron can be increased, is there an advantage to Warmline? If so, how much more Fibron per week is desirable?

Solution 2.1.1 (continued)

Consider Figure 2.1.3. If the amount of Fibron can be increased by an as-yet unspecified amount, then the Fibron line can be moved outwards, parallel to the

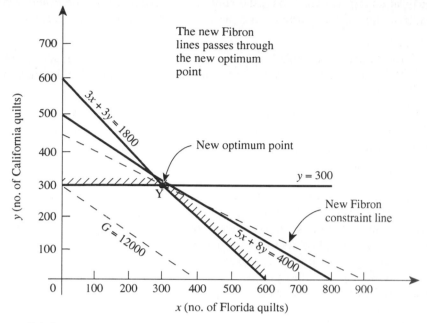

Figure 2.1.4

original – but how far is beneficial? The easiest way to proceed is to remove the original Fibron constraint and to focus on the other constraints. The resulting feasible region is shown in Figure 2.1.4.

Projecting the iso-profit line outwards the new optimum point is point Y, and the company should now produce 300 of each type of quilt. The revised weekly profit is

$$G = (30 \times 300) + (40 \times 300) = £21000$$

which is an improvement on the original profit of £20,000. So increasing the amount of Fibron is worthwhile, and the new quantity required is

$$(3 \times 300) + (6 \times 300) = 2700 \text{ kgs}$$

(since a Florida quilt requires 3 kgs of Fibron and a California quilt 6 kgs). The new Fibron line, shown dotted on the Figure, can be plotted as follows:

$$3x + 6y = 2700 \qquad \text{if } x = 0, \ y = 450; \text{ if } y = 0, \ x = 900$$

EXERCISES 2.1

1 A factory has 3 processing divisions A, B, C, having maximum daily capacities of 900 hours, 1200 hours and 1600 hours, respectively. Two products P and Q are manufactured. Production of one unit of P requires 4 hours in Division B and 8 hours in Division C. Production of one unit of Q requires 4 hours in Division A, 3 hours in Division B and 2 hours in Division C. The profit is £7 on each unit of P and £4 on each unit of Q.

(a) Assuming that, each day, the company produces x units of P and y units of Q, express the constraints, and the total weekly profit G, in terms of x and y.

(b) By drawing a suitable graph, determine the quantities of P and Q which should be produced each day to maximise profit, and calculate the maximum daily profit.

(c) Because of a power crisis, it is now decided to reduce daily processing time in *just one* of the divisions by 200 hours. In which division should the reduction be made if the profit loss is to be minimised, and what is the new maximum daily profit?

2　Aztec Electronics Ltd. manufactures an automatic oven and an automatic dishwasher, these products being dependent for their operation on the new Auton control circuit. Aztec is able to obtain up to 800 of these control circuits per week, and employs 2 circuits in the production of each oven and 5 circuits in the production of each dishwasher. Two departments, A and B, are involved in the production of the products. Assembly, by semi-skilled labour, takes place in department A, each oven requiring 3 man-hours and each dishwasher 2.5 hours. Department B is concerned with the operation of the Auton control circuits, and each oven requires 30 minutes specialist attention from an engineer, whereas a dishwasher requires 50 minutes.

The workforce, which comprises 15 semi-skilled employees and 3 engineers, works a 50 hour week. Aztec sells all the ovens produced at a profit of £80 each and all the dishwashers produced at a profit of £120 each. The company has a contract to supply 50 ovens per week to a particular customer.

(a) Determine the optimum quantities of ovens and dishwashers, and calculate the maximum weekly profit.

(b) The company now decides to increase the total time in department A or department B by a third but not both. In which department should this increase be made and what is the new figure for the weekly profit?

3　A tailor manufactures one style of overcoat and one style of jacket. The profit on an overcoat is £16 and on a jacket is £14.

An overcoat requires 6 yards of cloth, 5 yards of lining and takes 5 hours to produce. A jacket requires 4 yards of cloth, 2 yards of lining and requires 8 hours to make. A wholesaler can supply 540 yards of cloth and 390 yards of lining each week, and the tailor's labour force is sufficient to provide up to 800 hours/week. In order to maintain a balanced stock, the tailor has a policy of producing at least as many jackets as overcoats.

Determine the quantities of jackets and overcoats which the tailor should produce each week in order to achieve maximum profit, and calculate this maximum profit.

4　Sleepwell Ltd. manufactures mattresses in two qualities – 'Super' and 'Supreme'. Each 'Super' mattress requires 9.6 square metres of fabric, 40 kilograms of stuffing, and takes 1 machine hour to produce, whilst each 'Supreme' mattress requires 8 square metres of fabric, 60 kilograms of stuffing, and takes 2 machine hours to produce. Each month, 9600 square metres of fabric, 48000 kilograms of stuffing and 1500 machine hours are available for production. The profit on each 'Super' mattress is £60 and each 'Supreme' mattress is £80.

(a) Advise the company as to the quantity of each type of mattress which should be produced monthly to maximise profit, and calculate the maximum monthly profit.

(b) Following the introduction of new regulations, both types of mattress have to be treated with fire-proofing fluid and then dried in a special chamber under controlled conditions. The drying chamber is currently available for 400 hours per month. 10 mattresses (not necessarily of the same type) can be dried at one time and the drying process takes 4 hours.

Advise the company as to the revised quantities of 'Super' and 'Supreme' mattresses which should now be produced monthly, and calculate the reduced maximum monthly profit.

(c) Suppose, now, that the company can increase the number of hours per month for which the drying chamber is available. What increase in the drying hours per month would be required in order to achieve the maximum profit determined in (a)?

5 Groundhog Ltd. manufactures 2 types of tractor: the model S, up to 250 of which can be sold per month, and the Model T for which demand is at present unlimited. Assembly of these tractors is performed by hand, the Model S requiring 20 man-hours per unit and the model T, 15 man-hours per unit. The success of these machines is due mainly to the anti-corrosion treatment which they receive. Each tractor is sprayed with the revolutionary ZB-90 paint which is obtained from a supplier, the Model S requiring 50 litres of this paint and the Model T 75 litres.
  Assembly time for the tractors is limited to 6000 man-hours per month and the supply of ZB-90 is limited to 21,000 litres per month. You are advised that each Model S sells for £3500 and each Model T for £3000.

(a) By drawing a suitable graph, determine the number of each type of tractor which should be produced monthly to maximise revenue, and calculate the maximum monthly revenue.

(b) Because of a dispute with the union, it is anticipated that in the next month the available labour will be reduced to 5700 hours and, to avoid any loss of revenue, the management has decided to ask the supplier for an additional amount of ZB-90.

If the total monthly revenue is to be maintained at the level determined in (a), what additional amount of ZB-90 would it be necessary for the supplier to provide, and how many tractors of each type should be produced next month?

6 Thames Technical College is planning to run a series of new residential cookery courses this year, during the vacations, and plans to accommodate the applicants in the Hillside hall of residence. The hall will be available for 25 weeks during the year and for 4 days each week. The courses will be of two types: an intensive 2-day course and a more leisurely 4-day course, only one of which can be run at a time. It is estimated that the administrative cost associated with each 2-day course is £400 and with each 4-day course is £600. The technical college has allowed a budget of £18000 for the first year, to cover such charges.

After a preliminary survey, it has been decided that demand for the shorter 2-day course is unlimited, whereas there is only sufficient interest for up to 20 of the longer courses this year. The estimated profit from a 2-day course is £500 and from a 4-day course is £800.

(a) Determine the number of courses of each type which should be run during the first year, and calculate the corresponding maximum annual profit.

(b) If it were possible to use the hall of residence for an extra 4 weeks, by how much would the annual profit increase?

(c) It is anticipated that it may be possible to increase the profit for a 2-day course. By how much can the profit on such a course increase before it becomes necessary to revise the optimum number of courses determined in (a).
(N.B. Assume that the hall of residence is available for up to 25 weeks, as before.)

2.2 EXTENDING THE METHOD

The next example illustrates another common use of linear programming, which is the solution of a so-called portfolio problem, in which a sum of money is to be invested in a number of investment opportunities, with the aim of maximising the return on this money. In this example, a problem which involves three unknowns is reduced to one involving only two unknowns, which is then solved graphically. It should not be inferred that this approach is always possible but it is sometimes useful.

EXAMPLE 2.2.1

The Accountant for Aztec Ltd. wishes to invest £200,000 in total and is considering 3 investment opportunities.

INVESTMENT 1 – SHARES IN MIDAS ENGINEERING
Shares are expected to yield a profit of 50p in the pound over a 2 year period and £120,000 worth of shares may be purchased.

INVESTMENT 2 – BONDS
These will earn 20p in the pound over a 2 year period and bonds to the value of £60,000 in total may be purchased.

INVESTMENT 3 – INTERNAL PROJECTS UNDERTAKEN BY AZTEC LTD

A minimum investment of £50,000 is required and the profit yield is 15% in total over a 2 year period.

Required Assuming that the Accountant wishes to invest in all of these opportunities, how much should be invested in each?

Note: It is the policy of Aztec Ltd. that money invested outside of the company should in total earn at least 40%.

Solution 2.2.1

The problem is to find the amount of money which should be invested in each opportunity so as to maximise total profit. Therefore let

£x thousand be invested in Midas Engineering
£y thousand be invested in bonds
£z thousand be invested in internal projects

As before, the objective function and constraints must be expressed algebraically. For the objective function, total profit, we use the stated returns on investment. Money invested in Midas Engineering returns 50p, i.e. £0.5 in the pound, and so £x thousand produces a profit of £$0.5x$ thousand. Similarly, for bonds, £y thousand produces a profit of £$0.2y$ thousand. Internal projects yield a profit of £$0.15z$ thousand. (Note that the % must be written as $15/100$, before multiplying.) Therefore

$$G = 0.5x + 0.2y + 0.15z \qquad (\text{£000's}) \qquad (2.2.1)$$

Now consider the constraints. Firstly, the company wishes to invest *exactly* £200,000 in total and so

$$x + y + z = 200 \qquad (\text{£000's}) \quad \text{Total investment} \qquad (2.2.2)$$

It is the fact that this constraint is an *equation* which allows a 3 variable problem to be reduced to one involving only two. For example, we can eliminate z by writing

$$z = 200 - x - y \qquad (2.2.3)$$

However, such elimination of z will be postponed until we have expressed the remaining constraints algebraically.

For Midas Engineering shares and bonds, the constraints are based upon a comparison of the sums x, y actually invested and the maximum investments of £120 thousand and £60 thousand, respectively. Thus

$$x \leqslant 120 \qquad (\text{£000's}) \quad \text{Midas Engineering constraint}$$

$$y \leqslant 60 \qquad (\text{£000's}) \quad \text{Bonds constraint}$$

For internal projects, there are two constraints. The first is based upon the minimum investment of £50 thousand so

$$z \geqslant 50 \qquad (\text{£000's}) \quad \text{Internal projects constraint} \qquad (2.2.4)$$

The second constraint is more awkward. It states that money invested outside the company (at greater risk perhaps) should in total earn at least 40%. In this case, the money invested outside is £$(x+y)$ thousand and this must yield at least £0.4 $(x+y)$ thousand. But we have already looked at the profits yielded from the investments in Midas Engineering and bonds, since these were relevant to the objective function. Midas yields £$0.5x$ thousand and the bonds £$0.2y$ thousand. Putting all this information together, the constraint becomes

$$0.5x + 0.2y \geqslant 0.4(x+y)$$

$$0.5x + 0.2y \geqslant 0.4x + 0.4y$$

Rearranging and simplifying

$$0.5x - 0.4x \geqslant 0.4y - 0.2y$$

$$0.1x \geqslant 0.2y$$

$$x \geqslant 2y \qquad \text{external investment constraint}$$

Before stating the linear programme, it remains to eliminate z where appropriate using (2.2.3). Substituting for z in the objective function equation (2.2.1)

$$G = 0.5x + 0.2y + 0.15(200 - x - y)$$

$$= 0.5x + 0.2y + 30 - 0.15x - 0.15y$$

$$= 0.35x + 0.05y + 30$$

The only constraint involving z is (2.2.4). Thus

$$z \geqslant 50$$

$$200 - x - y \geqslant 50$$

$$x + y \leqslant 150$$

This makes sense – if at least £50,000 of the £200,000 must be invested in internal projects, then a maximum of £150,000 is available for outside investments.
    The linear programme is therefore

Maximise: $G = 0.35x + 0.05y + 30$

subject to the
constraints:

$x \leqslant 120$	Midas Engineering
$y \leqslant 60$	Bonds
$x \geqslant y \leqslant 150$	Internal projects
$x \geqslant 2y$	External investment
$x \geqslant 0,\ y \geqslant 0$	Additional

The first three constraints are of the type considered earlier and are plotted as follows:

$x = 120$	vertical line cutting the x-axis at 120
$y = 60$	horizontal line cutting the y-axis at 60
$x + y = 150$	if $x = 0$, $y = 150$; if $y = 0$, $x = 150$

The constraint $x \geqslant 2y$ requires particular consideration. The corresponding equation is $x = 2y$ and whether we substitute $x = 0$ or $y = 0$, the same point on the line is obtained – the origin. Another point is therefore required and for this any convenient value of x may be substituted. For example, substituting $x = 40$ gives $y = 20$.

The feasible region is shown in Figure 2.2.1.

The constraint is $x \geqslant 2y$ and so feasible points must be on or *below* this line. (Think of it this way: starting at *any* point on the line, at which $x = 2y$, it is necessary to move to the right, into the region below the line, in order to increase the value of x.)

For the iso-profit line, choose $G = 37$, say.

$$37 = 0.35x + 0.05y + 30$$

If $x = 0$, $y = 140$. If $y = 0$, $x = 20$.

The iso-profit line $G = 37$ is shown in Figure 2.2.1. Projecting the line outwards to the furthermost point of the feasible region identifies the optimum point (120, 30), point X on the graph. Therefore:

$$G = 0.35x + 0.05y + 30$$

$$= (0.35 \times 120) + (0.05 \times 30) + 30 = 73.5 \quad (\text{£ thousand})$$

Conclusion: Of the £200,000, £120,000 should be invested in Midas Engineering, £30,000 in bonds, and therefore £50,000 in internal projects. The maximum profit is £73,500.

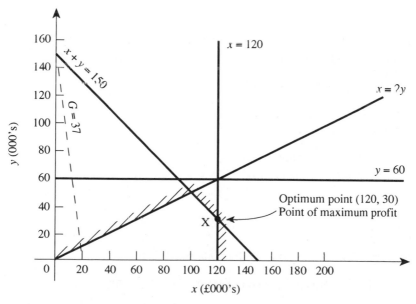

Figure 2.2.1

The final example considered is one of cost *minimisation*. The approach is basically the same, but the iso-cost line is projected *backwards* to obtain the optimum solution.

EXAMPLE 2.2.2

A manufacturer of animal foodstuffs is asked to supply 40 tons of feed per week to a particular customer and regulations state that this must contain a minimum of 25% fat and a minimum of 20% protein. To make up the order the manufacturer uses raw materials A and B, together with bulk feed (of negligible cost and content). The cost of one ton of A is £30 and one ton of B is £20. The supply of B is limited to 20 tons per week. The fat and protein contents of A and B are as follows: A contains 50% fat and 25% protein; B contains 20% fat and 40% protein.

(a) What quantities of A and B should the manufacturer use in fulfilling the order, so that his cost is minimised?
(b) If there were no bulk feed present, what would be the minimum cost of fulfilling the order?

Solution 2.2(a)

First we define the unknowns. Let

x = no. of tons of A y = no. of tons of B

used to fulfil the order. There are a number of constraints to express algebraically, and we will start with the nutritional constraints. Notice, in particular, how *percentages are converted to fractions* when expressing these constraints.

Fat constraint   The approach here is to first determine the *minimum* fat content of the feed, and then to decide how much fat is actually contained in x tons of A and y tons of B. We are told that the minimum fat content must be 25% or $\frac{1}{4}$ and this proportion is applied to the total weight, 40 tons, of the feed. So

Minimum fat content $= \frac{1}{4} \times 40 = 10$ tons

As for the amount of fat which the feed actually contains, we are told that A is $\frac{1}{2}$ fat and B is $\frac{1}{5}$ fat. Therefore:

x tons of A contains $\frac{1}{2} x$ tons of fat
y tons of B contains $\frac{1}{5} y$ tons of fat

and so

$\frac{1}{2} x + \frac{1}{5} y \geqslant 10$

$5x + 2y \geqslant 100$ multiply by 10 to remove fractions

Protein constraint   Since the feed must contain at least 20% protein

Minimum protein content $= \frac{1}{5} \times 40 = 8$ tons

Since A is $\frac{1}{4}$ protein and B is $\frac{2}{5}$ protein, the protein content of x tons of A and y tons of B is:

$\frac{1}{4}x + \frac{2}{5}y$ tons

Therefore

$\frac{1}{4}x + \frac{2}{5}y \geqslant 8$

$5x + 8y \geqslant 160$ 　　　　multiply by 20 to remove fractions

So much for the minimum nutritional constraints. There are now two maximum constraints to be determined.

Supply of B　　This constraint

$y \leqslant 20$

is similar to ones which you have seen before.

Size of order　　It is easy to overlook this constraint but note that the total quantity of A and B cannot be more than 40 tons. It can be less, however, since the feed can contain bulk feed. Thus:

$x + y \leqslant 40$

The linear program is therefore

　　　　Minimise:　　　$C = 30x + 20y$　　　total cost

　　　　subject to the
　　　　constraints:　　　$5x + 2y \geqslant 100$　　　Fat
　　　　　　　　　　　　　$5x + 8y \geqslant 160$　　　Protein
　　　　　　　　　　　　　$y \leqslant 20$　　　　　　　Supply of B
　　　　　　　　　　　　　$x + y \leqslant 40$　　　　　Size of order
　　　　　　　　　　　　　$x \geqslant 0, y \geqslant 0$　　　Additional

The constraints are plotted in the usual way. The relevant lines are

$5x + 2y = 100$
$5x + 8y = 160$
$y = 20$
$x + y = 40$

The constraints and feasible region are shown in Figure 2.2.2.
　　An iso-cost line is plotted, by using the equation

$C = 30x + 20y$

and choosing a value for C. The value 900 is convenient and so

$900 = 30x + 20y$　　　if $x = 0$, $y = 45$;　　　if $y = 0$, $x = 30$

This iso-cost line is shown in Figure 2.2.2 . It is representative of all cost lines in the sense that they are all parallel to this one.

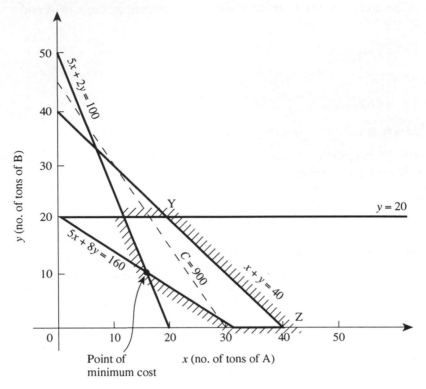

Figure 2.2.2

Finally, to find the point of minimum cost, this cost line is projected *backwards* as far as it will go, ensuring that contact is not lost with the feasible region. Therefore

Optimum point = (16, 10)

(Note that these coordinates can be checked by solving the equations:

$$5x + 2y = 100 \quad \text{and} \quad 5x + 8y = 160$$

simultaneously.)

Minimum value of $C = (30 \times 16) + (20 \times 10) = 680$

Conclusion: The 40 ton order should contain 16 tons of A, 10 tons of B, and therefore 14 tons of bulk feed. The minimum cost is £680.

Solution 2.2(b)

Suppose, now, that the feed contains no bulk feed. Then the 'size of order' constraint becomes

$$x + y = 40$$

and so is an *equation*, rather than an inequality. The feasible region is now the

line segment YZ, and is referred to as a **degenerate** feasible region. The least cost point is now Y = (20, 20) and

$$C = (30 \times 20) + (20 \times 20) = 1000$$

Conclusion: The feed should now contain 20 tons of A and 20 tons of B (no bulk feed). The minimum cost is £1000.

EXERCISES 2.2

1 A firm operates two plants each of which produces agricultural products in the form of fertiliser, weed killer and pesticide. Each hour plant A can produce 25 tons of fertiliser together with 15 tons of weed killer and 10 gallons of pesticide, whereas plant B can produce 50 tons of fertiliser together with 5 tons of weed killer and 75 gallons of pesticide. The plants are run intermittently as required.

On a particular day the firm has an order on hand for 2000 tons of fertiliser, 600 tons of weed killer and 1350 gallons of pesticide, and the plants are to be run until at least these quantities have been produced. If it costs £1000 an hour to run plant A and £2500 an hour to run plant B, for how long should each plant be run?

2 Barnes Ltd manufacture a popular canned stew which they advertise as being both high protein and low calorie. The main ingredients are meat and mixed vegetables, and the protein and calorie content of these, together with their costs, are tabulated below. (The stew also contains stock which is assumed to be of negligible content and cost.)

	Protein gms/gm	Calories per gm	Cost pence/gm
Meat	0.35	1.4	0.1
Mixed Vegetables	0.18	0.4	0.04

The meat content of each can is guaranteed to be at least 30% and the total protein content at least 20% (these percentages by weight being laid down in the portion control regulations). The maximum calorie content of each can is 210 calories.

Assuming that each (full) can weighs 280 gms, advise Barnes as to the quantities of meat and mixed vegetables which it should contain so as to minimise cost, and calculate the corresponding production cost per can.

3 A company manufacturing fish pastes and spreads is producing a display pack for the retail trade. The pack will contain an assortment of different pastes and spreads. Pastes and spreads have their own characteristic jars, spread jars being much taller than paste jars. Each variety of paste and spread will have a different type of label.

Each paste jar when full weighs 60 gms. and occupies an area of 8 sq. cms. Each spread jar when full weighs 90 gms. and occupies an area of 6 sq. cms. The cost of production per full jar is 15p for paste and 10p for spread.

The company requires that each display pack should contain at least 30 jars and weigh a minimum of 2000 gms. (The weight of the box itself is negligible). The space available for jars is limited to 210 sq. cms. (Ignore the space required for partitions.)

(a) Formulate a linear programming model to minimise the cost per display pack. Hence, determine graphically the number of paste jars and spread jars which each pack should contain. What is the minimum cost per pack?
(Note: Use a scale on both axes of 1 cm. for 2 jars.)

(b) After considering your solution, the manufacturer requires that a minimum of 10 paste jars should be included in each pack. Determine how many paste and spread jars each pack should now contain and find out how much more each display pack costs.

4   The matron in a children's home is concerned about the total daily intake of calories, protein and calcium which the 100 children in her care should have. The daily requirements for an average child are 2800 calories, 60 grams of protein and 1200 milligrammes of calcium.
   She decides that at least one quarter of the calories, at least one quarter of the calcium, and at least one half of the protein should be provided by the milk and bread in the childrens' diet. The nutritional content of these two products is tabulated below:

	Calories	Protein (grams)	Calcium (milligrammes)
Bread (per loaf)	620	20	90
Milk (per pint)	416	21	720

   If the cost of bread is 36p per loaf and of milk is 30p per pint, determine the quantities of milk and bread which she should order daily in order to minimise cost.

5   Boffo Ltd manufacture a liquid shampoo which is guaranteed to contain at least 20% of a magic ingredient, JT-47. This ingredient can be incorporated by using two additives X and Y. JT-47 constitutes half of additive X and a third of additive Y.
   The cost of 1 gallon of additive X is £25 and the cost of 1 gallon of additive Y is £20. However, these costs are based on a discount earned by Boffo Ltd only if they buy at least 200 gallons of X per week and 150 gallons of Y per week. The supply of X is limited to a maximum of 500 gallons per week.
   If Boffo Ltd have a contract to supply 1000 gallons of the shampoo each week to a particular customer, find the quantities of X and Y which should be bought weekly so as to minimise the cost of the additives. What is this minimum cost?

6   A company has to decide on a mixture of ingredients for a cat food. Three ingredients A, B, C are available and the costs of these per ton are £60, £48

and £40, respectively. The nutritional content of these is as follows:

A contains 40% protein, 40% fat, 15% carbohydrate, 5% ash
B contains 25% protein, 60% fat, 10% carbohydrate, 5% ash
C contains 90% carbohydrate, 10% ash.

The final mixture must contain a *minimum* of 20% protein and 36% fat. For sterilisation purposes, the amount of B must not exceed 60% of the final mixture.

Show that, if the mixture contains a fraction x of A and y of B, then the cost £C per ton of the mixture is given by

$$C = 20x + 8y + 40$$

Draw a suitable graph and mark the feasible region Hence, find the fractions of A, B, C in the minimum cost mixture, and calculate the minimum cost per ton.

If the costs of the ingredients A, B, C per ton change to £50, £60 and £40, respectively, calculate the new minimum cost per ton of the final mixture.

3

SIMPLEX ALGORITHM

When you have completed this chapter you will be able to:

- understand the role of slack variables
- represent a linear programming problem in tableau form
- use the Simplex algorithm to find an optimum solution
- handle mixed constraints using the Simplex algorithm
- apply the Simplex algorithm to minimisation problems

In the last chapter, we considered the graphical solution of linear programming problems. This approach requires that only two products are involved (although, there are those who claim to be able to think effectively in three dimensions). The Simplex algorithm provides a numerical approach which lends itself to computer implementation and allows any number of products to be considered. Moreover, it can be applied to both maximisation and minimisation problems.

3.1 MAXIMISATION PROBLEMS

At first sight the algorithm appears rather mysterious (to say the very least) and it is instructive to apply it to a problem which has already been solved graphically, in order to see exactly what the algorithm does. We will look again at Example 2.1.1, considered in detail in the last chapter, for which the unknowns x and y are defined as follows:

x = number of Florida quilts produced weekly

y = number of California quilts produced weekly

The linear program, as justified earlier, is stated thus:

Maximise:	$G = 30x + 40y$	Weekly profit
subject to the constraints:	$3x + 6y \leqslant 2400$	Fibron (kgs)
	$5x + 8y \leqslant 4000$	Nylon fabric (sq. m.)
	$3x + 3y \leqslant 1800$	Time (hours)
	$y \leqslant 300$	Demand
	$x \geqslant 0, \ y \geqslant 0$	Additional

(The graphical interpretation of the constraints and the feasible region is shown in Figure 3.1.1.)

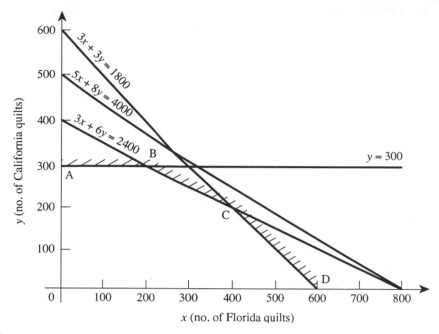

Figure 3.1.1

The algorithm explained

The algorithm is based upon the conversion of constraint inequalities to equations by introducing new variables called *slack variables*, which are traditionally denoted by s_1, s_2, etc. For example, consider the first constraint above concerned with the *maximum* availability of Fibron. The slack variable for this constraint, s_1, represents the spare amount of Fibron remaining after x Florida quilts and y California quilts have been produced. If all the Fibron is used, then $s_1 = 0$, whereas if 50 kilograms of Fibron remain, say, then $s_1 = 50$. One essential property of s_1 is that it is *non-negative*, which means that s_1 is zero or positive. The other essential property is that when s_1 is added to the total Fibron required for x Florida quilts and y California quilts, this equates to the maximum availability of Fibron. Thus

$$3x + 6y + s_1 = 2400$$

Slack variables s_2, s_3 and s_4 are *added* for the other constraints in a similar way, since the second and third constraints are also concerned with *maximum* resources, and the fourth constraint deals with maximum demand. Summarising, the first step in using the Simplex algorithm is as follows:

Step 1: Re-state the linear program, by converting all the constraint inequalities to **equations** through the introduction of new **non-negative** variables, called **slack variables**.

53

The linear program is now

Maximise:	$f = 30x + 40y$	Profit	
subject to the constraints:	$3x + 6y + s_1 = 2400$	Fibron	
	$5x + 8y + s_2 = 4000$	Nylon Fabric	(3.1.1)
	$3x + 3y + s_3 = 1800$	Time	
	$y + s_4 = 300$	Demand	

$$x \geqslant 0, \ y \geqslant 0, \ s_1 \geqslant 0, \ s_2 \geqslant 0, \ s_3 \geqslant 0, \ s_4 \geqslant 0$$

Note: the objective function (gross weekly profit) will be referred to as f here.

Although the slack variables s_1, s_2, s_3, s_4 have a different meaning to the *decision* variables x, y, *mathematically* these variables are all used in the same way. Figure 3.1.1 provides an illustration of this fact. The origin, point O, is one vertex of the feasible region and is the point at which two variables, x and y, are both zero. With the introduction of slack variables, this property is true for all the other vertices as well. At vertex A, $x = 0$ and $s_4 = 0$ (since on the demand line, there is no unfulfilled demand); at vertex B, $s_1 = 0$ and $s_4 = 0$ (there is no spare Fibron or demand); at vertex C, $s_1 = 0$ and $s_3 = 0$; and at vertex D, $y = 0$ and $s_3 = 0$. Thus, the algorithm is able to identify the vertices of the feasible region (where the optimum solution is to be found) by looking at points for which two of the variables are zero.

Similarly, when there are three or more decision variables, vertices of the feasible region, defined algebraically rather than graphically, will still be identified as points at which sets of variables are zero.

The Simplex algorithm is based upon the *manipulation of sets of equations*, such as (3.1.1). However, it is convenient to represent each of these by a **tableau**.

Step 2: Write down the initial tableau and the initial feasible solution.

Initial tableau

x	y	s_1	s_2	s_3	s_4	f	Quantity
3	6	1	0	0	0	0	2400
5	8	0	1	0	0	0	4000
3	3	0	0	1	0	0	1800
0	1	0	0	0	1	0	300
−30	−40	0	0	0	0	1	0
0	**1**	**0**	**0**	**0**	**1**	**0**	**300 M.R.**

Explanation of the initial tableau Consider, for example, the first constraint equation in (3.1.1):

$$3x + 6y + s_1 = 2400$$

This must be rewritten in terms of *all* the variables, before representing it as the first row of the tableau. Thus

$$3x + 6y + 1 \ s_1 + 0 \ s_2 + 0 \ s_3 + 0 \ s_4 + 0 \ f = 2400$$

The coefficients of the terms on the left-hand side are then placed in the first row and the first seven columns of the tableau, and the right-hand side is placed in the quantity column. The other constraint equations are then rewritten in the same way, and represented as the second, third and fourth rows of the tableau. However, the final row, representing the objective function f, requires further explanation. The equation

$$f = 30x + 40y$$

is rewritten so that it has a form consistent with the other equations. The most convenient rearrangment of the equation is

$$-30x - 40y + f = 0$$

Rewriting

$$-30x - 40y + 0\ s_1 + 0\ s_2 + 0\ s_3 + 0\ s_4 + 1\ f = 0$$

(as represented by the fifth row of the tableau). As you can see, the profit margins are now represented by *negative* values in the objective function row. You will always need to remember that *negative* values in the objective function row (the f-row) correspond to *positive* terms in the objective function. Therefore

increasing the variables corresponding to negative coefficients in the f-row increases the value of f.

The initial feasible solution, for which the original variables are zero, is

$$x = 0,\ y = 0,\ s_1 = 2400,\ s_2 = 4000,\ s_3 = 1800,\ s_4 = 300,\ f = 0 \qquad \text{the origin}$$

(Variables s_1, s_2, s_3 correspond to the maximum availability of each resource. s_4 corresponds to the maximum demand.)

Notice that in the initial tableau (as in all future tableaus), the nature of the **columns** beneath the variables indicates which variables are currently zero and which are non-zero.

- The non-zero variables are those for which the column comprises a single 1 and 0's.
- The value of each non-zero variable is obtained by reading across from the 1 in its column to the right-hand quantity column.

As an example of the second of these statements, consider the variable s_3 in the initial tableau. The 1 lies in the third row, and reading across this row to the right-hand quantity column, we obtain the value 1800 for s_3.

The Simplex algorithm now proceeds by increasing one of the *zero* variables (x or y), and obtaining a new feasible solution and a new tableau.

Step 3: Decide which **zero variable** to increase, and by how much it can be increased.

For the moment, we will adopt the approach of increasing the variable which corresponds to the **numerically largest negative f-coefficient**. The coefficients of x and y in the f-row are -30 and -40, and we therefore choose the variable y, for which the coefficient is numerically largest (i.e. largest when the negative signs are disregarded). Remember that a negative coefficient in the f-row indicates that f increases when the corresponding variable is increased.

The column for y and the rows of the tableau are used to decide the maximum amount that y can be increased. Consider the first row. To understand the approach it may be helpful to write down the corresponding equation:

$$3x + 6y + s_1 = 2400$$

Since x is zero, y can be increased provided that the slack variable (indicating the amount of the unused resource) does not become negative. So, for the maximum increase in y

$$6y = 2400 \qquad y = 400$$

To perform this same calculation using the tableau, the coefficient of y in the first row is divided into the number in the first row and *quantity* column. The same operation is performed for the other constraint rows, to find the maximum value of y for each. The relevant calculations, using the y-column coefficients, are therefore

$$y = 2400/6 = 400 \text{ (row 1)} \qquad y = 4000/8 = 500 \text{ (row 2)}$$
$$y = 1800/3 = 600 \text{ (row 3)} \qquad y = 300/1 = 300 \text{ (row 4)}$$

In order to ensure that no constraint is exceeded, the *smallest* value 300 is chosen. The approach is therefore as follows:

To decide the amount by which a zero variable can be increased, divide each *positive* coefficient in the column for that variable into the corresponding number in the quantity column, and take the smallest result.

The smallest value 300 arises from the fourth row, and division by the number 1 in this row and the y-column. The fourth row is called the **master row** for the first tableau and 1 is called the **pivot**. The master row is placed under the initial tableau, as shown, for reasons which will shortly become apparent.

(Actually, if the pivot is larger than one, then the row must be *divided by the pivot* to obtain the master row.)

Having decided to increase y to 300 units, it is now necessary to update the set of equations (3.3.1) to account for this value.

Step 4: Use the **master row** to convert each number in the **y-column,** other than the pivot, to **zero**.

This is done using the tableau but to understand what is happening, it is useful to look at the equations again. The demand equation

$$y + s_4 = 300$$

corresponds to the master row. The value on the right is the current value of y (although, as we have said, it is often necessary to divide the equation by the pivot to ensure that this is so).

It is tempting to simply substitute $y = 300$ into the other equations. However, in order to eliminate y from the other equations, whilst at the same time obtaining an updated set of equations which is *equivalent* to the first set, the equations must be manipulated by adding or subtracting multiples of equations. More precisely, *multiples of the master row equation* are added to or subtracted from the other equations. Consider the first row equation (for Fibron) for example:

$$3x + 6y + s_1 = 2400 \qquad (3.1.2)$$

Using the master row equation to eliminate the y term from this equation

$$
\begin{array}{ll}
3x + 6y + s_1 = 2400 & \\
\underline{6y + 6s_4 = 1800} & 6 \times \text{master row equation} \\
3x + s_1 - 6s_4 = 600 &
\end{array}
$$

The figure of 600 on the right is, in fact, the amount of Fibron left over when $y = 300$ units are produced. To see this look at the Fibron equation (3.1.2). The term $6y$ indicates that 6 kgs. of Fibron are used for each California quilt. Therefore, for 300 California quilts, $6 \times 300 = 1800$ kgs. of Fibron are used. Deducting this figure from 2400 kgs. of Fibron, 600 kgs. of Fibron remain.

The above calculation involving equations can be done more easily by using the first row of the tableau and the master row. Thus

For the first row of the next tableau
Calculate R1 − 6 × M.R.

3	**6**	1	0	0	0	0	2400	
0	**6**	0	0	0	6	0	1800	**6 × M.R.**
3	0	1	0	0	−6	0	600	

Remember that, having decided to increase y, y is now eliminated from the first equation. The master row is multiplied by 6 in order to reduce the number 6 in the **y-column** and the first row to zero.

For the second row of the next tableau
Calculate R2 − 8 × M.R.

5	**8**	0	1	0	0	0	4000	
0	**8**	0	0	0	8	0	2400	**8 × M.R.**
5	0	0	1	0	−8	0	1600	

The number 8 in the second row and **y-column** is reduced to zero.

For the third row of the next tableau
Calculate R3 − 3 × M.R.

3	**3**	0	0	1	0	0	1800	
0	**3**	0	0	0	3	0	900	**3 × M.R.**
3	0	0	0	1	−3	0	900	

The number 3 in the third row and **y-column** is reduced to zero.

For the new objective row – fourth row
Calculate R4 + 40 × M.R.

−30	−40	0	0	0	0	1		0	
0	**40**	0	0	0	40	0		12000	**40 × M.R.**
−30	0	0	0	0	40	1		12000	

Again a zero is achieved in the **y-column**.

Step 5: Create a new tableau by using the master row and the new rows obtained from the row operations.

Second tableau
The fourth row is the master row from the previous tableau, and the remaining rows are those calculated above.

x	y	s_1	s_2	s_3	s_4	f	Quantity	
3	0	1	0	0	−6	0	600	
5	0	0	1	0	−8	0	1600	
3	0	0	0	1	−3	0	900	
0	1	0	0	0	1	0	300	
−30	0	0	0	0	40	1	12000	
1	**0**	**1/3**	**0**	**0**	**−2**	**0**	**200**	**M.R.**

The feasible solution is now

$$x = 0, \ y = 300, \ s_1 = 600, \ s_2 = 1600, \ s_3 = 900, \ s_4 = 0, \ f = 12000$$

point A on graph

Remember that a non-zero variable is one for which the column consists of a single 1 and 0's elsewhere, and that the value in the 'quantity' column opposite the 1 is the current value of that variable. y has now become a non-zero variable, with current value 300. The algorithm is moving around the vertices of the feasible region shown in Figure 3.1.1.

We now proceed by repeating Steps 3 to 5 until the optimum solution is found. For this, all the coefficients in the f-row will be non-negative.

There is a *negative* coefficient still in the f-row, and so we increase the zero variable x. To decide the maximum amount to which x can be increased (Step 3), each *positive* number in the x column is divided into the quantity column value in the same row. Thus

$$x = 600/3 = 200 \quad \text{row 1} \qquad x = 1600/5 = 320 \quad \text{row 2}$$

$$x = 900/3 = 300 \quad \text{row 3}$$

The *smallest* value 200 corresponds to row 1 and division by 3, and 3 is therefore the pivot. Row 1 is divided by the pivot to obtain the master row, shown beneath the second tableau. It is now necessary (Step 4) to add or subtract multiples of the master row to or from the other rows in order to obtain zeroes in the *x-column* of the next tableau. For the new second row, the calculation is

R2 – 5 × M.R.

5	0	0	1	0	–8	0	1600	
5	0	5/3	0	0	–10	0	1000	5 × M.R.
0	0	–5/3	1	0	2	0	600	

For the new third row, the calculation is

R3 – 3 × M.R.

3	0	0	0	1	–3	0	900	
3	0	1	0	0	–6	0	600	3 × M.R.
0	0	–1	0	1	3	0	300	

No calculation is necessary for the fourth row, since the value in this row and the *x*-column is 0. For the new f-row the required calculation is R4 + 30 × M.R.

The new tableau (Step 5) for which the new first row is the master row, and the remaining rows are as calculated above, is as follows:

Third tableau

x	y	s_1	s_2	s_3	s_4	f	Quantity
1	0	1/3	0	0	–2	0	200
0	0	–5/3	1	0	2	0	600
0	0	–1	0	1	3	0	300
0	1	0	0	0	1	0	300
0	0	10	0	0	–20	1	18000
0	**0**	**–1/3**	**0**	**1/3**	**1**	**0**	**100 M.R.**

The corresponding feasible solution is

$$x = 200, \ y = 300, \ s_1 = 0, \ s_2 = 600, \ s_3 = 300, \ s_4 = 0, \ f = 18000$$

point B on graph

There is a *negative coefficient in the f-row* and s_4 column, and so the zero variable s_4 is increased. Dividing each *positive* number in the s_4 column into the corresponding 'quantity' figure gives

$s_4 = 600/2 = 300$ row 2 $s_4 = 300/3 = 100$ row 3

$s_4 = 300/1 = 300$ row 4

The *smallest* value is 100 which corresponds to row 3 and division by 3, and 3 is therefore the pivot. Therefore, row 3 divided by the pivot is the master row, as shown beneath the third tableau. It is now necessary to add or subtract multiples of the master row to or from the other rows in order to obtain zeroes in the s_4-*column* for the next tableau. The appropriate calculations are

$$R1 + 2 \times M.R.$$
$$R2 - 2 \times M.R.$$
$$R4 - M.R.$$
$$R5 + 20 \times M.R.$$

Fourth tableau

x	y	s_1	s_2	s_3	s_4	f	Quantity
1	0	$-1/3$	0	$2/3$	0	0	400
0	0	-1	1	$-2/3$	0	0	400
0	0	$-1/3$	0	$1/3$	1	0	100
0	1	$1/3$	0	$-1/3$	0	0	200
0	0	$10/3$	0	$20/3$	0	1	20000

All the coefficients in the *f-row* are now *non-negative* (and so correspond to 0 or negative terms in the objective function equation). For the zero variables s_1 and s_3 the terms are negative and so would cause profit to fall if either one of these variables is increased. The solution is therefore **optimum**.

Conclusion: To maximise f, $x = 400$, $y = 200$, $s_1 = 0$, $s_2 = 400$, $s_3 = 0$, $s_4 = 100$. The maximum value of f is 20,000. This is point C on the graph.

Therefore, there is no spare Fibron ($s_1 = 0$) and no spare time ($s_3 = 0$). 400 sq. metres of Nylon fabric are unused ($s_2 = 400$), and there is an unfulfilled demand of 100 California quilts ($s_4 = 100$). The maximum profit is £20,000.
    The above solution illustrates the essential steps of the Simplex algorithm which are summarised thus:

The Simplex Algorithm

Step 1: Re-state the linear program, by converting all the constraint inequalities to equations, using slack variables.

Step 2: Write down the initial tableau and the initial feasible solution.

Step 3: Decide which **zero variable** (if any) to increase, and by how much it can be increased.

   The chosen variable must correspond to a **negative** coefficient in the **f-row**. One approach is to choose the variable, or a variable, corresponding to the numerically largest negative f-row coefficient.

   For the chosen variable, each **positive** number in its column is divided into the corresponding 'quantity' value in the right-hand column. The number (or a number) for which the result of the division is smallest is called the **pivot**. The row containing the pivot is divided by the pivot (unless the pivot is 1) to obtain the **master row**.

Step 4: Use the **master row** to convert each number in the **column** for the variable chosen in Step 3, other than the pivot, to **zero**.

Step 5: Create a new tableau by using the master row and the new rows obtained from the row operations in Step 4.

Steps 3, 4 and 5 are now repeated until the solution is optimum. This will be so when every coefficient in the *f*-row is **non-negative**.

Note: Rather than choosing the variable in Step 3 for which the negative *f*-row coefficient is numerically largest, it is often more efficient to choose the variable which actually produces the largest *total* increase in the value of the objective function.

Alternative solution to previous problem

To understand the significance of the note above, notice that in finding the optimum solution, the algorithm moved from O to A to B to C, on the graph shown in Figure 3.1.1. C is the optimum point, and had the algorithm moved from O to D to C, the optimum solution would have been obtained earlier. It is possible to process the vertices in this order by choosing to increase the variable which *maximises* the *increase* in *f*.

As before, the initial tableau is

x	y	s_1	s_2	s_3	s_4	f	Quantity
3	6	1	0	0	0	0	2400
5	8	0	1	0	0	0	4000
3	3	0	0	1	0	0	1800
0	1	0	0	0	1	0	300
−30	−40	0	0	0	0	1	0
1	**1**	**0**	**0**	**1/3**	**0**	**0**	**600**

(Currently, x and y are both zero.) To see that it is better to increase x, rather than y, look at the objective function

$$f = 30x + 40y$$

(This can always be obtained from the objective row of the tableau.)

We saw earlier that y can be increased to 300 units, giving $f = 300 \times 40 = 12{,}000$. To find the amount by which x can be increased, each positive value in the x-column is divided into the corresponding quantity value on the right-hand side. The values obtained are

$$2400/3 = 800 \qquad 4000/5 = 800 \qquad 1800/3 = 600$$

and so x can be increased to 600 units, the smallest of these values, and the pivot is 3. As a result, $f = 30 \times 600 = 18{,}000$. Therefore f increases by an extra 6000 when increasing x. Since the limitation on x arises from the third row of the tableau, the master row is obtained by dividing this row by the pivot 3, and is shown under the above tableau, as usual. It forms the third row of the new tableau. The master row is now used to create a zero in the x-column for each of the first, second and fourth rows of the next tableau, by using the following row operations:

R1 − 3 × M.R.
R2 − 5 × M.R.
R5 + 30 × M.R.

The first of these calculations, for example, is

3	6	1	0	0	0	0	2400	
3	3	0	0	1	0	0	1800	3 × M.R.
0	3	1	0	−1	0	0	600	new first row

Second tableau

x	y	s_1	s_2	s_3	s_4	f	Quantity
0	3	1	0	−1	0	0	600
0	3	0	1	−5/3	0	0	1000
1	1	0	0	1/3	0	0	600
0	1	0	0	0	1	0	300
0	−10	0	0	10	0	1	18000
0	**1**	**1/3**	**0**	**−1/3**	**0**	**0**	**200**

The feasible solution is

$$x = 600, \; y = 0, \; s_1 = 600, \; s_2 = 1000, \; s_3 = 0, \; s_4 = 300, \; f = 18000 \quad \textbf{point D}$$

Notice that we have achieved, in the *second* tableau, the value of f given by the *third* tableau in the first version. Nonetheless, one more tableau is required. Fortunately, since only one coefficient in the objective row is now negative, it is clear that the zero variable y is the variable to increase. Dividing the positive values in the y-column into the quantity values gives

$$600/3 = 200 \qquad 1000/3 = 333\tfrac{1}{3} \qquad 600/1 = 600 \qquad 300/1 = 300$$

and so y can be increased to 200 units and the pivot is 3 (highlighted). The new master row is row 1 divided by 3, and is shown under the tableau. The row operations which produce zeroes in the y-column of the next tableau, for all entries except the pivot, are

R2 − 3 × M.R.
R3 − M.R.
R4 − M.R.
R5 + 10 × M.R.

Third tableau

x	y	s_1	s_2	s_3	s_4	f	Quantity
0	1	1/3	0	−1/3	0	0	200
0	0	−1	1	−2/3	0	0	400
1	0	−1/3	0	2/3	0	0	400
0	0	−1/3	0	1/3	1	0	100
0	0	10/3	0	20/3	0	1	20000

The optimum solution

$$x = 400, \ y = 200, \ s_1 = 0, \ s_2 = 400, \ s_3 = 0, \ s_4 = 100, \ f_{max} = \pounds 20000 \quad \textbf{point C}$$

has been reached. Therefore, in this version of the solution, we have saved one tableau by maximising the increase in f at the first stage. The payoff can sometimes be much greater.

However, the method of simply increasing the zero variable for which the negative coefficient in the objective row is numerically greatest proves to be effective in many cases. You may therefore wish to adopt this approach whilst getting to grips with the Simplex algorithm.

EXERCISES 3.1

1 A company manufactures two products P and Q, each of which is processed in three of the company's four divisions. At present, market demand is such that they are able to sell all of their production of P and Q. The processing times in each division for one unit of each product are given below.

Processing times (hours per unit)

Division	Product P	Product Q
A	4	3
B	2	1
C	2	3
D	2	0

In any week, the total processing time available in each of the company's four divisions is as follows:

Division	Total processing time available in hours per week
A	360
B	160
C	300
D	140

The revenue per unit is £60 for product P and £75 for product Q.

(a) If x, y denote the number of units of P and Q, respectively, produced per week, express the constraints and the weekly *revenue* function f in terms of x and y.

(b) Write down the initial tableau and the initial feasible solution.

(c) Use the Simplex algorithm to determine the quantities of P and Q which should be produced each week to maximise revenue, and state the maximum revenue.

(d) When revenue is maximised, which divisions, if any, have spare capacity?

(e) If the cost of producing one unit of P is £15 and one unit of Q is £45, calculate the weekly *profit* when revenue is maximised.

2 Suppose that the company in Exercise **1** wishes to arrange production so as to maximise profit rather than revenue. Use the Simplex algorithm to find the production mix which maximises profit, and state the maximum weekly profit.

3 Use the Simplex algorithm to find the optimum solution for the linear program

Maximise: $f = 10x_1 + 30x_2 + 40x_3$

subject to the
constraints:

$8x_1 + 2x_2 + 4x_3 \leqslant 1000$
$16x_1 + 4x_2 + 8x_3 \leqslant 2400$
$x_2 \leqslant 300$
$20x_1 + 2x_2 + 4x_3 \leqslant 800$
$x_1 \geqslant 0, \, x_2 \geqslant 0, \, x_3 \geqslant 0$

State the values of all the variables in the optimum solution.

4 Nouveau Fabrics produces woven fabric in three qualities – 'Standard', 'Superior' and 'Supreme'. Each unit length of 'Standard' fabric requires 2 kilograms of wool, 2 kilograms of cotton and 1 hour for production; each unit length of 'Superior', 4 kilograms of wool, 3 kilograms of cotton and 2 hours for production; and each unit length of 'Supreme', 2 kilograms of wool, 2 kilograms of cotton and 3 hours for production. The company is able to obtain up to 1000 kilograms of wool and 850 kilograms of cotton per week. Production time is limited to 800 hours per week.

The profit margins per unit length for 'Standard', 'Superior' and 'Supreme' are £13, £20 and £12, respectively. The demand for 'Supreme' is unlimited at present but the *combined* demand for 'Standard' and 'Superior' is estimated to be at most 400 units per week.

(a) If x, y, z denote the number of units of 'Standard', 'Superior' and 'Supreme', respectively, produced per week, express the constraints and the weekly profit function f in terms of x, y and z.

(b) Write down the initial Simplex tableau.

(c) Use the Simplex algorithm to obtain the optimum tableau. State the maximum profit, and the amount of each type of fabric which should be produced weekly to achieve this maximum. State the values of all the other variables.

5 (This question follows on from Exercise **4**)

(a) The management of Nouveau Fabrics suspects that it will be forced to decrease the profit per unit on 'Standard' fabric in the near future. Assuming that there is no change in demand for this fabric, use the tableaus which you have produced for **4** to determine the largest *decrease* possible in this profit margin, before the solution found in **4**(c) ceases to be optimum.
(b) The management has been negotiating for an increase in the weekly supply of cotton, and it has now been agreed that extra cotton can be made available. However, for this extra cotton, the cost per kilogram will be £C *more* than the normal cost upon which the profit margins of £13, £20 and £12 per unit are based.

By using the optimum tableau obtained in **4**(c), determine the range of acceptable values for C, if the management of Nouveau Fabrics wishes to raise total weekly profit above the optimum level calculated in **4**(c).

3.2 MIXED INEQUALITY AND MINIMISATION PROBLEMS

So far we have considered maximum constraints but many problems involve minimum constraints such as

$$2x + 3y \geqslant 100$$

To convert this constraint to an equation in order to apply the Simplex algorithm, it is tempting to simply **subtract** a slack variable s_1 so that

$$2x + 3y - s_1 = 100 \tag{3.2.1}$$

Actually, s_1 should be more accurately called an 'excess' variable, since it represents the amount by which $2x + 3y$ exceeds 100. The problem is that when the Simplex algorithm starts, it is necessary, or at least easiest, to assume that x and y are zero, in which case $s_1 = -100$. But the essence of the Simplex algorithm is that variables should not become negative, and to avoid this difficulty an extra variable s_2 is introduced for which

$$2x + 3y - s_1 + s_2 = 100$$

Such a variable s_2 is called an **artificial variable**. When $2x + 3y < 100$, $s_1 = 0$ and s_2 is positive. When $2x + 3y > 100$, $s_1 > 0$ and $s_2 = 0$. In both cases, neither of the variables is negative.

As the next example shows, the Simplex algorithm can be used to solve problems involving mixed constraints in the ordinary way.

EXAMPLE 3.2.1

A company produces three products A, B, C which require processing in two divisions X and Y. The table below shows the times in hours/unit required by these products in the two divisions, and the weekly maximum capacities in hours for the two divisions.

Times required per unit

		Products			Maximum capacity (hrs./week)
		A	B	C	
Divisions	X	5	3	4	360
	Y	3	2	5	400

The profit margins for A, B, C are £16/unit, £10/unit, £30/unit, respectively. The company has a contract to supply 60 units of A and/or C in total each week.

Determine the quantities of A, B, C which should be produced per week to maximise profit.

Solution 3.2.1

Let x_1, x_2, x_3 be the quantities of A, B, C, respectively, produced per week. Then the linear program is

Maximise: $f = 16x_1 + 10x_2 + 30x_3$ profit

subject to the constraints:
$5x_1 + 3x_2 + 4x_3 \leqslant 360$ Division A
$3x_1 + 2x_2 + 5x_3 \leqslant 400$ Division B
$x_1 + x_3 \geqslant 60$ Contract
$x_1 \geqslant 0, \ x_2 \geqslant 0, \ x_3 \geqslant 0$

The first step, as always, is to re-state the problem by converting the constraint inequalities to equations, using slack variables s_1, s_2, s_3 and the *artificial* variable s_4:

Maximise: $f = 16x_1 + 10x_2 + 30x_3$

subject to the constraints:
$5x_1 + 3x_2 + 4x_3 + s_1 = 360$
$3x_1 + 2x_2 + 5x_3 + s_2 = 400$
$x_1 + x_3 - s_3 + s_4 = 60$
$x_1 \geqslant 0, \ x_2 \geqslant 0, \ x_3 \geqslant 0, \ s_1 \geqslant 0, \ s_2 \geqslant 0, \ s_3 \geqslant 0, \ s_4 \geqslant 0$

Initial tableau

x_1	x_2	x_3	s_1	s_2	s_3	s_4	f	Quantity
5	3	4	1	0	0	0	0	360
3	2	5	0	1	0	0	0	400
1	0	1	0	0	-1	1	0	60
-16	-10	-30	0	0	0	0	1	0
1	0	1	0	0	-1	1	0	60 M.R.

The initial feasible solution is assumed to be

$$x_1 = 0, \ x_2 = 0, \ x_3 = 0, \ s_1 = 360, \ s_2 = 400, \ s_3 = 0, \ s_4 = 60$$

Remember that the non-zero variables for each tableau are precisely those for which the columns comprise a single 1 and 0's. Moreover, the value of any non-zero variable is obtained by reading across from the corresponding 1 to the value in the right-hand column. Notice that currently the third constraint equation is

$$x_1 + x_3 = 0 + 60 = 60 \qquad \text{since } s_3 = 0, \ s_4 = 60$$

The non-zero value of the artificial variable s_4 ensures that the solution is feasible, even though x_1 and x_3 are both zero. The constraint $x_1 + x_3 \geqslant 60$, will only be fulfilled **once the artificial variable s_4 has become zero**. Once s_4 has become zero, we will leave its column blank, thus effectively eliminating it from the calculation. Since x_1, x_2 and x_3 all correspond to negative f-row coefficients, we need to decide which variable to increase. The objective function is

$$f = 16x_1 + 10x_2 + 30x_3$$

For x_1, dividing the positive values in the x_1 column into the values in the quantity column produces the results

$360/5 = 72, \ 400/3 = 133\frac{1}{3}, \ 60/1 = 60$ smallest value 60 produces an increase in f value of $16 \times 60 = 960$

For x_2

$360/3 = 120, \ 400/2 = 200$ smallest value 120 produces an increase in f value of $10 \times 120 = 1200$

For x_3

$360/4 = 90, \ 400/5 = 80, \ 60/\mathbf{1} = 60$ smallest value 60 produces an increase in f value of $30 \times 60 = 1800$

Therefore, increase x_3. The pivot (highlighted) is 1 and the third row is the master row, as shown under the first tableau. (No division of the third row is required.) The appropriate row operations are now performed to create zero for every entry of the x_3 column of the next tableau, except the pivot. The operations are

$$R1 - 4 \times \text{M.R.}$$
$$R2 - 5 \times \text{M.R.}$$
$$R4 + 30 \times \text{M.R.}$$

For example, the first of these calculations is

5	3	**4**	1	0	0	0	0	360	
4	0	**4**	0	0	−4	4	0	240	$4 \times$ M.R.
1	3	0	1	0	4	−4	0	120	

Second tableau

x_1	x_2	x_3	s_1	s_2	s_3	s_4	f	Quantity
1	3	0	1	0	4	−4	0	120
−2	2	0	0	1	5	−5	0	100
1	0	1	0	0	−1	1	0	60
14	−10	0	0	0	−30	30	1	1800
−2/5	2/5	0	0	1/5	1	−1	0	20 M.R.

The feasible solution is

$$x_1 = 0, \; x_2 = 0, \; x_3 = 60, \; s_1 = 120, \; s_2 = 100, \; s_3 = 0, \; s_4 = 0, \; f = 1800$$

Notice that **the artificial variable s_4 is now zero**, indicating that the contract constraint is now satisfied – which it certainly is, since $x_3 = 60$. As explained above, the s_4 column will be left blank in the next tableau, to indicate that s_4 has now fulfilled its purpose.

Either x_2 or s_3 is now to be increased, and, to decide which, we need the objective function equation. This can always be obtained from the last row of the tableau. Thus

$$14x_1 - 10x_2 - 30s_3 + 30s_4 + f = 1800$$

$$f = 1800 - 14x_1 + 10x_2 + 30s_3 - 30s_4$$

For x_2 the profit is $10x_2$. Dividing the positive values in the x_2 column into the values in the right-hand column

$120/3 = 40, \; 100/2 = 50$ smallest value 40. Increase in f value
                                          $= 10 \times 40 = 400$

For s_3 the profit is $30s_3$.

$120/4 = 30, 100/5 = 20$ smallest value 20. Increase in f value
                                          $= 30 \times 20 = 600$

So, s_3 should be increased. The pivot (highlighted) is 5 and the second row is divided by 5 to create the master row. The appropriate row operations are

R1 − 4 × M.R.
R3 + M.R.
R4 + 30 × M.R.

Third tableau

x_1	x_2	x_3	s_1	s_2	s_3	s_4	f	Quantity
13/5	7/5	0	1	−4/5	0		0	40
−2/5	2/5	0	0	1/5	1		0	20
3/5	2/5	1	0	1/5	0		0	80
2	2	0	0	6	0		1	2400

There are no negative coefficients in the final, objective function, row of this tableau, and so the solution is optimum.

Conclusion: f has a maximum value of 2400 when $x_1 = 0$, $x_2 = 0$, $x_3 = 80$. ($s_3 = 20$, which means that, for the contract constraint, $x_1 + x_3$ actually exceeds 60 by 20 units for the optimum solution.)

Minimisation problems

For minimisation problems, the simplex algorithm can be used in much the same way as before. Minimum constraints occur frequently and artificial variables are used for these.

The problem of minimising a function is most easily handled by increasing zero variables which correspond to the **numerically smallest negative** coefficients in the objective row. Actually, for efficiency, we should increase the variable which produces the smallest increase in the objective function, but we shall opt for the 'numerically smallest' criterion for simplicity.

EXAMPLE 3.2.2

Minimise: $\qquad\qquad\qquad f = 20x_1 + 25x_2$

subject to the constraints: $\quad 4x_1 + 5x_2 \geqslant 1200$
$$x_1 \geqslant 100$$
$$2x_1 + 2x_2 \geqslant 560$$
$$x_1 \geqslant 0, \, x_2 \geqslant 0$$

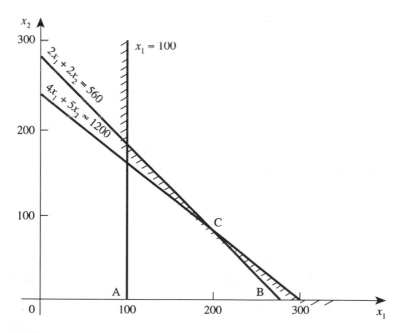

Figure 3.2.1

69

Solution 3.2.2

Introducing slack and artificial variables, the linear program becomes

Minimise: $\qquad f = 20x_1 + 25x_2$

subject to the constraints: $\quad 4x_1 + 5x_2 - s_1 + s_2 = 1200$

$$x_1 - s_3 + s_4 = 100$$
$$2x_1 + 2x_2 - s_5 + s_6 = 560$$
$$x_1 \geqslant 0,\ x_2 \geqslant 0,\ s_1 \geqslant 0,\ s_2 \geqslant 0,\ s_3 \geqslant 0,\ s_4 \geqslant 0,$$
$$s_5 \geqslant 0,\ s_6 \geqslant 0$$

For the purposes of illustration, the feasible region is shown in Figure 3.2.1.

The aim is to make the artificial variables zero and to obtain the smallest value of f for which this aim is achieved. As each artificial variable becomes zero, its column will be left blank so that it is not inadvertently increased in the future. The artificial variables will be marked with an * in each tableau.

Initial tableau

	x_1	x_2	s_1	s_2 *	s_3	s_4 *	s_5	s_6 *	f	Quantity
	4	5	−1	1	0	0	0	0	0	1200
	1	0	0	0	−1	1	0	0	0	100
	2	2	0	0	0	0	−1	1	0	560
	−20	−25	0	0	0	0	0	0	1	0
M.R.	1	0	0	0	−1	1	0	0	0	100

The initial feasible solution is assumed to be

$$x_1 = 0,\ x_2 = 0,\ s_1 = 0,\ s_2 = 1200,\ s_3 = 0,\ s_4 = 100,\ s_5 = 0,\ s_6 = 560,\ f = 0$$

(This is the origin of the graph.)

Since x_1 corresponds to the *numerically smallest negative* coefficient in the objective row, we increase x_1 by an amount determined by

$$1200/4 = 300,\ 100/1 = 100,\ 560/2 = 280 \qquad \text{smallest value 100 from row 2}$$

The pivot is 1 and row 2 is the master row (as shown above). This becomes the second row of the new tableau. The master row is now used to ensure a zero in the x_1 column for each of the other rows of the next tableau. The row operations are

R1 − 4 × M.R.
R3 − 2 × M.R.
R4 + 20 × M.R.

The first of these calculations is

4	5	−1	1	0	0	0	0	0	1200
4	0	0	0	−4	4	0	0	0	400
0	5	−1	1	4	−4	0	0	0	800

Second tableau

x_1	x_2	s_1	s_2 *	s_3	s_4 *	s_5	s_6 *	f	Quantity
0	5	−1	1	4	−4	0	0	0	800
1	0	0	0	−1	1	0	0	0	100
0	2	0	0	2	−2	−1	1	0	360
0	−25	0	0	−20	20	0	0	1	2000
M.R. 0	**1**	**0**	**0**	**1**	**−1**	**−1/2**	**1/2**	**0**	**180**

Reading from the tableau, the feasible solution (point A on the graph) is now

$$x_1 = 100,\ x_2 = 0,\ s_1 = 0,\ s_2 = 800,\ s_3 = 0,\ s_4 = 0,\ s_5 = 0,\ s_6 = 360,\ f = 2000$$

Although the feasible region is outside all the constraint lines, as shown in Figure 3.2.1, the algorithm is working outwards from the origin. x_1 is increased until one of the artificial variables becomes zero. In this case, s_4 becomes zero at point A, indicating that the second constraint $x_1 \geq 100$ is now satisfied (since x_1 has the value 100). s_4 has served its purpose, and its column will be left blank for the remainder of the solution. Looking at the objective function row, s_3 corresponds to the *numerically smallest negative* coefficient in the objective row, and so this variable is increased to 180. You are left to check that the master row (obtained by dividing row 3 by 2) is as shown above, and that the required row operations are

R1 − 4 × M.R.
R2 + M.R.
R4 + 20 × M.R.

Third tableau

x_1	x_2	s_1	s_2 *	s_3	s_4 *	s_5	s_6 *	f	Quantity
0	1	−1	1	0		2	−2	0	80
1	1	0	0	0		−1/2	1/2	0	280
0	1	0	0	1		−1/2	1/2	0	180
0	−5	0	0	0		−10	10	1	5600
M.R. 0	**1**	**−1**	**1**	**0**		**2**	**−2**	**0**	**80**

The feasible solution, at point B on the graph, is now

$$x_1 = 280,\ x_2 = 0,\ s_1 = 0,\ s_2 = 80,\ s_3 = 180,\ s_4 = 0,\ s_5 = 0,\ s_6 = 0,\ f = 5600$$

The artificial variable s_6 is now zero, indicating that the third constraint $2x_1 + 2x_2 \geq 560$ is now satisfied (since $x_1 = 280$). The column for s_6 will be left blank in the next tableau. The variable x_2 is increased next. The master row is row 1, and the row operations required for the next tableau are

R2 – M.R.
R3 – M.R.
R4 + 5 × M.R.

Fourth tableau

x_1	x_2	s_1	s_2	s_3	s_4	s_5	s_6	f	Quantity
			*		*		*		
0	1	−1	1	0		2		0	80
1	0	1	−1	0		−5/2		0	200
0	0	1	−1	1		−5/2		0	100
0	0	−5	5	0		0		1	6000

All the **artificial variables** are now zero and so all the ≥ constraints are fulfilled and the solution is optimum. In order to *decrease* f, it would be necessary to increase a variable with a *positive* coefficient in the objective function row (since a positive coefficient indicates a negative term in the objective function equation). The only variable is the artificial variable s_2, and this cannot be increased without violating the first constraint.

Conclusion: The optimum solution, at point C on the graph, is $x_1 = 200$, $x_2 = 80$, $s_1 = 0$, $s_2 = 0$, $s_3 = 100$, $s_4 = 0$, $s_5 = 0$, $s_6 = 0$. (The value of 100 for s_3 signifies that the minimum value of 100 for the second constraint is exceeded by 100 – this checks since $x_1 = 200$.)

EXERCISES 3.2

1 Use the Simplex algorithm to find the optimum solution for each of the following linear programs:

(a) Maximise: $\qquad\qquad\qquad\qquad\quad f = 5x + 20y$

       subject to the constraints: $\quad 2x + 6y \leqslant 300$
$\qquad\qquad\qquad\qquad\qquad\qquad\quad 2x + 3y \leqslant 240$
$\qquad\qquad\qquad\qquad\qquad\qquad\quad y \leqslant 30$
$\qquad\qquad\qquad\qquad\qquad\qquad\quad x \geqslant 20$
$\qquad\qquad\qquad\qquad\qquad\qquad\quad y \geqslant 0$

(b) Maximise: $\qquad\qquad\qquad\qquad\quad f = 20x_1 + 10x_2 + 5x_3$

       subject to the constraints: $\quad 5x_1 + 2x_2 + 4x_3 \leqslant 200$
$\qquad\qquad\qquad\qquad\qquad\qquad\quad 10x_1 + 6x_2 + 8x_3 \leqslant 450$
$\qquad\qquad\qquad\qquad\qquad\qquad\quad x_1 \geqslant 15$
$\qquad\qquad\qquad\qquad\qquad\qquad\quad x_2 \geqslant 20$

2 Use the Simplex algorithm to determine the optimum solution for the linear program

Minimise: $\qquad\qquad\qquad\qquad f = 20x + 40y$

subject to the constraints: $\qquad 2x + y \geqslant 100$
$\qquad\qquad\qquad\qquad\qquad\quad 4x + 3y \geqslant 240$
$\qquad\qquad\qquad\qquad\qquad\quad x \geqslant 0$
$\qquad\qquad\qquad\qquad\qquad\quad y \geqslant 20$

3 An oil company puts additives in its petrol to give improved performance and reduce engine wear. A quantity of petrol has been ordered and must contain at least 18 mgs. of additive A and 28 mgs. of additive B. The company can use two ingredients X and Y which have the following weights of additives:

Weights of additives in mgs. per litre

		Additive	
		A	B
Ingredient	X	1	2
	Y	3	4

For technical reasons, the quantity of petrol ordered must contain at least 3 litres of ingredient X. Both ingredients cost £10 per litre.

If the order contains x litres of ingredient X and y litres of ingredient Y, and the cost of the order is to be minimised, formulate a suitable linear program, and use the Simplex algorithm to find the least cost solution.

4 Use the Simplex algorithm to find the optimum solution for the linear program

Minimise: $\qquad\qquad\qquad\qquad f = 15x_1 + 30x_2 + 10x_3$

subject to the constraints: $\quad 2x_1 + x_2 + 3x_3 \geqslant 60$
$\qquad\qquad\qquad\qquad\qquad\quad 4x_1 + 2x_2 + 2x_3 \geqslant 80$
$\qquad\qquad\qquad\qquad\qquad\quad 2x_1 + 3x_3 \leqslant 120$
$\qquad\qquad\qquad\qquad\qquad\quad x_1 \geqslant 0,\ x_2 \geqslant 0,\ x_3 \geqslant 0$

4

PRODUCTION PLANNING AND FORECASTING

When you have completed this chapter you will be able to:

- express data correctly in matrix format
- perform matrix operations
- apply matrices to production planning
- understand the concept of matrix inverse
- calculate the inverse of a 2 × 2 matrix
- apply matrices to determine market changes

4.1   MATRICES AND MATRIX OPERATIONS

The aim here is to apply matrices, which were first introduced for mathematical and scientific purposes, to business problems. Matrices are arrays or tables of data and provide a natural way of describing many problems, particularly when a computer is to be used to obtain a solution. Before looking at particular applications, it is necessary to do some groundwork.

Definition 4.1.1 – matrix

An **m × n matrix** is a **rectangular array** (or **table**) of numbers (called the elements of the matrix) with **m rows** and **n columns**. The matrix is said to have dimensions $m \times n$.

The elements of a matrix are contained in brackets, and the matrix is usually denoted by a capital letter. For example

$$A = \begin{pmatrix} 1/2 & 0 & -3 \\ 1 & -2 & 4 \end{pmatrix} \quad \text{and} \quad B = \begin{pmatrix} 2 & 1 & 1/3 & 4 \\ 5 & -1 & 0 & -2 \\ 1 & 6 & 5 & 1/4 \end{pmatrix}$$

are 2 × 3 (2 rows, 3 columns) and 3 × 4 (3 rows, 4 columns) matrices. Note that

The number of rows is always written first.

So, for example, under no circumstances is A described as a 3 × 2 matrix. Given that many programming languages and software packages have built-in matrix facilities, a rigid approach to defining matrices is essential.

74

For an example of how matrices arise naturally in practice, consider the following table which refers to three products P1, P2, P3, and three processing divisions A, B, C, and describes the processing times in each division required to produce one unit of each product.

Processing times in hours per unit

	A	B	C
P1	1	1	0
P2	2	0	2
P3	1	2	1

In matrix form, this can be written as

$$T = \begin{pmatrix} 1 & 1 & 0 \\ 2 & 0 & 2 \\ 1 & 2 & 1 \end{pmatrix}$$ Use T for the matrix, say, with **time** requirements in mind

Obviously, the most natural approach is to write down the rows and columns as they stand, when forming the matrix. Alternatively, we could write

$$T = \begin{pmatrix} 1 & 2 & 1 \\ 1 & 0 & 2 \\ 0 & 2 & 1 \end{pmatrix}$$ writing the rows of the table as columns

What is important when using matrices is *consistency*.

Once data has been represented in matrix form, it is not necessary, or even desirable, to change the format subsequently.

Extending the previous example a little more, suppose that an order were to be received for 50 units of P1, 70 units of P2 and 80 units of P3. This information can also be written in matrix format as follows:

$$D = (50 \quad 70 \quad 80) \quad \text{or} \quad D = \begin{pmatrix} 50 \\ 70 \\ 80 \end{pmatrix}$$ use D, say, with **demand** in mind

$$1 \times 3 \qquad\qquad\qquad 3 \times 1$$

For such matrices, which have one row or one column, a separate terminology is introduced.

Definition 4.1.2 – vector

A **vector** is a matrix with just **one row** or **one column**. If the matrix has one row it is called a *row vector*; if it has one column it is called a *column vector*.

Note: You may be familiar with the term 'vector' in the context of science, where it refers to a quantity with magnitude, direction and sense, e.g. force, velocity. In fact, such a quantity can be represented by a row vector or column vector in the matrix sense of Definition 4.1.2, where the elements of the matrix are the components of the quantity – hence the terminology.

The usefulness of matrices arises from the fact that, as you will see, it is possible to develop a **matrix arithmetic**, which satisfies many of the rules which we take for granted for ordinary numbers.

Matrix operations

Scalar multiplication of a matrix

Scalar multiplication of a matrix means multiplication by a number. *Any* matrix A may be multiplied by *any* number n to obtain the matrix nA. The elements of nA are obtained by multiplying every element of A by n.

For example, consider the first version of the previous time matrix

$$T = \begin{pmatrix} 1 & 1 & 0 \\ 2 & 0 & 2 \\ 1 & 2 & 1 \end{pmatrix}$$

then

$$5T = \begin{pmatrix} 5 & 5 & 0 \\ 10 & 0 & 10 \\ 5 & 10 & 5 \end{pmatrix} \quad \text{multiplying each element by 5}$$

Whereas, the T matrix gives the production times per unit for P1, P2, P3, the matrix 5T obviously gives the times required for producing 5 units of each product.

Addition and subtraction of matrices

Two matrices A and B can be added or subtracted if they have **exactly the same dimensions**, i.e. the same number of rows and the same number of columns.

A + B is calculated by adding corresponding elements.

A – B is calculated by subtracting corresponding elements.

Again, using the previous example for the purposes of illustration, suppose that a modification to the products P1, P2, P3 means that P1 and P2 require an extra half hour per unit in division A, P1 and P3 require an extra quarter of an hour per unit in division B, and P3 requires an extra half hour per unit in division C. Then, the matrix E of *extra* times is

$$E = \begin{pmatrix} 1/2 & 1/4 & 0 \\ 1/2 & 0 & 0 \\ 0 & 1/4 & 1/2 \end{pmatrix}$$

The new times per unit can now be obtained by adding T and E as follows:

$$T + E = \begin{pmatrix} 1 & 1 & 0 \\ 2 & 0 & 2 \\ 1 & 2 & 1 \end{pmatrix} + \begin{pmatrix} 1/2 & 1/4 & 0 \\ 1/2 & 0 & 0 \\ 0 & 1/4 & 1/2 \end{pmatrix}$$

$$= \begin{pmatrix} 1.5 & 1.25 & 0 \\ 2.5 & 0 & 2 \\ 1 & 2.25 & 1.5 \end{pmatrix} \quad \text{add corresponding elements}$$

Matrix subtraction could be used to calculate reduced processing times.

Multiplication of matrices

The operations described so far are natural and easy to use. Matrix multiplication is neither of these. However, you must remember that it was introduced for mathematical and scientific reasons. Therefore, the view which should be taken is that these are the operations, as given – how can they be exploited for business purposes?
    If A, B are matrices, the matrix product AB is calculated as follows:

- To find the first row of AB multiply the first row of the left-hand matrix A by each column of the right-hand matrix B. Each calculation is placed in a separate column of AB.
- To find the second row of AB multiply the second row of the left-hand matrix A by each column of the right-hand matrix B. Again each calculation is placed in a separate column of AB. And so on.

(4.1.1)

To multiply a **row** of A by a **column** of B,

Each element of the row is multiplied by the corresponding element of the column and the products are added.

Notice the reference to 'corresponding' elements here. The implication is that, for the multiplication to be possible, each row of A and each column of B must have the same number of elements. The number of elements in each row of A is equal to the number of columns of A, and the number of elements in each column of B is equal to the number of rows of B Therefore, multiplication is possible provided that the number of *columns* of A is equal to the number of *rows* of B. This is most easily checked by writing down the matrices, in the order A, B, with their dimensions underneath.

$$\begin{array}{cc} A & B \\ m \times n & n \times p \end{array}$$
must be equal for
multiplication to be possible

A has n columns, B has n rows   (4.1.2)

What about the dimensions of the answer AB? Looking at (4.1.1), each row of A produces a row of AB and so AB has the same number of rows as A. Each row of

A is multiplied by the columns of B and the answers are placed in different columns. Therefore, AB has the same number of columns as B. This can be remembered as follows:

$$\underbrace{\begin{array}{cc} A & B \\ m \times n & n \times p \end{array}}$$

dimensions of AB are $m \times p$

To see how matrix multiplication is performed, consider the matrices

$$A = \begin{pmatrix} 2 & 3 & -1 & 4 \\ 4 & 2 & 0 & -6 \\ 1 & -3 & 5 & 1 \end{pmatrix} \qquad B = \begin{pmatrix} 2 & -3 \\ -4 & 2 \\ 1 & 3 \\ 0 & -1 \end{pmatrix}$$

A and B have different dimensions and yet the product can be calculated. First write down the dimensions of the matrices in the order in which they are to be multiplied:

A   B   'Inner' dimensions are equal – multiplication is
3×4 4×2 possible. Outer dimensions give size of answer – AB is 3×2.

To calculate AB, it is important to remember that

Only the **rows** of the **left-hand matrix** are used, and only the **columns** of the **right-hand matrix**.

1. To find the first row of AB

The *first* row of A is multiplied by each column of B. The two calculations are shown separately below:

first row × first column

$$AB = \begin{pmatrix} 2 & 3 & -1 & 4 \\ 4 & 2 & 0 & -6 \\ 1 & -3 & 5 & 1 \end{pmatrix} \begin{pmatrix} 2 & -3 \\ -4 & 2 \\ 1 & 3 \\ 0 & -1 \end{pmatrix} = \begin{pmatrix} -9 & \cdot \\ \cdot & \cdot \\ \cdot & \cdot \end{pmatrix}$$

3×4 4×2 3×2

The calculation is

$$(2 \times 2) + (3 \times -4) + (-1 \times 1) + (4 \times 0) = 4 - 12 - 1 = -9$$

(The first row element is multiplied by the first column element, the second row element by the second column element, etc. The individual results are added.)

first row × second column

$$AB = \begin{pmatrix} 2 & 3 & -1 & 4 \\ 4 & 2 & 0 & -6 \\ 1 & -3 & 5 & 1 \end{pmatrix} \begin{pmatrix} 2 & -3 \\ -4 & 2 \\ 1 & 3 \\ 0 & -1 \end{pmatrix} = \begin{pmatrix} -9 & -7 \\ \cdot & \cdot \\ \cdot & \cdot \end{pmatrix}$$

The calculation is

$$(2 \times -3) + (3 \times 2) + (-1 \times 3) + (4 \times -1) = -6 + 6 - 3 - 4 = -7$$

2. To find the second and third rows of AB

$$AB = \begin{pmatrix} 2 & 3 & -1 & 4 \\ 4 & 2 & 0 & -6 \\ 1 & -3 & 5 & 1 \end{pmatrix} \begin{pmatrix} 2 & -3 \\ -4 & 2 \\ 1 & 3 \\ 0 & -1 \end{pmatrix} = \begin{pmatrix} -9 & -7 \\ 0 & -2 \\ 19 & 5 \end{pmatrix}$$

For the **second** row of the answer, the calculations are, using the **second** row of A,

$(4 \times 2) + (2 \times -4) + (0 \times 1) + (-6 \times 0) = 0$ multiply by first column of B

$(4 \times -3) + (2 \times 2) + (0 \times 3) + (-6 \times -1) = -2$ multiply by second column of B

For the **third** row of the answer, the answers are, using the **third** row of A,

$(1 \times 2) + (-3 \times -4) + (5 \times 1) + (1 \times 0) = 19$ multiply by first column of B

$(1 \times -3) + (-3 \times 2) + (5 \times 3) + (1 \times -1) = 5$ multiply by second column of B

The calculation of AB is now complete. By contrast, BA cannot be calculated as the dimensions show

    B $\neq$ A   BA is not defined
4 × 2   3 × 4

So the **order in which matrices are multiplied is vital**.

We have now covered all the required operations. The next example provides some further sample calculations.

EXAMPLE 4.1.1

Consider the matrices

$$A = \begin{pmatrix} -1 & 3 \\ 3 & -4 \end{pmatrix} \qquad B = \begin{pmatrix} 2 & -2 & 4 \\ 3 & 5 & -3 \end{pmatrix} \qquad C = \begin{pmatrix} 3 \\ 4 \end{pmatrix}$$

$$D = \begin{pmatrix} 1 & -2 \\ 3 & 1 \end{pmatrix} \qquad E = (5 \quad -1) \qquad F = \begin{pmatrix} -1 & 4 & -3 \\ 6 & -2 & 2 \end{pmatrix}$$

Calculate (if possible)   **(a)** $3A + 4D$ **(b)** $2B - 2F + D$ **(c)** AB   **(d)** BA

                           (e) $A(B + F)$ **(f)** $(A - 2D)^2$ **(g)** CE

Verify that $A(B + F) = AB + AF$.

Solution 4.1.1(a)

$$3A + 4D = 3 \begin{pmatrix} -1 & 3 \\ 3 & -4 \end{pmatrix} + 4 \begin{pmatrix} 1 & -2 \\ 3 & 1 \end{pmatrix}$$
$$\qquad\qquad 2 \times 2 \qquad\qquad 2 \times 2$$

$$= \begin{pmatrix} -3 + 4 & 9 - 8 \\ 9 + 12 & -12 + 4 \end{pmatrix} = \begin{pmatrix} 1 & 1 \\ 21 & -8 \end{pmatrix}$$

Solution 4.1.1(b)

The dimension check

$$
\begin{array}{ccc}
2B & - & 2F & + & D \\
2 \times 3 & & 2 \times 3 & & 2 \times 2
\end{array}
$$

shows that this expression is not defined. D has different dimensions to 2B and 2F, and cannot be added.

Solution 4.1.1(c)

$$
\text{AB} = \begin{array}{c} \text{rows} \\ \left(\begin{array}{cc} -1 & 3 \\ 3 & -4 \end{array}\right) \\ 2 \times 2 \end{array} \begin{array}{c} \text{columns} \\ \left(\begin{array}{ccc} 2 & -2 & 4 \\ 3 & 5 & -3 \end{array}\right) \\ 2 \times 3 \end{array}
$$

Multiply first row of A by cols. of B to get first row of AB.

Multiply second row of A by cols. of B to get second row of AB.

Size of answer $= 2 \times 3$

$$
= \left(\begin{array}{ccc} (-1 \times 2) + (3 \times 3) & (-1 \times -2) + (3 \times 5) & (-1 \times 4) + (3 \times -3) \\ (3 \times 2) + (-4 \times 3) & (3 \times -2) + (-4 \times 5) & (3 \times 4) + (-4 \times -3) \end{array}\right)
$$

$$
= \left(\begin{array}{ccc} 7 & 17 & -13 \\ -6 & -26 & 24 \end{array}\right)
$$
$$
2 \times 3
$$

Solution 4.1.1(d)

$$
\begin{array}{ccc}
B & \neq & A \\
2 \times 3 & & 2 \times 2
\end{array}
$$

Product is not defined.

Solution 4.1.1(e)

To calculate $A(B + F)$, the matrix in the bracket must first be evaluated.

$$
B + F = \left(\begin{array}{ccc} 2 & -2 & 4 \\ 3 & 5 & -3 \end{array}\right) + \left(\begin{array}{ccc} -1 & 4 & -3 \\ 6 & -2 & 2 \end{array}\right)
$$

matrices must have same dimensions when adding

$$
= \left(\begin{array}{ccc} 1 & 2 & 1 \\ 9 & 3 & -1 \end{array}\right)
$$

$$
A(B + F) = \left(\begin{array}{cc} -1 & 3 \\ 3 & -4 \end{array}\right) \left(\begin{array}{ccc} 1 & 2 & 1 \\ 9 & 3 & -1 \end{array}\right) = \left(\begin{array}{ccc} 26 & 7 & -4 \\ -33 & -6 & 7 \end{array}\right)
$$
$$
\quad\quad\quad\quad\quad 2 \times 2 \quad\quad 2 \times 3 \quad\quad\quad\quad 2 \times 3
$$

Solution 4.1.1(f)

To find $(A - 2D)^2$, first calculate $A - 2D$.

$$
A - 2D = \left(\begin{array}{cc} -1 & 3 \\ 3 & -4 \end{array}\right) - 2\left(\begin{array}{cc} 1 & -2 \\ 3 & 1 \end{array}\right) = \left(\begin{array}{cc} -3 & 7 \\ -3 & -6 \end{array}\right)
$$

Squaring this matrix does not mean squaring its elements. We have to multiply the matrix by itself.

$$(A - 2D)^2 = \begin{pmatrix} -3 & 7 \\ -3 & -6 \end{pmatrix}\begin{pmatrix} -3 & 7 \\ -3 & -6 \end{pmatrix} = \begin{pmatrix} -12 & -63 \\ 27 & 15 \end{pmatrix}$$

Solution 4.1.1(g)

CE requires some thought. For this product, there is a column vector on the left and a row vector on the right. Nonetheless, for the left-hand matrix, only the *rows* are relevant and for the right-hand matrix, only the *columns* are necessary. Thus

$$CE = \begin{pmatrix} 3 \\ 4 \end{pmatrix} (5 \quad -1) = \begin{pmatrix} 15 & -3 \\ 20 & -4 \end{pmatrix}$$
$$2 \times 1 \quad 1 \times 2 \qquad 2 \times 2$$

Finally, we must verify that $A(B + F) = AB + AF$. In (e), we showed that

$$A(B + F) = \begin{pmatrix} 26 & 7 & -4 \\ -33 & -6 & 7 \end{pmatrix} \tag{4.1.3}$$

To calculate the right-hand side, the products AB and AF must be calculated. You should check that:

$$AB = \begin{pmatrix} 7 & 17 & -13 \\ -6 & -26 & 24 \end{pmatrix} \qquad AF = \begin{pmatrix} 19 & -10 & 9 \\ -27 & 20 & -17 \end{pmatrix}$$

and that $AB + AF$ is the matrix (4.1.3). The given matrix equation is therefore verified.

Note: The matrix property $A(B + F) = AB + AF$, where the bracket is removed and A is multiplied by each matrix inside, illustrates that matrix operations satisfy the rules of ordinary arithmetic. This particular rule is called a *Distributive Law*. Another example is $(AB)C = A(BC)$, assuming that the multiplications are defined. This is called the *Associative Law*. You will see that it has an important role to play in the next example. It is important to note, however, that AB is *not* usually the same as BA.

Production planning

Matrices can be used for production planning purposes, in order to determine the resources required to meet orders, calculate unit production costs and calculate the total costs of orders, for example. When applying matrices to a business context, it is essential that

- all matrix calculations are correct **dimensionally**
- all matrix calculations **make sense** within the **problem context**

The next example illustrates these issues.

EXAMPLE 4.1.2

A company produces three types of tent – the Alpine, the Arctic and the Polar. The input quantities required for production are as follows:

Table of input quantities per tent

	Canvas (sq. metres)	Plastic (sq. metres)	Tubing (metres)
Alpine	14	6	12
Arctic	12	7	9
Polar	8	5	8

The company purchases the canvas at £30/sq. metre, the plastic at £15/metre, and the tubing at £20/metre. To meet current demand, the company requires to produce 150 Alpine tents, 100 Arctic tents, and 50 Polar tents. Use matrix multiplication to

(a) determine the input quantities necessary to meet current demand
(b) calculate the cost of production per tent for each of the three types
(c) calculate the total cost of fulfilling the current demand.

Solution 4.1.2(a)
First the given table is expressed as a 3 × 3 resource requirement matrix

$$R = \begin{pmatrix} 14 & 6 & 12 \\ 12 & 7 & 9 \\ 8 & 5 & 8 \end{pmatrix}$$

The costs of the resources per unit are £30, £15 and £20 for canvas, plastic and tubing, respectively. In order to calculate the production cost per unit for each of the three tent types, these costs must be multiplied by the resource quantities given by R. It is therefore necessary to form the costs into a vector (a matrix with one row or one column). There are two related questions:

'should C be a **row** vector or a **column** vector?'   (only one of these is right)

'should we calculate **RC** or **CR**?'   (only one of these is right)

For this first example, we will adopt the approach of trying all possibilities, in order to show the pitfalls. With experience, it is possible to arrive at the correct combination more quickly. As stated earlier, the correct answer must be *correct dimensionally* and must *make sense* within the problem context.

First, we will try **writing the costs as a row vector**

$$C = (30 \quad 15 \quad 20)$$

The product

$$RC = \begin{pmatrix} 14 & 6 & 12 \\ 12 & 7 & 9 \\ 8 & 5 & 8 \end{pmatrix}(30 \quad 15 \quad 20)$$

$$\qquad\qquad 3 \times 3 \quad \neq \quad 1 \times 3$$

is not defined. However, the product

$$CR = \begin{matrix} & \text{Can.} & \text{Pla.} & \text{Tub.} \\ (& 30 & 15 & 20 \ ) \end{matrix} \quad \begin{matrix} & \text{Can.} & \text{Pla.} & \text{Tub.} \\ \text{Alp.} & 14 & 6 & 12 \\ \text{Arc.} & 12 & 7 & 9 \\ \text{Pol.} & 8 & 5 & 8 \end{matrix}$$

$$1 \times 3 \qquad\qquad 3 \times 3$$

is correct dimensionally. To decide if it makes sense, we label the rows and columns with the tent types and the resources. Bearing in mind that this calculation involves multiplying the row on the left by the columns of the matrix on the right, since this is the way that multiplication is defined, you can see that the calculation makes no sense within the business context. For example, if the row of costs is multiplied by the first column of the right-hand matrix, then costs for canvas, plastic and tubing are multiplied by quantities 14, 12 and 8 of *canvas*. Notice that the mismatch between the headings (Can., Pla., Tub.) when reading across the row on the left, and those (Alp., Arc., Pol.) when reading down the columns on the right, indicates that something is wrong.

Therefore, C cannot be a row vector, since we have run out of options. So

$$C = \begin{pmatrix} 30 \\ 15 \\ 20 \end{pmatrix}$$

The product

$$\begin{matrix} C & R \\ 3 \times 1 & 3 \times 3 \end{matrix}$$

is not defined and so the correct answer is

$$RC = \begin{matrix} & \text{Can.} & \text{Pla.} & \text{Tub.} \\ \text{Alp.} & 14 & 6 & 12 \\ \text{Arc.} & 12 & 7 & 9 \\ \text{Pol.} & 8 & 5 & 8 \end{matrix} \quad \begin{matrix} \text{Can.} & 30 \\ \text{Pla.} & 15 \\ \text{Tub.} & 20 \end{matrix}$$

$$3 \times 3 \qquad\qquad 3 \times 1$$

$$= \begin{pmatrix} 750 \\ 645 \\ 475 \end{pmatrix} \begin{matrix} \text{Alpine} \\ \text{Arctic} \\ \text{Polar} \end{matrix} \qquad \text{production costs in £/tent}$$

$$3 \times 1$$

Although we have looked at all possibilities, the format for the cost calculation can be deduced directly from the *nature of the calculation*. Bear in mind that it is the cost per tent which is required, and that the costs of the resources are multiplied by the quantities of the resources for each type of tent. Since these quantities per tent form the **rows** of R, the costs must therefore be in a **column**, and must be multiplied on the **right** of R, since only **row × column** multiplication is legitimate. So the above CR calculation must be the right one.

Solution 4.1.2(b)

To find the total of each input necessary to meet the demand on hand, a vector of demand figures is used:

$$D = (150 \quad 100 \quad 50) \quad \text{or} \quad D = \begin{pmatrix} 150 \\ 100 \\ 50 \end{pmatrix}$$

(again only one of these is correct). We could try all possibilities as in **(a)**. Alternatively, we can look directly at the *nature of the calculation*. For each resource, the input quantities must be multiplied by the quantities of the tents in order to find the total of the resource required. The input quantities appear as **columns** in R, and so D must be a **row** vector, and must be multiplied on the **left** of R, since only **row × column** multiplication is legitimate. The headings across the row on the left (Alp., Arc., Pol.) and down the columns on the right match.

$$DR = \begin{matrix} \text{Alp.} & \text{Arc.} & \text{Pol.} \\ (\,150 & 100 & 50\,) \end{matrix} \qquad \begin{matrix} & \text{Can.} & \text{Pla.} & \text{Tub.} \\ \text{Alp.} & 14 & 6 & 12 \\ \text{Arc.} & 12 & 7 & 9 \\ \text{Pol.} & 8 & 5 & 8 \end{matrix}$$

$$1 \times 3 \qquad\qquad\qquad 3 \times 3$$

$$= \begin{matrix} \text{Can.} & \text{Pla.} & \text{Tub.} \\ (\,3700 & 1850 & 3100\,) \\ (\text{sq. m.}) & (\text{sq. m.}) & (\text{m}) \end{matrix} \qquad \begin{matrix} \text{quantities required to fulfil} \\ \text{the order on hand} \end{matrix}$$

$$1 \times 3$$

Solution 4.1.2(c)

Finally, the total cost of the order is required. For this, we can either multiply the costs per tent determined in **(a)** by the demand D, or multiply the total input quantities for the order determined in **(b)** by the costs C. **Consistency** is important, and where a matrix has already been used, **the same format** should be used again. Therefore

either

$$D(RC) = \begin{matrix} \text{Alp.} & \text{Arc.} & \text{Pol.} \\ (\,150 & 100 & 50\,) \end{matrix} \qquad \begin{matrix} \text{Alp.} \\ \text{Arc.} \\ \text{Pol.} \end{matrix}\begin{pmatrix} 750 \\ 645 \\ 475 \end{pmatrix} = 200{,}750$$

$$1 \times 3 \qquad\qquad\qquad 3 \times 3 \quad 1 \times 1$$

or

$$(DR)C = \begin{matrix} \text{Can.} & \text{Pla.} & \text{Tub.} \\ (\,3700 & 1850 & 3100\,) \end{matrix} \qquad \begin{matrix} \text{Can.} \\ \text{Pla.} \\ \text{Tub.} \end{matrix}\begin{pmatrix} 30 \\ 15 \\ 20 \end{pmatrix} = 200{,}750$$

Conclusion: The total cost of the order is £200,750.

Notice that $(DR)C = D(RC)$, which is an example of the associative law referred to in the note following Example 4.1.1.

EXERCISES 4.1

1 The matrices A, B, C and D are defined by

$$A = \begin{pmatrix} 1 & -4 & 3 \\ -5 & 7 & 2 \end{pmatrix} \quad B = \begin{pmatrix} 2 & 7 \\ -1 & 4 \\ 5 & 1 \end{pmatrix} \quad C = \begin{pmatrix} -8 & 2 \\ 1 & 4 \end{pmatrix} \quad D = \begin{pmatrix} 3 & -1 & 0 \\ 1 & 5 & 4 \end{pmatrix}$$

Calculate, if possible,

   (a) $4A + 3D$ (b) $3A - 2B + 6D$ (c) BA (d) AB

   (e) CB (f) BC (g) $2C - C^2$

Show that $(A + D)B = AB + DB$.

2 Consider the matrices

$$A = \begin{pmatrix} 2 & 4 \\ 3 & -1 \\ -4 & 1 \end{pmatrix} \quad B = \begin{pmatrix} -3 & 2 & 4 \\ 2 & 0 & 1 \end{pmatrix}$$

$$C = \begin{pmatrix} 1 & 3 \\ 4 & -2 \end{pmatrix} \quad D = \begin{pmatrix} 2 & 1 \\ 5 & -2 \end{pmatrix} \quad E = \begin{pmatrix} 3 & 0 \\ -1 & 4 \\ 2 & 1 \end{pmatrix}$$

Calculate, if possible

   (a) AD   (b) DA   (c) $3D - 2C + 4B$ (d) $(2D - C)B$ (e) $D^2(C + D)$

Show that $(AB)E = A(BE)$.

3 R. Corkitt Ltd. produces three types of wine – Superior, Special and Ordinary. The quantities of the inputs required to produce one gallon of each type of wine are described in the following table:

Table of input quantities per gallon of wine

	Superior	Special	Ordinary
Grapes (kilos)	5	4	3
Sugar (kilos)	4	5	6
Labour (hours)	8	6	3

The company purchases the grapes at £2/kilo and the sugar at £1.50/kilo. The cost of labour is £10/hour. To meet current demand, the company requires to produce 70 gallons of Superior, 60 gallons of Special, and 40 gallons of Ordinary wine.

Use matrix multiplication to

(a) calculate the total quantities of the inputs necessary to meet current demand
(b) calculate the cost of production per gallon for each of the wines
(c) calculate the total production cost of meeting the order on hand, in two different ways, by using your answers to (a) and (b).

4 A farm produces wheat, corn and barley, and the inputs per acre for each of these crops are as follows:

Table of input quantities per acre

	Seed (bags)	Fertiliser (tons)	Pesticide (drums)
Wheat	6	10	7
Corn	4	16	4
Barley	9	20	9

The farmer estimates that, to meet his demand in the present year, he will require 40 acres of wheat, 50 acres of corn and 30 acres of barley. He pays £30/bag for seed, £20/ton for fertiliser and £25/drum for pesticide. He also pays delivery costs of £4/bag, £10/ton and £6/drum for seed, fertiliser and pesticide, respectively.
  Use matrix multiplication to calculate

(a) the total quantities of the inputs necessary to meet the demand
(b) the total purchase cost and the total delivery cost of the inputs per acre, for each of the three crops.

5 Rosenstern (Adhesives) Ltd manufactures packs of epoxy-based glue, each pack containing a tube of basic adhesive and a tube of hardener. Two types are available, type A being a faster-setting glue than type B, and the table below shows the quantities of basic adhesive and hardener contained in one pack of each type.

Quantities per pack

	Basic adhesive	Hardener
Type A	60 gm	40 gm
Type B	80 gm	20 gm

The basic adhesive and the hardener are themselves composed of three substances X, Y and Z and the quantities of these per gm of basic adhesive and per gm of hardener are as follows:

Quantities per gram

	X	Y	Z
Basic adhesive	0.7 gm	0.1 gm	0.2 gm
Hardener	0.3 gm	0.5 gm	0.2 gm

The costs per gm of X, Y and Z are 0.5p, 0.5p and 1p respectively. Currently the company has an order on hand for 3000 packs of type A and 2000 packs of type B glue. Present the information given in the form of 4 matrices, and use matrix calculations only to:

(a) determine the 2 × 3 matrix which, per pack, relates the glue types A and B to the substances X, Y and Z
(b) calculate the quantities of X, Y, Z required in making up the order for 3000 packs of type A glue and 2000 packs of type B glue
(c) determine the cost to Rosenstern per pack for each of the glue types A and B.

6 Robertsons Ltd produces 3 types of mechanical pump, P1, P2, P3, and has received orders for these from 3 customers C1, C2 and C3. The table below shows the numbers of each type of pump required by these customers.

Table 1 *Quantities demanded*

	C1	C2	C3
P1	15	30	40
P2	20	0	30
P3	20	25	0

The pumps are produced at 3 factories, F1, F2, F3, and the table below describes the costs incurred in delivering from each factory to each customer. The costs are the same for each type of pump.

Table 2 *Delivery costs per pump (£)*

	F1	F2	F3
C1	4	3	6
C2	7	5	4
C3	3	8	3

If A, B are 3 × 3 matrices having the same rows and columns as tables 1 and 2, respectively, calculate AB, and explain what the numbers in this matrix represent. Deduce the cheapest way of delivering the required pumps to the customers C1, C2 and C3, assuming that each factory fulfils the total requirement for just one type of pump.

4.2 INVERSE MATRICES AND SOLUTION OF MATRIX EQUATIONS

The overall aim here is **to solve matrix equations with the same ease with which we solve ordinary number equations**. However, first we consider an example which shows how matrix equations arise naturally.

EXAMPLE 4.2.1

A company manufactures three products P1, P2, P3, and has three processing divisions A, B, C. The table below shows the time (in machine hours) required by each product in each division.

Time requirements in hours per unit

	A	B	C
P1	1	1	0
P2	2	0	2
P3	1	2	1

If the total available weekly processing time is 2000 machine hours for division A, 1200 machine hours for division B, and 1600 machine hours for division C, and production of the products P1, P2 and P3 is to be planned to use *all* this available time, determine the quantities of P1, P2 and P3 which should be produced per week.

Solution 4.2.1

Let x units of P1, y units of P2 and z units of P3 be produced per week. Then, the appropriate equation for x, y, z is as follows:

$$\begin{array}{c} \begin{matrix} \text{P1} & \text{P2} & \text{P3} \end{matrix} \\ (\;x \quad y \quad z\;) \\ 1 \times 3 \end{array} \begin{array}{c} \begin{matrix} & \text{A} & \text{B} & \text{C} \end{matrix} \\ \begin{matrix} \text{P1} \\ \text{P2} \\ \text{P3} \end{matrix} \begin{pmatrix} 1 & 1 & 0 \\ 2 & 0 & 2 \\ 1 & 2 & 1 \end{pmatrix} \\ 3 \times 3 \end{array} = \begin{array}{c} (2000 \quad 1200 \quad 1600) \\ 1 \times 3 \end{array}$$

Notice that this equation is dimensionally correct, and makes sense since the headings across the row on the left and down the columns on the right match. If T denotes the 3×3 matrix of unit processing times, X is the row vector with elements x, y, z, and Y is the row vector of total available processing times, then the equation becomes:

$$XT = Y \qquad\qquad (4.2.1)$$

At this stage, we will break off and look at the way such equations are solved.

A method for solving matrix equations

The approach is firstly to think about how we solve a simple number equation such as

$$2x = 3$$

Obviously, if we *divide* by 2,

$$x = 3/2$$

The trouble is that, since it is not possible to divide matrices, this solution does not give us any hints as to how to proceed with matrix equations. Solving the above equation *by using multiplication only* is more instructive:

$2x = 3$

$\frac{1}{2}.2x = \frac{1}{2}.3$ multiply each side by the inverse of 2

$1.x = \frac{3}{2}$ cancel $2 \times \frac{1}{2}$ to 1

$x = \frac{3}{2}$ multiplication by 1 leaves x unchanged, and so 1 can be dropped from the calculation

This solution is more helpful from the matrix standpoint, and works for two reasons. Firstly, there is a number, 1, which when multiplied by any number x leaves x unchanged, and which can therefore be dropped from the calculation altogether. Secondly, the number 2 has an inverse, $1/2$, which can be used to cancel 2 down to 1, and thereby remove 2 from the left-hand side of the calculation, leaving just x.

What we now aim to do is to define a matrix equivalent of the number 1, and to use this to define the inverse of a matrix.

Identity matrices

An 'identity matrix' (sometimes called a 'unit matrix') is a matrix equivalent of the number 1. It is a **square** matrix which has 1's down the leading diagonal and zeros elsewhere. Such a matrix may be 1×1, 2×2, 3×3, etc. For example, the 2×2 identity matrix and the 3×3 identity matrix are, respectively,

$$\begin{pmatrix} 1 & 0 \\ 0 & 1 \end{pmatrix} \qquad \begin{pmatrix} 1 & 0 & 0 \\ 0 & 1 & 0 \\ 0 & 0 & 1 \end{pmatrix}$$

The essential property of an identity matrix **ID** is that, for any compatible matrix A,

$$\text{A } \mathbf{ID} = \text{A} \quad \text{and} \quad \mathbf{ID} \text{ A} = \text{A} \tag{1.2.2}$$

As a check, consider the following calculations involving the 3×3 identity matrix **ID**. The matrix A can be any matrix which is compatible with **ID**; which means it can be multiplied by the 3×3 identity matrix, either as A **ID** or **ID** A. A must therefore be a square 3×3 matrix.

$$\underset{\text{A}}{\begin{pmatrix} 1 & -2 & 3 \\ 0 & 4 & 6 \\ 2 & -1 & -4 \end{pmatrix}} \underset{\mathbf{ID}}{\begin{pmatrix} 1 & 0 & 0 \\ 0 & 1 & 0 \\ 0 & 0 & 1 \end{pmatrix}} = \underset{\text{A}}{\begin{pmatrix} 1 & -2 & 3 \\ 0 & 4 & 6 \\ 2 & -1 & -4 \end{pmatrix}}$$

$$\underset{\mathbf{ID}}{\begin{pmatrix} 1 & 0 & 0 \\ 0 & 1 & 0 \\ 0 & 0 & 1 \end{pmatrix}} \underset{\text{A}}{\begin{pmatrix} 1 & -2 & 3 \\ 0 & 4 & 6 \\ 2 & -1 & -4 \end{pmatrix}} = \underset{\text{A}}{\begin{pmatrix} 1 & -2 & 3 \\ 0 & 4 & 6 \\ 2 & -1 & -4 \end{pmatrix}}$$

Remember that an identity matrix is the matrix equivalent of the number 1. Using such a matrix, we can now start to talk about **inverse matrices** in much the same way that we talk about inverse numbers. The essential fact about $1/2$, in our number example, is that $1/2 \times 2 = 1$ and $2 \times 1/2 = 1$, and this suggests the appropriate definition for inverse matrices. Note that $1/2$ can also be denoted by 2^{-1} and this alternative notation proves to be more appropriate for matrices.

Inverse matrices

A **square matrix** A is said to have an inverse matrix if there is a matrix A^{-1} such that

$$A^{-1}A = AA^{-1} = \mathbf{ID} \tag{4.2.3}$$

where **ID** denotes the identity matrix which has the same size as A. Note that the matrix A must be square, since the definition states that the product of A and its inverse must be defined, whichever way around the product is performed.

There are two natural questions to ask:

- Does every square matrix have an inverse?
- Can a square matrix have more than one inverse?

The answer to both questions is **no**, although we will not look at the reasons here.

EXAMPLE 4.2.2

Consider the matrices

$$T = \begin{pmatrix} 1 & 1 & 0 \\ 2 & 0 & 2 \\ 1 & 2 & 1 \end{pmatrix} \qquad S = \frac{1}{4}\begin{pmatrix} 4 & 1 & -2 \\ 0 & -1 & 2 \\ -4 & 1 & 2 \end{pmatrix}$$

Check that S is the inverse matrix of T.

Solution 4.2.2

We need to check that $TS = \mathbf{ID}$ and $ST = \mathbf{ID}$, where **ID** is the 3×3 identity matrix. This is therefore basically an exercise in matrix multiplication. Thus

$$TS = \frac{1}{4}\begin{pmatrix} 1 & 1 & 0 \\ 2 & 0 & 2 \\ 1 & 2 & 1 \end{pmatrix}\begin{pmatrix} 4 & 1 & -2 \\ 0 & -1 & 2 \\ -4 & 1 & 2 \end{pmatrix}$$

$$= \frac{1}{4}\begin{pmatrix} 4 & 0 & 0 \\ 0 & 4 & 0 \\ 0 & 0 & 4 \end{pmatrix} = \begin{pmatrix} 1 & 0 & 0 \\ 0 & 1 & 0 \\ 0 & 0 & 1 \end{pmatrix}$$

Similarly

$$ST = \frac{1}{4}\begin{pmatrix} 4 & 1 & -2 \\ 0 & -1 & 2 \\ -4 & 1 & 2 \end{pmatrix}\begin{pmatrix} 1 & 1 & 0 \\ 2 & 0 & 2 \\ 1 & 2 & 1 \end{pmatrix} = \begin{pmatrix} 1 & 0 & 0 \\ 0 & 1 & 0 \\ 0 & 0 & 1 \end{pmatrix}$$

So S is the inverse matrix of T, i.e. $T^{-1} = S$.

N.B. In fact, it is not essential to check both TS and ST, since it can be shown that if *either* one of these products is equal to **ID**, then the other product must also equal **ID**.

Using identity and inverse matrices to solve equations

EXAMPLE 4.2.1 (continued)

So far, we have obtained the matrix equation in (4.2.1):

$$XT = Y$$

where T is the per unit time requirement matrix, X is a row vector of unknowns *x*, *y*, *z*, corresponding to the quantities of P1, P2 and P3 produced, and Y is the row vector of total available processing times in divisions A, B and C. Note that the same matrix T was considered in Example 4.2.2 (and the inverse matrix $T^{-1} = S$). Using T^{-1} and the 3×3 identity matrix **ID**, equation (4.2.1) can be rewritten as follows:

$$XTT^{-1} = YT^{-1} \qquad (T^{-1} \text{ must go on the } right \text{ because T is on the } right)$$

$$X \, \textbf{ID} = YT^{-1} \qquad (T \text{ times } T^{-1} \text{ cancels down to the identity matrix } \textbf{ID})$$

$$X = YT^{-1} \qquad (\text{multiplication of X by } \textbf{ID} \text{ leaves X unchanged, and so } \textbf{ID} \text{ can be dropped from the calculation})$$

If we substitute for X, T and Y, the required quantities of P1, P2 and P3 are obtained.

$$(x \quad y \quad z) = \frac{1}{4}(2000 \quad 1200 \quad 1600)\begin{pmatrix} 4 & 1 & -2 \\ 0 & -1 & 2 \\ -4 & 1 & 2 \end{pmatrix}$$

$$= (400 \quad 600 \quad 400)$$

Conclusion: 400 units of P1, 600 units of P2 and 400 units of P3 can be produced, if all the available time in divisions A, B and C is to be used.

Important note: It is not necessary to show all the steps involved in multiplying an equation by an inverse matrix. The essential step, for a general matrix equation, where X is a **row vector of unknowns**, is

if $\qquad XA = B$

then $\qquad X = BA^{-1}$ $\qquad$ cancel A from the **right** on one side, and write A^{-1} on the **right** on the other side

For a general matrix equation, involving a **column vector of unknowns**, the equivalent steps are as follows:

if $\qquad AX = B$

then $\qquad X = A^{-1}B$ $\qquad$ cancel A from the **left** on one side, and write A^{-1} on the **left** on the other side

A formula for the inverse of a 2 × 2 matrix

We will not describe how inverses are calculated for matrices of any size, since there are programming languages and software packages which will calculate inverses. However, there is a convenient formula for 2 × 2 matrices:

$$\text{If} \quad A = \begin{pmatrix} a & b \\ c & d \end{pmatrix}$$

$$\text{then} \quad A^{-1} = \frac{1}{ad - bc} \begin{pmatrix} d & -b \\ -c & a \end{pmatrix} \qquad (4.2.4)$$

This formula is only valid if $ad - bc \neq 0$. If it is zero, it can be shown that there is no inverse. For example,

$$\text{if} \quad A = \begin{pmatrix} 3 & 8 \\ -1 & 4 \end{pmatrix}$$

then, using (4.2.4)

$$A^{-1} = \frac{1}{(3 \times 4) - (8 \times -1)} \begin{pmatrix} 4 & -8 \\ -(-1) & 3 \end{pmatrix} = \frac{1}{20} \begin{pmatrix} 4 & -8 \\ 1 & 3 \end{pmatrix} \qquad (4.2.5)$$

The solution of simultaneous equations

Inverse matrices can usually be used to solve a set of simultaneous equations, provided it is first expressed in matrix form. Consider, for example, the equations

$$3x + 8y = 40$$
$$4y - x = -20 \qquad (4.2.6)$$

The first step is to write down the **matrix of coefficients** A corresponding to the x and y terms on the left-hand side of each equation. For the first equation, the coefficients are 3 and 8, whereas the coefficients are -1 and 4 for the second equation. Notice that these are the coefficients of the x and y terms, respectively, for each equation. We could, instead, read the coefficient of the y term first; what is important is that the x and y terms are considered in the same order for both equations. Thus:

$$A = \begin{pmatrix} 3 & 8 \\ -1 & 4 \end{pmatrix}$$

Equation (4.2.6) can now be rewritten as

$$\begin{pmatrix} 3 & 8 \\ -1 & 4 \end{pmatrix} \begin{pmatrix} x \\ y \end{pmatrix} = \begin{pmatrix} 40 \\ -20 \end{pmatrix} \qquad (4.2.7)$$

To see that this is so, note that the matrix product on the left-hand side gives

$$\begin{pmatrix} 3x + 8y \\ -1x + 4y \end{pmatrix}$$

For this column vector to be equal to the column vector on the right-hand side of (4.2.7), $3x + 8y$ and $-1x + 4y$ must be 40 and -20, respectively, and this is exactly what equation (4.2.6) states, (4.2.7) can further be written as:

$$AX = Y \qquad (4.2.8)$$

where X denotes the column vector formed from the unknowns x and y, and the column vector Y is formed from the right-hand sides 40 and -20 of equation (4.2.6). Notice that A is the matrix for which the inverse is given by (4.2.5). From the previous equation

$$X = A^{-1}Y \qquad A^{-1} \text{ must be on the left of Y, since A was on the left of X}$$

$$= \frac{1}{20}\begin{pmatrix} 4 & -8 \\ 1 & 3 \end{pmatrix}\begin{pmatrix} 40 \\ -20 \end{pmatrix}$$

$$\begin{pmatrix} x \\ y \end{pmatrix} = \frac{1}{20}\begin{pmatrix} 320 \\ -20 \end{pmatrix} = \begin{pmatrix} 16 \\ -1 \end{pmatrix}$$

So the solutions of the simultaneous equations are $x = 16$ and $y = -1$.

EXERCISES 4.2

1 (a) Express the simultaneous equations

$$3x + 4y = 6$$
$$2x + 5y = 4$$

in the matrix form

$$AX = Y$$

where A is a 2×2 matrix and X, Y are column vectors.

(b) Using the formula for the inverse of a 2×2 matrix, calculate the inverse matrix of A, and hence find the solution of the given equations.

2 Repeat parts (a) and (b) of Exercise 1 for the simultaneous equations

$$7y - 5x = 6$$
$$2x - 4y = 12$$

3 A company which manufactures three types of chemical C1, C2, C3, has three factories F1, F2, F3, and the table below, which is to be represented by the matrix A, shows the hourly outputs of these factories. For example, in 1 hour, factory F1 can produce 1 ton of C1, together with 2 tons of C2 and 1 ton of C3.

Factory outputs in tons/hour

	C1	C2	C3
F1	1	2	1
F2	1	1	2
F3	3	0	1

(a) Use matrix multiplication to determine the total quantities of C1, C2 and C3 which would be produced if factory F1 operates for 50 hours, F2 for 40 hours and F3 for 30 hours.

(b) At present, the company has a demand for 600 tons of C1, 300 tons of C2 and 500 tons of C3, and it has been decided that all three factories will be engaged in the production of these quantities.

If, in order to meet the demand on hand, x hours are required in factory F1, y hours in factory F2 and z hours in factory F3, write down a matrix equation which must be satisfied by x, y, z, and the matrix A. Check that

$$\frac{1}{8}\begin{pmatrix} 1 & -2 & 3 \\ 5 & -2 & -1 \\ -3 & 6 & -1 \end{pmatrix}$$

is the inverse matrix A^{-1} of A, and hence find the amount of time required in each factory, in order to meet the present demand.

4 Marvo Ltd. manufactures 3 types of washing machine – the Economy, the Super and the Special – and the only effective constraint on the production of these, at present, arises from the limited supply of 3 types of circuit board B1, B2 and B3. The supply of B1 is limited to 1500 boards per month, the supply of B2 to 900 boards per month, and the supply of B3 to 600 boards per month. The table below, to be represented by the matrix A, describes the numbers of these circuit boards required in producing one machine of each type.

Circuit boards required per machine

	Economy	Super	Special
B1	2	3	2
B2	1	2	1
B3	0	1	3

It is *claimed* that the matrix

$$B = \frac{1}{3}\begin{pmatrix} 5 & -4 & -3 \\ -3 & 6 & 0 \\ 1 & -2 & 1 \end{pmatrix}$$

is the inverse matrix of A but, in fact, two of the entries in the matrix are incorrect. By first calculating AB and BA, correct the errors in B. Hence, find the monthly outputs of the 3 machine types, assuming that production is planned to utilise all the available circuit boards.

5 Let

$$A = \begin{pmatrix} 1 & 0 & -1 \\ 2 & 1 & 2 \\ 3 & 1 & 4 \end{pmatrix}$$

Show that the matrix

$$A^{-1} = \frac{1}{3}\begin{pmatrix} 2 & -1 & 1 \\ -2 & 7 & -4 \\ -1 & -1 & 1 \end{pmatrix}$$

is the inverse matrix of A. Hence, solve the set of simultaneous linear equations

$$x \qquad - z = 1$$
$$2x + y + 2z = 0$$
$$3x + y + 4z = 2$$

6 If

$$A = \begin{pmatrix} 2 & 4 & 3 \\ 0 & 2 & 6 \\ 1 & 4 & 6 \end{pmatrix} \quad \text{and} \quad B = \begin{pmatrix} 2 & 2 & -3 \\ -2 & -3 & 4 \\ 1 & 2 & -2 \end{pmatrix}$$

calculate BA. Use your answer to solve the simultaneous linear equations

$$2x + 4y + 3z = 31$$
$$2y + 6z = 36$$
$$x + 4y + 6z = 44$$

and check your answers for x, y and z.

7 Consider the two sets of equations

$$u = y + 2z \qquad\qquad r = u + 3v + 4w$$
$$v = 3y - x + z \qquad\qquad s = 2v - 3u + w$$
$$w = 2x + 4y - 2z \qquad\qquad t = 2u - 4v$$

Write each of these sets of equations in matrix form, and hence determine the three equations which relate r, s, t to x, y and z.

4.3 MARKOV PROCESSES

A Markov process is an iterative process in which the outcome at each stage can be obtained from the previous outcome by applying certain *fixed* percentage or proportional changes. One common application of such a process is in the area of brand switching as the following example shows.

Consider a market shared by 2 brands of detergent – A and B – and suppose that a market survey has produced the following information about the proportions of people who stay with the same brand, or change brands, in consecutive months:

- of customers who bought brand A last month, 80% buy it again and 20% change to brand B
- of customers who bought brand B last month, 40% buy it again and 60% change to brand A.

95

(The essential assumption here is that these percentages remain the same from month to month.)

If, for a sample of 1000 people, say, 400 buy brand A and 600 buy brand B in the first month of observation, what figures can we expect for the second, third and fourth months, and can any conclusion be drawn from these? Matrices can be used to answer this question, provided that we first set up a **transition table** as follows:

Transition matrix

From

		A	B
To	A	0.8	0.6
	B	0.2	0.4

The figure of 0.8 indicates that 80% of people 'change' from A to A in the second month. This is simply a convenience; it means that 80% stay with A. The figure of 0.6 indicates that 60% of people change from brand B to brand A in the second month, and the other figures are similarly explained.

Now we use matrix multiplication to predict what happens in subsequent months, by introducing the transition matrix

$$T = \begin{pmatrix} 0.8 & 0.6 \\ 0.2 & 0.4 \end{pmatrix}$$

We need the multiplications to

- be dimensionally correct
- make sense for the particular context

Consider the second month:

- of the 400 people who bought brand A,

0.8×400 buy A again   and 0.2×400 change to B

- of the 600 people who bought brand B

0.6×600 change to brand A   and 0.4×600 buy brand B again

Therefore

$(0.8 \times 400) + (0.6 \times 600) = 680$ now buy A

$(0.2 \times 400) + (0.4 \times 600) = 320$ now buy B

and these figures are precisely those obtained from the matrix multiplication

$$\begin{pmatrix} 0.8 & 0.6 \\ 0.2 & 0.4 \end{pmatrix}\begin{pmatrix} 400 \\ 600 \end{pmatrix} = \begin{pmatrix} 680 \\ 320 \end{pmatrix} \begin{matrix} A \\ B \end{matrix}$$ second month

We can now multiply further:

$$\begin{pmatrix} 0.8 & 0.6 \\ 0.2 & 0.4 \end{pmatrix}\begin{pmatrix} 680 \\ 320 \end{pmatrix} = \begin{pmatrix} 736 \\ 264 \end{pmatrix} \begin{matrix} A \\ B \end{matrix}$$ third month

$$\begin{pmatrix} 0.8 & 0.6 \\ 0.2 & 0.4 \end{pmatrix} \begin{pmatrix} 736 \\ 264 \end{pmatrix} = \begin{pmatrix} 747.2 \\ 252.8 \end{pmatrix} \quad \begin{matrix} A \\ B \end{matrix} \quad \text{averages for the fourth month}$$

$$\begin{pmatrix} 0.8 & 0.6 \\ 0.2 & 0.4 \end{pmatrix} \begin{pmatrix} 747.2 \\ 252.8 \end{pmatrix} = \begin{pmatrix} 749.4 \\ 250.56 \end{pmatrix} \quad \begin{matrix} A \\ B \end{matrix} \quad \text{fifth month}$$

These figures approach closer and closer to what we can think of as a **steady state**, which we would estimate to be 750 buyers of A and 250 buyers of B.

It is interesting to ask whether the above trend in the figures would repeat itself if we considered a different breakdown of the buying preferences of the 1000 people in the first month. Suppose, for example, that 900 buy brand A and 100 buy brand B, initially. Then, multiplying as before,

$$\begin{pmatrix} 0.8 & 0.6 \\ 0.2 & 0.4 \end{pmatrix} \begin{pmatrix} 900 \\ 100 \end{pmatrix} = \begin{pmatrix} 780 \\ 220 \end{pmatrix} \quad \begin{matrix} A \\ B \end{matrix}$$

gives the buying preferences in the second month. The results for the third and fourth months are

$$\begin{pmatrix} 756 \\ 244 \end{pmatrix} \quad \begin{matrix} A \\ B \end{matrix} \qquad \begin{pmatrix} 751.2 \\ 248.8 \end{pmatrix} \quad \begin{matrix} A \\ B \end{matrix}$$

and again the implication is that the figures are approaching 750 buyers of A, 250 buyers of B, probably. If you choose a different breakdown of your own for the buying preferences of the 1000 people, and repeatedly multiply by T, you will again see the same tendency in the results over consecutive months.

If the buying preferences of the 1000 people happened to be 750 buyers of A and 250 buyers of B in the first month, then the steady state would have already been achieved since

$$\begin{pmatrix} 0.8 & 0.6 \\ 0.2 & 0.4 \end{pmatrix} \begin{pmatrix} 750 \\ 250 \end{pmatrix} = \begin{pmatrix} 750 \\ 250 \end{pmatrix} \quad \begin{matrix} A \\ B \end{matrix}$$

and this gives us the clue as to how to find the steady state mathematically, without repeated multiplications. The answer is to solve the equation

$$\begin{pmatrix} 0.8 & 0.6 \\ 0.2 & 0.4 \end{pmatrix} \begin{pmatrix} x \\ y \end{pmatrix} = \begin{pmatrix} x \\ y \end{pmatrix} \tag{4.3.1}$$

However, the values of x and y will depend on the sample size of people considered. It is therefore more convenient to let x and y be *proportions* of the market so that, in addition to the equation above,

$$x + y = 1$$

We therefore seem to have *three* equations in *two* unknowns but in fact (4.3.1) produces only one useful equation. We will leave you to finish off the details of this problem in Exercise 1, and look at a three product problem.

Note: For reasons which we will not go into, transition matrices do *not* have inverses, and so the equations must be solved in a more traditional way.

EXAMPLE 4.3.1

The market for a particular item is shared by three brands A, B, C, and a market survey has produced the table below, which describes the proportions of customers who buy the same brand again or change brands in consecutive months.

Monthly transition table

		From		
		A	B	C
	A	0.6	0.1	0.2
To	B	0.2	0.6	0.6
	C	0.2	0.3	0.2

Find the share of the market which each brand would hold in the steady state.

Solution 4.3.1

Suppose that A, B, C hold proportions x, y, z of the market, respectively, in the steady state. *Three* equations are necessary to find these *three* unknowns, and the most obvious of these is

$$x + y + z = 1 \qquad \text{proportions add to one} \qquad (1)$$

The remaining equations come from the fact that when the steady-state proportions of the market are multiplied by the transition matrix, they remain the same. Thus

$$\begin{pmatrix} 0.6 & 0.1 & 0.2 \\ 0.2 & 0.6 & 0.6 \\ 0.2 & 0.3 & 0.2 \end{pmatrix} \begin{pmatrix} x \\ y \\ z \end{pmatrix} = \begin{pmatrix} x \\ y \\ z \end{pmatrix}$$

Multiplying out the left-hand side and equating elements, as illustrated for the earlier example,

$$0.6x + 0.1y + 0.2z = x$$

$$0.2x + 0.6y + 0.6z = y \qquad \text{steady-state equations}$$

$$0.2x + 0.3y + 0.2z = z$$

Each of these equations can be simplified. For example, the first equation becomes

$$0.6x + 0.1y + 0.2z = x$$

$$0.6x + 0.1y + 0.2z - x = 0$$

$$-0.4x + 0.1y + 0.2z = 0 \qquad \text{multiply this equation by 10}$$

$$-4x + y + 2z = 0 \qquad (2)$$

For the second steady-state equation

$$0.2x + 0.6y + 0.6z = y$$

$$0.2x + 0.6y + 0.6z - y = 0$$

$$0.2x - 0.4y + 0.6z = 0$$

$$2x - 4y + 6z = 0 \tag{3}$$

Similarly, you should check that the third steady-state equation becomes

$$2x + 3y - 8z = 0 \tag{4}$$

In summary, we have the equations

$$x + y + z = 1 \tag{1}$$

$$-4x + y + 2z = 0 \tag{2}$$

$$2x - 4y + 6z = 0 \tag{3}$$

$$2x + 3y - 8z = 0 \tag{4}$$

To find the *three* unknowns, we choose *three* equations. Equation (1) is vital, and we will choose (3) and (4). (Whilst it is by no means obvious, it is the case that equation (2) will automatically be satisfied if (3) and (4) are satisfied.) So the equations to be used are (1), (3) and (4), and the simplest unknown to eliminate is x.

$(3) - 2 \times (1)$ gives

$2x - 4y + 6z = 0$	(3)
$2x + 2y + 2z = 2$	$2 \times (1)$
$-6y + 4z = -2$ subtracting	(5)

$(4) - (3)$ gives

$2x + 3y - 8z = 0$	(4)
$2x - 4y + 6z = 0$	(3)
$7y - 14z = 0$ subtracting	(6)

We now have two equations (5) and (6) in two unknowns to solve.
To eliminate z, use $7 \times (5) - 2 \times (6)$

$-42y + 28z = -14$	$7 \times (5)$
$14y - 28z = 0$	$2 \times (6)$
$-28y = -14$ adding	

Therefore, $y = -14/-28 = 1/2$. This value can be substituted into either one of the equations (5) and (6). Using (5),

$$-6y + 4z = -2$$
$$(-6 \times 1/2) + 4z = -2$$
$$z = 1/4$$

Finally, substitute into the proportions equation (1)

$$x + 1/2 + 1/4 = 1 \qquad x = 1/4$$

Conclusion: Brands A, B, C will command $1/4$, $1/2$ and $1/4$ of the market in the steady-state.

Note: The existence of a steady state is based upon the assumption that the transition matrix does not change; but it will from time to time. However, the *assumption* that it is constant allows a company to *forecast* its market share and to take action if necessary.

EXERCISES 4.3

1 Consider the detergent example discussed earlier. Starting with the steady-state equation

$$\begin{pmatrix} 0.8 & 0.6 \\ 0.2 & 0.4 \end{pmatrix}\begin{pmatrix} x \\ y \end{pmatrix} = \begin{pmatrix} x \\ y \end{pmatrix}$$

show that the equations

$$-2x + 6y = 0$$
$$2x - 6y = 0$$

are obtained, and that these are essentially the same. Using one of these equations, and the equation

$$x + y = 1$$

determine the proportion of the market which each brand would capture in the steady state.

2 Consider the market for a product which is shared by two brands A and B, and for which the following information is available:

- of those who buy brand A in a particular week, 80% buy it again and 20% change to brand B
- of those who buy brand B in a particular week, 40% change to brand A and the remainder stay with brand B.

(a) Considering a sample of 900 people, of whom 400 initially buy brand A and 500 buy brand B, determine the market share for A and B over the next two weeks.

(b) Determine the proportion of the market captured by each brand in the steady state.

3 The market for a particular type of malt whisky is shared by three brands X, Y, Z, and the table below describes the proportions of customers who buy the same brand again or change brands in consecutive years.

Annual transition table

		From		
		X	Y	Z
	X	0.4	0.6	0.6
To	Y	0.3	0.3	0.1
	Z	0.3	0.1	0.3

(a) If currently, 1000 people buy X, 1500 people buy Y and 800 buy Z, determine the market behaviour for the next two years.

(b) Determine the proportion of the market which each brand can expect to capture in the steady state.

4 Repeat parts (a) and (b) of Exercise 3 for the following transition table:

Annual transition table

		From		
		X	Y	Z
	X	0.8	0.2	0.2
To	Y	0	0.2	0.2
	Z	0.2	0.6	0.6

5 The following information describes the monthly changes in the market shared by 3 products X, Y and Z.

- 20% of those who bought brand X last month buy it again, and the remainder choose Y and Z in equal numbers
- 20% of those who bought Y last month buy it again, and the remainder choose X and Z in equal numbers
- of those who bought Z last month, 40% choose it again, whilst of the remainder twice as many choose X as choose Y.

Write down the steady-state equation in matrix form, and hence find the proportion of the market which each brand can expect to hold in the steady-state.

6 Fabron Ltd. manufactures a fabric for use by upholsterers and shares the market with two competitors. The information below, where brand X is manufactured by Fabron and brand Y, brand Z are manufactured by its competitors has been observed about the people who buy the same brand again or change brands in consecutive months:

- Of those who bought brand X, 50% buy it again, 30% change to brand Y and 20% change to brand Z.

- Of those who bought brand Y, 50% buy it again and four times as many people change to brand X as brand Z.
- Of those who bought brand Z, 40% buy it again and twice as many people change to brand Y as brand X.

(a) Write down the monthly transition table.

(b) Determine the proportion of the market which each brand can expect to capture in the long term.

(c) The sales manager of Fabron Ltd. believes that, with the right marketing policy, the company could capture 0.5 of the market in the long term, by reducing the proportion, 0.3, of customers who change from brand X to brand Y, to a smaller figure p, whilst at the same time increasing the proportion of customers who continue to buy brand X. (All other proportions in the transition table may be assumed to remain unchanged.)

Assuming that the sales manager is right, determine the proportions of the market which brand Y and brand Z would hold in the long term, and calculate the required value of p.

5

INTEREST: MONEY AND TIME

When you have completed this chapter you will be able to:

- understand the difference between simple and compound interest
- calculate future balances, interest rates and time periods
- understand the concept of continuous % growth
- apply arithmetic and geometric progressions to business problems

5.1 SIMPLE AND COMPOUND INTEREST

Whether we look at individuals or organisations, the fact that 'money earns money' is always an important guiding principle. An individual may wish to calculate the expected growth in an invested sum, or wish to know how much to invest to achieve a target amount. An organisation may need to invest in order to meet the cost of replacement equipment or an expansion programme. There may be a single payment involved or a sequence of payments.

In this chapter, we will lay the foundations for such considerations by first looking at a single payment into an account, perhaps in a Bank or Building Society. The important factors are the size of the initial investment, the interest rate, and the duration of the investment, which influence the amount in the account at any one time. To make progress mathematically it is therefore necessary to introduce symbols for these:

P = **principal (initial investment)**

R = **% rate of interest per period** (the period may be less than a year)

t = **number of compounding periods**

A_t = **amount at the end of t compounding periods**

Two interest schemes will be considered: *simple interest*, where the interest earned is the same throughout and is based on the original investment, and *compound interest*, where the interest earned increases as the amount in the account increases.

Simple interest

Before obtaining a general formula, it is useful to see what happens when a specific sum, £300 say, is invested at a specific simple interest rate of 4% per half-year, say. The assumption of simple interest is that the interest earned in *any* half year is 4% of the *original* investment and so

Interest earned in each half-year $= \dfrac{4}{100} \times 300$

$= 0.04 \times 300 = £12$

% rate is divided by 100 before multiplying by the principal

and

New amount (at end of t half-years) $= 300 + 12t$

Replacing the numbers in the above calculation by the general symbols introduced above:

Interest earned in each half-year $= \dfrac{R}{100} \times P = \dfrac{PR}{100}$

New amount after t periods is

$$A_t = P + \frac{PR}{100}.t = P + \frac{PRt}{100}$$

P is a common factor, and so factorising, we obtain the required formula:

$$A_t = P\left(1 + \frac{Rt}{100}\right)$$
total amount after t periods – simple interest (5.1.1)

Before giving an example, a word on current practice in applying interest rates is required. Account information is usually presented *per year*, and this information can be inserted directly into formula (5.1.1), if interest is actually added annually. If interest is added more than once a year, it is the *period* rate and number of *periods* which are relevant to the formula. The calculation of the number of *periods* is obvious. For example, if interest is compounded quarterly (4 times per year), and a sum of money is invested for 5 years, then the number of interest-compounding periods is $5 \times 4 = 20$. However, for the interest rate per period, some *convention* or agreement is necessary as to how the period rate is obtained from the annual rate, and, in practice, it is the *average* rate per period which is adopted. For example, if the annual rate is 6% and interest is compounded quarterly, the period rate is taken to be $6/4 = 1.5\%$. In summary,

No. of interest compounding periods =

no. of years × no. of periods per year (5.1.2)

Interest rate per period = annual rate/no. of periods per year

EXAMPLE 5.1.1

£300 is invested in an account which earns simple interest at the rate of 3% per quarter. Calculate the balance after 6 years.

Solution 5.1.1

$$A_t = P\left(1 + \frac{Rt}{100}\right)$$

where $P = 300$, $R = 3$ (% per quarter), $t = 6 \times 4 = 24$ quarters

$$A_{24} = 300\left(1 + \frac{3 \times 24}{100}\right) = 300\,(1.72) = 516$$

Conclusion: £300 grows to £516.

Compound interest

The basic assumption for compound interest is that interest is *based upon the increasing balance*, and this case therefore differs from that of simple interest for the second period onwards. For the first period, using the example of £300 invested at 4% per half year as before,

$$A_1 = 300 + (0.04 \times 300) = 312 \qquad \text{end of first half-year} \tag{5.1.3}$$

The sum of £312 now becomes the initial sum for the second period. Thus

$$A_2 = 312 + (0.04 \times 312) = 324.48 \qquad \text{end of second half-year} \tag{5.1.4}$$

and continuing,

$$A_3 = 324.48 + (0.04 \times 324.48) = 337.46 \qquad \text{end of third half-year}$$

This process of substituting each new balance in as principal could be continued to determine the amount after any number of periods, but this would be tedious and a general formula is required. To deduce the formula, it is necessary to write the above calculations in a different way. Since 300 is a common factor on the right-hand side of (5.1.3), we can factorise to obtain

$$A_1 = 300\,(1 + 0.04) = 300(1.04) \tag{5.1.5}$$

Similarly, 312 is a common factor for the right-hand side of (5.1.4) and so

$$A_2 = 312\,(1 + 0\,04) = 312(1.04)$$

But relating A_2 to the original principal by substituting for A_1 according to (5.1.5),

$$A_2 = 300(1.04)(1.04) = 300\,(1.04)^2$$

A similar approach leads to

$$A_3 = 300\,(1.04)^2\,(1.04) = 300(1.04)^3$$

and so on. It is now clear that what determines the way the balance grows is repeated multiplication by 1.04. In general

$$A_t = P\left(1 + \frac{R}{100}\right)^t \qquad \textbf{total amount after } \textit{t} \textbf{ periods} \atop \textbf{– compound interest} \tag{5.1.6}$$

We will now look at a number of examples illustrating the use of the above formula. Since the formula contains four quantities, we need to be able to calculate any one of these, *given* the values of the other three. For this purpose, a calculator and a number of different techniques are required.

Each of the three examples will illustrate a different technique. Example 5.1.2 shows how the 'power button' on a calculator can be used to calculate a value for A_t, the total amount in the account. In Example 5.1.3, a value for R, the period interest rate, is calculated by using the 'root key' on a calculator. Finally, in Example 5.1.4, a time period t is calculated by using logarithms, the values of which will also be provided by the calculator.

EXAMPLE 5.1.2

£850 is invested in an account which earns compound interest at the rate of 10% p.a. Calculate the amount in the account at the end of 8 years, if interest is compounded quarterly.

Solution 5.1.2

Note: Answering this question will require the use of the 'power key' on the calculator, which will usually be marked x^y *or* y^x.

Interest is compounded more than once per year, and so, as explained above, it is necessary to find the % interest rate per *period*, R, and the number, t, of compounding *periods*, before applying formula (5.1.6). Since interest is compounded 4 times per year, the average rate per (quarterly) period is $10/4 = 2.5\%$, and there are $8 \times 4 = 32$ periods in 8 years. Thus

$$A_t = P(1 + R/100)^t \qquad \text{where } P = 850, R = 2.5, t = 32$$

Therefore

$$A_{10} = 850 \ (1 + 2.5/100)^{32}$$
$$= 850 \ (1.025)^{32} \qquad\qquad\qquad (5.1.7)$$
$$= 850 \times 2.203756938$$
$$= £1873.19 \quad \text{(to the nearest penny)}$$

Conclusion: The total amount in the account at the end of 8 years is £1873.19.

Note: In (5.1.7), the value of $(1.025)^{32}$ could be found by multiplying 1.025 by itself 32 times, but this would be tedious; imagine how much more tedious the calculation would be if interest were compounded monthly, and therefore 96 times over 8 years! However, the following calculator steps make life easier:

enter **1.025**	
press the x^y or y^x key	(using the 'shift' or 'second function' key if necessary)
enter **32**	
press the = key	(2.203756938)

The next example deals with the calculation of an interest rate.

EXAMPLE 5.1.3

A sum of £600 is invested in an account which earns monthly compounded interest. Determine the *annual* rate of interest for this account, if the total amount in the account at the end of 5 years is £1350.

Note: Answering this question will require the use of the 'root key' on your calculator, which will usually be marked $x^{1/y}$ *or* $y^{1/x}$ *or* $x\sqrt{y}$.

Solution 5.1.3

As in the previous example, the account information is presented annually, and indeed it is the annual interest rate which is required. However, the important point when applying formula (5.1.6) is that interest is compounded more than once per year. The monthly interest rate and the number of months of the investment are therefore used, and the answer obtained for R is monthly. Thus

$$A_t = P\,(1 + R/100)^t \qquad \text{where } P = 600, \; t = 5 \times 12 = 60 \text{ (months)}, \; A_t = 1350$$

and so

$$1350 = 600\,(1 + R/100)^{60} \qquad \text{(remember, } R \text{ is the monthly rate)}$$

$$2.25 = (1 + R/100)^{60}$$

Since $1 + R/100$ to the power 60 is 2.25, $1 + R/100$ is the 60th root of 2.25. The previous equation is therefore rewritten thus:

$$1 + R/100 = \sqrt[60]{2.25} \quad \text{or} \quad 1 + R/100 = 2.25^{1/60}$$

(The difference here is only the way in which the 60th root is written; when you are solving problems, use the notation which matches that on your calculator.) Finally

$$1 + R/100 = 1.013607$$

$$R/100 = 0.013607$$

$$R = 1.3607\% \text{ per month}$$

The annual rate of interest is therefore $12 \times 1.3607 = 16.33\%$ p.a. (to 2 d.p.).

Note: the appropriate calculator steps are:

enter **2.25**

press the $x\sqrt{y}$ or $x^{1/y}$ or $y^{1/x}$ key   (using the 'shift' or 'second
                                                                function' key, if necessary)

enter **60**
press the $=$ key   (1.013607)

The final example in this section deals with logarithms. If you are doubtful about the use of logs in the solution re-read section 1.3 of Chapter 1.

EXAMPLE 5.1.4

A sum of £2000 is invested in an account for which interest is compounded semi-annually. If the annual rate of interest is 5% p.a., find the time taken for this amount to treble.

Since the time period is unknown, the 'log' key on your calculator will be required as well as the property for logs which states that

$$\log N^p = p \times \log N$$

(See section 1.3 of the first chapter.)

Note: The 'log' key calculates logs to the base 10. You might also notice a key 'ln' which also calculates logs, but to a different base. This will prove useful for the next section.

Solution 5.1.4

To find the time period, the compound interest formula is applied thus:

$$A_t = P(1 + R/100)^t$$

where $P = 2000$, $A_t = 4000$, $R = 5/2 = 2.5$ (half-yearly interest) and t is the number of half-years

$$4000 = 2000(1.025)^t$$

$$2 = (1.025)^t \qquad\qquad (5.1.8)$$

In this equation, *it is the power t which is unknown.* Of course, trying values of t would produce an answer but this can be a slow process. The efficient, mathematical way to find t is to use logs. Applying the log function to each side of (5.1.8)

$$\log 2 = \log (1.025)^t$$

Now using the property for logs, which was re-stated above:

$$\log 2 = t \times \log (1.025) \qquad \text{think of this as 'moving the power } t \text{ to the front of the log'}$$

Using the log key on the calculator

$$0.3010 = t \times 0.0107 \qquad \text{accuracy is not critical here, since we will round up ultimately to find } t$$

$$t = \frac{0.3010}{0.0107} = 28.13 \qquad \text{the logs are ordinary numbers – powers of 10 in fact – and are divided in the ordinary way}$$

(Note that, once the logs have been evaluated, it is easy to find t but only because the use of logs allows us to convert t from a power to a multiplier.)

We now know that, in theory, the original investment is doubled after 28.13 half-years. However, in practice, interest is added at the *end* of each half-year, and so the target amount is reached, in fact exceeded, after 29 half-years.

Conclusion: It takes 14.5 years for the original investment to double.

EXERCISES 5.1

1   £1000 is invested in an account which earns simple interest. Find the final balance of the account if

  (a) the rate of interest is 7% p.a. and the sum is invested for 6 years
  (b) the rate of interest is 9% per half-year and the sum is invested for 4 years.

  For case (a), how long does the original investment of £1000 take to double?

2   A sum of £1200 is invested and earns compound interest at the rate of 9% p.a. Calcualte the balance after 6 years if interest is compounded

  (a) annually   (b) semi-annually   (c) monthly.

  For each of the cases (a) and (b) find the time taken for the balance to first exceed £3000.

3   Mrs Jones invests £1000 in each of two accounts. The first account offers interest at the annual rate of 9%, compounded quarterly; whereas the second account offers interest at an annual rate of 8%, compounded semi-annually, for the first 4 years, after which the annual rate increases to 10%, compounded semi-annually.

  If Mrs Jones withdraws £500 from the first account at the end of the second year, find the total balance of the two accounts at the end of 6 years.

4   £700 is invested in an account which earns compound interest at the rate of 8% per annum, compounded semi-annually, until the balance reaches or first exceeds £1000. Thereafter, the interest rate is increased to 12% p.a., and interest is compounded quarterly.

  Calculate the balance of the account 8 years after the initial investment.

5   (a) £800 is invested in account X which earns compound interest at the rate of 10% p.a., compounded semi-annually. Calculate the amount in the account at the end of 5 years.

  (b) The interest for account Y is compounded quarterly. What annual rate of interest for this account would make accounts X and Y equally attractive? State your answer to the first decimal place.

6   At the end of 1993, Mr Smith invested £2000 in an account which earns interest at the rate of 10% p.a., compounded quarterly, with the aim of accumulating £3700. His aim, originally, was to leave the money invested until the target is achieved, and to make no further payments.

However, Mr Smith has now been told that the interest rate will be reduced to 6% p.a., compounded quarterly, at the end of June 1996, and he therefore intends to invest an extra sum at that time, in order that his target will still be achieved on the same date as before.

What extra investment is required?

7 A sum of money is invested in an account in which interest is compounded annually. If the interest earned in the first year is £174 and that earned in the second year is £194.88, determine the principal and the annual rate of interest

5.2 CONTINUOUS COMPOUNDING

Since compound interest is calculated on the increasing balance of an account, the more often interest is compounded, e.g. quarterly, monthly, daily, the faster the invested amount will grow. However, the invested amount cannot increase without bound and it is interesting to look at precisely what the limitation on the growth is, as we approach closer and closer to an idealised state in which we *imagine* that interest is added continuously. We have to imagine such continuous growth, since, in practice, it is always necessary to pause to perform some intermediate calculation, and so a truly continuous situation is not possible. However, there is nothing artificial about compounding interest very frequently, e.g. hourly. Indeed, overnight investment of money by large companies is commonplace.

The continuous growth model which we are about to describe can be applied to any quantity which we view as increasing continuously, provided that the annual % rate of growth is fixed. For example, it might be applied to costs and profits or to populations. The model can be used to represent both increases and decreases, by using a positive or negative rate, respectively.

For the purposes of illustration, we will look at a sum of £1, invested for 4 years at an annual interest rate of 12%. Table 5.2.1, based on formula (5.1.6), shows the effect of compounding more and more frequently. The average 6-monthly, 3-monthly and monthly interest rates are, respectively, $12/2 = 6$, $12/4 = 3$ and $12/12 = 1$. For the weekly rate we will approximate the rate of $12/52$ by 0.231.

The table suggests that the successive differences will continue to get smaller and smaller, and that the balance is approaching closer and closer to, but not quite reaching, some *limiting value* (close to 1.6161 at a guess!); it is this value which would be regarded as the value of £1, at the end of 4 years, when interest is *compounded continuously*.

It should be noted that this limiting value does not correspond to compounding interest a specific number of times, but is implied by the calculations obtained by compounding more and more often. Presumably the limiting value is determined only by the number of *years* of the investment and the *annual* rate of interest. The aim now is to determine a formula for the limiting value in terms of these two quantities.

Table 5.2.1

Compounding interval	Calculation	Balance (end of 4 years)	Successive differences
Annually	$(1.12)^4$	1.5735	
6-monthly	$(1.06)^8$	1.5938	0.0203
3-monthly	$(1.03)^{16}$	1.6047	0.0109
monthly	$(1.01)^{48}$	1.6122	0.0075
weekly	$(1.00231)^{208}$	1.6160	0.0038

A formula for continuous growth

Since R and t are reserved for the period interest rate and number of compounding periods for an investment, R_a and t_a will be used for the annual interest rate and the number of years. A useful first step in obtaining a formula for continuous growth in terms of R_a and t_a is to look at the compound interest formula (5.1.6) used to calculate the balances in the previous table. Assuming an investment of £1 as before, (5.1.6) states that

$$A_t = (1 + R/100)^t \tag{5.2.1}$$

and the limiting value obtained from the table is the value which this expression approaches as the number of compounding periods t becomes larger and larger, causing the period rate R to become smaller and smaller.

There are similarities between this and a standard mathematical result (standard to mathematicians, that is!) which states that, for any number x, the expression

$$(1 + x/n)^n \tag{5.2.2}$$

where n is a positive whole number, approaches the limiting value e^x, as n becomes larger and larger (in mathematical terms, $n \to \infty$). The number e is called the **exponential constant** and e^x is called the **exponential function**. There is nothing obvious about this result or the value 2.718 ... of e; you are asked to accept this result and to appreciate that the values of e^x can be obtained from a calculator. However, we can demonstrate the result *numerically*, for a specific value of x and specific values of n, increasing in size. For example, let $x = 0.2$. Then

if $n = 10$ $(1 + 0.2/10)^{10} = (1.02)^{10} = 1.21899$

if $n = 50$ $(1 + 0.2/50)^{50} = (1.004)^{50} = 1.22092$

if $n = 100$ $(1 + 0.2/100)^{100} = (1.002)^{100} = 1.22116$

if $n = 500$ $(1 + 0.2/500)^{500} = (1.0004)^{500} = 1.22135$

Compare these values with the value of $e^{0.2}$ which, by calculator, is 1.22140. These results are consistent with the claim that we are approaching closer and closer to the value of the exponential function.

Let us now return to the similarities between compounding interest more and more often, and the standard result for the exponential function stated above. The

111

balances in the table are obtained by making the *power* in (5.2.1) larger and larger, and the same is true of the power in (5.2.2). However, for the standard result, the value of n is divided within the bracket, and so we will rewrite (5.2.1) so that we are dividing by t within the bracket.

To do this, let k be the number of times that interest is compounded per year. Then, the relationships between the annual and period interest rates, and the times in years and periods, are as follows:

$$R = R_a/k \quad \text{and} \quad t = kt_a$$

Therefore, $k = t/t_a$ and substituting into the first equation

$$R = \frac{R_a}{t/t_a} = \frac{R_a t_a}{t}$$

Substituting into (5.2.1)

$$A_t = \left(1 + \frac{R_a t_a}{100 t}\right)^t = \left(1 + \frac{R_a t_a/100}{t}\right)^t$$

The right-hand side of this equation is now exactly of the form stated in (5.2.2) when $R_a t_a/100$ is substituted for x and t is used instead of n. Therefore, the limiting value of the balance of the account as interest is compounded more and more often is

$$e^{R_a t_a/100}$$

This is therefore regarded as the balance, after t_a years at R_a % p.a, when interest is compounded continuously. For example, if $R_a = 12\%$ and $t_a = 4$ years, as in the previous table, then the above formula predicts the value

$$e^{12 \times 4/100} = e^{0.48} = \pounds 1.6161 \qquad \text{to 4 d.p.}$$

and so our earlier guess from Table 5.2.1 was appropriate!

The balance for a principal of $\pounds P$ is obtained by multiplying the previous formula by P. If we now drop the subscript a, which was only used to distinguish between compounding more than once per year and annually, the **continuous compounding formula** is obtained.

$$A_t = P\, e^{Rt/100} \tag{5.2.3}$$

where R = annual % rate of interest and t = number of years.

Note that it is always the data per **annum** which is used in this formula.

EXAMPLE 5.2.1

£200 is invested in an account which earns interest at the annual rate of 8%, compounded continuously.

(a) Calculate the balance of the account at the end of 6 years.

(b) Find the time taken for the balance of the account to double.

Note: answering this part will require the use of the 'exponential key' on the calculator, which will usually be marked **e^x** *or* **exp x.**

Solution 5.2.1(a)

Using formula (5.2.3), the balance is given by

$$A_t = P\,e^{Rt/100} \qquad \text{where } P = 200,\ R = 8,\ t = 6$$

Therefore

$$A_6 = 200\,e^{8 \times 6/100} = 200\,e^{0.48}$$

$$= £323.21$$

Solution 5.2.1(b)

Note: Answering this part will require the use of the 'log to the base e key' on your calculator, which should be denoted by **log e** *or* **ln***.*

If you are doubtful about the use of logs in the calculation which follows, re-read section 1.3 of Chapter 1. Let t years be the time taken for the balance to double to £400. Then

$$400 = 200\,e^{8t/100}$$

$$2 = e^{8t/100}$$

Therefore

$$\ln 2 = 8t/100 \qquad \text{by definition, } \ln 2 \text{ is the } power \text{ to which the base e must be raised to produce the result 2}$$

$$0.69315 = 8t/100 \qquad \text{by calculator}$$

$$t = 8.7 \text{ years}$$

(The answer is not rounded to a whole number, since interest is compounded continuously.)

General formulation of exponential models

The important formula (5.2.3) is applicable to other areas such as population growth and the growth of certain quantities in economics, such as Gross National Product. It is therefore useful to state a general version of the formula as follows:

$$y = y_0\,e^{kt} \tag{5.2.4}$$

where y_0 is the initial value of y when $t = 0$ and the constant k (either positive or negative) is the growth factor. If R is the percentage rate of growth, $k = R/100$, and a negative value of k indicates that y actually decreases as t increases.

This type of exponential growth for y_0, k positive, where y grows indefinitely large provided that t is allowed to be indefinitely large, is represented graphically as in Figure 5.1.1.

When growth is limited, the exponential model takes on a different form

$$y = A - B\,e^{-kt} \qquad \text{where } A,\ B,\ k \text{ are constants with } B,\ k \text{ positive} \tag{5.2.5}$$

and graphically this is represented as in Figure 5.1.2.

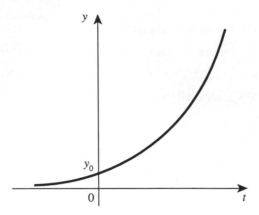

Figure 5.1.1 $y = y_0 e^{kt}$ (y_0, k positive constants)

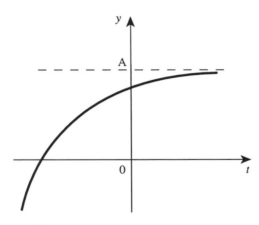

Figure 5.1.2 $y = A - Be^{-kt}$ (A, B, k constants)

Such a curve might represent, for example, the growth in demand for a new product or the output from an industrial process as it approaches its maximum output.

EXERCISES 5.2

1 An account earns continuously compounded interest.

(a) If the initial investment is £2200 and the annual interest rate is 12%, calculate the balance at the end of 7 years.

(b) If the annual interest rate is 12%, what principal grows to £4000 in 4 years?

(c) For an initial investment of £2200, what annual interest rate would achieve the same balance as that determined in (a) after 5 years?

2 £3400 is invested in an account which earns continuously compounded interest.

(a) After how many years will the balance first exceed £6500, if the annual interest rate is 11%

(b) What interest rate would cause the original £3400 to double in 8 years?

3 The yearly maintenance cost £y of a computer is related to its average monthly use x (in hundreds of hours) by the expression

$$y = 3500 - 2500 \, e^{-0.02x}$$

If the annual maintenance bill is not to exceed £1200, what maximum monthly usage of the computer should be allowed?

4 x days after the start of a 'run', a batch production process is producing at the rate of n items/day where

$$n = 200 \, (1 - e^{-0.1x})$$

When does the production rate first exceed 80 items/day?

5.3   REGULAR EQUAL PAYMENT SCHEMES

Consider an account earning compound interest at the rate of 6% p.a., and suppose that £100 is invested for 5 years. Then the balance after t years is given by the compound interest formula (5.1.6) as follows:

$A_t = P(1 + R/100)^t$ where $P = 100$, $R = 6$

$A_t = 100(1.06)^t$ where $t = 0, 1, 2, 3, 4, 5$

The successive balances are therefore

$100, 100(1.06), 100(1.06)^2, 100(1.06)^3, 100(1.06)^4, 100(1.06)^5$ (5.3.1)

and this is an example of a geometric progression.

Geometric progressions and applications

A geometric progression (G.P.) is a sequence of numbers for which

- the first number can have any value (denoted by a),
- each subsequent number is obtained by multiplying the previous one by some constant number (called the **common ratio** and denoted by r).

The entries in the sequence are called **terms**, and the number of terms is denoted by n.

So (5.3.1) is a G.P. with 6 terms. It starts with the number 100, and then each number is obtained by multiplying the previous one by 1.06. Thus $a = 100$, $r = 1.06$ and $n = 6$.

Another example is

1, 1/2, 1/4, 1/8, 1/16

which is a G.P. for which $a = 1$, $r = 1/2$ and $n = 5$, and which can be written as

$$1, 1\ (1/2), 1\ (1/2)^2, 1\ (1/2)^3, 1\ (1/2)^4 \qquad \text{(5 terms)}$$

Notice that the *final power* in this case and in (5.3.1) *is one less than the number of terms* (since the first term corresponds to r^0, which is 1).

In general, a G.P. with first term a, common ratio r and n terms will have the form

$$a,\ ar,\ ar^2,\ ar^3, ...,\ ar^{n-1}$$

We saw above that the successive balances from a *single* investment form a G.P. The same is true of the balances from a number of *equal* payments, made at regular intervals, as the examples which follow will illustrate, and the total balance is calculated by adding up the terms of the G.P. Fortunately, there is a convenient formula for doing this.

For a G.P. with first term a, common ratio r and n terms, the sum S_n of the terms is given by

$$S_n = \frac{a(r^n - 1)}{r - 1} \qquad \text{if } r > 1 \tag{5.3.2}$$

or

$$S_n = \frac{a(1 - r^n)}{1 - r} \qquad \text{if } r < 1$$

As an illustration of regular investment problems, two examples will be considered.

EXAMPLE 5.3.1

At the end of 1990, £500 was invested in an account which earns compound interest at the rate of 10% p.a., compounded semi-annually. At the end of each subsequent half-year, a further sum of £500 has been invested.

(a) Calculate the total balance of the account at the end of 1996.

(b) Find the time required for the balance to first exceed £12,000.

Solution 5.3.1(a)

The half-yearly payments into the account are as follows:

end of year	90		91		92		93		94		95		96
	500	500 500	500	500 500	500	500 500	500	500 500	500	500 500	500

To calculate the total balance, the compound interest formula (5.1.6) is applied to *each* payment. Therefore the future amount resulting from each payment is

$$A_t = P(1 + R/100)^t$$

where $P = 500$, $R = 10/2 = 5$ and t (half-years) varies with the payment

$$A_t = 500(1.05)^t$$

Therefore, at the end of 1996,

first payment yields $500(1.05)^{12}$ invested for 12 half-years
second payment yields $500(1.05)^{11}$
⋮
last but one payment yields $500(1.05)$
last payment yields 500

Writing these values in reverse order

Total balance at end of 1996
$= 500 + 500(1.05) + 500(1.05)^2 + \cdots + 500(1.05)^{12}$

This is a geometric progression for which $a = 500$ (lowest power term), $r = 1.05$ (each term is obtained from the previous one by multiplying by 1.05), $n = 13$ terms (the powers of 1.05 vary from 0 to 12). So, using the first version of formula (5.3.2),

$$\text{Total balance} = \frac{a(r^n - 1)}{r - 1} \qquad \text{use this version since } r > 1$$

$$= S_{13} = \frac{500((1.05)^{13} - 1)}{1.05 - 1} = \frac{500 \times 0.885649142}{0.05} \qquad (5.3.3)$$

$$= 8856.49$$

Conclusion: Balance is £8856.49 at the end of 1996.

Solution 5.3.1(b)
To find the time taken for the balance to first exceed £12000, look again at (5.3.3). The G.P. will now have n terms and we solve the equation

$$\frac{500((1.05)^n - 1)}{0.05} = 12000$$

Rearranging,

$$(1.05)^n - 1 = \frac{12000 \times 0.05}{500} = 1.2$$

$$(1.05)^n = 2.2$$

This is an exponential equation of the type considered in Section 1.5 of the first chapter, for which logs are used (to the base 10, say). Therefore

$$\log(1.05)^n = \log 2.2$$

$$n \log(1.05) = \log 2.2$$

$$n \times 0.0212 = 0.3424 \qquad \text{find logs from calculator}$$

$$n = 16.15$$

Rounding *up*, since interest is added at the end of each half-year, $n = 17$ *terms*. Therefore, 16 half-years are required, one less than the number of terms.

Conclusion: 8 years are required to exceed £12,000.

The final example deals with a **reserve fund**. A company will make regular investments into such a fund, in order to meet some planned future expenditure.

EXAMPLE 5.3.2

A company will need to replace its air-conditioning plant at the end of 1998 and estimates that the price of the new plant will be £500,000. In order to meet the replacement cost, the accountant has, since the end of 1993, invested a fixed sum at the end of each year in a reserve fund earning interest at the rate of 15% p.a. Assuming that the present air-conditioning plant will have a scrap value of £150,000, and that the fund will be just sufficient to meet replacement cost, what is the required annual investment?

Solution 5.3.2

Unlike the previous example, the annual payment is now the unknown, and must be sufficient to ensure that the total balance at the end of 1998 is

   $500,000 - 150,000 = 350,000$ the replacement cost

If the annual payment is X, say, then the payment scheme is as follows:

end of year	93	94	95	96	97	98
	X	X	X	X	X	X

To calculate the total balance, we apply

   $A_t = P(1 + R/100)^t$
   where $P = X$, $R = 15$ and t (years) varies with each payment
   $A_t = X(1.15)^t$

Therefore, at the end of 1998,

   first payment yields $X(1.15)^5$
   second payment yields $X(1.15)^4$
   $\vdots$
   last but one payment yields $X(1.15)$
   last payment yields X

Total balance at end of $1998 = X + X(1.15) + X(1.15)^2 + \cdots + X(1.15)^5$. This is a geometric progression for which

   $a = X$, $r = 1.15$, $n = 6$ terms

Therefore, using (5.3.2)

   Total balance $S_6 = \dfrac{X((1.15)^6 - 1)}{0.15} = 350,000$ equate to replacement cost

Rearranging

$$X = \frac{350,000 \times 0.15}{(1.15)^6 - 1} = 39982.92$$

Conclusion: Required annual payment is £39,982.92.

Geometric progressions are appropriate for compound interest problems. However, a different type of progression is sometimes useful (see Exercises 5.3, questions 6 and 7).

Arithmetic progressions

An arithmetic progression (A.P.) is a sequence of numbers for which

- the first number can have any value (denoted by a),
- each subsequent number is obtained by *adding* some constant number (called the **common difference** and denoted by d) to the previous number

So, for example,

$$5, 7, 9, 11, 13, 15, 17, 19 \tag{5.3.4}$$

is an arithmetic progression with $a = 5$, $d = 2$ and 8 terms.

In general, an A.P. with first term a, common difference d and n terms will have the form

$$a, a + d, a + 2d, a + 3d, \ldots, a + (n - 1)d$$

For an A.P. with first term a, common difference d and n terms, the sum S_n of the terms is given by

$$S_n = \frac{n}{2} (2a + (n - 1)d)$$

So, for example, the sum of the A.P. (5.3.4) for which $a = 5$, $d = 2$, $n = 8$, is

$$S_8 = \frac{8}{2} (2 \times 5 + 7 \times 2) = 96 \qquad \text{which checks with ordinary addition of the numbers}$$

EXERCISES 5.3

1 An account earns compound interest at the annual rate of 8%. Calculate the balance of the account at the end of 1998 if

(a) Interest is compounded quarterly, and, starting with an initial payment of £400 into the account at the end of 1990, £400 is paid in at the end of each quarter.

(b) Interest is compounded half-yearly, and, starting with an initial payment of £600 at the end of 1990, £600 is paid in at the end of each half-year.

2 Earthworms Ltd. has a reserve fund to cover the cost of replacing an excavator at the end of 1997.The present excavator (purchased on 1 January 1990) cost £300,000 and it is estimated that it will have a scrap value of £50,000. The company has chosen to base its calculations on an average inflation rate of 15% p.a. Commencing on 31 December 1990, a fixed sum has been paid into the fund at the end of each year.

(a) Calculate the replacement cost of the excavator.
(b) Determine the required annual payment into the fund, assuming a rate of return from the fund of 12% p.a.

3 Calculate the time required for the balance of an account to first exceed £10,000

(a) assuming the same account and payment details as those given in Exercise 1(a)
(b) assuming the same account and payment details as those given in Exercise 1(b).

4 A company has just bought a machine costing £6500, and estimates that its useful life will be 8 years, after which it will be sold as scrap for £300. The company decides to set up a reserve fund to cover the cost of a replacement machine in 8 years time, and to this end equal amounts are to be invested at yearly intervals in an account which earns 8% p.a. compound interest, the first investment to be made immediately. Due to inflation, it is estimated that the cost of this machine will be £22,000. How much must be invested each year to cover the cost of a replacement machine, allowing for the scrap value of the present one, if

(a) interest is compounded annually?
(b) interest is compounded semi-annually?

5 On December 31 1991, Longhorne Transport Ltd. established a reserve fund in an account which earned 10% per annum interest, compounded semi-annually. The first deposit, on 31 December 1991, was to be followed at half-yearly intervals by further deposits of the same amount. The Longhorne accountant had calculated the amount of these half-yearly deposits to be £845 with the objective of producing a specific balance at the end of 1996.

At the end of 1993, however, Longhorne were advised that, with effect from 1 January 1994, the interest rate on the reserve fund was to be reduced to 8% per annum, compounded semi-annually. The Longhorne accountant therefore decided that an increase must be made in the half-yearly deposits into the reserve fund, starting with the deposit on 30 June 1994, so that the balance at the end of 1996 is still sufficient.

Show that the intended balance at the end of 1996 is approximately £12,000, and find the increase in deposit necessitated by the reduction in the interest rate.

6 An account earns simple interest at the annual rate of 10%. £800 is invested in the account and a further £800 is invested at the end of each subsequent year.

120

Use the formula for the sum of an arithmetic progression to find the total balance after 12 years.

7 During the first year of employment, Mr Smith's annual salary was £2800, and at the end of each year he receives an increment of £400. Use the formula for the sum of an arithmetic progression to determine Mr Smith's total earnings over a 10 year period.

Mr Jones started work at the same time as Mr Smith and his starting salary was £4000. Each year he receives an increment of £200. After how many years will Mr Smith's total earnings first exceed the total earned by Mr Jones?

6

DISCOUNTED CASH FLOW ANALYSIS

After working through this chapter you will be able to

- understand the ' time value of money' concept
- perform net present value calculations
- apply criteria for judging the viability of investments
- perform depreciation calculations
- apply geometric progressions to the analysis of investments

6.1 INVESTMENT APPRAISAL

Whatever the activities of a company, sensible and effective investment of capital will be essential. The company will want a good return from money invested, and will have in mind an expectation of the profits which should be achieved, based upon the results of past ventures.

However complicated the investment, it will usually involve present-day capital outlay, with a view to returns from the investment in the *future*, and it is therefore important to have an understanding of what importance should be attached to the timing of money in this type of situation.

The time value of money

If we had to choose between receiving £1000 present day, or in two years time, there would be no doubt what decision we would make. The present-day sum is clearly worth more, not only because it should buy more in terms of goods and services, but because, if invested now, it would grow in two years to significantly more than £1000. Both these issues are important, but it is the latter which we will focus on in this chapter.

As an example of how to deal with sums of money occurring at different times, let us consider the problem faced by Mr Jones, who has been asked by a friend to invest capital in his new business.There is, of course, a significant element of risk in doing this, but risk is not an issue considered here. We will concentrate instead on what conclusions Mr Jones should draw, based purely on monetary terms.

Suppose, then, that Mr Jones has been asked to invest £12,000 now, and that he will receive the following amounts:

£6000	£9000
end of 2 years	end of 3 years

As it stands, we cannot decide whether this is a good deal for Mr Jones or not. We need to know what Mr Jones believes his money can earn *elsewhere*, if he does not take up the above offer. Let us suppose that he believes that his money will grow by 10% p.a., if invested elsewhere.

We will proceed by calculating the sum of money which, if invested elsewhere at 10% p.a., would grow sufficiently to provide the same future cash amounts as those which Mr Jones would receive from the project. If this is greater than £12,000, then Mr Jones would benefit from the project (in purely monetary terms); if it is lower, he will not benefit. The approach is to use the compound interest formula (5.1.6), from the last chapter, to calculate, for each of the future amounts, the principal which, if invested elsewhere, will grow to that amount.

For the sum of £6000 in two years, we use

$$A_t = P_1 \left(1 + R/100\right)^t \qquad \text{where } A_t = 6000, \ t = 2, \ R = 10$$

and so

$$6000 = P_1 \left(1 + 10/100\right)^2$$

$$P_1 = 6000/(1.1)^2 = £4958.68$$

Similarly, for the return of £9000 in three years

$$9000 = P_2 \left(1 + 10/100\right)^3$$

$$P_2 = 9000/(1.1)^3 = £6761.83$$

Therefore

Total investment = 4958.68 + 6761.83 = £11720.51   for money invested
required   elsewhere

Thus, if investing elsewhere, it would cost Mr Jones £11,720.51 to achieve the cash amounts as offered by his friend, for which he is being asked to pay £12,000. Therefore, in present day terms, Mr Jones is making a profit of

$$11720.51 - 12000 = -£279.49 \qquad \text{i.e. a loss of £279.49}$$

and the project is not worthwhile.

When companies appraise projects, the analysis is often no different in principle to that presented above, but it is couched in a different language, for which the terms have an agreed meaning. The incoming amounts from the project are referred to as **inflows**, and the costs as **outflows**. A **base date** is set, usually the start of the project, and it is the timing of each cash flow (whether inflow or outflow) relative to this date which is important. The rate of return available *elsewhere*, against which the project is judged, is called the **discount rate**, since it is the rate which must be 'discounted' or 'allowed for' in deciding the value of the cash flows involved, and the term **present value** carries with it an implicit understanding that it is the *principal* which grows to a future sum.

Rearranging the formula $A_t = P(1 + R/100)^t$ we obtain the **present value formula**:

$$P = \frac{A_t}{(1 + R/100)^t} \qquad (6.1.1)$$

where P is the present value of a future amount sum A_t, payable in t periods time, assuming a discount rate of $R\%$ per period.

Using this terminology, the analysis for Mr Jones is now presented as follows:

Base date: start of project

Discount rate: 10% p.a.   (expected rate of return on capital elsewhere)

Apply the present value formula

$$P = \frac{A_t}{(1 + R/100)^t} = \frac{A_t}{(1.1)^t}$$

Total present value of inflows $= \dfrac{6000}{(1.1)^2} + \dfrac{9000}{(1.1)^3}$

$$= 4958.68 + 6761.83 = £11720.51$$

Total present value of outflows $= 12000$

Net present value of inflows $= 11720.51 - 12000 = -£279.49$ as before

Of course, these calculations are all based upon the rate of return of 10% p.a. which Mr Jones expects to earn *elsewhere* on his money. If this rate turns out to be lower, then Mr Jones would have to invest more elsewhere to achieve the future amounts offered by his friend, and it is more likely that he would want to take up his friend's offer. For example, suppose that, in reality, he is only able to earn 7% p.a. elsewhere. Then the corresponding calculations are as follows:

Total present value of inflows $= \dfrac{6000}{(1.07)^2} + \dfrac{9000}{(1.07)^3}$

$$= 5240.63 + 7346.68 = £12587.31$$

Total present value of outflows $= 12000$

Net present value of inflows $= 12587.31 - 12000 = £587.31$

In this case, Mr Jones is making a profit of £587.31 in present value terms, and so the venture is worthwhile (provided he accepts the risks).

A criterion for deciding the viability of an investment

As the previous example demonstrates, the net present value of inflows is the profit from a venture over and above the expected % rate of return elsewhere – the discount rate – and therefore provides a basis for acceptance or rejection. The criterion is as follows:

Net present value (N.P.V.) of inflows =

Total present value (T.P.V.) of inflows – Total present value of outflows

If N.P.V. of inflows > 0   accept the investment

If N.P.V. of inflows < 0   reject the investment

Two more examples will be considered, exploring different aspects of investment appraisal.

EXAMPLE 6.1.1

Yorkshire Properties purchased a small block of flats for £50,000 on 31 December 1993 and plans to retain the property for 4 years. The following amounts, from renting out the property, are expected:

Date	Dec. 31 1994	Dec. 31 1995	Dec. 31 1996	Dec. 31 1997
Total rent for year	5000	5800	7000	8500

The company estimates that the property will appreciate in value by 20% p.a., but anticipates that it will require rewiring, at a cost of £2300, at the end of 1995. A discount rate of 25% p.a. is to be adopted in appraising the investment.

(a) Calculate the net present value of inflows for the investment. Is the investment worthwhile?

(b) Determine the minimum annual rate at which the property can appreciate in value if the company is not to make a loss on the investment.

Solution 6.1.1 (a)

Two versions of the answer to this part of the question are given, the first making use of tables for presenting the present values of inflows and outflows. The use of tables allows for an organised approach to present value problems, and this can be helpful, particularly when there is a number of inflows and outflows to be considered, and intermediate calculations such as the determination of a resale value are required.

Base date: 31 Dec. 1993   the obvious base date, since the flats were purchased on this date

Discount rate: 25% p.a.

Apply the present value formula (6.1.1)

$$P = \frac{A_t}{(1+R/100)^t} = \frac{A_t}{(1.25)^t}$$

1 *Cash inflows*

The annual rents £5000, £5800, £7000 and £8500 clearly qualify for this category and, in addition, the company will receive the *resale value* of the flats after 4 years. Since an appreciation rate acts upon the increasing value of the property, it

125

can be treated in the same way as a compound interest rate. Therefore using formula (5.1.6), where A_t is the value of the property after 4 years

$$A_t = P(1 + R/100)^t \quad \text{where } P = 50000, R = 20, t = 4$$

$$A_t = 50000(1.20)^4 = 103680$$

The inflow table, in which the timing of each inflow is recorded relative to the base date, is therefore as follows:

Cash inflow (£)	Timing	Calculation $P = A_t/(1.25)^t$	Present value (£)
5000	End of 1 yr	$5000/(1.25)$	4000.00
5800	End of 2yrs	$5800/(1.25)^2$	3712.00
7000	End of 3yrs	$7000/(1.25)^3$	3584.00
8500	End of 4 yrs	$8500/(1.25)^4$	3481.60
103680	End of 4 yrs	$103680/(1.25)^4$	42467.33
(Resale value)			57244.93

T.P.V. of inflows = £57244.93.

Although the question does not ask for an interpretation of the results, it is worth reiterating the meaning of present values. The total present value of £57,244.93 is the sum which the company would need to invest *now* (i.e. at the base date), *elsewhere*, at 25% p.a., in order to obtain the same inflows as the flats project. So £57,244.93 is the total amount received in present day terms.

2 *Cash outflows*
The major cash outflow is the purchase cost of £50,000, paid out presumably on the base date, but there is also an anticipated outlay of £2300 two years on from the base date. Thus:

Cash outflow (£)	Timing	Calculation	Present value (£)
50000	Immediate	–	50000
2300	End of 2 yrs	$2300/(1.25)^2$	1472
			51472

T.P.V. of cash outflows = £51472.

This sum of money is sufficient to meet the initial cost and allows enough extra money to meet the maintenance cost after 2 years, provided that this extra sum is invested now, elsewhere, at 25% p.a. £51,472 is therefore the total cost of the project in present day terms.
    Finally

Net present value of cash inflows for project $= 57244.93 - 51472$

$$= 5772.93$$

Conclusion: £5772.93 is the profit in present value terms, over and above the 25% p.a. which the company expects to receive from its investments. Since this net present value is positive, the project is worthwhile.

Alternative Solution 6.1.1 (a)

If you prefer, the answer can be expressed more briefly as follows:

Base date: 31 Dec. 1993
Discount rate: 25% p.a.

$$\text{T.P.V. of inflows} = \frac{5000}{1.25} + \frac{5800}{(1.25)^2} + \frac{7000}{(1.25)^3} + \frac{8500}{(1.25)^4} + \frac{103680}{(1.25)^4}$$

$$= 4000 + 3712 + 3584 + 3481.60 + 42467.33 = 57244.93$$

$$\text{T.P.V. of outflows} = 50000 + \frac{2300}{(1.25)^2}$$

$$= 50000 + 1472 = 51472$$

$$\text{N.P.V. of inflows} = 57244.93 - 51472 = £5772.93$$

Solution 6.1.1(b)

Since the company expects 25% p.a. from its investments, a return of less than this figure must be regarded as a loss. As stated in **(a)**, the net present value of inflows is the profit from the investment over and above the 25% p.a. and so the resale value must be calculated so as to avoid a negative N.P.V. Thus, we require that

$$\text{N.P.V. of inflows} \geq 0$$

and the worst case

$$\text{N.P.V. of inflows} = 0$$

corresponds to the minimum % appreciation rate, which we will denote by R, say. This is equivalent to the equation

$$\text{T.P.V. of inflows} = \text{T.P.V. of outflows} \qquad (6.1.2)$$

Using this equation, we could launch into a calculation of R. However, it is easier to find the minimum resale value after 4 years, which we will denote by X, and then use the compound interest formula (5.1.6) to find R. (Since $P = 50000$ and $t = 4$, the only missing piece of information is the value of X.)

Using the present values of the rents, and the rewiring cost, found in **(a)**, and discounting the resale value

$$\text{T.P.V. of inflows} = 4000 + 3712 + 3584 + 3481.60 + \frac{X}{(1.25)^4}$$

$$= 14777.60 + \frac{X}{(1.25)^4}$$

$$\text{T.P.V. of outflows} = 51472$$

Substituting into (6.1.2)

$$14777.60 + \frac{X}{(1.25)^4} = 51472$$

$$X = 36694.40 \ (1.25)^4 = £89585.94$$

Now applying formula (5.1.6) to find the annual appreciation rate

$$A_t = P \ (1 + R/100)^t \qquad \text{where } A_t = 89585.94, \ P = 50000, \ t = 4$$

$$89585.94 = 50000 \ (1 + R/100)^t$$

$$1.79171875 = (1 + R/100)^t$$

$$1 + R/100 = \sqrt[4]{(1.79171875)} \qquad$$ if you are doubtful about this,

$$= (1.79171875)^{1/4} \qquad$$ look back at the calculation of the interest rate in Example 5.1.3

$$= 1.156957644$$

$$R = 15.6957644$$

Conclusion: The minimum acceptable rate of appreciation for the property is 15.7% p.a. (to 1 decimal place).

Note: The calculator steps for finding the root are as follows:

---

enter **1.79171875**

press the $x^{1/y}$ or $y^{1/x}$ or $^x\!\sqrt{y}$ key

enter **4**

press the = key

EXAMPLE 6.1.2

Copycat Ltd. is planning to acquire a specialised printer, which it is claimed does not require servicing, and has two options open to it:

- *Purchase of the printer*
  The cost will be £2500, and Copycat will need to purchase cartridges, each capable of printing 600 pages, at a cost of £90 each. It is estimated that the printer would be sold at the end of 5 years for £800.
- *Hire of the printer*
  The charge is £1500, payable annually in advance. Cartridges are included in this charge and faults with the printer will be repaired free of charge.

(All other operating costs for the printer, including cost of paper, are incurred whether the company rents or buys, and can be disregarded for the purposes of comparison.)

Copycat plans to print 4800 pages in the first year, and envisages that this number will increase by 800 pages per year (over the 5-year period). If Copycat's capital earns interest at the rate of 14% p.a., should the company rent or buy?

Solution 6.1.2

There are two significant differences between this example and the last. Firstly, it is not concerned with profitability of the printer but with cost, and so it is the **net present value of outflows** which is adopted rather than the net present value of inflows. Therefore inflows are subtracted from outflows. Secondly, the outflows when *purchasing* the printer are not given directly but require calculation.

The present value calculations will be based upon the following:

Base date: date of acquisition

Discount rate: 14% p.a.

Apply the present value formula

$$P = \frac{A_t}{(1 + R/100)^t} = \frac{A_t}{(1.14)^t}$$

1 *Outright purchase*

The outflows to be considered are the purchase cost of £2500 and the cost of cartridges. (All other operating costs are to be disregarded.) For the first year,

4800 pages will be produced, requiring $4800/600 = 8$ cartridges
Cost $= 8 \times 90 = £720$

Each year thereafter,

800 additional pages will be produced, requiring $1\frac{1}{3}$ cartridges.
Additional cost for year $= 4/3 \times 90 = £120$

(It is reasonable to consider part of a cartridge, since the remainder can be used at the start of the next year.) Allowing for the annual increase in cost of £120, the annual costs of cartridges for the five year period are therefore £720, £840, £960, £1080 and £1200. The outflows must now be discounted, and we shall assume that they are incurred at year ends for the purpose of analysis.

Cash outflow (£)	Timing	Calculation $P = A_t/(1.14)^t$	Present value (£)
2500	immediate	–	2500.00
720	End of 1 yr	$720/(1.14)$	631.58
840	End of 2yrs	$840/(1.14)^2$	646.35
960	End of 3 yrs	$960/(1.14)^3$	647.97
1080	End of 4 yrs	$1080/(1.14)^4$	639.45
1200	End of 5 yrs	$1200/(1.14)^5$	623.24
			5688.59

T.P.V. of outflows = £5688.59

There is one cash inflow, resulting from the resale of the copier.

Cash inflow	Timing	Calculation	Present value (£)
800	End of 5 yrs	$800/(1.14)^5$	415.49
			415.49

T.P.V. of cash outflows = £415.49

Therefore

N.P.V. of cash outflows = 5688.59 – 415.49 = £5273.10

2 Hire option
Care has to be taken with the timing of the cash outflows for this option. Each payment is made at the *start* of year, and the first payment is made immediately.

Cash outflow (£)	Timing	Calculation $P = A_t/(1.14)^t$	Present value (£)
1500	immediate	–	1500.00
1500	End of 1 yr	$1500/(1.14)$	1315.79
1500	End of 2 yrs	$1500/(1.14)^2$	1154.20
1500	End of 3 yrs	$1500/(1.14)^3$	1012.46
1500	End of 4 yrs	$1500/(1.14)^4$	888.12
			5870.57

T.P.V. of cash outflows = £5870.57

Conclusion: The outright purchase option is cheapest. However, the hire option includes the fixing of faults, and so, if opting for outright purchase, the company must hope that the copier is reliable.

EXERCISES 6.1

1 A company is to invest in just one of three projects A, B and C, the inflows from which are tabulated below. Projects A and C each cost £9000, whereas B costs £10,000.

End of Year	A	B	C
1	3000	—	—
2	3000	7000	—
3	3000	—	16000
4	3000	7000	—
5	2500	—	—
6	2500	7000	—

Calculate the net present value of inflows for each project, using a discount rate of 18% p.a., and advise the company as to which project to choose.

2 An engineering firm is to acquire a computerised lathe and has 2 options open to it. It could purchase the lathe outright for £20,000 and maintain the machine itself. The expected life of the machine is 8 years and the maintenance costs over this period are expected to be as follows:

End of 2 years	End of 4 years	End of 6 years
£700	£1500	£2500

It is estimated that the machine would have a scrap value of £2000.

Alternatively, the lathe manufacturer offers a contract under which the lathe can be hired. The annual charge is £4000, payable in advance, in return for which the lathe will be maintained free of charge. If the engineering firm can obtain a return of 15% p.a. on its capital, should it hire or buy?

3 (a) Innovations PLC is to launch a new product at the start of 1996. The cost to be met at the time of the launch is £40,000 and, over a four year trial period, the annual end-of-year profit from the product (after production costs have been deducted) is expected to be £20,000.

If Innovations PLC currently adopts a discount rate of 20% p.a., calculate the net present value of inflows for this venture.

(b) Innovations PLC is now approached by Sellars Associates—a firm of marketing consultants. Sellars proposes a contract under which a marketing strategy for the new product would be developed, which it is claimed would double the annual profit (over the trial period).

Under the contract, Sellars would be paid an initial sum at the start of 1996, and a sum of £10,000 at the start of each subsequent year of the trial period.

Assuming that the forecast of increased annual profit is correct, and that Innovations PLC would only sign the contract if the net present value of inflows for the new product increased by at least 50%, what is the maximum sum the company would be willing to pay to Sellars when the product is launched?

For the remaining questions, assume that cash flows which are incurred at different times during the year are timed at year end for the purposes of investment appraisal.

4 Maitland Engineering is to produce a new type of bearing and must decide on the type of machine to be bought for this purpose. Two alternatives are available, each with a life of 4 years. The first alternative costs £20,000 and is not expected to have any scrap value. The cost of machine time is £6 for each unit produced, and in addition the company would need to meet the cost of employing four operators. The second alternative costs £35,000 and has a much greater degree of automation. As a result, only one operator is required. The cost of machine time per unit produced is £7, and it is estimated that this machine would have a scrap value of £10,000. Maitland Engineering estimates that demand will be 10,000 bearings in the first year, and that demand will increase by 10% per year thereafter. Production will be planned to exactly meet demand.

Assuming that an operator would earn a salary of £6000 p.a., and adopting a discount rate of 20% p.a., determine which machine is the cheapest.

5 Frobisher PLC publish a book by the well known author R. Duncan entitled *Computers – Do They Really Count?* The book went on sale on 31 October 1994. The cost of production is £12 per copy and the selling price £20 per copy. It is envisaged that the book will remain on sale for 4 years. Frobisher has already paid the author £60,000 (this sum was paid on 31 October 1993, when the book was commissioned) and the author will receive a royalty of £4 for each copy sold. It has been agreed that the book will be revised when it has been on sale for 2 years and that Frobisher will pay the author a fee of £30,000 at that time.

It is estimated that sales of the book will total 30,000 in the first year but will decrease by 20% each year thereafter. These figures take into account the proposed revision of the book. Production will be planned so as to exactly meet estimated demand.

Assuming that the demand estimates prove to be accurate, and adopting a discount rate of 25% p.a., calculate the net present value of inflows to Frobisher for this venture.

6 The Knot Timber Company has just added a new type of veneered chip board to its range of products, and has purchased the required machinery at a cost of £200,000. This machinery has a life of four years and an estimated scrap value of £10,000. It is capable of producing 60,000 metres of chip board annually. The company expects fixed costs of £60,000 and variable costs of 90p/metre in the first year of production, and anticipates a selling price of £3/metre. Subsequently all costs are expected to rise by 5% p.a. and the company plans to increase the selling price by 10% p.a.

Assuming that the company adopts a discount rate of 20% p.a., calculate the net present value of inflows for this investment.

6.2 AN ALTERNATIVE APPROACH TO INVESTMENT APPRAISAL – INTERNAL RATE OF RETURN

So far we have looked at project appraisal relative to a figure, the discount rate, *set* within a company, for the annual percentage rate of return which the company ought currently to be earning on its capital. A net present value of inflows is thus calculated which is the profit yielded by a project, over and above the expected discount rate.

However, it is possible instead to look at a project *in its own right* (without reference to a set discount rate) and to produce a figure for the **annual percentage rate of return** which is *implicit* from the inflows and outflows for the project. This rate of return can be calculated solely by using these flows, and, for this reason, the term 'Internal Rate of Return' is used (abbreviated to I.R.R.).

But how can such a rate be calculated? The net present value of inflows represents the profit yielded by the project over and above a particular rate of return. Therefore, the project makes more than the rate of return, if the net present value is positive, or less if the net present value is negative. However, it is the case when the net present value of inflows *is* zero which interests us here. In this case, the particular rate of return is *exactly* that yielded by the project. We therefore have a criterion:

To determine the Internal Rate of Return of a project, find the percentage rate of return for which the net present value of inflows is zero. (6.2.1)

In practice, two aspects of this criterion are worthy of note. Firstly, it is only in the most exceptional cases that a formula can be used to calculate the Internal Rate of Return. Secondly, it is usually necessary to decide upon the required degree of accuracy for the I.R.R., and to settle for a net present value which is as close to zero as possible. The following examples will make this clear.

EXAMPLE 6.2.1

Consider a project which produces the following cash inflows:

End of 1 year	End of 2 years	End of 3 years
£10000	£13000	£18000

If the cost of the project is £30,000, calculate the internal rate of return to the nearest whole percent.

Solution 6.2.1

From (6.2.1) we need to find the rate of return for which the net present value of inflows is zero, or at least as close to zero as possible. Denoting the rate by $R\%$, we need to find the integer (i.e. whole number) value of R for which

$$\text{N.P.V. of inflows} = \frac{10000}{(1+R/100)} + \frac{13000}{(1+R/100)^2} + \frac{18000}{(1+R/100)^3} - 30000 \quad (6.2.2)$$

is as near to zero as possible. It is important to note that, since the cash inflows are *divided* by powers of $1 + R/100$, the N.P.V. gets smaller as R gets larger, and larger as R gets smaller. Thus

$$\text{N.P.V} \downarrow R \uparrow \qquad \text{N.P.V} \uparrow R \downarrow$$

We need a strategy for 'tracking down' the I.R.R., since its value is not obvious from the inflows and outflows. The following strategy allows a good starting value of R to be found, which can then be improved:

- Try various values for R in order to find a **range** in which the I.R.R. lies – values of 10%, 20%, 30%, etc. are convenient. If the N.P.V. has **opposite signs** for two **consecutive** values, then the N.P.V. must be zero for a value of R between these. *Note*: If no sign change is found, suspect a value for R of 10% or less.

Try R = 10% p.a.
Substituting for *R* in (6.2..2)

$$\text{N.P.V. of inflows} = \frac{10000}{1.1} + \frac{13000}{(1.1)^2} + \frac{18000}{(1.1)^3} - 30000$$

$$= 33358.38 - 30000 = £3358.38$$

Try R = 20% p.a.
Substituting for *R* in (6.2.2)

$$\text{N.P.V. of inflows} = \frac{10000}{1.2} + \frac{13000}{(1.2)^2} + \frac{18000}{(1.2)^3} - 30000$$

$$= 27777.78 - 30000 = -2222.22$$

The net present value of inflows changes from positive to negative when *R* increases from 10 to 20, and so the N.P.V. must be zero somewhere in this interval. If the value of the N.P.V. at one of these values of *R* were to be very close to zero, then the sensible next step would be to investigate the N.P.V. close to this value. However, in the present case the N.P.V. values are roughly comparable and so the average of the two rates is used.

Try R = 15% p.a.
Substituting for *R* in (6.2.2)

$$\text{N.P.V. of inflows} = \frac{10000}{1.15} + \frac{13000}{(1.15)^2} + \frac{18000}{(1.15)^3} - 30000$$

$$= 30360.81 - 30000 = 360.81$$

Since this N.P.V. is in hundreds, we must be close to the I.R.R. We therefore investigate the possibility of making the N.P.V smaller, by increasing *R* to the next whole number value.

Try R = 16% p.a.

$$\text{N.P.V. of inflows} = \frac{10000}{1.16} + \frac{13000}{(1.16)^2} + \frac{18000}{(1.16)^3} - 30000$$

$$= 29813.65 - 30000 = -186.35$$

There is no point in going any further. If we were to increase *R* to 17%, then the N.P.V. will be smaller than −186.35 and therefore further away from zero.

Conclusion: The internal rate of return for the project is 16% p.a. to the nearest whole percent.

Note: The same technique can be used to find *R* to the first decimal place, or to a greater degree of accuracy. Since *R* lies between 15% and 16%, we would calculate the N.P.V. for *R* = 15.5% and so on.

A criterion for investment appraisal using the internal rate of return

The net present value of inflows assesses the profitability of a project in monetary terms, using the discount rate – the interest rate which a company currently believes should apply to all its projects. By contrast, the internal rate of return assesses the percentage yield from the project per year. The criterion for decision making is therefore

If I.R.R. < discount rate   reject project

(6.2.3)

If I.R.R. > discount rate   accept project

Application of internal rates of return

The calculation of internal rates of return for *past* projects provides a company with one means of obtaining a realistic figure for the set discount rate to be applied to *future* projects. For example, the *average* internal rate of return for recent projects might be adopted as the discount rate.

EXERCISES 6.2

1 The cash inflows from a project which commenced on 1/1/92, and which cost £6000, are as follows:

Year end	1992	1993	1994	1995	1996
Return (£)	2000	3000	2000	1000	1000

(a) Calculate the net present value of inflows for the project at 1/1/92, if a discount rate of 17% p.a. is adopted.

(b) Estimate the internal rate of return of the project, to the nearest whole percent.

2 A project costs £17,200 and is expected to yield the following cash amounts:

£10,000	£20,000
End of two years	End of three years

(a) Find the internal rate of return of the project correct to the nearest whole percent.

(b) Find a more accurate value for the internal rate of return of this project, correct to the first decimal place.

3 Repeat parts (a) and (b) of Exercise 2 for a project costing £25,500, which is expected to yield the following amounts:

£8000	£15,000	£25,000
End of 1 year	End of 2 years	End of 3 years

4 Preston Plastics has just paid £900,000 for equipment which is capable of producing a specialised type of moulding. It is estimated that the profit will be £40/unit, where this figure is based upon production costs only, and takes no account of the cost of purchasing or servicing the equipment. The equipment will be used to its full capacity throughout, and will produce 10,000 units in the first year. However, as a result of wear, the quantity produced is expected to fall each year by 800 units.

Preston Plastics plans to keep the equipment for five years and to have it serviced at the end of the first year and the third year. The cost of a service will be £1200 per thousand mouldings, or part of a thousand, produced since the last service. The equipment was serviced without charge at the time of installation.

(a) Assuming that the company adopts a rate of return on invested capital of 25% per annum, and that the equipment has no scrap value, calculate the net present value of inflows for this investment.

(b) Suppose that, in reality, the company does not service the equipment at all, and sells it at the end of three years for £200,000. Calculate the internal rate of return of the investment to the nearest whole percent.

6.3 DEPRECIATION

Many items depreciate in value, i.e. reduce in value, as they get older; cars, washing machines, computers are common examples. Methods are therefore required for calculating the **depreciated value** of an item (sometimes called the **book value** or **written-down value**), at each stage of its life, and each method is based upon an assumption about the way in which the value of an item should be reduced during its lifetime.

Two methods will be considered here. The first assumes that the annual depreciation of an item remains fixed throughout its useful life; whereas the second method assumes that the annual depreciation slows down as the item gets older.

Straight-line method of depreciation

The assumption here is that an item reduces in value by a **fixed amount** £D each year. For example, if an item is initially valued at £2500, and depreciates each year by £400, then after 4 years the depreciated value is

$$V_4 = 2500 - 4 \times 400 = £900$$

In general, the value after t years is

$$V_t = V_0 - Dt \tag{6.3.1}$$

where V_0 = initial value, V_t = value after t years, D = annual depreciation.

Reducing-balance method of depreciation

For this method, annual depreciation is based on a **fixed percentage**, which is applied each year to the written-down value of the item at the start of that year. A formula for the depreciated value can therefore be obtained by taking the compound interest formula (5.1.6), which *adds* a fixed percentage per year, and changing the addition to a subtraction. Therefore

$$V_t = V_0 \, (1 - R/100)^t \tag{6.3.2}$$

where V_0 = initial value, V_t = value after t years and R = % depreciation rate p.a.

This approach to depreciation is illustrated in the following example.

EXAMPLE 6.3.1

A computer is purchased for £1500. If it depreciates each year by 20% of its written-down value at the start of that year, calculate its value at the end of 5 years by

(a) constructing a suitable table
(b) using the appropriate formula.

Solution 6.3.1(a)
Each row of the required table starts with the value of the computer at the start of the year, and the depreciation for the year is 20% of this value. Subtracting the depreciation gives the end-of-year value of the computer, which is in turn the starting value for the next year. The table is therefore

Year	Start of year	Depreciation	End of year
1	1500	300	1200
2	1200	240	960
3	960	192	768
4	768	153.60	614.40
5	614.40	122.88	491.52

So the written-down value of the computer at the end of 5 years is £491.52.

Solution 6.3.1(b)
Using formula (6.3.2)

$$V_t = V_0 \, (1 - R/100)^t \qquad \text{where } V_0 = 1500, \, R = 20, \, t = 5$$

Therefore

$$V_5 = 1500 \, (1 - 20/100)^5$$

$$= 1500 \, (0.8)^5$$

$$= £491.52 \quad \text{(as before)}$$

Note Whilst the approaches used in (a) and (b) of this example are both valid, the use of the formula is clearly more efficient when only the final value of an item is required.

So far we have considered the way in which depreciated values are calculated, once the *depreciation rate is known*. In practice, this rate must be calculated by using the appropriate depreciation formula and the following information:

- the useful life of the item
- an estimate of the value of the item at the end of its useful life

The next example shows how a depreciation rate is calculated. Note that the calculation for the reducing-balance method is very similar to that of a compound interest rate (see Example 5.1.3).

EXAMPLE 6.3.2

It is estimated that a newly acquired company car, costing £11,000, will be retained for 4 years, and then be sold for £5000. Calculate the annual rate of depreciation if

(a) the straight-line depreciation method is used
(b) the reducing-balance depreciation method is used.

Solution 6.3.2(a)

Using (6.3.1)

$$V_t = V_0 - Dt \qquad \text{where } V_0 = 11000, \ t = 4, \ V_t = 5000$$

$$5000 = 11000 - 4D$$

Rearranging

$$D = \frac{11000 - 5000}{4} = £1500/\text{year}$$

Solution 6.3.2(b)

In this case, the annual rate of depreciation is expressed as a percentage R. From (6.3.2)

$$V_t = V_0(1 - R/100)^t \qquad \text{where } V_0 = 11000, \ t = 4, \ V_t = 5000$$

$$5000 = 11000 \ (1 - R/100)^4$$

Therefore

$$0.454545 = (1 - R/100)^4$$

and so $1 - R/100$ is the 4th root of 0.454545. This is expressed as

$$1 - R/100 = 0.454545^{1/4} \quad \text{or} \quad 1 - R/100 = \sqrt[4]{0.454545}$$

(Choose the notation for the root which matches that on your calculator.) Thus

$$1 - R/100 = 0.821097$$

$$R/100 = 1 - 0.821097 = 0.178903$$

$$R = 17.89\%/\text{year}$$

The calculator steps for finding the root are as follows:

enter **0.454545**

press the $x^{1/y}$ or $y^{1/x}$ or $^x\sqrt{y}$ key

enter **4**

press the = key   (0.821097)

Note: The annual depreciation rates found above could now be used to determine the written-down values of the car at various stages in its life.

EXERCISES 6.3

1 A machine costing £5000 has a life of 6 years. Calculate the written-down value at the end of its life if

(a) the straight-line method is adopted, and the annual depreciation is £700

(b) the reducing-balance method is used, and the depreciation rate is 22% p.a.

2 It is estimated that a newly acquired video camera, costing £3000, will have a useful life of 6 years and be worth £600 at the end of this period.

(a) Find the annual depreciation if

(i) the straight-line method is used
(ii) the reducing-balance method is used.

(b) Determine the book-value of the camera after 3 years for each of the methods of depreciation indicated above.

3 The Albatross Margarine Co. has the choice of two new packaging machines A and B. Machine A costs £4000 and is expected to yield profits of £1800 at the end of each year for four years. It will depreciate by £650 per year and be sold for scrap at its written-down value. Machine B costs £5000 and is expected to yield profits of £2000 at the end of each year for 4 years. It is estimated that this machine will depreciate each year by 20% of its written-down value at the beginning of that year, and will be sold for scrap at its written-down value.

If invested money can earn compound interest at the rate of 15% p.a., which machine do you recommend?

4 Crosland Fabrics PLC are to purchase a new trimming machine, costing £100,000, at the end of 1997. It has an estimated life of 6 years and is expected to yield a profit of £20,000 at the end of each year. It is anticipated that the machine will depreciate in value each year by 15% of its written-down value at the beginning of that year.

(a) Calculate the net present value of inflows for this investment, using a discount rate of 10% p.a.

(b) Some doubt has been cast on the depreciation rate of 15%, and it has been suggested that the rate may, in reality, prove to be higher. If the company is not to make a loss on this investment, what is the largest acceptable depreciation rate?

6.4 MORE REGULAR PAYMENT SCHEMES

In section 5.3 of the last chapter, the formula for the sum of a geometric progression was used to calculate total future balances, when a number of *equal* payments are made into an account at *regular* intervals. This formula is equally applicable to problems involving present values, provided that the same assumption of equal, regular cash flows is retained, as the following example shows.

EXAMPLE 6.4.1

A project costs £120,000 and is expected to yield a profit of £40,000 at the end of each year for 8 years. Assuming a discount rate of 25% p.a., calculate the net present value of inflows for this investment.

Solution 6.4.1

To calculate the total present value of inflows, the present value formula (6.1.1) must be applied to each cash inflow. Thus

$$P = \frac{A_t}{(1 + R/100)^t} = \frac{A_t}{(1.25)^t}$$

$$\text{T.P.V. of inflows} = \frac{40000}{1.25} + \frac{40000}{(1.25)^2} + \frac{40000}{(1.25)^3} + \cdots + \frac{40000}{(1.25)^8}$$

This is a geometric progression with $a = 40000/1.25$, $r = 1/1.25$ (every term is obtained from the previous one by multiplying by $1/1.25$), $n = 8$ terms. Therefore, using the second version of the formula for the sum of a G.P. given in 5.3.2, the sum of n terms is given by

$$S_n = \frac{a(1 - r^n)}{1 - r} \qquad \text{use this version since } r < 1$$

$$\text{Total present value of inflows} = \frac{40000}{1.25} \times \frac{1 - (1/1.25)^8}{1 - 1/1.25}$$

$$= 32000 \times \frac{0.83222784}{0.2} = 133156.45$$

Therefore

Net present value of inflows = 133,156.45 − 120,000 = £13,156.45

There are numerous other problems to which present values and geometric progressions can be applied. These problems include mortgages and hire-purchase, and first an understanding of how these payment schemes operate is required.

Mortgages

Whether or not you have a mortgage, you will probably not need convincing that the mortgage market is a minefield. Offers of reduced starting payments for first-time buyers, and variable rates, abound. However, the basis of any mortgage is that a mortgage loan is a project undertaken by a Bank, Building Society, etc., for which the outflow is the amount loaned, and the inflows are the repayments received from us, the customers. Thus, from the loan company's point of view,

Net present value of inflows = Total present value of all repayments
– Amount loaned

where the **discount rate** in this case is the **mortgage rate**. The understanding is that the Bank, Building Society, etc. earns *exactly* this annual rate of return on its money. Therefore, **the net present value of inflows is zero** and so

Amount loaned (now) = Total present value of all repayments   (6.4.1)

where the **base date** is the date on which the mortgage starts. It is this equation which is used to calculate repayments on mortgages.

A similar equation to (6.4.1) can be used to find the total amount still owed at the end of any year. Thus

Total amount outstanding at the end of any year   (6.4.2)
= Total present value of the remaining repayments

where the base date is now the year end at which the amount outstanding is to be calculated.

Important note
For mortgages, interest is (normally) charged on an annual basis, even though repayments are made several times per year, e.g. monthly. Therefore, the term repayment in equations (6.4.1) and (6.4.2) can be taken to mean *total annual repayment*, and, when calculating present values, each total annual payment can be regarded as occurring at the *end of the year*. Once the total annual payment has been found, using equation (6.4.1), the monthly payment, for example, can easily be calculated.

Hire-purchase problems

Provided that, each time interest is added, it is charged on the *outstanding* balance, i.e. the amount still owed at that time, the situation is very similar to that for a mortgage. In this case, the cash price of an item is the amount loaned. Thus

Cash price of item = Total present value of repayments   (6.4.3)

where the discount rate is the interest charged by the company financing the loan, and the base-date is the date of acquisition of the item.

EXAMPLE 6.4.2

A mortgage of £30,000 is to be repaid over 25 years. Assuming a mortgage rate of 12% p.a., calculate the total annual repayment.

Solution 6.4.2

Let the total annual repayment be £X, say. Applying the present value formula to each payment.

$$P = \frac{A_t}{(1 + R/100)^t} = \frac{X}{(1.25)^t}$$

$$\text{T.P.V. of inflows} = \frac{X}{1.12} + \frac{X}{(1.12)^2} + \frac{X}{(1.12)^3} + \cdots + \frac{X}{(1.12)^{25}}$$

This is a geometric progression with $a = X/1.12$, $r = 1/1.12$, $n = 25$ terms. Therefore

$$S_n = \frac{a(1 - r^n)}{1 - r} \qquad \text{use this version since } r < 1$$

$$\text{Total present value of inflows} = \frac{X}{1.12} \times \frac{1 - (1/1.12)^{25}}{1 - 1/1.12} = \frac{X(1 - (1/1.12)^{25})}{0.12}$$

Finally, using (6.4.1),

$$\frac{X(1 - (1/1.12)^{25})}{0.12} = 30000$$

Rearranging

$$X = \frac{30000 \times 0.12}{1 - (1/1.12)^{25}} = 3825.00$$

Conclusion: The total annual repayment is £3825.00.

Note: The monthly repayment is $3825.00/12 = £318.75$

EXERCISES 6.4

1 A project costs £60,000 and is expected to yield £11,000 at the end of each year for 12 years. Calculate the net present value of inflows for this investment, assuming a discount rate of 14% per annum.

2 A mortgage of £16,000 is to be repaid over 20 years.

   (a) If the mortgage rate is 8% p.a. throughout the period of the loan,

      (i) calculate the total annual repayment, and hence determine the monthly repayment
      (ii) calculate the total amount still owed at the end of 6 years.

(b) If the mortgage rate is suddenly increased to 11% p.a. before repayments start, and stays at that rate throughout the period of the loan, but the annual repayment determined in (a)(i) is adopted, show that the loan can never be repaid, whatever the repayment period.

3   A colour T.V. set is to be purchased under a hire purchase agreement, which states that an instalment of £28.50 is to be paid at the end of each month for 12 months. If the retailer charges compound interest (on the outstanding balance) at the annual rate of 18%, compounded monthly, calculate the cash price of the T.V. set.

4   A project costs £70,000 and is expected to yield a fixed inflow at the end of each year for 10 years. Calculate the minimum annual inflow which will make this project at least as attractive as the project considered in Exercise 1. Adopt a discount rate of 14% p.a., as before.

5   Maitland Engineering has asked for your advice on two aspects of its operation, the first related to the future replacement of existing machinery, and the second to the acquisition of additional warehousing.

(a) The machinery is to be replaced at the end of 1998 and, for this purpose, the company has, since 31 December 1992, invested a sum of £3000 at the end of each quarter, in a reserve fund earning interest at the rate of 14% p.a., compounded quarterly. Advise the company as to the balance of the fund at the end of 1998.

(b) The company is about to receive a loan of £100,000 for the purchase of warehousing and has asked for your independent assessment of the repayment period. If £8000 is to be repaid at the end of each month and interest is to be charged at the rate of 2% per month, in which month will repayment be completed?

6   A company wishes to purchase a new machine and has two alternatives available. Machine A costs £5000 and is expected to yield profits of £1100 per year for 6 years, after which it will be sold for £1500. Machine B costs £9000 and is expected to yield £1500 each year for 7 years, after which it will be sold at its written-down value. It is predicted that machine B will depreciate each year by 16% of its written-down value at the beginning of that year.

    Assuming that the company's rate of return on its capital is 10% p.a., determine the N.P.V. of inflows for each machine, and decide which offers the better investment.

7   With the aim of financing an annuity for his son, Mr Smith plans to have a sum of £10,000 available at the end of 1996. To achieve this aim, he has been investing in two accounts A and B. At the end of 1987, he invested £2000 in account A which offers interest at the annual rate of 8%, compounded quarterly. He has made no further payments into this account. To supplement account A, and to exactly achieve his target of £10,000, he has invested a

fixed sum at the end of each year in account B, commencing at the end of 1988. Account B offers interest at the rate of 10% per annum, compounded annually at year ends.

(a) Show that the balance of account A at the end of 1996 is approximately £4080, and find the fixed annual payment into account B.

(b) At the end of 1996, Mr Smith intends to close account A and transfer the balance to account B. He will make no further payment *into* account B. By making withdrawals from this account, he plans to pay his son a sum of £2000 at the end of 1997 and at the end of each subsequent year.

Over how many years will he be able to do this?

8 A car costing £3400 is purchased by payment of a deposit of £850, and the balance paid by means of a number of quarterly instalments of £300, together with a final smaller payment at the end of the last quarter. If interest is charged on the outstanding balance at the rate of 16% p.a., compounded quarterly, find the number of £300 instalments required and the amount of the last instalment.

7

COST, REVENUE AND PROFIT

When you have completed this chapter you will be able to:

- use graphs to analyse costs, revenue and profit for the company
- solve equations in a business context
- use algebra to model market issues

7.1 COSTS, REVENUE AND PROFIT FOR THE COMPANY

In this section, we shall consider a particular product produced by a company, and use numerical, graphical and algebraic methods to analyse the costs, revenue and profits associated with that product. Issues such as determining the break-even point, and achieving a viable profit level, are important.

Firstly, notation is required for some important quantities. For clarity, we will adhere to the following:

x = output (quantity produced and sold)
C = total production cost
p = selling price per unit
R = total sales revenue
G = total gross profit

There are certain properties and assumptions concerning these quantities which form the basis for *all* that follows. For revenue and profit, the most basic properties are

$R = px$ **Total sales revenue = price × quantity sold**

$G = R - C$ **Gross profit is the difference between revenue and cost**

(7.1.1)

For total cost, we will assume that this is made up of two types of costs, those which vary with output and fixed costs, and write

    $C =$ **Variable costs + Fixed costs**   (7.1.2)

The following are examples of costs falling into these two categories:

- *Fixed costs (or indirect costs)*
  cost of maintenance of machinery
  cost of rental of premises.

- *Variable costs*
  cost of raw materials
  cost of machine time.

Obviously the preceding statements about costs, revenue and profit are very general indeed, and to make progress we now need to make very specific assumptions about these quantities. The simplest starting point is to look at linear models.

Linear models for cost, revenue and profit

The linear assumption for total cost is that the total variable costs are *proportional* to the output x. In other words, the variable cost *per unit* is constant. If the variable costs per unit are denoted by V, then the linear cost equation is given by

$$C = Vx + F \qquad \text{where } V = \text{variable cost per unit}$$
$$F = \text{fixed costs per period} \qquad (7.1.3)$$

V is the *slope* of the cost line and F is the *intercept* on the vertical axis. The linear assumption for revenue is that

$$R = px \qquad \text{where the selling price is constant} \qquad (7.1.4)$$

This would apply in a competitive market, where a price is agreed by the companies in the market (see Section 7.2). The next example shows the type of problems which can be tackled, given the straight-line assumption.

EXAMPLE 7.1.1

For one of its products, a company experiences a fixed cost of £12,000 per month and a variable cost of £40 for each unit produced. The company can sell all that it produces at a price of £90 per unit.
(a) Determine equations for the total monthly cost, revenue and profit in terms of the monthly output x.
(b) Determine the break-even output level algebraically.
(c) Plot a graph showing the variation of total monthly cost and total monthly revenue with x, for output in the range 0 to 600 units, and identify the break-even point.
(d) Find, algebraically, the output level at which average cost is £64 per unit.
(e) What increase in the fixed costs would result in break-even at 400 units per month?

Solution 7.1.1(a)

Since the given costs are based upon a constant variable cost per unit and a fixed monthly cost,

$$C = Vx + F \qquad \text{where } V = 40 \text{ and } F = 12000$$

$$C = 40x + 12000 \qquad (7.1.5)$$

For revenue,

$$R = px \qquad \text{where price } p = 90$$

$$R = 90x \qquad (7.1.6)$$

Finally, gross profit G is obtained from the equation

$$G = R - C$$

Therefore, substituting for revenue and cost,

$$\begin{aligned} G &= 90x - (40x + 12000) \\ &= 90x - 40x - 12000 \end{aligned}$$
the bracket is essential when subtracting a sum of terms for C

$$G = 50x - 12000 \tag{7.1.7}$$

Note: It is often useful to apply some intuition to an equation, once obtained. In this case, substituting $x = 0$ into the equation gives the *negative* value $G = -12000$, which is reassuring since when the company produces nothing, variable costs and revenue will be zero, and the fixed costs cause a profit *loss* of £12,000. If the bracket had been omitted when determining the equation, the resulting *positive* constant should have sounded alarm bells.

Solution 7.1.1(b)
At break-even

$$R = T$$

Therefore, using equations (7.1.5) and (7.1.6)

$$90x = 40x + 12000$$

$$50x = 12000$$

$$x = 12000/50 = 240$$

Conclusion: The output level for break-even is 240 units/month.

Solution 7.1.1(c)
Since C and R are both linear functions, only two points need be plotted for each, so the following table suffices:

x	0	600
$C = 40x + 12000$	12000	36000
$R = 90x$	0	54000

The graph is shown in Figure 7.1.1.

Solution 7.1.1(d)
To answer a question about average cost algebraically, it is first necessary to have an *equation* for this quantity. Denoting the average cost per unit by A,

$$A = \frac{C}{x}$$

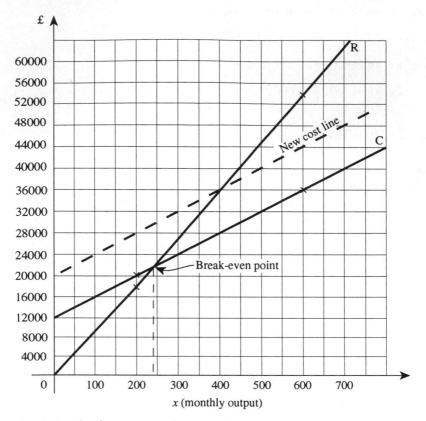

Figure 7.1.1 Graph of revenue and cost against output

Substituting for C

$$A = \frac{40x + 12000}{x}$$

$$64 = \frac{40x + 12000}{x} \qquad \text{multiply each side by } x$$

$$64x = 40x + 12000$$

$$24x = 12000$$

$$x = 12000/24 = 500$$

Conclusion: Average cost is £64/unit when the output is 500 units/month.

Solution 7.1.1(e)

Given that break-even now occurs at 400 units per month, there are two ways of determining the new fixed costs. On the one hand, we can draw a new cost line with the same slope as the original (since unit variable costs remain the same), which intersects the revenue line at $x = 400$. This is the dotted line shown in Figure 7.1.1, and so the new fixed cost is equal to the intercept 20,000.

Alternatively, we can denote the new fixed costs by F, and equate the cost and revenue functions at the break-even point. Therefore

$$40x + F = 90x \quad \text{where } x = 400$$

$$16000 + F = 36000 \quad F = 20000$$

The new fixed costs are £20,000.

Quadratic models for cost, revenue and profit

Having considered the case of constant price, we will now extend our analysis to a company which is a monopoly, and is therefore able to vary demand by varying the price. In such a case, it is possible to obtain an algebraic relationship between prices, and the number of units demanded at that price, provided that the general relationship is known. For example, it may be thought to be linear or quadratic. The next example should make these ideas clear.

EXAMPLE 7.1.2

An engineering company produces a specialist bearing for which production costs are categorised as follows:

Fixed cost   £4200 per week

Variable cost   £45 per unit

Demand is dependent on price, and it has been found, for example, that demand is 40 units per week at a price of £250 per unit but increases to 60 units per week if the price is reduced to £190 per unit. It is assumed that the relationship between price and demand is *linear*.

If x units are produced and sold each unit,

(a) Express the price p in terms of x, and hence calculate the weekly demand when the price is £220/unit.
(b) Express total weekly cost and total weekly revenue in terms of x.
(c) Plot the graph of cost and revenue against x, and find the output levels at which the company breaks-even.
(d) Use the graph to find the output level at which profit is maximised.

Solution 7.1.2(a)

The essential first step is to write down the general form of the equation for p in terms of x, in this case the equation of a straight line. Thus

$$p = ax + b \tag{7.1.7}$$

The values of a and b can either be obtained graphically or by simultaneous equations. (See sections 1.2 and 1.6 of Chapter 1.) We shall opt for the second alternative. Substituting $x = 40$, $p = 250$ into (7.1.7)

$$250 = 40a + b$$

whereas using $x = 60$, $p = 190$

$$190 = 60a + b$$

Subtracting the first equation from the second (or vice-versa), gives the value of a:

$$190 = 60a + b$$
$$250 = 40a + b$$
$$\overline{-60 = 20a} \qquad a = -3$$

Substituting for a in the first equation, say,

$$190 = -180 + b \qquad b = 370$$

The required price equation (or *demand function*) is now obtained by substituting for a and b in (7.1.7). So

$$p = 370 - 3x \tag{7.1.8}$$

The advantage of deducing this *equation* from the two pairs of given data is clear, since it is now possible to predict the demand given any realistic price. In particular, if the price is £220, then

$$220 = 370 - 3x$$

$$x = 50 \text{ units per week}$$

Solution 7.1.2(b)

For cost, $C = Vx + F$, where $V = 45$ and $F = 4200$. Therefore

$$C = 45x + 4200 \tag{7.1.9}$$

For revenue $R = px$, and substituting for p from equation (7.1.8),

$$R = (370 - 3x)x$$

Therefore

$$R = 370x - 3x^2 \qquad \text{a quadratic model for revenue} \tag{7.1.10}$$

Solution 7.1.2(c)

The essential first step in plotting the graph is to decide the *output* range. $x = 0$ is a convenient starting value for the range, and so an upper limit is required. For this purpose, look at the demand function

$$p = 370 - 3x$$

Obviously it is not practical for the price to fall to zero but it is mathematically convenient to solve the extreme case

$$p = 0$$

in which case

$$370 - 3x = 0$$

$$x = 123 \text{ approximately}$$

A range for x starting at zero but falling somewhere short of 123 therefore seems reasonable. (The approach has been helpful since it is now clear that a range of values in 10's is appropriate, rather than a range in 100's, for example.) A range of 0 to 100 allows both break-even points to be shown.

Since C is a linear function of x, only two points are required for plotting. However, revenue is to be represented by a smooth curve and so considerably more points are required. The following table suffices:

$$C = 45x + 4200$$

$$R = 370x - 3x^2$$

x	0	10	20	30	40	50	60	70	80	90	100
R	0	3400	6200	8400	10000	11000	11400	11200	10400	9000	7000
C		5100					6900				

For example

if $x = 30$ $R = 370 \times 30 - 3(30)^2 = 8400$

The graph is therefore as in Figure 7.1.2. The company breaks even at 15 bearings/month and 94 bearings/month.

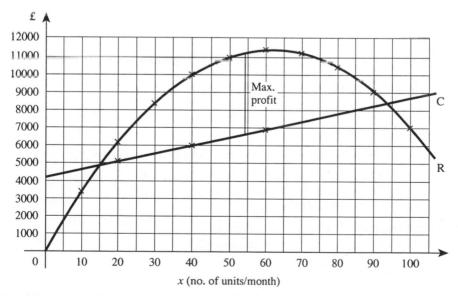

Figure 7.1.2 Graph of cost and revenue against output

Solution 7.1.2(d)

To find the output level for maximum profit, it is possible to count squares as shown on the graph. The output level for maximum profit is 54 units per week.

Having related price to demand, and obtained equations for revenue, cost and profit, it is now possible to answer *algebraically* the same types of question as those posed earlier. For example, identifying the output for break-even, output levels for target profit, etc. The following example provides a sample of the types of problems which can be answered.

EXAMPLE 7.1.3

Consider again the production of bearings, as described in Example 7.12, for which the total weekly cost £C and total weekly revenue £R satisfy the equations

$$C = 45x + 4200 \quad \text{and} \quad R = 370x - 3x^2$$

when x units are produced and sold per week.

(a) Determine, algebraically, the smallest output level for break-even.

(b) Find, algebraically, the two output levels at which total weekly profit is £4000 per week.

(c) It is envisaged that it will be necessary to increase the variable cost per unit in the near future. If, as a result, the profit at the output level determined in (b) will be reduced by 20%, what increase in variable costs is envisaged.

(d) The company now introduces a rust-proofing process for which an *additional* cost £C_1 is incurred, where fixed costs are £1000 per week and variable costs are proportional to the *square* of the output x. If break-even now occurs at 20 units per week, determine the new total weekly cost in terms of x, and find the output level at which total cost is £8800 per week.

Solution 7.1.3(a)

At the break-even point $R = C$

Substituting for C and R gives the quadratic equation

$$45x + 4200 = 370x - 3x^2$$

(If you are doubtful about solving equations of this type, look again at section 1.5 of Chapter 1.) Thus

$$45x + 4200 - 370x + 3x^2 = 0 \qquad \text{rearranging to obtain zero on one side}$$

$$-325x + 4200 + 3x^2 = 0 \qquad \text{next write terms in descending powers}$$

$$3x^2 - 325x + 4200 = 0 \tag{7.1.11}$$

Use the quadratic formula

$$x = \frac{-b \pm \sqrt{(b^2 - 4ac)}}{2a}$$

where $a = 3$, $b = -325$, $c = 4200$. (Note the inclusion of the negative sign for b.)

$$x = \frac{-(-325) \pm \sqrt{(325^2 - 4 \times 3 \times 4200)}}{6}$$

$$= \frac{325 \pm \sqrt{55225}}{6} = \frac{325 \pm 235}{6}$$

$$= 15 \text{ or } 93\tfrac{1}{3}$$

Rather than using the quadratic formula, equation (7.1.11) can be factorised as follows:

$$(x - 15)(3x - 280) = 0$$

Therefore either $x - 15 = 0$, giving $x = 15$, or $3x - 280 = 0$, giving $x = 93\tfrac{1}{3}$. The problem with using factorization for business problems of this type, however, is that the usually large figure for the fixed cost can make the factors difficult to find.

Conclusion: The smallest output at which the company breaks even is 15 units per week.

Solution 7.1.3(b)

The first step in algebraically answering a question about weekly profit G, or any quantity for that matter, is to find the appropriate equation. Using the general relationship

$$G = R - C$$

therefore

$$G = 370x - 3x^2 - (45x + 4200) \qquad \text{(remember the bracket when}$$
$$\text{subtracting)} \qquad (7.1.12)$$

$$= 370x - 3x^2 - 45x - 4200$$

$$= -3x^2 + 325x - 4200 \qquad \text{use descending powers}$$

Substituting $G = 4000$

$$4000 = -3x^2 + 325x - 4200$$

$$3x^2 - 325x + 8200 = 0 \qquad (7.1.13)$$

This equation is very similar to (7.1.11). In fact, solving $G = 0$ provides an alternative to $R = T$ for finding the break-even point. Therefore, in brief:

$$x = \frac{325 \pm \sqrt{(325^2 - 4 \times 3 \times 8200)}}{6} = \frac{325 \pm 85}{6}$$

$$x = 40 \text{ or } 68\tfrac{1}{3}$$

Conclusion: Profit is £4000 per week at outputs of 40 units/week and $68\tfrac{1}{3}$ units per week. (Ignore the fraction since it is bearings which are produced)

153

Solution 7.1.3(c)

So far we have reached conclusions by using the strict principles of algebra. However, this part of the question demonstrates that it is sometimes worth looking for a short cut.

We are told that an increase in the variable cost per unit is anticipated which will reduce the £4000 profit in **(b)** by 20%, i.e. by £800. Writing the new total cost as $T = Vx + 4200$ (where V is the variable cost per unit), we could replace the original cost equation by this in equation (7.1.12) and substitute $x = 40$, $G = 3200$, in order to find V. However, it is simpler to argue as follows.

Let the *increase* in variable cost per unit $= i$. Therefore

Increase in total variable costs at an output of 40 units $= 40i$

Since this increase in total costs accounts for the fall in profits

$$40i = 800 \qquad i = 20$$

Conclusion: The anticipated increase in the variable cost per unit is £20.

Solution 7.1.3(d)

Finally, we are asked to deduce a modified cost equation. Since the variable costs for the rust-proofing process are proportional to x^2, they are kx^2, where k is a constant, and so

$$C_1 = kx^2 + 1000$$

The new total weekly cost equation is

$$C = 45x + 4200 + kx^2 + 1000$$
$$= kx^2 + 45x + 5200$$

To find k, we use (yet again) the break-even criterion

$$R = C$$

but in this case the value of x is known.

$$370x - 3x^2 = kx^2 + 45x + 5200 \qquad \text{substitute } x = 20$$
$$6200 = 400k + 900 + 5200$$
$$100 = 400k \qquad k = 0.25$$

So the weekly total cost is

$$C = 0.25x^2 + 45x + 5200 \qquad \text{this is now a quadratic model for cost}$$

Finally, substitute $C = 8800$

$$8800 = 0.25x^2 + 45x + 5200$$
$$0.25x^2 + 45x - 3600 = 0$$

Now use the quadratic formula

$$x = \frac{-b \pm \sqrt{(b^2 - 4ac)}}{2a}$$

where $a = 0.25$, $b = 45$, $c = -3600$. (In this case, it is c which is negative.)

$$x = \frac{-45 \pm \sqrt{(45^2 - 4 \times 0.25 \times (-3600))}}{0.5}$$

$$= \frac{45 \pm \sqrt{5625}}{0.5} = \frac{-45 \pm 75}{0.5} \qquad x = 60 \text{ or } -240$$

Since it is an output level which is required, the negative value can be ignored.

Conclusion: At an output of 60 bearings per week, total cost is £8800.

EXERCISES 7.1

1 For one type of chemical produced by a company, the fixed weekly cost is £9000 and the variable cost per ton is £30. Each ton produced is sold at a price of £60.

(a) Express total cost, total revenue and total profit in terms of the number x of tons produced and sold per week.
(b) Plot the total cost and total revenue functions on the same graph (using a range for x from 0 to 700 tons). Determine, from the graph, the level of output at which break-even occurs.
(c) Calculate the break-even output level algebraically.
(d) Find, from the graph, the output level which will yield a profit of £6000 per week.
(e) Use algebra to check your answer to (d).
(f) If costs remain the same, what increase in the selling price per ton would be needed to break-even at 200 tons per week?

2 A firm finds that the total weekly cost £C of producing x units per week of its product is given by

$$C = 2.5x^2 + 25x + 6000$$

and that the total weekly revenue £R resulting from the sale of these x units is given by

$$R = 445x - 3.5x^2$$

(a) Plot the total weekly cost and total weekly revenue functions on the same graph, and *use this graph* to determine

(i)   the output level at which the company first breaks-even
(ii) the output levels at which total weekly profit is £750
(iii) the output level at which profit is greatest.

(b) Determine, *algebraically*, the smallest output level at which the company breaks-even, and the corresponding selling price per unit.

3   For one of the fabrics produced by a company, the total weekly cost of producing x unit lengths per week, and the selling price £p/unit length required to sell x unit lengths per week, are given by the equations

$$C = 40x + 6000$$
$$p = 250 - 1.5x$$

(a) Calculate the smallest output level at which the company breaks-even, and the corresponding total weekly revenue.
(b) Find the output level at which the average cost per unit length is £115.
(c) Determine the output levels at which total weekly revenue is £2400.
(d) Find the output levels at which total weekly profit is £1200.
(e) Following an advertising campaign, the relationship between the selling price £p per unit length and the demand x unit lengths has changed, although it remains of the form

$$p = ax + b \qquad \text{where } a, b \text{ are constants}$$

If break-even now occurs at an output level of 40 unit lengths, and the selling price at twice this level of output is £120 per unit length, calculate the values of a and b.

4   A manufacturer finds that, if his product is priced at £170 per unit, the weekly demand is 20 units, and if the price is £100 per unit, the weekly demand is 55 units. His fixed weekly costs are £2800 and his variable costs are £30 per unit.

(a) Write down the total weekly cost £C as a function of x, where x is the weekly output.
(b) Assuming the price £p is a *linear* function of x, find equations for the price and the total revenue £R, in terms of x. Hence find the output levels at which total weekly revenue is £2700.
(c) Show that the weekly profit £G satisfies the equation

$$G = -2x^2 + 180x - 2800$$

(d) Plot the graph of weekly profit against x. Hence find the output levels at which weekly profit is £1050, and the corresponding prices.
(e) Use algebra to confirm the weekly outputs at which profit is £1050 per week.

5   The total weekly cost £C of producing x units of a particular product is given by

$$C = x^2 + 30x + 2700$$

The selling price £p/unit required to sell this quantity x is calculated from the equation

$$x = 90 - \tfrac{1}{3}p$$

(a) Express total weekly revenue R in terms of x.

(b) Determine the output levels at which break-even occurs.

(c) Find the output levels at which total weekly cost is £8100 and £4075.

(d) Find the output levels at which average cost per unit is £134.

6 The Cameron Optical Company produces a variety of cameras and accessory lenses. You are asked to consider the Series X camera for which the following information is available:

- Total weekly production cost $£C$ is a linear function of the weekly output and fixed costs amount to £9450/week.
- The price $£p$/unit is a quadratic function of the weekly demand x units and the demand at three price levels has been recorded as follows:

Weekly demand x	30	35	50
Price $£p$/unit	320	315	240

- The company breaks even at 30 units per week.

Express p in terms of x and find the weekly demand at a price of £75/unit. Also express total weekly cost, revenue and gross profit in terms of x, assuming that the company produces so as to meet its demand.

7 A manufacturer finds that when the selling price of its product is $£p$/unit, the weekly volume of sales x is given by

$$x = 24 - 2\sqrt{p}$$

The total weekly cost $£C$ when producing x units/week is given by

$$C = 0.25x^3 + 420$$

Find the smallest level of production at which break-even occurs, and calculate the average production cost per unit.

7.2 SUPPLY AND DEMAND; MARKET EQUILIBRIUM

So far we have considered costs, revenue and profit from the point of view of a particular company, and we have looked at the way that these quantities vary with the output level x units for a product, in order to maximise profit for example. It was therefore appropriate to write equations in terms of x.

Here we assume that the market for a good is made up of a number of different companies. As well as demand for the good, there is also the issue of how much each company in the market is willing to *supply* at a particular price, based on considerations of the type considered in section 7.1. Often, the companies will wish to collectively set a price so as to achieve a balance between demand and supply, and it is therefore natural to use the price p as the independent variable when stating equations for the quantities which influence the choice of price.

It should be noted that there is a clash between mathematics and business practice, when plotting or sketching graphs for the market. Since p is the independent variable, the convention, mathematically, would be to use the *horizontal* axis to plot the values of p. However, in practice, you will find that the vertical axis is normally used for p.

Demand function

This relates the total amount x_d units which the companies in the market *can sell*, i.e. the demand, to the price p. The simplest assumption is that x_d is a *linear* function of p, in which case

$$x_d = ap + b$$

where a is the slope of the line and b is the intercept on the x_d axis. Since demand *decreases* as p increases, a will normally be *negative* for such an equation.

Of course, the assumption of linearity will not always be appropriate. The relationship may be quadratic, and have the form

$$x_d = ap^2 + bp + c \qquad \text{where a, b, c are constants}$$

or some other function altogether.

Supply function

This relates the total amount x_s which the companies in the market are *willing to supply* to the price p. Again, the simplest assumption is that x_s is a *linear* function of p, in which case

$$x_s = cp + d$$

where c is the slope and d is the intercept on the x_s axis. (We use c, d here, rather than a, b, in order to distinguish the supply function from the demand function.)

Unlike the demand function, we would expect the slope c to be *positive*, since x_s would normally be expected to *increase* as p increases. It may be that the higher price encourages the existing companies in the market to supply more, or that a higher price attracts new companies into the market.

As for the demand function, there will be times when a linear assumption for supply is inappropriate. For a quadratic relationship, for example, the equation would take the form

$$x_s = cp^2 + dp + e \qquad \text{where c, d, e are constants}$$

Market equilibrium

In order to achieve a balance between supply x_s units and demand x_d units, the market price is set so that it satisfies the equation

$$\boldsymbol{x_d = x_s}$$

EXAMPLE 7.2.1

The demand function for a good is given by

$$x_d = 800 - 10p$$

where x_d thousand units are demanded per month at a price of £p/unit.

Supply of the good, which is thought to be a *quadratic* function of price, has been observed at three different price levels, and the results are as follows:

Price p (£/unit)	5	10	20
Supply x_s (thousands of units per month)	600	900	2100

A sketch graph of these functions is shown in Figure 7.2.1.

(a) Determine the equation of the supply function
(b) Calculate the price and quantity at market equilibrium.

Solution 7.2.1(a)

Since x_s is a quadratic function of p, we start with

$$x_s = ap^2 + bp + c \tag{7.2.1}$$

and substitute the given pairs of values to obtain three simultaneous equations. (These are solved using the approach described in section 1.6 of Chapter 1.) Substituting $x_s = 600$ when $p = 5$

$$a5^2 + 5p + c = 600$$

$$25a + 5b + c = 600 \tag{1}$$

Similarly, the other equations are

$$a10^2 + 10b + c = 900$$

$$100a + 10b + c = 900 \tag{2}$$

$$400a + 20b + c = 2100 \tag{3}$$

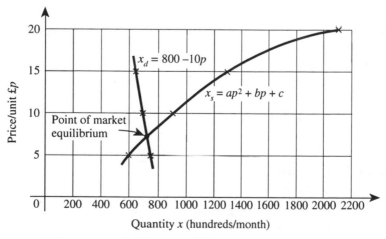

Figure 7.2.1 Hypothetical market situation: graph of supply/demand

We now eliminate c to obtain two equations in two unknowns:

$(2) - (1)$ gives

$$100a + 10b + c = 900$$
$$25a + 5b + c = 600$$
$$75a + 5b = 300 \qquad (4)$$

$(3) - (2)$ gives

$$400a + 20b + c = 2100$$
$$100a + 10b + c = 900$$
$$300a + 10b = 1200 \qquad (5)$$

To eliminate b, we use $(5) - 2 \times (4)$

$$300a + 10b = 1200$$
$$150a + 10b = 600$$
$$150a = 600 \qquad a = 4$$

Substituting for a in equation (4), say

$$(75 \times 4) + 5b = 300 \qquad b = 0$$

Substituting for a and b in (1), say

$$(25 \times 4) + c = 600 \qquad c = 500$$

Checking in equation (2)

Left-hand side $= (100 \times 4) + 500 = 900$ as required

Therefore, from (7.2.1),

$$x_s = 4p^2 + 500$$

Solution 7.2.1(b)

At market equilibrium

$$x_d = x_s$$
$$800 - 10p = 4p^2 + 500$$
$$4p^2 + 10p - 300 = 0$$

Using the quadratic formula

$$p = \frac{-b \pm \sqrt{(b^2 - 4ac)}}{2a} \qquad \text{where } a = 4, b = 10, c = -300$$

(Note the inclusion of the negative sign for the value of c.)

Therefore

$$p = \frac{-10 \pm \sqrt{(10^2 - 4 \times 4 \times (-300))}}{8}$$

$$= \frac{-10 \pm \sqrt{4900}}{8} = \frac{-10 \pm 70}{8} = 7.50 \text{ or } -10$$

Rejecting the negative value, the price at market equilibrium is £7.50 per unit.

Either the demand function *or* the supply function can be used to determine the equilibrium quantity, but substitution into both provides a useful check on the value of p.

$$x_d = 800 - (10 \times 7.50) = 725$$

$$x_s = 4(7.50)^2 + 500 = 725$$

Conclusion: At market equilibrium, the price is £7.50 per unit and the quantity is 725 thousand units per month.

EXERCISES 7.2

1 The demand function for a good is described by the equation

$$x_d = 1720 - 13p$$

where x_d is the number of units demanded per week and p is the price in £/unit. The supply function relating the number x_s of units supplied each week to the price p is known to be *linear*, and the following table shows the weekly supply at two different prices:

Price p (£/unit)	50	100
Weekly supply x_s	850	1450

(a) Express x_s in terms of p.
(b) Find the price and quantity at market equilibrium.

2 (a) For a particular good, the quantity demanded x_d units and quantity supplied x_s units are given in terms of the price £p/unit by the equations

$$x_d = 4p + 500 \qquad x_s = 800 - 8p$$

Calculate the price and quantity at market equilibrium.

(b) The weekly demand for a particular blend of tea has been found to be 10400 packets when the price is 24 pence per packet, and 9800 packets when the price is 28 pence per packet.

(i) Assuming that the relationship between the demand x_d and the price p is *linear*, determine x_d in terms of p.

(ii) If the weekly supply (in hundreds of packets) for this tea is related to the price (in pence per packet) by the equation

$$x_s = 0.2p^2 + 0.5p + 20$$

determine the price and quantity at market equilibrium.

(Hint for (b): Take care to work with the *same* units in both the demand and supply equations.)

3   The relationship between the total number x_d of units of a good demanded per week and the price £p/unit is given by

$$x_d = 2000 - 0.4p^2$$

The total number x_s of units which the market is willing to supply each week at a price of £p/unit is thought to be of the form

$$x_s = ap^2 + b \qquad a, b \text{ are constants}$$

and the following data have been observed:

p	30	60
x_s	1940	2480

(a) Determine x_s in terms of p.
(b) Find the price and quantity at market equilibrium.

4   (a) The market for a particular good is such that the number x_d of units demanded per week, and the number x_s of units supplied per week, are given in terms of the price £p/unit by the equations

$$x_s = 0.4p^2 + 21p + 30$$
$$x_d = 300 - 0.2p^2$$

Determine the price and quantity at market equilibrium.

(b) The supply function now changes to one of the form

$$x_s = 0.6p^2 + ap + 30 \qquad \text{where } a \text{ is a constant}$$

Assuming that the demand function remains unchanged, and that the quantity at market equilibrium is now 255 units per week, determine the value of a.

5   The total monthly supply x_s for a particular good increases as the price p increases, and an investigation of the market has yielded the following data:

p (£/unit)	20	30	50
x_s (no. of units supplied per month)	1000	1600	3400

(a) By assuming that

$$x_s = ap^2 + bp + c \qquad \text{where } a, b, c \text{ are constants}$$

and solving a set of simultaneous equations, show that

$$x_s = p^2 + 10p + 400$$

(b) If the total monthly demand x_d for this good is given by

$$x_d = 1000 - p^2$$

find the price and quantity at market equilibrium.

8

MARGINALS

After completing this chapter you will be able to

- understand the difference between average and instantaneous rates of increase
- differentiate from first principles
- apply differentiation rules
- determine and identify stationary points
- understand elasticity and the implications for revenue

8.1 CALCULATING RATES OF INCREASE

In the last chapter, we looked at *total* costs, revenue and profit for the company. As well as the current values of these quantities, it is important to be aware of the *rates* at which they would change, perhaps as a result of a change in output or price, for example. The rates of increase of cost, revenue and profit are called **marginal cost, marginal revenue** and **marginal profit**, respectively, and there are two distinct approaches to calculating these.

Calculating average rates of increase

Consider a quantity y which is a function of the quantity x. To calculate an *average* rate of increase of y with respect to x, it is necessary to consider a specific starting value of x and an increase Δx in this value which produces an increase Δy in y. (Negative increases are allowed which actually signify decreases.) Then

$$\text{Average rate of increase of } y \text{ with respect to } x = \frac{\Delta y}{\Delta x}$$

As an illustration, consider Figure 8.1.1 which shows a straight-line graph and also the graph of $y = x^2$.

If $x = 3$ and $\Delta x = 2$, then the average rate of increase of y with respect to x for the line is

$$\frac{\Delta y}{\Delta x} = \frac{15}{2} = 7.5$$

and obviously this is the *slope* of the line. It is in the nature of the line that the same value is obtained whatever the starting value x and increase Δx. For the curve

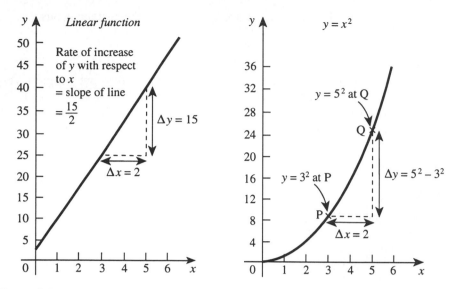

Figure 8.1.1

$y = x^2$, the situation is different since the average rate of increase changes when x or Δx changes. For the given values of x and Δx, where x increases from 3 to 5:

$$\frac{\Delta y}{\Delta x} = \frac{5^2 - 3^2}{2} = 8$$

The problem with an average rate of increase is that it requires both x and Δx to be specified. However, it is possible to measure a rate of increase *at* a specified value of x, without reference to the increase in x. Mathematically, at least, this makes life much easier.

Calculating instantaneous rates of increase

The obvious question is how can an instantaneous rate of increase be calculated *at* a specified value of x (a specified output level for a product perhaps). The answer is to consider a number of different increases in x (positive or negative), all measured from the specified x value, *which are made progressively smaller and smaller*. For each increase, the *average* rate of increase of y with respect to x is measured in the hope that a *trend* in the average rates will *imply* a value for the instantaneous rate. An example should make this clear.

EXAMPLE 8.1.1

Suppose that the total daily revenue £R from the sale of x tons of a particular fertiliser is given by

$$R = 50x - x^2$$

and that the current sales level is 15 tons per day. By considering suitable increases in the sales level, deduce a likely value for the instantaneous rate of increase in R with respect to x at $x = 15$.

Solution 8.1.1

Consider increases in sales level 0.5, 0.3. 0.1. 0.01 which get progressively smaller. (There are infinitely many other choices which we could make.) The table below shows the average rates of increase of R with respect to x, all measured from $x = 15$, corresponding to the different increases in x. For example, if x increases from 15 to 15.1, the new revenue is

$$50\,(15.1) - (15.1)^2 = 526.99$$

Therefore

$$\Delta R = 526.99 - 525 = 1.99 \qquad \text{the original revenue 525 is subtracted every time}$$

$$\frac{\Delta R}{\Delta x} = \frac{1.99}{0.1} = 19.9$$

x	R	Δx	ΔR	$\dfrac{\Delta R}{\Delta x}$	Average rate of increase of R with respect to x (£/unit)
15	**525**	—	—		—
15.5	534.75	0.5	9.75	9.75/0.5	= 19.50
15.3	530.91	0.3	5.91	5.91/0.3	= 19.70
15.1	526.99	0.1	1.99	1.99/0.1	= 19.90
15.01	525.1999	0.01	0.1999	0.1999/0.01	= 19.99
15.005	525.09998	0.005	0.09998	0.09998/0.005	= 19.996

Since the value of x approaches closer and closer to 15, as we move down the table, the average rate of increase in the final column should become more and more representative of the rate of increase of R at $x = 15$. We therefore hope that these average rates will show evidence of approaching some value, called a **limiting value**, and we are not disappointed. For, as the value of x becomes closer and closer to 15, and the increase Δx becomes smaller and smaller, the change in each successive rate of increase slows down, and the average rates are clearly approaching some limiting value, which is *probably* 20. Therefore, we conclude that

Rate of increase of R with respect to x (at $x = 15$) = £20/unit (probably)

In other words, the *marginal revenue* is £20/unit. (In Exercise 1 you will see that the average rates of increase behave in the same way if we approach 15 from below rather than above.)

Of course, you may find this approach rather unscientific, since we do not know that the limiting value is 20 for sure – although it is certainly close to 20. Indeed, we will not be sure until we look at the revenue function algebraically. But the above analysis is useful for two purposes. Firstly, it shows that by measuring average rates of increase, which are perfectly obvious, and then measuring over smaller and smaller increases measured from the target output level ($x = 15$ in this case), it is possible to talk sensibly about a rate of increase at a specific output level; a concept which at first sight is certainly not obvious. Secondly, it shows that for a case where we do not have an equation, but the values in column (2) can be observed, it is still possible to estimate an instantaneous rate of increase.

The notation dy/dx is introduced for the instantaneous rate of increase of y with respect to x. Therefore

$$\frac{dy}{dx} = \lim_{\Delta x \to 0} \frac{\Delta y}{\Delta x} \qquad (8.1.1)$$

and dy/dx is called the **derivative of y with respect to x**.

Measuring instantaneous rates of increase graphically

Figure 8.1.2 is a sketch graph of some function y of x.

Consider a particular value of x corresponding to point P on the curve, and an increase Δx in x. Then if Q is the point corresponding to $x + \Delta x$,

$$\frac{\Delta y}{\Delta x} = \text{slope of chord PQ} \qquad \text{a chord is a line joining two points on a curve}$$

As $\Delta x \to 0$, that is the increase in x becomes smaller and smaller, the slope of PQ approaches closer and closer to the slope of the tangent to the curve drawn at P. But, as indicated by (8.1.1), $\Delta y/\Delta x$ approaches closer and closer to dy/dx, and so, putting these two facts together:

$$\frac{dy}{dx} = \text{tangent to the } y\text{-curve at P} \qquad (8.1.2)$$

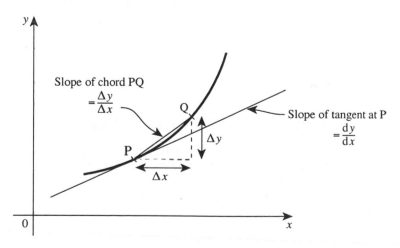

Figure 8.1.2

167

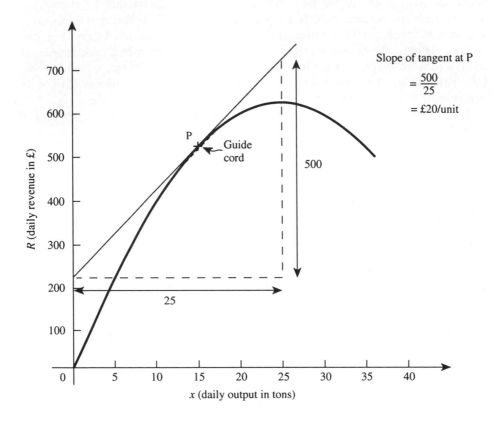

Figure 8.1.3 $R = 50x - x^2$

Consider, again, the revenue function of Example 8.1.1. Figure 8.1.3 shows the graph of this function and the tangent drawn at $x = 15$. Accuracy in drawing the tangent is improved by choosing a value of x slightly below $x = 15$ and a value of x which is an equal amount above $x = 15$, joining the corresponding points on the curve by a chord, and drawing the tangent parallel to this chord. The tangent slope is 20 as shown, thus confirming the value of dy/dx obtained earlier.

Determining instantaneous rates of increase algebraically

As demonstrated both numerically and graphically, the essence of **differentiation** – the process of determining an *instantaneous* rate of increase dy/dx – is to calculate average rates of increase of y with respect to x, measured from some specific value of x, and to determine the limit as the increase in x is made smaller and smaller. This approach is summarised as follows:

- Consider a specific value of x and increase x to $x + \Delta x$
- Find an equation for Δy, and deduce an equation for $\Delta y/\Delta x$

- Determine dy/dx from the definition

$$\frac{dy}{dx} = \lim_{\Delta x \to 0} \frac{\Delta y}{\Delta x} \qquad\qquad (8.1.3)$$

When an algebraic relationship exists between y and x, this procedure is called **differentiation from first principles**.

EXAMPLE 8.1.2

Consider the revenue function

$$R = 50x - x^2$$

between daily revenue and the daily sales x tons. Use differentiation from first principles to obtain an equation for marginal revenue.

Solution 8.1.2

We are asked to find dR/dx from first principles. Consider the output level x (tons per day), and an increase Δx in x which results in an increase ΔR for R. We follow the procedure (8.1.3) and the first step is to apply the revenue equation to the new output level $x + \Delta x$. The new revenue $R + \Delta R$ is

$$R + \Delta R = 50(x + \Delta x) - (x + \Delta x)^2$$

and so

$$R + \Delta R = 50x + 50\,\Delta x - x^2 - 2x\,\Delta x - (\Delta x)^2$$

Next, we subtract the original revenue equation to obtain

$$
\begin{array}{ll}
R + \Delta R = & 50x + 50\,\Delta x - x^2 - 2x\,\Delta x - (\Delta x)^2 \\
R = & 50x \qquad\qquad\quad -x^2 \\
\hline
\Delta R = & 50\,\Delta x \qquad -2x\,\Delta x - (\Delta x)^2
\end{array}
$$

Therefore

$$\frac{\Delta R}{\Delta x} = \frac{50\,\Delta x - 2x\,\Delta x - (\Delta x)^2}{\Delta x} \qquad\qquad \text{divide the top by } \Delta x$$

$$= 50 - 2x - \Delta x$$

Finally

$$\frac{dR}{dx} = \lim_{\Delta x \to 0} \frac{\Delta R}{\Delta x} = \lim_{\Delta x \to 0} 50 - 2x - \Delta x \qquad \text{replace } \Delta x \text{ by 0 to find the limit}$$

$$\frac{dR}{dx} = 50 - 2x \qquad \text{as required}$$

Note: Substituting $x = 15$, $dR/dx = 50 - 2 \times 15 = £20/\text{unit}$. This proves that our earlier estimate is indeed correct.

As you can see, obtaining an equation for dy/dx algebraically, directly from the definition, can be time consuming. However, there are *rules* which can be used to convert an equation for the total quantity to an equation for the rate of increase. There are several such rules but only the simpler ones will be considered here.

Basic rules

To state these rules, it is assumed that y is some function of x.

	Total quantity y	Rate of increase dy/dx	
A	K	0	
B	Kx	K	K is a constant
C	Kx^n	Knx^{n-1}	

(8.1.4)

Rules A and B are easier to accept than rule C. Rule A states that a constant has a zero rate of increase which is clear enough. Rule B states that the rate of increase of a straight-line function $y = Kx$ is K. This is reasonable, since K is the slope of the line, and, as we pointed out at the start of the chapter, the slope is the rate of increase. We will not prove rule C but notice that when it, and rule B, are applied to the revenue function

$$R = \underset{B}{50x} - \underset{C}{1x^2} \qquad \text{for rule C multiply by power 2 and then subtract 1 from power}$$

the result

$$\frac{dR}{dx} = 50 - 1 \times 2x^{2-1} = 50 - 2x$$

is the same as that obtained from first principles. In arriving at dR/dx, the following principle has been applied:

Individual rates of increase are added (or subtracted) in order to determine the rate of increase of some overall quantity. (8.1.5)

EXAMPLE 8.1.2

Differentiate each of the following functions
  (a) $y = 3x^5 - 6x^3 + 10x - 20$
  (b) $y = (5x^3 - 3x^2)(2x^2 + 4x)$
  (c) $y = 50x^4 - \dfrac{5}{x^3}$
  (d) $y = (\sqrt{x})^3 + 4$

Solution 8.1.2(a)

The first step is to decide which rule will be used for each term.

$$y = \underset{C}{3x^5} - \underset{C}{6x^3} + \underset{B}{10x} - \underset{A}{20}$$

Thus

$$\frac{dy}{dx} = 3 \times 5x^{5-1} - 6 \times 3x^{3-1} + 10 - 0$$

$$\frac{dy}{dx} = 15x^4 - 18x^2 + 10$$

For the remaining examples, we will rely heavily upon the use of indices (see section 1.3 of Chapter 1).

Solution 8.1.2(b)

Before applying the basic rules, it is necessary to rewrite the equation. This is done by removing the brackets and using the index law

$$x^{mn} = x^{m+n}$$

to multiply out. *Simply applying the rules to each bracket produces the wrong answer.* Thus

$$\begin{aligned}
y &= (5x^3 - 3x^2)(2x^2 + 4x) \qquad \text{rewrite} \\
&= 10x^5 + 20x^4 - 6x^4 - 12x^3 \\
&= \underset{c}{10x^5} + \underset{c}{14x^4} - \underset{c}{12x^3}
\end{aligned}$$

Now this is in a similar format to the example in **(a)**, and the basic rules can be applied.

$$\frac{dy}{dx} = 10 \times 5x^{5-1} + 14 \times 4x^{4-1} - 12 \times 3x^{3-1}$$

$$\frac{dy}{dx} = 50x^4 + 56x^3 - 36x^2$$

Solution 8.1.2(c)

Before differentiating, it it necessary to rewrite y so that the second term is expressed in terms of a negative power:

$$y = 50x^4 - \frac{5}{x^3}$$

$$= \underset{c}{50x^4} - \underset{c}{5x^{-3}} \qquad \text{rewrite before differentiating}$$

$$\frac{dy}{dx} = 50 \times 4x^3 - 5 \times (-3)x^{-4}$$

$$= 200x^3 + 15x^{-4} \qquad \text{this answer is good enough}$$

$$\frac{dy}{dx} = 200x^3 + \frac{15}{x^4} \qquad \text{can be rewritten}$$

Solution 8.1.2(d)

$$y = x^{3/2} + 4 \qquad \text{rewrite before differentiating}$$
$$\phantom{y = x^{3/2} + 4} \; \underset{C}{} \; \underset{A}{}$$

$$\frac{dy}{dx} = \tfrac{3}{2}x^{3/2-1} + 0$$

$$= \tfrac{3}{2}x^{1/2} \qquad \text{good enough}$$

$$= \tfrac{3}{2}\sqrt{x} \qquad \text{can be rewritten}$$

Marginal quantities

Since the derivative measures rate of increase, it can be used to reason about marginal quantities. Thus:

$$\text{Marginal revenue} = \frac{dR}{dx} \qquad \text{Marginal cost} = \frac{dC}{dx}$$

$$\text{Marginal profit} = \frac{dG}{dx}$$

Furthermore, since $G = R - C$

$$\frac{dG}{dx} = \frac{dR}{dx} - \frac{dC}{dx}$$

which translates to the familiar statement that

Marginal profit = Marginal revenue – Marginal cost
M.G. = M.R. – M.C.

So, for example, if

$$C = 2x^3 + 100 \qquad \text{where } x \text{ is the output}$$
$$R = 200x - 3x^2$$

then differentiating

Marginal cost $= 6x^2$ Marginal revenue $= 200 - 6x$
Marginal profit $= (200 - 6x) - 6x^2 = 200 - 6x - 6x^2$

To calculate the rate of increase of profit at an output of 5 units, say

$$\text{M.G.} = 200 - (6 \times 5) - (6 \times 25) = \pounds20/\text{unit}$$

For a *small* increase in output from 5 to 5.3, say, we deduce that the *approximate* increase in profit is $20 \times 0.3 = \pounds6$, since the rate of increase of $\pounds20/\text{unit}$ will remain approximately constant over the small increase from 5 to 5.3 units.

For the rate of increase of revenue at an output of 35 units, say,

$$\text{M.R.} = 200 - (6 \times 35) = -\pounds10/\text{unit} \quad \text{revenue is actually decreasing by } \pounds10/\text{unit}$$

EXERCISES 8.1

1 Consider the revenue function of Example 8.1.1

$$R = 50x - x^2$$

where x tons is the daily sales level. For the sales level of 15 tons per week, copy and complete the following table for sales levels approaching 15 from below, and confirm that the same rate of increase £20/unit as in Example 8.1.1 is obtained:

x	R	Δx	ΔR	$\dfrac{\Delta R}{}$	Average rate of increase of R with respect to x (£/unit)
15	525	—	—	—	—
14.5					
14.8					
14.9					
14.96					

2 Determine dy/dx for each of the following functions:

(a) $y = 6x^3 - 3x$ (b) $y = 8x^4 - 2x^5 + 3x^2 - 10$

(c) $y = \frac{1}{2}x^4 - \frac{1}{3}x^6 + \dfrac{2}{x^3} - 6x + 3$

(d) $y = \frac{1}{4}x^{5/2} - 2x^{1/3} + 5x - 40$ (e) $y = (\sqrt[3]{x})^2 - 5x$

(f) $y = 2(\sqrt[4]{x})^7$ (g) $y = \dfrac{1}{3x} + 10x^2$

3 Determine dy/dx for

(a) $y = x^3(x^2 + 3x - 4)$ (b) $y = 3 + (2x^2 + 5)^2$ (c) $y = (1 - x^4)^2$

(d) $y = \dfrac{2x^5 - 3x^3 + 3}{x^3}$ (e) $y = x^{1/2}(4x^3 - 3x^{1/2} + 2)$

4 Differentiate each of the following functions from first principles:

(a) $y = 5x^2 + 20$ (b) $y = 6x^3$ (c) $y = 1/x$

5 The total cost £C and revenue £R for a small farm are related to the number q acres farmed as follows:

$$C = 2q^2 + 100q + 4000$$
$$R = -\frac{1}{3}q^3 + 17q^2 + 1100q$$

(a) Determine equations for marginal cost, marginal revenue and marginal profit in terms of q.

(b) Determine the rates of increase of cost, revenue and profit (in £/acre), if 40 acres are currently farmed.

Use your answer for the rate of increase of revenue to find the approximate increase in revenue, if the number of acres farmed is increased from 40 to 40.2.

(c) Find the acreage at which marginal cost is £220/acre.

6 For one of the chemicals produced by Bates Ltd., the total daily cost £C and total daily revenue £R are described by the equations

$$C = 8x^2 + 20x + 13000$$
$$R = 1500x - 2x^3$$

where x tons is the daily output.

(a) Copy, and complete, the table below, showing average rates of increase of total daily cost C, with respect to output x, measured relative to the output level of 5 tons per day. Use the table to estimate the rate of increase of C, with respect to x, at this output level.

x	C	Δx	ΔC	$\dfrac{\Delta C}{\Delta x}$
5	13300			
5.2				
5.1				
5.04				
5.01				

(b) Determine equations for the rate of increase of total daily revenue, and the rate of increase of total daily cost, in terms of x.

(c) Calculate the rate of increase of total daily cost when the output level is 20 tons per day.

(d) Calculate the output level at which total daily revenue is increasing 3 times faster than total daily cost.

7 For a particular product manufactured by a company, the total weekly cost £C and total weekly revenue £R are given by

$$C = 50x + 2000 \qquad R = 180x - 2x^2$$

when the output level is x units per week.

(a) Plot R against x for x in the range 0 to 90 units.

(b) Determine, graphically, the value of dR/dx when

    (i) $x = 30$ units/week
    (ii) $x = 70$ units/week

(c) Check your answers to (b) by differentiating R to find marginal revenue.

(d) Determine marginal cost and marginal profit in terms of x.

(e) Use your answer to (d) to calculate the rates of increase of total weekly cost and total weekly profit, with respect to output, at an output level of 20 units per week.

(f) The company now introduces a modified production process for which the total weekly cost $£C_1$ is given by the equation

$$C_1 = ax^2 + 60x + 4000$$

where a is a constant.

Assuming that the rate of increase of total weekly cost with respect to output is three times greater when the output is 50 units/week than it is when the output is 10 units/week, determine the value of a.

8.2 STATIONARY POINTS AND CURVE SKETCHING

Consider a quantity y which is a function of the quantity x. It is often important to determine maximum or minimum points on the y-curve (if any), since this information may be used for decision making or for sketching the curve. These **maximum and minimum points** are collectively referred to as **turning points**, and the derivative dy/dx proves useful for finding them.
  In the previous section, we looked at two important interpretations of dy/dx:

• For each value of x, dy/dx measures the (instantaneous) **rate of increase** of y with respect to x, at that value.
• For each value of x, dy/dx measures the **slope of the tangent** at the point on the y-curve corresponding to x.

It is the second of these which provides a way of finding maximum or minimum points because, as Figure 8.2.1 shows, the tangent to the curve is horizontal at

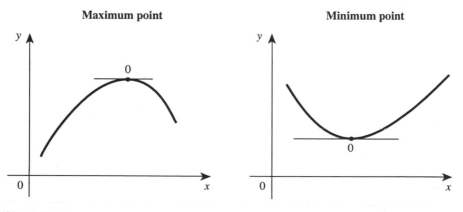

Figure 8.2.1

175

such points and so has *zero* slope. Thus

$$\frac{dy}{dx} = 0 \quad \text{at a maximum or minimum point}$$

However, there may be other points on a curve at which the tangent has zero slope, and $dy/dx = 0$. These points, called **points of inflexion**, are illustrated in Figure 8.2.2.

The term **stationary points** is used to describe **all points at which $dy/dx = 0$**. (At such points, the rate of increase, dy/dx, is zero, and so y is neither increasing nor decreasing. y is therefore, in that sense, stationary.)

Using the first derivative to test the nature of a stationary point

In Figures 8.2.1 and 8.2.2, we observed that $dy/dx = 0$ at maximum points, minimum points and points of inflexion. However, what does separate these types of points is the behaviour of dy/dx on **either side** of the point. Since the value of dy/dx is the slope of the tangent, then as Figure 8.2.3 shows:

- dy/dx is **positive** to the left of a **maximum** point, becomes **zero** at the point itself, and then becomes **negative**. dy/dx therefore **decreases** as we move from left to right through a maximum point.
- dy/dx is **negative** to the left of a **minimum** point, becomes **zero** at the point itself, and then becomes **positive**. dy/dx therefore **increases** from left to right through a minimum point.
- dy/dx **does not change sign** at a **point of inflexion**.

Application to marginal quantities

Using the criterion for a maximum point, *maximum* profit occurs at $x = a$ if

M.G. > 0	when $x < a$	M.G. = marginal profit
M.G. $= 0$	when $x = a$	
M.G. < 0	when $x > a$	

Point of inflexion

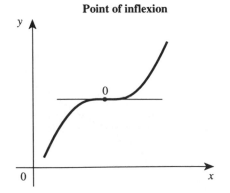
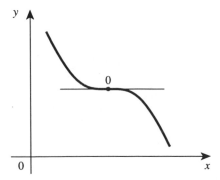

Figure 8.2.2

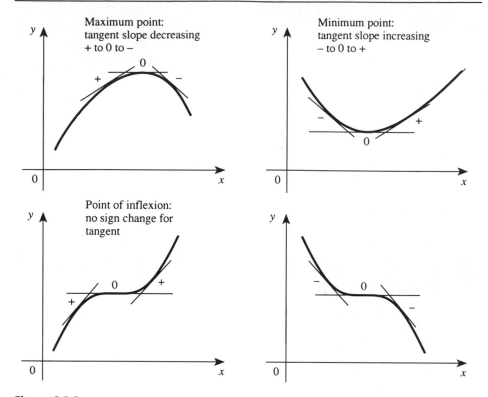

Figure 8.2.3

Since

M.G. = M.R. – M.C.   difference between marginal revenue and marginal cost

we deduce that *maximum* profit occurs at $x = a$ if

M.R. > M.C.   when $x < a$

M.R. = M.C.   when $x = a$

M.R. < M.C.   when $x > a$

EXAMPLE 8.2.2

Find the stationary points of the function

$$y = x^4 - 4x^3 + 10 \tag{8.2.1}$$

and determine their nature.

Solution 8.2.2

At a stationary point

$$\frac{dy}{dx} = 0$$

Therefore

$$4x^3 - 12x^2 = 0 \qquad \text{no constant term, so take out a common factor}$$
$$4x^2(x - 3) = 0$$

It follows that

$$x = 0 \quad \text{or} \quad x - 3 = 0, \text{ i.e. } x = 3$$

Using (8.2.1)

if $x = 0$, $y = 10$

if $x = 3$, $y = 3^4 - (4 \times 3^3) + 10 = -17$

The stationary points are therefore $(0, 10)$ and $(3, -17)$.

Identification of points
For $x = 0$, choose a value of x slightly below, say -0.5, and a value of x slightly above, say 0.5. Similarly, for $x = 3$, choose 2.5 and 3.5. We now complete the following table:

x	-0.5	0	0.5	x	2.5	3	3.5
dy/dx	$-\backslash$	$\underline{0}$	$\backslash-$	dy/dx	$-\backslash$	$\underline{0}$	$/+$

(The lines indicate the tangent slope at each point. At the stationary points, the slope is zero and the lines are horizontal.)
  The tangent slopes shown are based upon the following calculations:

$$\frac{dy}{dx} = 4x^3 - 12x^2$$

Therefore

if $x = -0.5$ $dy/dx = 4(-0.5)^3 - 12(-0.5)^2 = -3.5$ negative slope

if $x = 0.5$ $dy/dx = 4(0.5)^3 - 12(0.5)^2 = -2.5$ negative slope

if $x = 2.5$ $dy/dx = 4(2.5)^3 - 12(2.5)^2 = -12.5$ negative slope

if $x = 3.5$ $dy/dx = 4(3.5)^3 - 12(3.5)^2 = 24.5$ positive slope

Notice, that it is not the values of dy/dx which we are interested in but whether these are positive or negative.
  The table is completed using these values. For example, if $x = -0.5$, then the downward line signifies negative tangent slope. From the table, we see that

(0, 10) is a **point of inflexion**   no change of sign for tangent slope at this point

(3, -17) is a **minimum point**   tangent slope changes from negative to zero to positive

The second way of identifying stationary points relies on the use of a second derivative.

The second derivative

The second derivative, denoted by d^2y/dx^2, is obtained by differentiating dy/dx. It therefore measures the rate of increase of the first derivative or tangent slope:

$$\frac{d^2y}{dx^2} = \frac{d}{dx}\left(\frac{dy}{dx}\right)$$

For example, if

$$y = 5x^4 - 3x^2 + 2x - 3$$

then, using the basic rules of differentiation

$$\frac{dy}{dx} = 20x^3 - 6x + 2$$

$$\frac{d^2y}{dx^2} = 60x^2 - 6 \qquad \text{applying the rules again}$$

Using the second derivative to test the nature of a stationary point

Whilst the technique of looking at the first derivative *always* works, when identifying a stationary point, it is sometimes useful to use a second derivative test instead, which is derived from the first derivative case. This test is sometimes quicker, but it does not cover all cases as we shall see.

The test is stated as follows:

$$\frac{d^2y}{dx^2} > 0 \quad \textbf{at a minimum point}$$

(8.2.2)

$$\frac{d^2y}{dx^2} < 0 \quad \textbf{at a maximum point}$$

Note. If $d^2y/dx^2 = 0$, the test fails, and dy/dx must be considered instead.

To derive the test for a **maximum** point, recall that the first derivative dy/dx changes from positive to zero to negative as we move from left to right through the point, and so **dy/dx decreases** as x increases. Thus

Rate of increase of dy/dx is negative

Put another way

$$\frac{d}{dx}\left(\frac{dy}{dx}\right) < 0$$

$$\frac{d^2y}{dx^2} < 0 \quad \text{at a maximum point}$$

The test for a **minimum** point is derived in a similar way, using the fact that dy/dx **increases** as we pass from left to right through the point

The next example illustrates the use of the second derivative.

179

EXAMPLE 8.2.2

The total weekly cost C in £ when producing x units of a certain product is given by

$$C = 0.5x^2 + 60x + 1000$$

and the total weekly revenue £R from the sale of these x units is given by

$$R = 240x - 1.5x^2$$

(a) Find the output level at which profit is at a maximum, and calculate the maximum weekly profit.
(b) Calculate the fall in profit if the firm's objective were to maximise revenue rather than profit.
(c) Determine the output level at which average cost per unit is least.

Solution 8.2.2(a)

It is first necessary to find the equation for profit G.

$$G = R - C$$
$$= 240x - 1.5x^2 - (0.5x^2 + 60x + 1000)$$
$$= 240x - 1.5x^2 - 0.5x^2 - 60x - 1000$$
$$G = 180x - 2x^2 - 1000 \qquad\qquad (8.2.3)$$

Therefore

$$\frac{dG}{dx} = 180 - 4x$$

Maximum profit occurs at a stationary point and so

$$\frac{dG}{dx} = 0 \qquad \text{marginal profit is zero}$$

$$180 - 4x = 0$$
$$4x = 180$$
$$x = 45$$

To check for a maximum point, we differentiate again.

$$\frac{d^2G}{dx^2} = \frac{d(180 - 4x)}{dx} = -4 \qquad \text{differentiating } dG/dx$$

The *negative* value confirms that a maximum point occurs when $x = 45$.
Finally, using (8.2.3)

$$G = (180 \times 45) - (2 \times 45^2) - 1000 = 3050$$

Conclusion: A maximum profit of £3050 is achieved at an output of 45 units/week.

Solution 8.2.2(b)

Here we need to find the output at which maximum revenue occurs, and then calculate the profit at this output. This profit figure can then be compared with the maximum profit. Since

$$R = 240x - 1.5x^2$$

Therefore

$$\frac{dR}{dx} = 240 - 3x$$

For maximum revenue

$$\frac{dR}{dx} = 0 \qquad \text{marginal revenue} = 0$$

$$240 - 3x = 0$$
$$3x = 240$$
$$x = 80$$

Checking for a maximum

$$\frac{d^2R}{dx^2} = -3 \qquad \text{negative sign confirms maximum}$$

The corresponding profit from (8.2.3) is

$$G = (180 \times 80) - (4 \times 80^2) - 1000 = 600$$

Since maximum profit is £3050, the fall in profit per week is $3050 - 600 = £2450$.

Conclusion: Fall in profit is £2450 when revenue is maximised.

Solution 8.2.2(c)

We must first find an equation for the average cost per unit:

$$A = \frac{0.5x^2 + 60x + 1000}{x}$$

$$= 0.5x + 60 + 1000/x \qquad \text{divide out by } x \qquad (8.2.4)$$

$$= 0.5x + 60 + 1000x^{-1} \qquad \begin{array}{l}\text{rewrite using a negative} \\ \text{power before differentiating}\end{array}$$

$$\frac{dA}{dx} = 0.5 + 1000(-1)x^{-1-1} = 0.5 - 1000x^{-2}$$

At the minimum point

$$\frac{dA}{dx} = 0$$

Therefore

$$0.5 - \frac{1000}{x^2} = 0 \qquad \text{rewrite using an inverse power in order to solve equation}$$

$$\frac{1000}{x^2} = 0.5$$

$$0.5x^2 = 1000$$
$$x^2 = 1000/0.5 = 2000$$
$$x = 44.72 \text{ units per week}$$

Checking for a minimum

$$\frac{d^2A}{dx^2} = \frac{d}{dx}\left(\frac{dA}{dx}\right) = \frac{d}{dx}(0.5 - 1000x^{-2})$$
$$= -1000(-2)x^{-2-1} = 2000x^{-3} = 2000/x^3$$

Substituting $x = 44.72$

$$\frac{d^2A}{dx^2} = \frac{2000}{(44.72)^2} \qquad \text{positive value confirms a minimum}$$

Using (8.2.4)

$$A = (0.5 \times 44.72) + 60 + 1000/44.72$$
$$= £104.72/\text{unit}$$

Conclusion: An output of 44.72 units/week minimises the average cost/unit. The minimum is £104.72/unit.

EXAMPLE 8.2.3

The profit G (in thousands of pounds) for a particular firm over a ten year period, from the end of 1984 ($t = 0$) to the end of 1996, is given by

$$G = \tfrac{2}{3}t^3 - 14t^2 + 90t - 60 \qquad (8.2.5)$$

where t is the number of years elapsed.
   Determine the stationary points of the profit function G, and hence sketch its graph.

Solution 8.2.3
The stationary points occur when $dG/dt = 0$.

$$\frac{dG}{dt} = 2t^2 - 28t + 90 \qquad (8.2.6)$$

Therefore

$$2t^2 - 28t + 90 = 0$$
$$t^2 - 14t + 45 = 0$$

(8.2.7)

Factorising

$$(t-5)(t-9) = 0$$

$$t = 5 \quad \text{or} \quad t = 9 \text{ (years)}$$

You might prefer to solve equation (8.2.7) by using the quadratic formula as follows:

$$a = 1, b = -14, c = 45$$

$$t = \frac{-b \pm \sqrt{(b^2 - 4ac)}}{2a}$$

$$= \frac{14 \pm \sqrt{(14^2 - 4 \times 1 \times 45)}}{2 \times 1} = \frac{14 \pm 4}{2} = 5 \text{ or } 9 \text{ (years)}$$

Since the question asks for the stationary *points*, and points are specified by two coordinate values, we must now calculate the values of G. Thus

for $t = 5$ $G = (\frac{2}{3} \times 5^3) - (14 \times 5^2) + (90 \times 5) - 60 = 123.33$

for $t = 9$ $G = (\frac{2}{3} \times 9^3) - (14 \times 9^2) + (90 \times 9) - 60 = 102$

The stationary points are therefore (5, 123.33) and (9, 102). To determine their nature, we use the second derivative, obtained by differentiating the first derivative dG/dt. Using (8.2.6)

$$\frac{d^2G}{dt^2} = 4t - 28$$

if $t = 5$ $\dfrac{d^2G}{dt^2} = -8 < 0$ second derivative is *negative*, so (5, 123.33) is a maximum point

if $t = 9$ $\dfrac{d^2G}{dt^2} = +8 > 0$ second derivative is *positive*, so (9, 102) is a minimum point

The stationary points prove invaluable, if the profit function is to be sketched with confidence. However, it is also useful to determine where the curve cuts the two axes, if it is convenient to do so. It is easy to show that the curve cuts the vertical axis at $(0, -60)$, simply by substituting the value $t = 0$ into the G equation. However, to find the point at which the curve cuts the t-axis requires us to solve the equation $G = 0$, that is

$$\tfrac{2}{3}t^3 - 14t^2 + 90t - 60 = 0$$

This is a cubic equation (involving t^3). We have not considered the solution of cubic equations; it will be relatively difficult to solve and it may only be possible

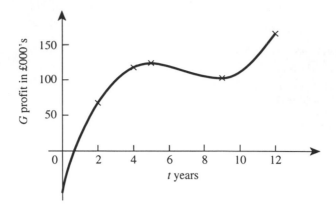

Figure 8.2.4

to obtain an approximate solution for t. In any event, we would certainly not attempt to solve it for the purposes of a sketch!

Since we are asked to sketch the graph of G over a finite range (from $t = 0$ to $t = 12$), there is one other obvious point on the graph which it is useful to calculate – the point at $t = 12$ (the top end of the range) at which $G = 156$ (using equation 8.2.5). The co-ordinates of the points obtained so far are shown in the following table:

t	0	5	9	12
G	-60	123.33	102	156

The final consideration in producing the sketch is to decide whether we have enough points or not. To decide this, we construct suitable axes and mark the points we have already. The sketch graph is shown in Figure 8.2.4 and it should be noted that, since we are sketching, and not plotting, the curve for G, there is no necessity for graph paper. Obviously, we would be guessing at the shape of the curve between $t = 0$ and $t = 5$, whereas elsewhere the shape of the curve is apparent, given that it must be smooth. We therefore calculate two further points, with co-ordinates as follows:

t	2	4
G	69.3	118.7

and it is now possible to draw, with confidence, a smooth curve representing the profit G.

EXERCISES 8.2

1 Home Electronics Ltd. manufactures a small computer for which the total weekly production cost £C and the total weekly revenue £R are given by

$$C = \tfrac{1}{2}x^2 + 10x + 2400$$
$$R = 240x - 2x^2$$

when x computers are produced and sold each week.

(a) Calculate the output level at which revenue is maximised and calculate the maximum weekly revenue.

(b) Calculate the output level at which profit is maximised and calculate the maximum weekly profit.

(c) Determine the reduction in weekly profit if the company's policy were to minimise average cost per unit rather than maximise profit.

2 Vampy Ltd. manufactures a type of powerful vacuum cleaner, for which demand varies with price. At a price of £55 per unit, 20 units are sold per day, whereas daily sales are 60 units at a price of £45 per unit. It is calculated that daily production costs £C are given by

$$C = \tfrac{1}{4}x^2 + 10x + 1050 \qquad\qquad (1)$$

when x cleaners are produced per day.

(a) Express the selling price £p/unit in terms of the daily demand x.

(b) How many cleaners does the company need to produce and sell each day to maximise profit, and what is the maximum daily profit? Show that marginal cost and marginal revenue are equal at this output level.

(c) A business consultant advises that a more accurate version of the total daily cost equation is obtained by adding an extra term $\tfrac{1}{40}x^3$ to the right-hand side of (1), and reducing the constant from 1050 to 250.

Based upon this model for total costs, what is the new maximum daily profit?

3 The total weekly production cost £C for a particular product is given by

$$C = 22x + 750$$

when x units are produced per week. The advertising cost £C_A necessary to sell these x units per week, and the weekly revenue £R resulting from the sale of these x units, are given by

$$C_A = 18x + 0.1x^3 + 750$$

$$R = 340x - 2.25x^2$$

(a) Find the optimum production level (at which maximum profit occurs), and calculate the maximum weekly profit.

(b) Find the level of output at which the advertising cost per unit is a minimum, and determine this minimum average cost.

4 The cost £C of producing x units of a certain commodity is given by

$$C = \tfrac{1}{4}x^2 + 20x + 400$$

Find the level of production at which minimum average cost per unit occurs, and calculate this minimum value. Show that at this output level, marginal cost is equal to average cost per unit.

5 The monthly profit £G for a product is given by the equation

$$G = 10x + 10x^2 - 0.1x^3 - 1000$$

where x is the number of units produced and sold per month. Find

(a) the value of x for which the marginal profit is zero

(b) the production required to maximise the monthly profit

(c) the value of the maximum monthly profit

(d) the value of x for which the marginal profit is greatest.

Sketch the graph of the profit against the number of units produced and sold per month, showing all important features, and calculate

(e) the values of x which give zero profit

(f) the smallest break-even quantity

(g) the change in the profit when the number of units produced and sold is increased from 40 to 50 units/month.

6 The marginal revenue and marginal cost, both in £/unit, for a commodity are given by

$$\text{M.C.} = x^2 + 7x + 20$$

$$\text{M.R.} = 20x - x^2$$

when x thousand units are produced and sold per annum. Find the value of x for which maximum profit occurs.

7 The revenue £R from the sale of x units of a particular product is given by

$$R = 90x - x^2$$

Fixed production costs are put at £850/week and profit is maximised at a production level of 25 units per week, the total weekly production cost at this level being £1600. Determine the equation for total weekly cost C in terms of output x, assuming that it has the form

$$C = ax^2 + bx + c \qquad \text{where } a, b, c \text{ are constants}$$

8 For each of the following functions, determine its stationary points and identify their nature. Hence make a neat sketch of the graph of the function.

$$y = 2x^3 - 3x^2 - 12x + 25 \qquad x \text{ in the range } -2 \text{ to } 3$$

$$y = 2x^4 - 8x^3 + 9x^2 - 10 \qquad x \text{ in the range } -1 \text{ to } 3$$

$$y = 5x^4 + 2x^5 + 20 \qquad x \text{ in the range } -3 \text{ to } 1$$

8.3 ELASTICITY

Elasticity measures the *responsiveness* of demand or supply for a good to a change in price, and two approaches to this measurement are possible.

Arc price elasticity of demand

Consider a good for which the price is p, and an increase in price Δp leads to a (negative) increase Δx in demand(see Figure 8.3.1). To measure the responsiveness of demand to change in price, it is tempting to simply calculate the ratio

$$\frac{\Delta x}{\Delta p}$$

Certainly, it is reasonable to calculate the change in demand relative to the change in price by calculating the *ratio* of increase in demand to increase in price. However, since we wish to measure responsiveness, it is the **relative** or **proportionate** change in demand and the relative change in price which are important.

The appropriate approach, therefore, is to calculate

$$E_D = \frac{\text{Proportionate increase in demand}}{\text{Proportionate increase in price}}$$

Expressed in terms of the symbols Δx and Δp, this becomes

$$E_D = \frac{\Delta x / x}{\Delta p / p}$$

and this formula can be rewritten more tidily as follows:

$$E_D = \frac{\Delta x}{x} \times \frac{p}{\Delta p}$$

$$E_D = \frac{p}{x} \cdot \frac{\Delta x}{\Delta p}$$

(8.3.1)

The problem with this is that it requires both a price and price increase to be specified (from which the demand and demand increase can be determined).

Point price elasticity of demand

In order to measure instantaneous (i.e. point) rates of increase in section 8.1, the strategy was to first determine the average rate of increase over an arc, and then to find the limit as $\Delta x \to 0$. The approach is the same here and using (8.3.1) we obtain

$$E_D = \lim_{\Delta p \to 0} \frac{p}{x} \cdot \frac{\Delta x}{\Delta p} \qquad \text{(now change } \Delta \text{ to } d \text{ when taking the limit)}$$

(8.3.2)

$$E_D = \frac{p}{x} \times \frac{dx}{dp}$$

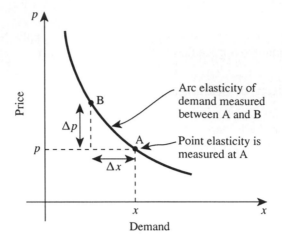

Figure 8.3.1

Price elasticity of demand and revenue

The aim of this section is to establish an important relationship between the rate of increase of revenue with respect to price, dR/dp, and the price elasticity of demand. The approach is similar to the 'first principles' procedure in section 8.1, and we start by considering a given price p (with associated demand x) and assuming an increase Δp in the price, which causes an increase Δx in demand. Thus

$$R = px \qquad\qquad \text{original revenue}$$

$$R + \Delta R = (p + \Delta p)(x + \Delta x) \qquad \text{new revenue}$$

Multiplying out the right-hand side of the second equation:

$$R + \Delta R = px + p.\Delta x + x.\Delta p + \Delta x.\Delta p$$

and subtracting the original revenue equation we obtain

$$
\begin{aligned}
R + \Delta R &= px + p.\Delta x + x.\Delta p + \Delta x.\Delta p \\
R &= px \\
\hline
\Delta R &= p.\Delta x + x.\Delta p + \Delta x.\Delta p
\end{aligned}
$$

It remains to divide the above equation by Δp, and then take the limit as $\Delta p \to 0$. Therefore

$$\frac{\Delta R}{\Delta p} = p.\frac{\Delta x}{\Delta p} + x + \Delta x \qquad \text{remember } p, \text{ and hence } x, \text{ are given,}$$
$$\text{and only } \Delta x, \Delta p \text{ vary in this equation}$$

$$\frac{dR}{dp} = \lim_{\Delta p \to 0} \frac{\Delta R}{\Delta p} \qquad\qquad \text{the increase in demand } \Delta x \to 0, \text{ as } \Delta p \to 0$$

$$= p.\frac{dx}{dp} + x$$

We are now very close to achieving the desired relationship between dR/dp *and* E_D, since the first term on the right-hand side of the last equation is very close to the formula for E_D given in (8.3.2). Indeed, rewriting the equation as

$$\frac{dR}{dp} = x \cdot \frac{p}{x} \cdot \frac{dx}{dp} + x$$

and taking x out as a common factor gives

$$\frac{dR}{dp} = x(E_D + 1) \tag{8.3.3}$$

Using equation (8.3.3) and the theory put forward in section 8.2, it is now possible to deduce criteria for E_D which determine the behaviour of R. This is an important step forward because it allows us to talk about the responsiveness of demand to changes in price, whilst at the same time understanding clearly whether such changes will increase or decrease the total revenue. Applying the properties of the derivative given on page 176 to p and R (rather than x and y), we see that R will increase if $dR/dp > 0$ and R will decrease if $dR/dp < 0$; alternatively, if $dR/dp = 0$, R will be at a maximum. But, since the demand x is positive in equation (8.3.3), $dR/dp > 0$, $dR/dp = 0$ or $dR/dp < 0$, depending on whether $E_D + 1 > 0$, $E_D + 1 = 0$ or $E_D + 1 < 0$, respectively; that is, depending on whether $E_D > -1$, $E_D = -1$ or $E_D < -1$. Therefore

if $E_D > -1$	revenue **increases** if p increases	demand is called **inelastic** in this case	
if $E_D = -1$	revenue is at a **maximum**	this case is called **unitary elasticity**	(8.3.4)
if $E_D < -1$	revenue **decreases** if p increases	demand is called **elastic** in this case	

Elasticity of supply

This measures the responsiveness of supply to change in price and

$$E_S = \frac{p}{x} \cdot \frac{dx}{dp} \qquad \text{E_S will always be \textit{positive}, since supply increases as price increases}$$

EXAMPLE 8.3.1

Consider the demand function

$$p = 150 - 10\sqrt{x}$$

relating the price $£p$/unit to the demand x (hundred) units per year.

Express E_D in terms of p. Hence, determine whether an increase in price will result in increased or decreased revenue, when the price is £10/unit.

Solution 8.3.1

This is an exercise in applying formula (8.3.2) and therefore involves finding a formula for dx/dp. This seems to pose a problem, since the subject of the demand equation is p and it is therefore natural to find dp/dx. However,

$$\frac{dx}{dp} = \frac{1}{\dfrac{dp}{dx}} \qquad \text{this is often useful}$$

and so we can find dp/dx and then invert it to find dx/dp. For dp/dx, it is necessary to rewrite the square root in the demand function as a fractional index. Thus

$$p = 150 - 10x^{1/2}$$

$$\frac{dp}{dx} = -10 \cdot \tfrac{1}{2}x^{-1/2} = -5x^{-1/2}$$

Writing dp/dx in a more useful form, and then inverting

$$\frac{dp}{dx} = -\frac{5}{\sqrt{x}}$$

$$\frac{dx}{dp} = -\frac{\sqrt{x}}{5}$$

Therefore, from (8.3.2)

$$E_D = -\frac{p}{x} \cdot \frac{dx}{dp} = -\frac{p}{x} \cdot \frac{\sqrt{x}}{5} = -\frac{p}{5\sqrt{x}} \qquad (8.3.5)$$

So far, so good. But the question requires a formula in terms of p, and the final step is to eliminate $\sqrt{x}$ by rearranging the original demand equation. Thus

$$p = 150 - 10\sqrt{x}$$
$$10\sqrt{x} = 150 - p$$

$$5\sqrt{x} = \frac{150 - p}{2} \qquad \text{(the } E_D \text{ formula contains } 5\sqrt{x}\text{)}$$

Substituting in (8.3.5)

$$E_D = -\frac{p}{5\sqrt{x}} = -\frac{p}{\dfrac{150 - p}{2}}$$

$$E_D = -\frac{2p}{150 - p}$$

For the final part of the question, substitute $p = 10$ into this formula. Thus

$$E_D = -\frac{20}{140} = -\frac{1}{7}$$

Demand is therefore inelastic and revenue will increase as the price is raised above £10/unit.

EXERCISES 8.3

1   When a particular product was first introduced, the demand function was given by the equation

$$x = 500 - 10p$$

where x is the number of units demanded at a price of £p/unit. However, a more realistic equation for the present day product is

$$x = 400 - 0.25p^2$$

(A practical price range of £10/unit to £30/unit applies to each equation.)

(a) Find a formula for the price elasticity of demand in terms of p, for each of the above equations.

(b) Compare the present response of demand to change in price with the original response when

   (i) $p = £10$/unit   (ii) $p = £30$/unit

2   The quantity x of a particular good demanded daily at a price of £p/unit satisfies the equation

$$p = 60 - 0.12x^3$$

(a) Find a formula for the price elasticity of demand in terms of p.

(b) Determine whether demand is elastic or inelastic when

   (i) $p = £30$/unit   (ii) $p = £50$/unit

and state, in each case, whether revenue will increase or decrease when the price is increased.

(c) Express revenue in terms of x and hence find the quantity and price at which revenue is maximised. Verify that this is the point of unitary elasticity.

3   In a particular market location, the annual demand for potatoes is given by

$$x_d = 2 - 0.02p$$

where the quantity x_d demanded annually is measured in thousands of tonnes and the price p is in pence per kg. The corresponding supply relationship is also linear and it has been observed that the market is willing to supply 900 tonnes per year at a price of 10 pence/kg and 1250 tonnes per year at a price of 15 pence/kg.

(a) Calculate the price and quantity at market equilibrium.

(b) Compare the response of demand to change in price with the supply response at the equilibrium point.

4 The price £p/unit, and the weekly demand x units at that price, for a particular product, are related by an equation of the form

$$x = ap^2 + bp + c$$

Given the table below, determine values for a, b, c, and hence find the price at which revenue is maximised.

p	10	20	30
x	140	100	40

9

INTEGRATION AND PARTIAL DIFFERENTIATION

When you have completed this chapter you will be able to

- determine indefinite integrals
- understand the relationship between integral and area
- apply the definite integral to the market
- find partial derivatives
- find stationary points for functions of more than one variable

9.1   INTEGRATION

The process of **indefinite integration** provides the **reverse operation** to differentiation. Given the *marginal cost* of a product, for example, indefinite integration can be used to deduce the equation for *total cost*. If y is a function of x, any function which has *derivative y* is called an **indefinite integral of y,** and is denoted by

$$\int y \, dx$$

The basic rules of differentiation, as given in (8.1.4), are

	y	dy/dx	
A	K	0	
B	Kx	K	K is a constant
C	Kx^n	Knx^{n-1}	

The basic rules of integration, obtained by reversing rules B and C, are as follows:

	y	$\int y \, dx$	
B1	K	Kx	K is a constant
C1	Kx^n	$\dfrac{Kx^{n+1}}{n+1}$	$n \neq -1$

As an example of applying rule B1,

$$\int 10 \, dx = 10x + K_1 \qquad \text{applying rule B1 with } K = 10$$

The presence of the constant of integration K_1, which can have any value and which enables us to include all possible answers, explains the term 'indefinite integral'. To check that $10x + K_1$ is the indefinite integral of the function $y = 10$, we differentiate

$$\frac{d}{dx}(10x + K_1) = 10 + 0 = 10 \quad \text{the constant disappears when differentiating}$$

(You might like to think of the introduction of a constant of integration as being the reverse of rule A above.) As an illustration of rule C1, which reverses rule C, consider the function $y = x^2$ and let the function y_1 of x be an indefinite integral of y. Then

$$\frac{dy_1}{dx} = x^2 \tag{9.1.1}$$

From rule C, we know that the equation for y_1 must contain x^{2+1}, since one is subtracted from the power during differentiation. But we also know that x^3 is multiplied by 3 during differentiation, and this figure does not appear in (9.1.1). So, it is necessary to divide by 3. Therefore

$$y_1 = \frac{x^{2+1}}{2+1} + K = \frac{x^3}{3} + K$$

The first term illustrates rule C1 and the constant K must be included to cover all possibilities for y_1. As a final check

$$\frac{dy_1}{dx} = \tfrac{1}{3}.3x^{3-1} = x^2$$

and so y_1 is indeed the indefinite integral of $y = x^2$. Two more substantial examples are as follows:

$$\int \underset{\text{C1}}{(6x^4} - \underset{\text{C1}}{8x^2} + \underset{\text{C1}}{\tfrac{1}{3}x} - \underset{\text{B1}}{6)}\,dx = \frac{6}{4+1}x^{4+1} - \frac{8}{2+1}x^{2+1} + \frac{\tfrac{1}{3}}{1+1}x^2 - 6x + K$$

$$= \tfrac{6}{5}x^5 - \tfrac{8}{3}x^3 + \tfrac{1}{6}x^2 - 6x + K$$

$$\int x^{\tfrac{1}{2}}(2x^2 - x^3)\,dx = \int \underset{\text{C1}}{(2x^{\tfrac{5}{2}}} - \underset{\text{C1}}{x^{\tfrac{7}{2}})}\,dx \qquad \text{rewrite before integrating}$$

$$= \frac{2}{\tfrac{5}{2}+1}x^{\tfrac{5}{2}+1} - \frac{1}{\tfrac{7}{2}+1}x^{\tfrac{7}{2}+1} + K = \tfrac{4}{7}x^{\tfrac{7}{2}} - \tfrac{2}{9}x^{\tfrac{9}{2}} + K$$

As we said earlier, indefinite integration can be used to recover total quantities from marginal quantities. For example, suppose that the marginal cost and marginal revenue (in £/unit) for a particular product are given by

M.C. $= x + 20$

M.R. $= 620 + 11x - x^2$

Then

$$C = \int (x + 20)\,\mathrm{d}x = \tfrac{1}{2}x^2 + 20x + K \qquad K \text{ is a constant}$$

$$R = \int (620 + 11x - x^2)\,\mathrm{d}x$$

$$= 620x + \tfrac{11}{2}x^2 - \tfrac{1}{3}x^3 + L \qquad L \text{ is a constant} \tag{9.1.2}$$

Additional information is required, if the constants are to be evaluated. If we know, for example, that revenue is zero when x is zero, then substituting in (9.1.2)

$$0 = 0 + L \qquad L = 0$$

Therefore

$$R = 620x + \tfrac{11}{2}x^2 - \tfrac{1}{3}x^3$$

If we also know the output level at which break-even occurs is 5 units/week, say, then

$$R = T \qquad \text{when } x = 5$$

$$620x + \tfrac{11}{2}x^2 - \tfrac{1}{3}x^3 = \tfrac{1}{2}x^2 + 20x + K$$

$$(620 \times 5) + (\tfrac{11}{2} \times 5^2) - (\tfrac{1}{3} \times 5^3) = \tfrac{1}{2}5^2 + (20 \times 5) + K$$

$$K = 3083.33 \qquad \text{fixed costs}$$

Therefore

$$C = \tfrac{1}{2}x^2 + 20x + 3083.33$$

The definite integral

Let y be a function of x. Then the **definite integral of y with respect to x, over the interval from a to b**, is defined to be the **area** bounded by the curve for y,

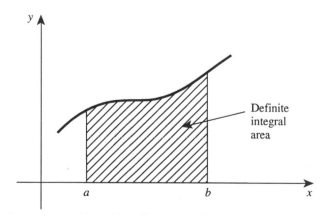

Figure 9.1.1(a)

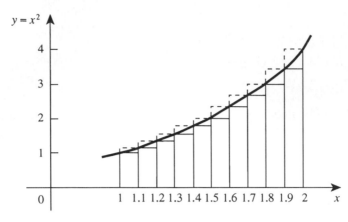

Figure 9.1.1(b)

the x-axis and the lines $x = a$, $x = b$. This area is shown in Figure 9.1.1(a). The notation for the definite integral is

$$\int_a^b y\, dx$$ the reason for using a notation similar to that for the indefinite integral will become apparent later

Defining the integral as an area is only useful if we know how an area is measured. The approach is to divide the area into a number of strips, each corresponding to a *small* increase Δx in x. Consider, for example, the area bounded by the function $y = x^2$, the x-axis, and the lines $x = 1$, $x = 2$, shown in Figure 9.1.1(b). We have divided the area into 10 strips, and approximated the area of each strip by an inner rectangle and an outer rectangle, as shown. (Rectangles are used because their areas are easy to find.) Of course there is an

Table 9.1.1

Strip	Width of strip (Δx)	Height of inner rectangle ($y_1 = x^2$)	Area of inner rectangle ($y_1\, \Delta x$)	Height of outer rectangle ($y_2 = x^2$)	Area of outer rectangle ($y_2\, \Delta x$)
1	0.1	1	0.100	1.21	0.121
2	0.1	1.21	0.121	1.44	0.144
3	0.1	1.44	0.144	1.69	0.169
4	0.1	1.69	0.169	1.96	0.196
5	0.1	1.96	0.196	2.25	0.225
6	0.1	2.25	0.225	2.56	0.256
7	0.1	2.56	0.256	2.89	0.289
8	0.1	2.89	0.289	3.24	0.324
9	0.1	3.24	0.324	3.61	0.361
10	0.1	3.61	0.361	4.00	0.400
			2.185		2.485

error in using a rectangle rather than the strip, but in due course we will ensure that the error becomes smaller and smaller by using more and more strips of narrower and narrower width. Table 9.1.1 enables us to find the total area of the inner rectangles, as an *underestimate* of the area under the curve (the definite integral), and the total area of the outer rectangles, as an *overestimate* of the area under the curve.

As an illustration of these calculations, consider the first strip. The starting value of x is 1 and so the height of the inner rectangle is 1^2 – the value of the function $y = x^2$ when $x = 1$. The height of the outer rectangle is $1.1^2 = 1.21$. The areas of these rectangles are $1 \times 0.1 = 0.1$ and $1.21 \times 0.1 = 0.121$, respectively. The calculations for the other strips are similar. (Of course, the height of each outer rectangle is the same as the height of the next inner rectangle.) We conclude that an underestimate for the area under the curve $y = x^2$ is 2.185 and an overestimate is 2.485 (a difference of 0.3). If we now use more and more strips, we get better and better estimates. For example

Number of strips	Total area of inner rectangles	Total area of outer rectangles
20	2.259	2.409
40	2.296	2.371

Therefore, the area under the curve lies between 2.296 and 2.371 (a difference of only 0.08), and the evidence is that the underestimates and overestimates are approaching the same limiting value. This value is *defined* to be the area under the curve, i.e. the definite integral. Thus

$$\int_b^a y \, dx = \lim_{\Delta x \to 0} \sum y \, \Delta x \qquad \text{the summation } \Sigma \text{ is either over inner rectangles or outer rectangles} \qquad (9.1.3)$$

(You will see that this interpretation proves useful when the definite integral is applied to business problems later.)

For the above example a *possible* value for the area would be around 2.33, based upon the figures of 2.296 and 2.371. In fact, since we know the equation of the function, $y = x^2$, we will be able to calculate the value exactly in due course – but some preliminary work is required.

Having defined the definite integral to be an area under the curve, it may seem odd that the same term 'integral' should be used for this and the apparently unrelated idea of reversing differentiation. However, we will now look at an important result, called the **Fundamental Theorem of the Calculus** which relates these two ideas.

Consider the graph of a general function y of x, shown in Figure 9.1.2, and let A be the shaded area bounded by the curve, the x – axis, the line $x = a$ and the vertical line through some general value of x. A is itself a function of x, since it can be determined for each value of x, and so it is possible to consider dA/dx – the rate of increase of A with respect to x. The technique of 'differentiation by first principles', described in (8.3.1), is used.

Consider a particular value of x, for which the function has value y and the area is A. Then, an increase Δx causes an increase Δy in the value of the function

197

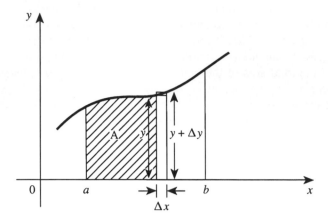

Figure 9.1.2

and an increase ΔA in the area. Observe that ΔA is larger than the area of the smaller rectangle drawn but smaller than the area of the larger rectangle, where

Area of smaller rectangle $= y\,\Delta x$

Area of larger rectangle $= (y + \Delta y)\,\Delta x$

Therefore

$$y\,\Delta x < \Delta A < (y + \Delta y)\,\Delta x \qquad \text{divide by } \Delta x$$

$$y < \frac{\Delta A}{\Delta x} < y + \Delta y$$

Now, if $\Delta x \to 0$, then $\Delta y \to 0$ and so $y + \Delta y \to y$. So, $\Delta A/\Delta x$ is 'sandwiched' between the value y and a value which approaches closer and closer to y, as Δx is made smaller and smaller. Thus

$$\frac{\mathrm{d}A}{\mathrm{d}x} = \underset{\Delta x \to 0}{\text{limit}}\ \frac{\Delta A}{\Delta x}$$

$$\frac{\mathrm{d}A}{\mathrm{d}x} = y$$

and so, by definition

$$A = \int y\,\mathrm{d}x + K \qquad A \text{ is therefore an indefinite integral of } y \qquad (9.1.4)$$

The constant can be evaluated by substituting $x = a$. For this value $A = 0$, since the area A is measured from the line $x = a$ and so

$$0 = [y\,\mathrm{d}x]_{x=a} + K$$

$$K = -[y\,\mathrm{d}x]_{x=a} \qquad \text{right-hand side is the indefinite integral of } y$$
$$\qquad\qquad\qquad\quad \text{evaluated at } x = a$$

Substituting for K in (9.1.4)

$$A = \int y \, dx - [y \, dx]_{x=a}$$

Therefore, substituting $x = b$

Area bounded by the y-curve, the x-axis and the lines $x = a$, $x = b$ is

$$\left[\int y \, dx \right]_{x=b} - \left[\int y \, dx \right]_{x=a} \qquad (9.1.5)$$

Restated, this becomes

$$\int_a^b y \, dx = \left[\int y \, dx \right]_{x=b} - \left[\int y \, dx \right]_{x=a}$$

$$= \left[\int y \, dx \right]_a^b \qquad \text{this is simply a notation for the right-hand side} \qquad (9.1.6)$$

If we now return to the area bounded by the curve $y = x^2$, the x-axis, and the lines $x = 1$, $x = 2$, then

$$\text{Area} = \int_1^2 y \, dx = \int_1^2 x^2 \, dx = [x^3/3]_1^2 \qquad \text{using the indefinite integral } x^3/3$$

$$= [x^3/3]_{x=2} - [x^3/3]_{x=1}$$

$$= \tfrac{8}{3} - \tfrac{1}{3} = \tfrac{7}{3} = 2.33$$

(So our earlier guess of 2.3 was good.)

EXAMPLE 9.1.1

(a) Plot the curves $y = -x$ and $y = x^3$ in the range $x = -2$ to 3. By evaluating a suitable definite integral, calculate the area enclosed between these curves and the lines $x = 1$, $x = 3$.

(b) Plot the curves $y = x^2$ and $y = 4x - x^2$ in the range $x = 0$ to 4. Calculate the area enclosed between these two curves.

Solution 9.1.1(a)

The graph of $y = -x$ is a straight line which passes through the points $(2, -2)$ and $(3, -3)$. The graph of $y = x^3$ is plotted for $x = -2, -1, 0, 1, 2, 3$. The graph is therefore as shown in Figure 9.1.3.

Two separate calculations are required in order to find the shaded area. Area A is given by

$$\int_1^3 x^3 \, dx = [x^4/4]_1^3$$

$$= \tfrac{81}{4} - \tfrac{1}{4} = 20$$

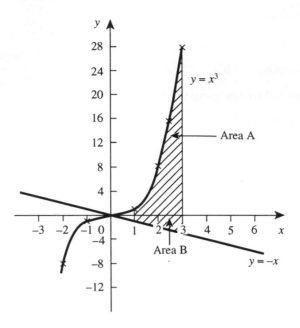

Figure 9.1.3

For area B

$$\int_1^3 -x\,dx = -\int_1^3 x = -[x^2/2]_1^3$$
$$= -\left(\tfrac{9}{2} - \tfrac{1}{2}\right) = -4$$

This last area is negative since the curve is below the x-axis, Therefore, to find the actual total area, *the negative sign is ignored.*

Conclusion: Total area $= 20 + 4 = 24$.

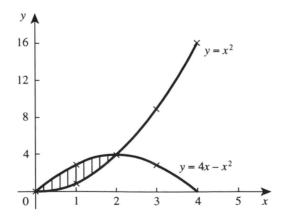

Figure 9.1.4

Solution 9.1.1(b)

The graph is as shown in Figure 9.1.4.

The shaded area is

$$\int_0^2 (4x - x^2)\,dx - \int_0^2 x^2\,dx \qquad subtract \text{ areas under the two curves}$$

$$= [2x^2 - x^3/3]_0^2 - [x^3/3]_0^2$$

$$= [8 - \tfrac{8}{3}] - \tfrac{8}{3} = \tfrac{8}{3}$$

Conclusion: Total area $= 8/3$.

Application of the definite integral to the market

Figure 9.1.5(a) shows the demand curve for a good, for which it is assumed that there is an equation relating p to x, and for which an equilibrium price p_e and equilibrium quantity x_e have been set, relative to some supply curve (not shown).

The aim here is to try to assess the implications for the consumers, if the quantity of the good available varies below the equilibrium quantity. (Rather than viewing the price of the good as controlling demand, we are here looking at how much the consumers would be willing to pay for given quantities of the good.)

Let the area under the curve between 0 and x_e be divided into strips of width Δx as shown, and let each strip be approximated from inside by a rectangle, in the manner considered earlier. Each strip corresponds to an increase Δx in the quantity of the good. For a typical strip, the consumers would be willing to pay £p/unit for the extra Δx units. Therefore, the consumers would be willing to pay $p\,\Delta x$ for the extra units – and this is the area of the rectangle. If we sum over all the rectangles, then

$$\sum p\,\Delta x$$

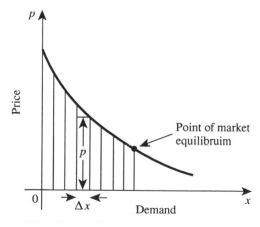

Figure 9.1.5(a) Demand curve

201

is a measure of the total amount which the consumers would be willing to pay for the good, if the quantity varies below the equilibrium quantity. If we now let $\Delta x \to 0$ (making the strip width smaller and smaller), the limit of the above sum is the definite integral

$$\int_0^{x_a} p \, dx$$

and this is the area between the demand curve, the x-axis, the p-axis and the line $x = x_e$. So this area can be thought of as measuring the total amount which the consumers would be willing to pay for the good, if the quantity varies below the equilibrium quantity. By contrast, the total amount that the consumers pay at the equilibrium price is $p_e x_e$ – which is the area of the rectangle shown in Figure 9.1.5(b). The difference between these two areas, which is shaded, is defined to be the **consumers' surplus**. It therefore measures the difference between the total amount people would willingly pay for varying amounts of a good and the total amount they pay at the equilibrium price. This is the benefit to the consumer of buying at a set equilibrium price. It is of help in cost-benefit analysis. Thus

$$\textbf{Consumers' surplus} = \int_0^{x_e} p \, dx - p_e x_e \qquad (9.1.7)$$

So far we have assumed that the demand equation relates p, as subject, to x. If, instead, it relates x to p, then the area measured by the definite integral is the area between the curve and the p-axis and so

$$\textbf{Consumers' surplus} = \int_{p_e}^{p_0} x \, dp \qquad (9.1.8)$$

where p_0 is the **intercept** of the demand curve with the p-axis.

Similarly, it is possible to look at benefits from the producer's point of view. More specifically, it is possible to look at the benefit of supplying less than the equilibrium quantity to those producers who would be willing to supply less than this quantity. (It is assumed that the equilibrium price and quantity have been set

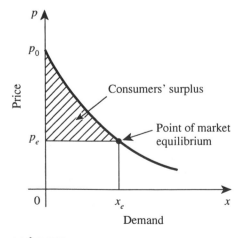

Figure 9.1.5(b) Demand curve

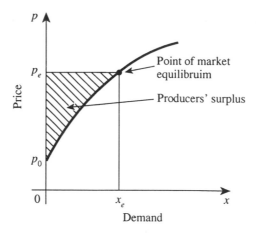

Figure 9.1.6 Supply curve

with respect to some demand function.) Consider the supply function of Figure 9.1.6.

The area *under* the supply curve between $x = 0$ and $x = x_e$ can be thought of as a measure of the total revenue from the good received by producers who are willing to supply below the equilibrium quantity. (To see this, divide the area into strips and approximate these by rectangles.) What these producers actually receive is $p_e x_e$ – the area of the large rectangle. The difference between these areas, which is shaded, is defined to be the **producers' surplus** – it measures the benefit to producers of supplying at the higher equilibrium level. The formula for producers' surplus is

$$\textbf{Producers' surplus} = p_e x_e - \int_0^{x_e} p \, dx \qquad (9.1.9)$$

or

$$\textbf{Producers' surplus} = \int_{p_0}^{p_e} x \, dp \qquad (9.1.10)$$

An example should make the use of these formulae clear.

EXAMPLE 9.1.2

(a) Given the demand and supply functions

$$p = 150 - 0.4x^2$$

$$p = 15 + 0.2x^2$$

calculate the consumers' surplus.

(b) For the supply equation $\qquad x = 4p^2 + 40p - 300$

calculate the producers' surplus, assuming that the price at market equilibrium is £10/unit.

Solution 9.1.2(a)

Since p is expressed in terms of x for these equations, we use the formula

$$\text{Consumers' surplus} = \int_0^{x_e} (150 - 0.4x^2)\, dx - p_e x_e$$

At market equilibrium,

Price at which units are supplied = price at which units are demanded

$$15 + 0.2x^2 = 150 - 0.4x^2$$
$$0.6x^2 = 135$$
$$x^2 = 225 \qquad x = 15 \text{ units}$$

The equilibrium price $= 15 + (0.2 \times 225) = 60$. Thus

$$\begin{aligned}
\text{Consumers' surplus} &= \int_0^{15} (150 - 0.4x^2)\, dx - 60 \times 15 \\
&= [150x - \tfrac{4}{30}x^3]_0^{15} - 900 \\
&= [150 \times 15 - \tfrac{4}{30}(15)^3] - 900 \\
&= 1800 - 900 = 900
\end{aligned}$$

Conclusion: Consumers' surplus $= 900$.

Solution 9.1.2(b)

Since x is the subject of the supply equation, formula (9.1.10) is the natural one to use. Therefore

$$\text{Producers' surplus} = \int_{p_0}^{p_e} (4p^2 + 40p - 300)\, dp$$

where p_0 is the intercept of the supply curve on the p-axis (i.e. the value of p for which $x = 0$) and $p_e = 10$. To find the intercept

$$0 = 4p^2 + 40p - 300$$

So

$$p = \frac{-b \pm \sqrt{[b^2 - 4ac]}}{2a} \qquad \text{where } a = 4, b = 40, c = -300$$

$$= \frac{-40 \pm \sqrt{[40^2 - 4 \times 4 \times (-300)]}}{8} = \frac{-40 \pm 80}{8}$$

$$= 5 \text{ or } -15 \qquad \text{negative price is not possible}$$

Therefore $p_0 = 5$ and

$$\begin{aligned}
\text{Producers' surplus} &= \int_5^{10} (4p^2 + 40p - 300)\, dp \\
&= [4p^3/3 + 20p^2 - 300p]_5^{10} \\
&= [4000/3 + 2000 - 3000] - [500/3 + 500 - 1500] \\
&= 1000/3 - (-2500/3) = 3500/3
\end{aligned}$$

Conclusion: Producers' surplus $= 3500/3$.

EXERCISES 9.1

1 Determine

(a) $\int (2x^3 - 3x + 6)\,dx$

(b) $\int (6x^5 - \frac{1}{2}x^3 - 1)\,dx$

(c) $\int \frac{x^3 + 10}{x^2}\,dx$

(d) $\int (4x + \sqrt{x})\,dx$

(e) $\int (x^2 - 2x + 3)x^{\frac{1}{2}}\,dx$

(f) $\int (2x^4 - 4x^5 + 3x)\,dx$

(g) $\int \left(3x^6 - \frac{4}{x^3}\right)dx$

(h) $\int (10x^{\frac{3}{2}} + 3x^{\frac{1}{2}})\,dx$

(i) $\int_1^3 (4x^3 - 6x^2 + 2)\,dx$

(j) $\int_2^4 \left(4x^2 - \frac{2}{x^2}\right)dx$

2 A particular curve has gradient given by

$$\frac{dy}{dx} = 3x^2 - \frac{2}{3} + \frac{3}{x^2}$$

Given that the curve passes through the point $(3, 20)$, find its equation.

3 (a) Plot the graph of the function $y = 5/x^2$ in the range $x = 1$ to 5. By evaluating a suitable definite integral, calculate the area bounded by this curve, the x-axis, and the lines $x = 1$, $x = 5$.

(b) Plot the curve $y = x^2 + 3$ and the line $y = 4x$ in the range -3 to 4. Calculate the area enclosed between these curves.

(c) Plot the curve $y - 2x^3 - 2$ and the line $y - 7x$ in the range 3 to 3.

(i) Calculate the area enclosed between the line $y = 7x$, the curve $y = 2x^3 - 2$, and the x-axis, which lies above the x-axis.

(ii) Calculate the area which is between the line $y = 7x$ and the curve $y = 2x^3 - 2$, and which lies to the right of the y-axis.

4 The marginal cost M.C. and marginal revenue M.R. (in £/unit) for a particular product are given by

M.R. $= 380 - 2x$
M.C. $= 4x + 20$

when x units are produced and sold per week.

(a) Determine the total cost C and total revenue R in terms of x, assuming that the company breaks even at 70 units per week.

(b) Determine the output level at which profit is a maximum, and calculate the maximum profit.

(c) Calculate the smallest level of production at which the company breaks even.

5 The marginal cost and revenue (in £/unit) for a particular product are given by

$$\text{M.C.} = 200 + 4x$$
$$\text{M.R.} = 800 - 6x - x^2$$

when x units are produced and sold each week. Fixed costs are put at £6750/week
Find the level of output at which maximum profit is achieved.
Determine equations for total weekly cost and total weekly revenue in terms of x, and hence calculate the maximum weekly profit.

6 Stevenson Ltd. batch manufactures rolls of plastic-coated paper using a process for which production costs £C/hour are known to increase, and output n rolls/hour is known to decrease, as 'run' time increases. The company has attempted to model these factors and has obtained the equations:

$$C = 400 + 0.5 \ t^2$$
$$n = 20 - 0.01 \ t^2$$

where t is the number of hours elapsed (the process being started at time zero).
Assuming that each roll sells at a price of £300, determine the time at which a 'run' should be terminated. By evaluating a suitable definite integral, calculate the total profit per 'run' when this operating time is adopted.

7 (a) Calculate the consumers' surplus for the following demand equations, and the given equilibrium price or quantity:

(i) $p = 900 - 2x^2$ $x = 20$

(ii) $p = 100 - 2x$ $p = 30$

(b) Calculate the producers' surplus for the following supply functions, and the given equilibrium price or quantity:

(i) $x = 10p - 100$ $p = 40$

(ii) $x = 2p^2 - 800$ $x = 450$

8 Calculate the consumers' surplus and producers' surplus for the demand and supply functions

$$p = 150 - 5x \qquad p = 0.5x^2 + 50$$

9 Calculate the consumers' surplus and producers' surplus for the demand and supply functions

$$x = 1250 - 0.5p^2 \qquad x = 0.6p^2 - 510$$

9.2   FUNCTIONS OF MORE THAN ONE VARIABLE

In Chapter 7, we looked at costs, revenue and profit associated with a single product. If there were two related products, say, then it would be reasonable to look at a joint cost function for these. For example, this might have the form

$$z = x^2 + xy^2 + 8y$$

Part of the graph of this function (for x in the range 0 to 4 and y in the range 0 to 2) is shown in Figure 9.2.1.

The graph is a *surface* in 3 dimensions. If $x = 2$ and $y = 1$, for example, then

$$z = 4 + 2 + 8 = 14$$

and a point P is plotted at 14 on the z scale, vertically above the point $(2, 1)$ in the $x - y$ plane (the plane containing the x and y axes), as shown in the diagram.

The way that z changes with x and y can be very complicated indeed, and can easily defy imagination. One important way of dealing with this complexity is to allow the variables x and y to change *one at a time*; that is, y is held constant while x changes or x is held constant while y changes. For each of these alternatives, z can be regarded as a function of one variable, and we can measure the rate of increase of z with respect to x or y as described in Chapter 8.

For the purposes of illustration, let $x = 2$ and $y = 1$ for the function above (point P on the diagram). If y is held constant at 1, and x is allowed to vary, then

$$z = x^2 + x + 8 \qquad \text{this is a function of one variable} \qquad (9.2.1)$$

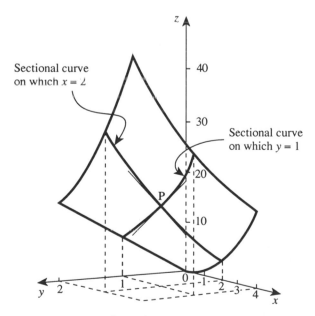

Figure 9.2.1 Part of surface $z = x^2 + xy^2 + 8y$

207

Using the rules of differentiation (8.1.4)

$$\frac{dz}{dx} = 2x + 1$$

Substituting $x = 2$, $dz/dx = 5$ and so the rate of increase of z with respect to x, with y held constant, when $x = 2$ and $y = 1$, is 5. Similarly, we would want to be able to find the rate of increase of z with respect to x, with y held constant, for *any* values of x and y.

To do this, we differentiate assuming that y is constant, rather than substituting for a particular value of y. However, to indicate that we are dealing with a function of *more than one* variable, with one of the variables held constant, we use the symbol ∂ to indicate the derivative (rather than d) and call the derivative a **partial derivative**. (More correctly, it is a first-order partial derivative.) So consider

$$z = x^2 + xy^2 + 8y$$

To find the partial derivatives, the basic rules A, B and C of differentiation (8.1.4) are used. For $\partial z/\partial x$, y is held constant and it may be helpful to write the equation for z with the constants highlighted. Thus

$$z = \underset{C}{x^2} + \underset{B}{y^2 x} + \underset{A}{\mathbf{8y}}$$ for the middle term, it is easier to write the constant at the front

and

$$\frac{\partial z}{\partial x} = 2x + y^2$$ substituting $x = 2$ and $y = 1$ gives the same rate of increase 5 as before

To find $\partial z/\partial y$, write the equation as

$$z = \underset{A}{\mathbf{x^2}} + \underset{C}{\mathbf{x}y^2} + \underset{B}{8y}$$

$$\frac{\partial z}{\partial y} = 2xy + 8$$

Consider another example:

$$z = 4x^3y^5 - 4x^4y^2 - 20xy + 6x - 10$$

For $\partial z/\partial x$, write this as

$$z = \mathbf{4y^5}x^3 - \mathbf{4y^2}x^4 - \mathbf{20y}\,x + \mathbf{6}x - \mathbf{10}$$ constants highlighted

Partially differentiating with respect to x, with y constant

$$\frac{\partial z}{\partial x} = 4y^5 3x^2 - 4y^2 4x^3 - 20y + 6$$

$$= 12x^2y^5 - 16x^3y^2 - 20y + 6$$

For $\partial z/\partial y$, x is held constant. So

$$z = 4x^3y^5 - 4x^4y^2 - 20xy + 6x - 10 \qquad \text{constants highlighted}$$

$$\frac{\partial z}{\partial y} = 4x^3 5y^4 - 4x^4 2y - 20x$$

$$= 20x^3y^4 - 8x^4y - 20x$$

A similar approach can be used to partially differentiate, for example

$$z = 2x^{1/2}y^4 - 2xy + x^3y^{-1/2}$$

You should convince yourself that

$$\frac{\partial z}{\partial x} = x^{-1/2}y^4 - 2y + 3x^2y^{-1/2}$$

$$\frac{\partial z}{\partial y} = 8x^{1/2}y^3 - 2x - \tfrac{1}{2}x^3y^{-3/2}$$

Note: For a function u of three variables x, y and z, the partial derivatives would be $\partial u/\partial x$, $\partial u/\partial y$ and $\partial u/\partial z$.

Interpreting partial derivatives graphically

Consider again the surface in Figure 9.1.1 drawn for $z = x^2 + xy^2 + 8y$, and consider the point P for which $x = 2$, $y = 1$. The vertical plane $x = 2$ shown in the diagram meets the surface in a **sectional curve** on which x is constantly 2, which therefore has the equation $z = 4 + 2y^2 + 8y$. The partial derivative $\partial z/\partial x$ at P is the derivative of this function of *one* variable at the point P, since it is the derivative with respect to x, with y held constant at 1, evaluated at $x = 2$. Therefore, from section 8.1, it is the **slope of the tangent** at P to the sectional curve drawn. Similarly, for the sectional curve in which the plane $y = 1$ meets the surface, the slope of the tangent at P is the value of $\partial z/\partial y$ at P.

There are important consequences as Figure 9.2.2 shows.

For surface (a) and surface (b), the tangent at P to the sectional curve AB on which x is a constant, and the tangent at P to the sectional curve CD on which y is a constant, are horizontal – which means they have **zero slope**. P is a maximum point for (a) and a minimum point for (b). The surface (c) has what is called a **saddle point** at P (for obvious reasons), and the tangents to the sectional curves at P are also horizontal. Maximum, minimum and saddle points are collectively called **stationary points**. Since the tangent slopes are the values of the partial derivatives at P, we conclude that

At a stationary point, all the (first-order) partial derivatives are zero

We will look at how stationary points are found, but how they are identified (using second-order partial derivatives) is beyond the scope of this book.

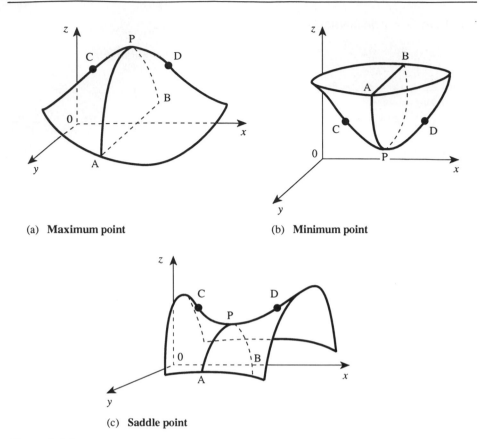

(a) **Maximum point** (b) **Minimum point**

(c) **Saddle point**

Figure 9.2.2

EXAMPLE 9.2.1

The demand relationships for two products produced by a company are given by

$$p_1 = 130 - 2x$$
$$p_2 = 320 - 4y$$

where x units of the first product and y units of the second product are sold per week at prices of $£p_1$/unit and $£p_2$/unit, respectively. The joint weekly cost $£C$ of producing these x units and y units is given by

$$C = 40x + 2xy + 2y^2 + 2000$$

Determine the quantities of the two products which should be produced weekly to maximise profit and calculate the maximum profit.

Solution 9.2.1

First an equation for the total weekly profit G is required. The total weekly revenue equations for the two products are

$$R_1 = (130 - 2x)x = 130x - 2x^2$$
$$R_2 = (320 - 4y)y = 320y - 4y^2$$

So

$$G = R_1 + R_2 - C$$
$$= 130x - 2x^2 + 320y - 4y^2 - (40x + 2xy + 2y^2 + 2000)$$
$$= 130x - 2x^2 + 320y - 4y^2 - 40x - 2xy - 2y^2 - 2000$$
$$G = 90x - 2x^2 + 320y - 6y^2 - 2xy - 2000 \qquad (9.2.2)$$

The partial derivatives are

$$\frac{\partial G}{\partial x} = 90 - 4x - 2y \qquad\qquad \frac{\partial G}{\partial y} = 320 - 12y - 2x$$

For maximum profit, we need to find the stationary point of the function, for which the partial derivatives are equated to zero. Thus

$$90 - 4x - 2y = 0 \qquad\qquad 320 - 12y - 2x = 0$$
$$4x + 2y = 90 \quad (1) \qquad\qquad 2x + 12y = 320 \quad (2)$$

These simultaneous equations are solved as described in section 1.6 of Chapter 1. Thus

Using $2 \times (2) - (1)$

$$
\begin{array}{ll}
4x + 24y = 640 & 2 \times (2) \\
\underline{4x + 2y = 90} & \\
22y = 550 & y = 25
\end{array}
$$

Substituting for y in equation (2)

$$2x + (12 \times 25) = 320 \qquad\qquad x = 10$$

Checking in (1)

Left-hand side $= (4 \times 10) + (2 \times 25) = 90$, as required

Equation (9.2.2) is used to calculate the maximum profit.

$$G = 90x - 2x^2 + 320y - 6y^2 - 2xy - 2000$$
$$= (90 \times 10) - 2(10)^2 + (320 \times 25) - 6(25)^2 - (2 \times 10 \times 25) - 2000$$
$$G = 2450$$

Conclusion: A maximum profit of £2450 is produced when 10 units of the first product and 25 units of the second are produced weekly.

EXERCISES 9.2

1 (a) Find $\partial z/\partial x$ and $\partial z/\partial y$ for each of the following functions:

(i) $z = 2x^4 + 4x - \frac{1}{2}y^3 + 6y^2 - 100$

(ii) $z = \frac{3}{2}x^2y^4 + 3y^2 - 9xy + 36x - 3y$

(iii) $z = x^2y - xy^3$

(b) Determine $\partial u/\partial x$, $\partial u/\partial y$ and $\partial u/\partial z$ for the function

$$u = 5x^3z^{1/2} - 10y^6x^2 + 2y^4z^3$$

2 The demand relationship for a particular product is given by

$$p_1 = 420 - 10x$$

where x is the weekly sales level at a price of £p_1 per unit. For a second product, the relationship between the price £p_2 per unit and the weekly sales level y is given by

$$p_2 = 650 - 2y^2$$

The joint total weekly cost £C of producing x units of the first product and y units of the second is given by

$$C = 20x + 50y + 1000$$

(a) Express the total weekly revenue R, and total weekly profit G, from the two products, in terms of x and y.

(b) Find the output levels which will maximise profit and the associated selling prices/unit. What is the maximum weekly profit?

3 Repeat parts (a) and (b) of Exercise 2 under the new assumptions that

$$p_1 = 56 - \tfrac{1}{4}x$$

$$p_2 = 94 - \tfrac{1}{2}y$$

$$C = \tfrac{1}{4}x^2 + 4xy + y^2 + 300$$

4 In order to increase profitability, the management of Floggit Incorporated are considering whether they should increase their advertising expenditure and reduce the number of sales offices in the country, or whether it would be preferable to reduce their advertising and increase the number of sales offices. They have arrived at the conclusion that the monthly profit £G is given by:

$$G = 88A - 2A^2 - 100 + 168S - 4S^2 - 4AS$$

where S is the number of sales offices in the country and A is the advertising expenditure in £1000's per month.
  Use partial differentiation to find the values of S and A for which the monthly profit is maximised.

5 A company is anxious to reduce its joint stock holding costs £C for two particular products and believes that these costs are given by the function

$$C = 60000 - 60y - 13.5x^2 + 0.2y^2 + 0.1x^3$$

where x and y are the quantities of these products held in stock.
  Use partial differentiation to show that this function has two stationary points.

6 The combined weekly profit £G from the two Viewmaster models manufactured by Easivu Ltd. is given by

$$G = 90x^2 - 2x^3 + 100y - y^2 - 25000$$

where x is the number of Viewmaster I models and y is the number of Viewmaster II models produced each week.

Show that this function has two stationary points.

10

STOCK (INVENTORY) CONTROL

When you have completed this chapter you will be able to:

- understand how costs are categorized for stock control calculations
- calculate economic order quantities and their associated costs
- understand how quantity discounts influence decision making
- understand the implications of variable demand on ordering policies

10.1 INTRODUCTION

All companies have items which are ordered in batches, or produced in batches, and then stored. These are items which are used on a day-to-day basis but for which it is simply not realistic to obtain them as and when needed. They might be packs of frozen food used by a restaurant, electrical components required by a car manufacturer, D.l.Y. items to be sold by a retailer, or even spare parts required for machinery.

Whatever the item, stock control (sometimes called inventory control) is principally concerned with deciding an order policy for the item, which means determining how many items should be ordered in each batch, and when an order should be placed.

Factors which influence the batch ordering or production policy

Obviously the quantity of the item required for the year, the **demand quantity**, must be taken into account. If, for example, the company expects to use 1000 items in a year, and orders the item from the supplier in equal-sized batches (say), then it could, for example, order 50 items 20 times per year; obviously, this is only one of many possibilities. This type of calculation, however, assumes that the company decides to meet all of the demand, and to avoid shortages, but such a decision will depend upon the **type of demand**. If the demand rate is steady, and therefore predictable, it is realistic to avoid shortages, but for variable demand, avoiding shortages means allowing for the maximum demand rate, and accepting a high stock level. On the other hand, incurring shortages can create difficulties. How much of the demand a company decides to meet (the service rate) depends upon the **storage costs** and the **penalties associated with shortages**. In fact, we have touched upon one of the main aims of stock control:

Aim 1: *To maintain a balance between holding too little or too much stock.*

Holding too little stock results in customers having to wait longer than necessary for their goods or going elsewhere, resulting in loss of goodwill and profits. It can also cause considerable disorganization. The consequences of a high stock level will include high storage costs and an excessive amount of capital tied up in stock. If borrowed, this capital will incur interest charges; alternatively, it may be capital which could earn interest if invested elsewhere.

Another factor which can influence the stock level is the time it takes the supplier to deliver the goods ordered – called the **lead time**. If the lead time is uncertain, then it is likely that either larger orders will be placed, or that orders will be placed when the stock level is already relatively high, to guard against undue delays. The overall effect, in either case, is to increase the stock level, and to encounter the types of problems described above. If the lead time is constant, it may be possible to maintain a lower stock level (see the stock level graph 10.2.1 and the discussion which follows it) but this will depend upon the demand pattern.

There is one other factor which we need to mention, and for this we will return to the annual demand of 1000 items considered earlier. As we have said, 50 items, ordered 20 times in the year, would suffice, as would, for example, 500 items, ordered twice in the year. The larger the batch quantity, the higher the stock level, but the fewer the orders per year. Which of these two policies is better will depend not only upon the storage costs but on the **ordering costs** (or **set-up costs**) associated with placing and receiving orders, where the emphasis here is upon costs, such as delivery charges, which are additional to the actual cost of buying the items. Obviously, the 1000 items have to be paid for, whichever ordering policy is chosen. We are thus led to another important aim of stock control which is:

Aim 2: *To provide a balance between holding high stock levels, and ordering or producing batches too frequently.*

When calculating holding costs and set-up costs, it may be necessary to categorise a number of different costs. Some of the more common are listed below.

Sample cost breakdown

(a) *Set-up costs* The following costs might be taken into account in evaluating this:

   (i)   Staff administrative costs concerned with raising orders and monitoring the progress of orders
   (ii) Cost of telephone calls
   (iii) Delivery charges
   (iv) Costs incurred when setting up machinery (in the case of batch manufacture).

(b) *Holding costs* This will include, for example:

   (i)   The 'opportunity cost of capital tied up in stock'
   (ii) All operational costs directly associated with storing goods, e.g. costs of labour, heating or refrigeration, stores transport, etc.
   (iii) Deterioration or obsolescence costs.

(i) is so important, it warrants further explanation.

215

Opportunity cost of capital tied up in stock

This is usually based upon the rate of return that the company estimates it can obtain on capital which it invests elsewhere. For example, suppose that a supplier charges £50 per unit, or that it costs £50 per unit to batch manufacture an item. If the company can obtain 20% p.a., say, by investing its capital elsewhere, then it *loses* $0.20 \times 50 = £10$ interest on the £50 which it pays for the item. This cost can be thought of as the cost of lost opportunity.

10.2 THE BASIC ECONOMIC ORDER QUANTITY (E.O.Q.) MODEL

This model, also called 'Wilson's Model', represents a first attempt to develop a stock control model which will permit the mathematical calculation of an 'optimum' batch quantity (the E.O.Q.). Having considered a number of factors which should influence the order policy, it will be necessary to make assumptions about these. We will list the assumptions first, and then comment upon them.

Assumptions of the E.O.Q. model

1 Stock is ordered in equal-sized batches.

2 The demand rate for the item, ordered and stored, is constant.

3 Demand is to be exactly met. No stock-outs are allowed, i.e. stocks available are always sufficient to meet demand.

4 The time between placing a replenishment order and receiving the items into stock (the 'lead-time') is constant.

5 The total cost of an order is made up of a fixed cost ('set-up cost'), independent of order size, and a variable cost that is directly proportional to the order size.

6 The total cost per unit time of holding a quantity of stock is proportional to the quantity held.

Assumption 1 is solely a simplifying assumption. Assumptions 2 and 3 are concerned with the demand pattern and the proportion of the demand which is to be met. The more complicated variable demand case will be considered later. The assumption of constant demand will be more appropriate for some situations than others. For a restaurant, say, using packs of frozen food, and with a dedicated clientele, this might be realistic. On the other hand, a car manufacturer, ordering electrical components, would probably expect a more erratic demand pattern. The assumption of no shortages is there for simplicity – there are stock control models, with constant demand, which allow shortages.

Assumption 4 for lead-times also simplifies matters, and again may be more appropriate in some situations than others. A large and powerful retail chain, for example, could certainly insist on a constant lead-time, whereas a small company may be at the mercy of its suppliers.

Finally, consider the last two assumptions. The proportional cost referred to in 5 is, of course, the cost of buying the item. The remaining part of 5 concerns the set-up cost per order, which is assumed to be *independent of order size*. The rationale here is that it takes the same time to make out a small order as a large one, and that when the order is delivered, the cost of a half-empty delivery van, say, is the same as for a full one. Of course such an argument has limits – a large quantity may require two vans, rather than one, for example. However, it may be that over the range of order quantities which are under consideration by a company, the assumption of a fixed set-up cost per order is realistic.

The essential point about assumption 6, is that the holding cost is *the same for each unit stored*; in which case, it makes sense to talk about the holding cost per unit. Certainly, this is reasonable as far as the opportunity cost of capital tied up in stock is concerned. However, for warehousing costs, a higher stock level may result in a steeper rise in holding costs than a smaller level. Extra warehousing may be required or it may simply take much more time to organize the stock. Certainly, the holding costs vary with the stock level; the simplest assumption is that is is proportional to this level.

In view of the assumptions, the graph of stock level against time is shown in Figure 10.2.1. The sloping, parallel, straight-line portions of the graph reflect the assumption of steady demand. There is one other very important aspect of the graph; namely, that a batch is received precisely when the stock level dwindles to zero. This is guaranteed by assumptions 2 and 4. Since demand is steady, the company knows when it will run out of stock, and, because of the constant lead-time, the company can ensure a batch delivery when needed, by ordering sufficiently in advance. From the graph, the average stock level is clearly $Q/2$.

The intention now is to look at the determination of an **optimum order policy**. Such a policy will stipulate when orders should be placeed, and the order size. 'When' was discussed above. So the problem now is to calculate the optimum batch size.

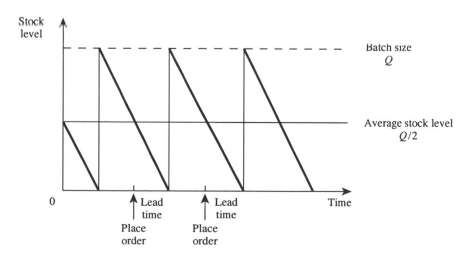

Figure 10.2.1 Stock level against time

217

Modelling the costs involved

For this model, the costs to be considered are those concerned with buying and holding stock, and setting-up orders. The intention now is to first find a formula for each of these, and hence to obtain a formula for the total annual cost of inventory. It will then be possible to find a formula for the batch quantity which minimizes the total inventory cost.

These formulae will be expressed in terms of the following symbols:

f **set-up cost per order** (independent of order size)

p **cost price per item** (normally viewed as the stock value per item)

h **cost of holding stock per unit per year**

d **annual demand from customers**

Q **order quantity**

T **total annual cost of inventory**

I **total annual indirect costs**

It will also be convenient, in the short term, to introduce the symbols B, H and S for the annual buying cost, holding cost and set-up cost. However, these will only be a means to an end. The easiest cost to consider is the annual buying cost B, since this is simply the product of the cost price per unit and the annual demand. Thus

$$B = pd$$

For H, the annual holding cost, the relevant factors are the unit holding cost h and the stock level. As the earlier graph of stock level against time shows, the stock level varies linearly (i.e. along a straight line) between a maximum of Q, which occurs when a new batch arrives, and zero. (Note that it is not in any way based upon the demand d.) Consequently, if we multiply h by the average stock level of $Q/2$, then any errors in underestimating holding costs, when the stock level is above $Q/2$, are counter-balanced by overestimates, when the stock level is below this average. Thus

$$H = h \times Q/2 = \frac{hQ}{2}$$

gives a legitimate measure of annual holding costs.

Next, we consider S. This must be based upon the set-up cost per order f and the number of orders, where

Number of orders $= d/Q$ (10.2.1)

For example, if annual demand is 200 units and the batch size is 10, then 20 orders are required, i.e. 200/10 orders. Thus:

$$S = f \times d/Q = \frac{fd}{Q}$$

Finally, remembering to add the annual indirect costs I, the total annual cost of inventory is

$$T = B + H + S + 1$$

$$T = pd + \frac{hQ}{2} + \frac{fd}{Q} + I \tag{10.2.2}$$

Having obtained the algebraic form of T, it would now be possible to proceed directly to the ultimate goal of finding a formula for the optimum batch quantity. However, before doing so, it is useful to apply the model to a specific example, in order to 'get a feel' for the determination of d, f, p and h, and the graphs of the costs involved.

EXAMPLE 10.2.1

Consider an item, used by an engineering company at a steady rate, for which the number of units demanded per year is 8400. The item is ordered in equal-sized batches from a supplier, and a clerical cost of £20 is incurred in placing each order. The supplier charges £42 per item, and makes a charge of £60 per delivery. Rental of warehousing incurs a cost of £20,000 per year.

(a) Assuming that the company adopts a rate of return on invested capital of 20% per annum, express the annual total cost of inventory T in terms of the batch quantity Q.
(b) If 1500 units are ordered each time, how many orders are placed each year, and what is the associated total annual cost of inventory.

Solution 10.2.1(a)
To find the T equation, we must attribute values to d, f, p and h.

$$d = 8400 \qquad \text{(annual demand)}$$

The 'acid test' for a cost to contribute to the set up cost f is that it should be per order and independent of order size. Both the cost £20 of placing an order and the delivery charge of £60 fit the bill. (Indeed, such costs were talked about when costs were classified at the beginning of this chapter.) Thus

$$f = 20 + 60 = 80 \qquad \text{(set-up cost per } \textit{order}\text{)}$$

$$p = 42 \qquad\qquad\quad \text{(cost price per } \textit{item}\text{)}$$

For h, we are looking for any holding costs which are per item per annum. In this case, only the opportunity cost of capital tied up in stock applies. As explained earlier, this is calculated using the capital outlay per item (the cost price p) and the rate of return on invested capital as follows:

$$h = 0.20 \times 42 = 8.4 \qquad \text{(holding cost per } \textit{unit} \text{ per } \textit{annum}\text{)}$$

Here £8.40 is the interest lost when the company commits £42 to buying stock, rather than investing it elsewhere.

We must also deal with the annual warehouse rental cost of £20,000. Since this cost is unaffected by the order policy (presumably), it is an indirect cost to be added at the end of the T equation.

We are now in a position to find the required equation for T. Using (10.2.2)

$$T = (42 \times 8400) + \frac{8.4Q}{2} + \frac{80 \times 8400}{Q} + 20000$$

$$= 352800 + 4.2Q + \frac{672000}{Q} + 20000$$

(10.2.3)

Solution 10.2.1(b)

Substituting the given order quantity $Q = 1500$ into the above equation

$$T = 352800 + (4.2 \times 1500) + \frac{672000}{1500} + 20000$$

$$= 352800 + 6300 + 448 + 20000$$

$$= 379,548$$

The total annual cost of inventory is therefore £379,548 when ordering 1500 items each time. Finally, using (10.2.1)

Number of orders $= 8400/1500 = 5.6$ per year

Note that it might be tempting to round the number of orders up to 6 orders per year. But this is wrong, since $6 \times 1500 = 9000$ items would be ordered per year, and this contradicts assumption 3, which states that the company orders so as to exactly meet demand. In fact, 5.6 is the *average* number of orders per year. If you prefer a whole number, this can be viewed as 28 orders over 5 years. Note that these orders are equally-spaced (see the stock level graph given earlier).

A graphical view of the costs

The sketch graph of S, H and the sum of these is shown in Figure 10.2.2. Note that the sketch shows

$$T_1 = S + H$$

and that the buying cost $B = pd$ has been omitted. This is for convenience only. B is a constant, unaffected by the batch size, and does not affect the shape of the total cost curve.

Consider the graph of S. Common sense tells us that S will be large for small order quantities, when many orders are placed, and small for fewer, larger orders. This is borne out by the previous example where $S = 672000/Q$. It is the fact that Q is divided which makes the curve behave as it does. On the other hand, as the equation $H = 4.2Q$ of the previous example illustrates, H is proportional to Q, and the graph of H is a straight line through the origin. H increases as Q increases.

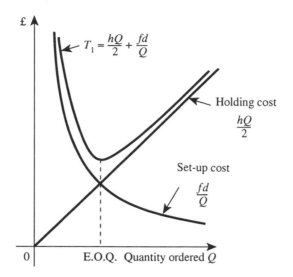

Figure 10.2.2 Graph of annual holding cost, annual set-up cost and the total of these

As a result, T_1 (and T) is dominated by S, and so is large for small orders, and is also large for large orders, when it is dominated by H. Therefore, the graph of T_1 (and T) has a characteristic U shape, and there is clearly an order quantity, called the **Economic Order Quantity (E.O.Q.)**, which minimizes both T_1 and T. It can be shown that **S and H are equal at this order quantity.**

Determining a formula for the E.O.Q.

We shall see that a general formula for the E.O.Q. can be obtained using the formula for T and differentiation. However, first it may be helpful to apply the same approach to the specific T equation (10.2.3) of the previous example.

EXAMPLE 10.2.2

Given that the total annual cost of inventory T is given by

$$T = 352800 + 4.2Q + \frac{672000}{Q} + 20000$$

determine the Economic Order Quantity (E.O.Q.)

Solution 10.2.2

Before differentiating the T equation, it must be rewritten using a negative index:

$$T = 352800 + 4.2Q + 672000Q^{-1} + 20000$$

Differentiating

$$\frac{dT}{dQ} = 4.2 + 672000(-1)Q^{-2} \qquad (10.2.4)$$

221

At the E.O.Q., which minimizes the value of T

$$\frac{dT}{dQ} = 0$$

Therefore

$$4.2 - \frac{672000}{Q^2} = 0$$

Rearranging

$$\frac{672000}{Q^2} = 4.2$$

$$672000 = 4.2Q^2$$

$$Q^2 = 672000/4.2 = 160000$$

$$Q = \sqrt{160000} = 400 \text{ items per order}$$

To complete the calculation, we must now find the second derivative of T and check that it is *positive* when $Q = 400$, in which case a minimum value is achieved. Therefore differentiating equation (10.2.4) for dT/dQ

$$\frac{d^2T}{dQ^2} = 672000(-1)(-2)Q^{-3} = \frac{1344000}{400^3} \quad \text{when } Q = 400$$

and so the second derivative is positive, and a minimum value is obtained. Thus, the economic order quantity, which minimizes T, is 400 items per order.

If we now return to the general equation (10.2.2) for T

$$T = pd + \frac{hQ}{2} + \frac{fd}{Q} + I$$

and apply the same approach as in the previous example, then the result will be a formula for the E.O.Q. which will serve us for the rest of this chapter.

If we rewrite the general equation (10.2.2) as

$$T = pd + (h/2)Q + (fd)Q^{-1} + I$$

and compare with the T equation of the previous example:

$$T = 352800 + 4.2Q + 672000Q^{-1} + 20000$$

we see that the expressions in bold type are simply constants. The first term and the last will disappear when we differentiate; whereas the constants $h/2$ and fd, which are combined with the variable Q, will simply be left where they are. Thus

$$\frac{dT}{dQ} = h/2 + fd(-1)Q^{-2} = 0 \tag{10.2.5}$$

for minimum T. Therefore

$$\frac{h}{2} - \frac{fd}{Q^2} = 0$$

$$\frac{h}{2} = \frac{fd}{Q^2}$$ (incidentally, this equation can be used to show
     that $S = H$ at the E.O.Q.)

$$hQ^2 = 2fd$$

$$Q^2 = \frac{2fd}{h}$$

and we obtain

$$Q = \sqrt{\frac{2fd}{h}}$$

To check that a minimum for T does occur, we differentiate the equation for dT/dQ in (10.2.5). Therefore

$$\frac{d^2T}{dQ^2} = (-1)(-2)fd\,Q^{-3} = \frac{2fd}{Q^3}$$

which is positive when Q has the square root value above (indeed, for any positive value of Q). We therefore have a general-purpose formula:

The optimum order quantity which minimizes the total annual cost of inventory

$$T = pd + \frac{hQ}{2} + \frac{fd}{Q} + I$$

is given by

$$\textbf{E.O.Q.} = \sqrt{\frac{2fd}{h}}$$ (10.2.6)

EXAMPLE 10.2.3

A company uses a particular component at a steady rate and the total demand amounts to 3800 units per year. The components are ordered in batches from a supplier and the cost of placing each order is £10. The cost price from the supplier is £6 per component. Storage space running costs are £1 per component per year.

Assuming a notional interest rate on invested capital of 15% p.a., determine the optimum order quantity and the corresponding total annual cost of inventory.

Solution 10.2.3

The key to finding the optimum order quantity and associated cost is to determine d, f, p and h.

$d = 3800$ annual demand
$f = 10$ set-up cost per *order*, independent of order size
$p = 6$ cost price per *unit*

For h, there are two categories of costs to be taken into account. One, an operational cost of £1, is explicitly given. But there is also the substantial opportunity cost of capital tied up in stock, highlighted below, which is based upon the capital outlay per unit (the price p) and the notional rate of return. So

$$h = (\mathbf{0.15 \times 6}) + 1 = 1.9 \quad \text{holding cost per } unit \text{ per annum}$$

and

$$\text{E.O.Q.} = \sqrt{\frac{2fd}{h}} = \sqrt{\frac{2 \times 10 \times 3800}{1.9}} = 200$$

Using this value of Q

$$T = pd + \frac{hQ}{2} + \frac{fd}{Q} + I$$

$$T = (6 \times 3800) + \frac{1.9 \times 200}{2} + \frac{10 \times 3800}{200} + 0$$

$$= 22800 + 190 + 190 = 23180$$

Note that the annual holding cost and annual set-up cost, both £190, are equal for the optimum order quantity, as illustrated by the graph of costs given earlier.

Conclusion: The optimum order quantity is 200, components and the corresponding total annual cost of inventory is £23,180.

Batch production

So far, the emphasis has been on batch **ordering**. However, the E.O.Q. stock control model can be adjusted to the case where a company **produces** an item itself in **batches**. In this case, p is the production cost per unit, f is the set-up cost per batch (which would include the cost of setting up the machinery, and any other costs incurred per batch, which are independent of the batch size), h is the holding cost per unit per annum and d is the annual demand. The **E.B.Q. (Economic Batch Quantity)** is given by the formula

$$\text{E.B.Q.} = \sqrt{\frac{2fd}{h}}$$

EXAMPLE 10.2.4

Consider the batch production of a particular type of fertiliser for which demand is 250 tons per calendar month. The following information is available:

Fertiliser production rate	5 tons/hour
Indirect plant costs	£10000/annum
Direct costs of operating plant	£300/hour
Cost of setting-up	£400/'run'
Cost of raw materials	£20/ton
Fertiliser storage space running costs	£3/ton/annum
Indirect warehousing costs	£20000/annum

If the company adopts a notional rate of return on invested capital of 15% p.a., calculate the optimum batch size and the corresponding total annual cost of inventory.

Solution 10.2.4

$$d = 250 \times 12 = 3000 \qquad annual \text{ demand}$$
$$f = 400 \qquad \text{set-up cost per } batch \text{ (or 'run')}$$

To calculate p, some thought is required. Since p is the direct production cost *per ton*, the raw materials cost of £20 per ton must be part of the calculation. In addition, the direct cost of operating the plant per ton must also play a part. This is $300/5 = £60$ per ton, where the direct plant costs *per hour* have been divided by the production rate per hour. Thus

$$p = 20 + 60 = 80$$

The calculation of h is similar to that in the previous example. Both the opportunity cost of capital per ton per annum (based upon the production cost per ton) and the direct storage space running costs per ton per annum must be included, so

$$h = (0.15 \times 80) + 3 = 15$$

Finally

$$I = 10000 + 20000 \qquad \text{annual indirect cost}$$

Therefore

$$\text{E.B.Q.} = \sqrt{\frac{2fd}{h}} = \sqrt{\frac{2 \times 400 \times 3000}{15}} = 400$$

Using this value of Q

$$T = pd + \frac{hQ}{2} + \frac{fd}{Q} + I$$

$$T = (80 \times 3000) + \frac{15 \times 400}{2} + \frac{400 \times 3000}{400} + 30000 = 276000$$

Conclusion: The optimum 'run' size is 400 tons; annual inventory cost is £276,000.

EXERCISES 10.2

1 A hotel chain is considering its batch ordering policy for a particular type of wine. This sells at a steady rate and the annual demand amounts to 800 crates. The cost price per crate is £16 and the cost of placing an order is estimated to be £5. If a notional interest rate of 25%, p.a. is to be adopted and the supplier makes a delivery charge of £20 per order, calculate the optimum order quantity and the total annual cost of inventory.

2 Askitt Ltd expects to use 2400 tons of butterbran during the coming year, at a cost of £70/ton, and, because the supplier passes on his high set-up cost, the set-up cost to Askitt is £450/order, regardless of order size. Storage of the butterbran involves an indirect warehousing cost of £5000/annum and there is also a direct cost of £10/ton/annum entailed in preventing deterioration during storage. Assuming that the cost of holding stock is 20% per annum of stock value, advise Askitt as to the order quantity which should be adopted, the time interval between orders, and the total annual cost of inventory.

3 Trents Tents Ltd. markets a range of tents, and for one such tent the demand is 100 units per month. The tents are obtained in batches from a foreign supplier who makes a delivery charge of £3000 per batch, and charges £120 for each tent. Trents adopts a notional interest rate of 25% per annum in all inventory calculations. Rental of warehousing incurs a cost of £15 per unit stored per annum.

(a) Advise the company as to the optimum order quantity and the minimum annual cost of inventory.

(b) Trents decides to adopt the order quantity determined in (a) but decides that an order should be placed only when the stock level falls to 100 units, despite the fact that lead-time is 2 months. The company is aware that there will be demand that cannot be immediately fulfilled, but for each unit demanded when none is in stock, the company is prepared to make a special delivery to the customer as soon as stock becomes available. The cost of this action is estimated to be £5 per unit.

Sketch the graph of stock level against time (assuming that the stock level is 300 units at time 0) and show that this order policy leads to a reduction in the total annual cost of inventory. State the revised total annual cost.

(*Hint:* Since the 'no shortages' assumption has been abandoned in (b), you will need to think about how the graph of stock level against time changes. Note that the other assumptions of the E.O.Q. model stated in this section remain the same, and that parts of the equation

$$T = pd + \frac{hQ}{2} + \frac{fd}{Q} + I$$

remain valid.)

4 Jones Ltd uses 2000 of a particular type of container each year, at a steady rate, and has two options open to it. On the one hand, the company can order the containers in batches from Smart Containers Ltd. The price per unit is £80 and the estimated cost of placing each order is £10. The supplier makes a delivery charge of £50/order.

Alternatively, Jones Ltd could produce the container itself in batches by purchasing suitable machinery. Production would entail an indirect cost of £6000 per annum and machine time costs £20/unit. The cost of setting up the machinery for each batch is £500 and the cost of raw materials is £40/unit. Cleaning up after each batch entails a cost of £300.

Storage of the containers entails a direct cost of £8/unit/annum, and Jones Ltd estimates its return on invested capital to be 20% per annum.

Calculate the total annual cost of inventory associated with each of the two alternatives.

10.3 QUANTITY DISCOUNTS

Here we continue with the batch ordering model introduced in the previous section and consider a common practice of suppliers which is to offer incentives, so that customers will purchase **larger orders**. One such incentive is a reduction in the cost price of an item, provided that a sufficiently large quantity of the item is ordered each time. For example, the supplier might offer to reduce the cost price by 5%, provided that 500 units at least are ordered each time.

The advantages of such a 'quantity discount' to the company placing the order are a reduction in the annual cost of buying stock, since the price has been reduced, and a reduction in the annual cost of setting up the orders, since orders are larger and fewer. However, the major disadvantage is that the larger order quantity will increase the stock level and hence significantly increase annual holding costs.

The key question is 'Would a particular company benefit from the discount?' If the company has a relatively low holding cost per unit, with warehousing to spare, and a high set-up cost per order (perhaps due to high delivery charges), then it will probably be happy to reap the benefits of fewer orders, without worrying about the higher stock level. On the other hand, if its holding costs are high, and its set-up costs are low, it would probably prefer to order more often, and keep its stock level down. The key question can therefore be re-phrased thus:

'Will the savings in purchase and set-up costs resulting from the discount outweigh the increase in annual holding costs?'

The procedure for answering this question involves first assessing the effect of the price reduction as though it were unconditional, and not dependent upon any minimum quantity set by the supplier, and then looking at the implications of the minimum quantity imposed.

Effect of an unconditional price reduction

Suppose, for example, that the basic (non-discount) price for an item is £80 per unit, and that the supplier now offers a discount of 5% on the cost price. We shall assume for the purposes of this illustration that

$d = 1800$ an annual demand of 1800 units per annum
$f = 50$ set-up cost of £50 per order

(these will be unaffected by the price reduction, of course), and that the company ordering adopts a rate of return on invested capital of 10% p.a.

At the basic price

$p = 80$
$h = 0.1 \times 80 = 8$ opportunity cost of capital per unit per annum

and at the reduced price

$p = 0.95 \times 80 = 76$ view this as either 5% deducted from £80 or 95% of £80

or

$p = 80 - (0.05 \times 80) = 76$

$h = 0.1 \times 76 = 7.6$ *lower capital outlay per unit means lower opportunity cost of capital per unit per annum*

Thus, for each batch size Q:

$$T = pd + \frac{hQ}{2} + \frac{fd}{Q} + I$$

$$= (80 \times 1800) + \frac{8Q}{2} + \frac{50 \times 1800}{Q} + 0$$

$$= 144000 + 4Q + \frac{90000}{Q} + 0 \quad \text{at basic price}$$

and

$$T = (76 \times 1800) + \frac{7.6Q}{2} + \frac{50 \times 1800}{Q} + 0$$

$$= 136800 + 3.8Q + \frac{90000}{Q} + 0 \quad \text{at discount price}$$

Comparing the T equations at the two prices, we see that, at the discount price, the cost of buying the stock is reduced (by £7200), as predicted earlier, and that, because of the reduction in the holding cost per unit per annum, the annual holding cost is smaller ($3.8Q$ as compared with $4Q$). The example therefore illustrates a useful fact: **a reduction in the cost price reduces the annual cost of inventory, whatever the value of Q.** Put another way, the curve for T

corresponding to the discount price lies below the T curve for the non-discount price, as shown in Figures 10.3.1 and 10.3.2. It follows that the lowest point on the discount price T curve is below the lowest point on the non-discount T curve. Thus **the minimum total annual cost at the discount price is less than the minimum total annual cost at the original price**.

We can test this last statement for the current example by calculating the E.O.Q. for each of the two prices. The economic order quantities at the original and reduced price are, respectively

$$\text{E.O.Q.} = \sqrt{\frac{2fd}{h}} = \sqrt{\frac{2 \times 50 \times 1800}{8}} = 150 \text{ units per order}$$

$$\text{E.O.Q.} = \sqrt{\frac{2fd}{h}} = \sqrt{\frac{2 \times 50 \times 1800}{7.6}} = 154 \text{ units per order (approx.)}$$

These values illustrate another useful fact: **a reduction in the cost price has relatively little effect on the E.O.Q.**; it increases the E.O.Q. only slightly.

Finally, if we substitute these E.O.Q. values into the relevant T equations, we see that

$$T = 144000 + (4 \times 150) + \frac{90000}{150} = 145200 \qquad \text{at basic price}$$

$$T = 136800 + (3.8 \times 154) + \frac{90000}{154} = 137969.62 \qquad \text{at discount price}$$

These calculations confirm that the minimum total annual cost of inventory is indeed lower at the discount price.

Now that we have an understanding of the implications of a price reduction, which, if unconditional, must be beneficial as we have shown, we can now turn our attention to the real issue which is a price discount, offered by the supplier, based upon a **minimum order quantity**.

A procedure for assessing quantity discounts

As the previous example indicated, the **ideal** order quantity is that calculated at the **discount price**, using the **square root formula**. This order quantity is cheapest at the discount price, and cheaper than the cheapest non-discount alternative (again based upon the square root formula, but the non-discount price). However, because of the minimum order quantity set by the supplier, two cases have to be considered, and these are shown graphically in Figures 10.3.1 and 10.3.2. In both graphs, the T curve at the discount price is shown below the non-discount T curve, with the minimum cost point shifted slightly to the right of its non-discount counterpart, as explained previously. The dotted portions of the discount curves are outside the discount range and therefore not applicable.

229

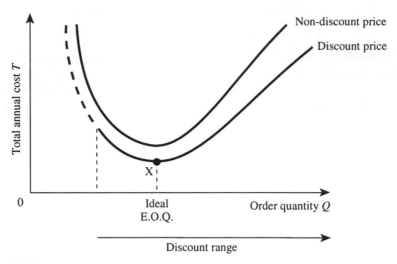

Figure 10.3.1

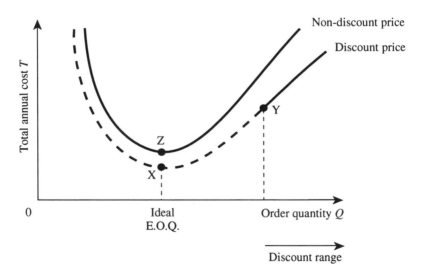

Figure 10.3.2

For the first case (Figure 10.3.1), the ideal E.O.Q., corresponding to point X, is in the discount range, and so can, and should, be adopted. Clearly point X is the lowest cost point overall. For the second case (Figure 10.3.2), the ideal E.O.Q. is not in the range, and, if the discount is to be adopted, a next best alternative order quantity, in the discount range, must be chosen. This quantity is clearly the least quantity earning the discount, since inventory costs are increasing in the discount range. Thus, if the discount is to be adopted, the order quantity at point Y should be chosen. But, now that the ideal order quantity has been rejected, it is not clear that the lowest cost at discount is actually better than that at non-discount; a comparison of the inventory costs at points Y and Z is required.

In summary, the procedure for investigating a quantity discount is as follows:

1 Consider the **discount case**, and calculate the **ideal E.O.Q.** using the discount price and the square root formula.

2 (a) If the ideal E.O.Q. is **in the discount range**, it must result in a lower total cost than the non-discount case.
   (b) If the ideal E.O.Q. is not in the discount range, then:

   • choose the **next best alternative at discount**, which is the **least order quantity earning the discount**, and calculate the associated annual inventory cost
   • calculate the E.O.Q. at the **non-discount price**, and the associated annual inventory cost
   • choose the cheapest alternative.

Note: It may be necessary to compare a number of discount cases.

EXAMPLE 10.3.1

An item is used at a steady rate amounting to 2500 units per annum. It is ordered in batches from a supplier and the total cost of receiving and placing each order is put at £64. The basic price per item is £40 and holding costs are estimated to be 20% p.a. of stock value.

(a) If the supplier offers a discount of 2% on cost price for orders of 1000 items or more, determine the optimum order quantity and the corresponding annual cost of inventory.

(b) The supplier now decides to charge an additional delivery charge of £240 per order, but reduces the minimum quantity earning the discount to 400 items. Calculate the revised optimum order quantity and the minimum total annual inventory cost.

Solution 10.3.1(a)
Following the procedure above, we first consider the discount case and calculate the ideal E.O.Q. As described in step 1 of the procedure, this is given by the square root formula evaluated at the discount price.

Discount case (orders of 1000 units or more required)

$d = 2500 \qquad f = 64$
$p = 0.98 \times 40 = 39.2$ (98% of £40)
$h = 0.2 \times 39.2 = 7.84$ (only the opportunity cost of capital per unit per annum, which is 20% of £39.2, is relevant to h here)

Thus

$$\text{Ideal E.O.Q.} = \sqrt{\frac{2fd}{h}} = \sqrt{\frac{2 \times 64 \times 2500}{7.84}} = 202 \text{ (approx) units per order}$$

This ideal quantity is *below* the discount range of 1000 or more, and so must be *rejected*; therefore part 2(b) of the procedure applies. The next best alternative at discount, which is the *least quantity earning the discount*, is $Q = 1000$.

The minimum total annual cost of inventory at discount is therefore

$$T = (39.2 \times 2500) + \frac{7.84 \times 1000}{2} + \frac{64 \times 2500}{1000} = 0$$

$$T = \underset{\text{buying}}{98000} + \underset{\text{holding}}{3920} + \underset{\text{setting-up}}{160} = £102080 \text{ p.a.} \qquad (10.3.1)$$

Following 2(b) of the procedure, we must now calculate the minimum annual cost at the non-discount price, and compare the total cost with that above. (We have itemized the costs in (10.3.1) so as to make this comparison clearer.)

Non-discount case

$d = 2500$
$f = 64$
$p = 40$
$h = 0.2 \times 40 = 8$

Thus

$$\text{E.O.Q.} = \sqrt{\frac{2fd}{h}} = \sqrt{\frac{2 \times 64 \times 2500}{8}} = 200 \text{ units per order}$$

There is no minimum order quantity for the non-discount case, of course, and so

$$T = pd + \frac{hQ}{2} + \frac{fd}{Q} + I$$

$$= (40 \times 2500) + \frac{8 \times 200}{2} + \frac{64 \times 2500}{200} + 0$$

$$= \underset{\text{buying}}{100000} + \underset{\text{holding}}{800} + \underset{\text{setting-up}}{800} = £101600 \qquad (10.3.2)$$

Conclusion: The discount proves to be *not* worthwhile since it costs £480 more per year. Thus the optimum order quantity is 200 items and the total annual cost of inventory is £101,600.

Note that a comparison of the buying, holding and set-up costs for the T calculations (10.3.1) and (10.3.2) reinforces the points made at the start of this section. In this example, the substantial increase in holding costs for the discount case outweighs the decrease in buying and set-up costs.

Solution 10.3.1(b)
Again we start with the discount case, and calculate the ideal E.O.Q.

Discount case (orders of 400 units or more required)

$d = 2500$
$f = 64 + 240 = 304$ (extra delivery charge of £240 per batch)
$p = 0.98 \times 40 = 39.2$ (as before)
$h = 0.2 \times 39.2 = 7.84$ (as before)

Thus

$$\text{E.O.Q.} = \sqrt{\frac{2fd}{h}} = \sqrt{\frac{2 \times 304 \times 2500}{7.84}} = 440 \text{ (approx) items per order}$$

Now, the ideal E.O.Q. is in the discount range and so, as described in step 2(a) of the procedure, it is cheaper than the *non-discount* alternative. Finally

$$T = (39.2 \times 2500) + \frac{7.84 \times 440}{2} + \frac{304 \times 2500}{440} + 0 = £101452.07$$

which is also cheaper than discount case **(a)**.

Conclusion: The optimum order quantity is now 440 items, with an associated annual inventory cost of £101,452.07.

EXERCISES 10.3

1 A company uses a particular item at a steady rate and orders this in batches from a supplier. Demand for this item is 1200 units/annum. The basic price is £20/item and the cost of placing an order is £7.50. The company adopts a notional rate of return on invested capital of 15% per annum. Storage of the item involves a direct cost of £2/item/annum. The supplier offers two discount possibilities: a discount of 4% on cost price for orders of 300 items or more, or a discount of 8% on cost price for orders of 600 items or more.

(a) Determine the order quantity which should be adopted and the corresponding total annual cost of inventory.

(b) Suppose, now, that the company only has sufficient storage space for 100 items but that additional storage cabinets, each capable of storing up to 200 items, can be leased at an annual cost of £800 each.

Does this information lead you to revise your recommendation to the company and, if so, what order quantity should now be adopted?

2 Stevenson Ltd. uses 1000 metres per month of a specialized laminated paper, which is imported in batches from a supplier. The set-up cost per order is £150 and storage space running costs are estimated to be 50p per metre per annum. The basic price per metre is £10 but the supplier offers a discount of 5% on cost price for orders of 3000 metres or more. Stevenson adopts a return on invested capital of 20% per annum in all inventory calculations.

(a) Show that the discount is worthwhile, and state the optimum order quantity, together with the total annual cost of inventory. State, also, the time interval between orders, and the reorder level (i.e. the stock level at which an order should be placed), assuming that lead-time is 2 months.

(b) Stevenson now decides to negotiate with the supplier for an improved discount on cost price for orders of 3000 metres or more.

Calculate the smallest percentage discount which Stevenson would find acceptable, if the company wishes to reduce the total annual inventory cost by at least £4000.

3 A manufacturer estimates that the demand for a certain item is 3600 per year. The items cost £5 each, and the firm adopts a notional interest rate of 16% p.a. The cost of placing each order is put at £10. A discount of 10% on cost price is allowed on orders of 250 to 799 units, and 15% on orders of 800 items or more. Find the optimum order size and the minimum total annual cost of inventory.

10.4 STOCK CONTROL WITH UNCERTAIN DEMAND

In this section, we no longer assume that demand is constant, but instead make the assumption that it is **randomly** distributed. There are some important implications of variable demand: firstly, it is no longer realistic for a company to avoid shortages; secondly, a company must decide what demand quantity to adopt in calculating the order quantity; and thirdly, it is no longer clear when orders should be placed. The assumptions 2 and 3 stated in section 10.2 are therefore no longer valid; but the other assumptions, concerning a constant batch size, the nature of holding/set-up costs, and constant lead-time, are retained.

Abandoning the no-stockout assumption

Consider a very simple probability distribution of demand for an item which is ordered in batches:

No. of items demanded per month	Probability
0	0.1
20	0.4
40	0.4
60	0.1

In order to be certain of not running out of stock, it would be necessary to order so as to meet the highest demand of 60 units per month; indeed, the demand may stay at this highest level for an extended period of time. The problem is that, *in the long run*, demand will be less than this maximum for 90% of the time, stocks will accumulate and holding costs will be high. Realistically, therefore, stock-outs will be allowed. However, it is assumed that the company will meet any unfulfilled demand immediately stocks become available.

Determining the order quantity

Having decided to allow shortages, the company must decide what demand figure to use in calculating the order quantity. We shall assume here that the **expected (or**

average) demand figure will be used. For the above example, this is calculated by multiplying the monthly demand figures by their probabilities. Therefore

$$\text{Expected monthly demand} = (0 \times 0.1) + (20 \times 0.4) + (40 \times 0.4) + (60 \times 0.1)$$
$$= 30$$

Therefore, $d = 30 \times 12 = 360$ units per annum, and this, together with estimates of f and h, can be inserted into the square-root E.O.Q. formula (10.2.6).

Deciding when orders should be placed

For an order policy, it is necessary to know when orders should be placed, as well as the order quantity. In the original model (section 10.1), both demand and lead-time were constant. It was clear when stock would run out and how long should be allowed for delivery, and so it was easy to determine the **times** at which orders should be placed. Although the assumption of constant lead-time has been retained, the uncertain demand pattern now makes it difficult to predict when shortages will occur, and therefore a time at which to order. One possible approach is to determine a stock level, rather than a time. Whenever the stock level reaches this **reorder level**, an order would be placed.

The graph of stock level against time, which reflects all the aspects discussed so far, is shown in Figure 10.4.1

Calculating the reorder level

A sensible reorder level allows for the expected or average demand during lead-time, since it is while waiting for a delivery that shortages may occur. However, it is usually advantageous to choose a reorder level above the average, in order to reduce the costs associated with shortages, which as we said in the introduction to

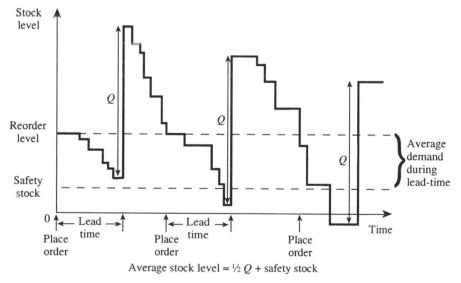

Figure 10.4.1 Stock control under uncertain demand

235

this chapter may result in loss of business, or costs entailed in making special deliveries. The amount by which the reorder level exceeds the average demand during lead-time is called the **safety stock** or **buffer stock**; it is there to protect against very severe shortages. Thus:

Reorder level = Average demand during lead-time + Safety stock   (10.4.1)

As is so often the case in stock control calculations, the calculation of the optimum reorder level is based upon finding a balance between two extremes. One extreme is holding too much safety stock, for which extra holding costs are incurred. The other extreme is holding too little safety stock, and thereby incurring increased costs arising from shortages. The approach is to **experiment with different reorder levels**, and to complete a suitable table.

Consider again the distribution of monthly demand given above which has a mean of 30. We shall assume that lead-time is one calendar month, so that the distribution above is also the distribution of demand during lead-time. From equation (10.4.1)

Reorder level = 30 + safety stock   (10.4.2)

and so the reorder level should be 30 or more. We could try 30, 31, 32, 33, 34, etc. There are many different possibilities, and for that reason we shall restrict the analysis, here and elsewhere, to a set of convenient figures for the reorder levels, e.g. multiples of 5, 10, etc. A table is now drawn up of the form shown below. The first three columns are concerned with holding safety stock, and the next three columns with the costs of shortages. The final column is obtained by adding costs, and the aim is to find the reorder level which minimizes this sum.

A complete example will be considered in a moment, but as an illustration of how the table is completed, consider the three reorder levels shown in column (1). From (10.4.2) the corresponding safety stock levels are obtained by deducting 30, as shown in (2).

Table of costs

(1) Reorder level	(2) Safety stock (s)	(3) Annual cost of holding safety stock	(4) Expected shortfall per lead time	(5) Expected annual shortfall	(6) Expected annual cost of shortfall	(7) Additional cost of safety stock and shortfall
30	0	0	7	168	672	672
40	10	60	2	48	192	252
50	20	120	1	24	96	216

For the purposes of this illustration, we shall assume that the holding cost per unit per annum h is £6, say, and that an optimum order quantity of 15 units per order, say, has already been calculated using the square-root formula (10.2.6). We shall assume also that a cost of £4, say, is incurred for each unit demanded when none is in stock during lead-time.

Since the holding cost for any stock is obtained by multiplying the quantity by h, the safety stock figures are multiplied by £6 to obtain the third column. So much for the holding costs; it is now necessary to account for the shortages, which occur while waiting for stock, and for this another table is required.

Table of shortages per lead-time

Demand during lead-time (one month)	Probability	Reorder levels		
		30	40	50
0	0.1	0	0	0
20	0.4	0	0	0
40	0.4	10	0	0
60	0.1	30	20	10

Consider, for example, the first column corresponding to the reorder level of 30. When the stock level reaches this level, an order is placed, and in the month spent waiting for stock, the demand can be 0, 20, 40 or 60. Since 30 units of stock are on hand when the order is placed, a shortage only occurs for a demand of 40 or 60. The shortage will be 10 units or 30 units, respectively. The other columns are completed in a similar way.

Using the columns, the expected or average number n of units out of stock per lead-time can be calculated for each of the reorder levels. From the first column, multiplying the shortages by the probabilities,

$$n = (0 \times 0.1) + (0 \times 0.4) + (10 \times 0.4) + (30 \times 0.1)$$
$$= 7 \qquad \text{(reorder level 30)}$$

For the second column

$$n = (0 \times 0.1) + (0 \times 0.4) + (0 \times 0.4) + (20 \times 0.1)$$
$$= 2 \qquad \text{(reorder level 40)}$$

Similarly

$$n = 10 \times 0.1$$
$$= 1 \qquad \text{(reorder level 50)}$$

Note that the average shortfall per lead-time decreases as the level of safety stock increases, as one would expect. The figures for n are placed in column (4) of the table of costs, and these figures are then scaled up to annual figures by multiplying by the number of lead-times per year, i.e. the number of orders per year. Since the expected annual demand was calculated to be 360, and an order quantity of 15 was assumed, the number of lead-times = 360/15 = 24. So the figures in column (4) are multiplied by 24 to obtain column (5). Column (6) is then obtained by multiplying column (5) by £4, which is the cost of being one unit out of stock. Finally, column (7) is the sum of the holding costs and costs of shortages calculated in (3) and (6). If the table were to be completed, the figures in column (7) should decrease to a minimum and then start to increase again. The reorder level at which the minimum value occurs is therefore the optimum reorder level.

The next example shows the complete process.

EXAMPLE 10.4.1

The demand per week for a particular item sold by a D.l.Y. Centre is described by the following probability distribution:

Weekly demand	Probability
0	0.13
5	0.27
10	0.27
15	0.19
20	0.09
25	0.04
30	0.01

The D.l.Y. Centre orders the item in batches from a supplier. The cost of setting up an order is £4 and the cost price per item is £32. Lead-time is one week, and for each item demanded when none is in stock during this period, the D.l.Y. Centre makes a special delivery to the customer as soon as stock is received. The cost of this action is £3 per item.

Adopting a notional rate of return on invested capital of 20% per annum, and assuming a 50 week year, determine

(a) the optimum order quantity,

(b) the optimum reorder level (considering only reorder levels which are multiples of 5, for simplicity),

Solution 10.4.1(a)

As explained earlier, the optimum order quantity is based upon the *expected* (or average) annual demand. From the given weekly probability distribution

Expected weekly demand
$$= (0 \times 0.13) + (5 \times 0.27) + (10 \times 0.27) + (15 \times 0.19)$$
$$+ (20 \times 0.09) + (25 \times 0.04) + (30 \times 0.01)$$
$$= 10 \text{ items per week}$$

Therefore,

$$d = 10 \times 50 = 500 \text{ items per year}$$

and

$$f = 4$$
$$p = 32$$
$$h = 0.2 \times 32 = 6.4 \qquad \text{(opportunity cost of capital)}$$

Hence

$$\text{E.O.Q.} = \sqrt{\frac{2 \times 4 \times 500}{6.4}} = 25 \text{ items per order}$$

Note: $500/25 = 20$ orders are placed per year. This will be useful in **(b)**.

Solution 10.4.1(b)

The approach here is to experiment with different reorder levels. First, the **range of reorder levels** must be determined. From (10.4.1)

Reorder level = expected demand during lead-time + safety stock

Since we know that lead-time is one week, and from (a), the expected weekly demand is 10 items

Reorder level = 10 + safety stock

Therefore, the relevant reorder levels are 10, 15, 20, etc. (i.e. reorder levels starting at 10 items, and increasing in steps of 5).

(Note that the ease of calculating the expected demand during lead-time depended upon the time interval (one week) for the given distribution of demand being the same as the lead-time. If this were not the case, we would need to adopt an altogether different approach.)

Having established the range of reorder levels, we next consider shortages.

The table of shortages per lead-time shows the number of items out of stock *per lead-time*, for different combinations of demand and reorder level. Since lead-time is one week, the distribution of demand given in the question can be used. (If you are doubtful about the table, and the calculation of expected shortfalls which follows it, re-read the previous example. The approach is always the same.)

Table of shortages per lead-time

Demand during lead-time (one week)	Probability	Reorder levels				
		10	*15*	*20*	*25*	*30*
0	0.13	0	0	0	0	0
5	0.27	0	0	0	0	0
10	0.27	0	0	0	0	0
15	0.19	5	0	0	0	0
20	0.09	10	5	0	0	0
25	0.04	15	10	5	0	0
30	0.01	20	15	10	5	0

The columns of the table, used in conjunction with the probabilities, can now be used to calculate the **average number (n) of units out of stock per lead-time**, for the different reorder levels.

Using the first column,

$$n = (5 \times 0.19) + (10 \times 0.09) + (15 \times 0.04) + (20 \times 0.01)$$
$$= 2.65 \qquad \text{(reorder level = 10)}$$

Using the second column,

$$n = (5 \times 0.09) + (10 \times 0.04) + (15 \times 0.01)$$
$$= 1 \qquad \text{(reorder level = 15)}$$

239

Similarly

$$n = (5 \times 0.04) + (10 \times 0.01)$$
$$= 0.3 \qquad \text{(reorder level} = 20)$$

$$n = 5 \times 0.01$$
$$= 0.05 \qquad \text{(reorder level} = 25)$$

$$n = 0 \qquad \text{(reorder level} = 30)$$

A cost analysis now completes the calculation of the optimum reorder level.

Table of costs

Reorder level	Safety stock (s)	(3) Annual cost of holding safety stock	Expected shortfall per lead time	Expected annual shortfall (a)	(6) Expected annual cost of shortfall	Additional cost of safety stock and shortfall
		$(s \times h$ $= s \times 6.4)$	(n)	$(n \times \text{orders/yr}$ $= n \times 20)$	$(a \times 3)$	$(3) + (6)$
10	0	0	2.65	53	159	159
15	5	32	1	20	60	92
20	**10**	**64**	**0.3**	**6**	**18**	**82**
25	15	96	0.05	1	3	99

The values in the final column reach a minimum in the third row. So the optimum reorder level is 20 items.

EXERCISES 10.4

1 The distribution of demand per calendar month for a particular type of pump sold by Morley Ltd. is described below, and has a mean of 50.

Monthly demand	Probability
0	0.01
10	0.04
20	0.08
30	0.13
40	0.17
50	0.18
60	0.15
70	0.10
80	0.07
90	0.04
100	0.02
110	0.01

The pumps are ordered in batches from a supplier who charges a price of £20/unit. Morley Ltd. estimates that the cost of holding stock is 20% per annum of stock value and that the cost of placing an order is £12. Lead-time is one calendar month, and for pumps demanded when none are in stock during this period, the company estimates that the cost is £5 per pump (this being an estimate of the cost of loss of goodwill).

Determine

(a) the optimum order quantity

(b) the optimum reorder level, considering only those levels which are multiples of 10

(c) the total annual cost of inventory.

2 The table below shows the distribution of weekly demand (with a mean of 25) for one type of outboard motor marketed by Aquamatic Ltd., and obtained in batches from a supplier.

Weekly demand	Probability
0	0.01
5	0.03
10	0.08
15	0.14
20	0.18
25	0.18
30	0.14
35	0.10
40	0.07
45	0.04
50	0.02
55	0.01

Aquamatic Ltd. pays the supplier £160 for each motor and the supplier makes a delivery charge of £72/batch. Aquamatic estimates the cost of storage to be £2/unit/annum. Lead-time is one week, and for each unit demanded when none is in stock, during this period, Aquamatic Ltd. offers a concessionary price to the customer, and the cost of this action to the company is £16/unit. The company adopts a rate of return on invested capital of 10% p.a. A 50 week year is to be assumed.

(a) The optimum order quantity for the motors, sufficient to meet average demand, has already been calculated, and is 100 motors per order. Considering only those reorder levels which are multiples of 5, determine the optimum reorder level.

(b) An important assumption underlying the answer to (a) is that stock-outs *are* allowed. If, instead, the company adopted a policy of never running out of stock, what is the optimum order quantity? (N.B. It is not necessary to consider reorder levels here.)

3 Chemico Ltd. markets a range of chemicals which are ordered in batches from a supplier. For one of these, demand is variable as described by the following table:

Monthly demand (tons)	Probability
0	0.10
10	0.12
20	0.17
30	0.24
40	0.17
50	0.11
60	0.05
70	0.03
80	0.01

The cost of placing each order is £40, and each ton costs £180. Lead-time is one month and, for each ton demanded when none is in stock during this period, Chemico make a special delivery, at a cost of £15, as soon as stock becomes available.

Assuming that Chemico adopts a notional rate of return of 10% p.a. in all inventory calculations, determine the optimum order quantity and the optimum reorder level. Determine, also, the total annual cost of inventory. (For the reorder level calculations, consider only reorder levels which are multiples of 10.)

11

ORGANIZING AND HANDLING DATA

When you have completed this chapter you will be able to:

- distinguish between data and statistics and between primary and secondary data
- distinguish between discrete and continuous data
- describe the processes involved in gathering data by questionnaire
- distinguish between different types of statistical survey
- organize numerical data by ranking and by grouping
- count frequencies and group frequencies of organized data
- store numerical data in tables

Perhaps one of the more important aspects of business analysis is the ability to predict the future or, at least, to be able to make some sort of assessment regarding the occurrence of future events. Any assessment of the future requires a knowledge of the past and present and before any predictions can be made we need to be able to describe the past and present in rational terms. Very often the information required is contained within numerical data which needs to be gathered, organized and analysed. This is the role of *statistics*.

11.1 DATA AND STATISTICS

The discipline of *statistics* is concerned with the gathering, the organization and the eventual analysis of data, and the data we shall be concerned with will be numerical data: collections of numbers. One of the by-products of the eventual analysis of the data is a further, smaller collection of numbers that can be taken to represent the data in a more compact form. These numbers derived from the data are called *statistics*.

EXAMPLE 11.1.1

Distinguish briefly between:

(a) data and statistics

(b) continuous and discrete data.

Solution 11.1.1(a)

A **datum** is a number or a sequence of alphanumeric characters – the word **data** being the plural of the singular datum. When a datum is placed within a context so as to give it *meaning*, the datum then carries **information**. What is meant by the words *meaning* and *information* will be assumed for our purposes to be self-evident. They are, indeed, not self-evident but a detailed discussion of meaning and information is not appropriate here. For example, the number 9780201624199 is a datum as is the sequence of alphanumeric characters B858BHD. When the number 9780201624199 is placed beneath the black and white stripes of a bar-code on a can of beans the number is given context and carries with it information sufficient for a computer to account for the sale of the beans when the can passes the laser beam at a supermarket checkout. When the second datum is placed on a car's number plate as B 858 BHD it is given context and carries meaning – the first letter B indicates the year and the letters HD indicate the place in which the car was registered. Numerical data representing *quantities* rather than non-numerical data which can be used to represent *qualities* have the advantage that they can be manipulated according to all the rules of arithmetic and such numerical data forms the basic stock of a study of statistics.

Having gathered and organized a collection of numerical data what remains is still a collection of numbers. Somehow we need to be able to describe the information that the numbers contain in a form that is understandable. To do this we can resort to a graphical display of the data in the form of bar charts, pie charts or even pictograms. The problem with this form of display is that it only gives a general idea of the information contained within the data. Often we require a more precise, quantitative description of the information and this is where the notion of a statistic comes in.

A **statistic** is a single number that describes a specific feature of a collection of numerical data. For example, if the heights of five people are measured in metres (m) as:

1.85 m   2.01 m   1.96 m   1.75 m   1.88 m

then the **sum** of their heights is:

9.45 m

The number 9.45 is a *statistic* and represents the *sum* or *total* property of the data. Part of the study of statistics is the study of how we can glean these specific numbers from the numerical data so as to describe the information in the data in the most efficient manner possible. This aspect of the study of statistics is called *descriptive statistics*. It should be noted that descriptive statistics usually only has real worth when comparing one collection of data with another.

Data is obtained by measuring attributes: the heights of ..., the weights of ..., the number of .... The entities whose attributes are being measured are referred to as the *population* from which the data is derived. Very often the population is so large that it is not possible to measure the attributes of it in its entirety. For example, to measure the weight of each head of barley in a complete crop would present a virtually impossible task. The best that can be done is to measure a sample drawn from the full crop. This leads to a second and further aspect of the study of statistics which deals with attempting to describe the properties of a large population from a knowledge of a small sample drawn from the population. This aspect of the study of statistics is called *inferential statistics* and requires a coupling of descriptive statistics and the notion of probability. Unlike descriptive statistics, inferential statistics can have worth when applied to a single collection of data as can be readily understood when considering the gathering of data for an opinion poll.

Solution 11.1.1(b)

Data is obtained by measuring. Whether you are measuring the lengths of pieces of string, recording the time it takes to bake a cake or simply counting the number of sheep through a gate you are obtaining data by measuring. Such data can be distinguished as being either *continuous* or *discrete* depending upon the nature of that which is being measured. For example, if the data came from measuring something that varied against a continuous scale such as length or time then the data would be described as **continuous data**. If, on the other hand, the data came from measuring something that varied, not continuously, but in jumps such as the number of sheep then the data would be described as **discrete**. Sometimes, data appears to be discrete when it is continuous. For example, if times were being measured and the data was recorded only to the nearest hour the data would appear to be discrete when in fact it is continuous; what matters is the *scale against which the data is measured*. As a further example, when measuring the heights of students the data gathered would be recorded only to the nearest centimetre thereby giving it the appearance of being discrete. However, the heights are actually measured against a continuous scale; for a person to grow from a height of 1.5 m to a height of 1.7 m they have to attain every possible height in between. Consequently, the heights of the students are considered to be continuous data.

11.2 SOURCES OF DATA

Sources of data are to be found everywhere. Whether you wish to find out for yourself by conducting your own statistical survey or whether you wish to use results found by someone else's survey for your own purposes there is no shortage of data.

EXAMPLE 11.2.1

Describe the differences between primary and secondary data, indicating sources of such data and the limitations of secondary data.

Solution 11.2.1

There are two different types of statistical data, *primary* data and *secondary* data. **Primary data** or *first-hand data* is data that has been gathered for a well specified purpose during a statistical survey. For example, if you were to stand in the High Street and question passersby about their taste in music you would be

245

conducting a statistical survey and gathering primary data – gathering your data first-hand. **Secondary data** or *second-hand data* is data that has already been gathered for one purpose but is now going to be used for another purpose. For example, the National Lottery publish all the data relating to past lottery draws on the Internet. Two such sets of data consist of:

The number of times a given number has been drawn
The last date a given number was drawn

This data was gathered to demonstrate the past performance of the National Lottery. Once published, this data can now be used to estimate the likely performance in future lottery draws. It can be used to work out the odds of selecting a winning combination of six numbers the following week and as such it forms secondary data – data that was gathered to describe the past behaviour of the lottery balls but is now being used to predict the future behaviour of the lottery balls.

Sources of primary data

Primary data is data that is gathered first-hand. The data is gathered for a specific purpose and the data collector is fully aware of both how it has been gathered and the subsequent processing it has undergone. As a result the accuracy and the relevance of the primary data is fully comprehended by those responsible for collecting it. Because it requires a substantial labour force to gather primary data the only organisations capable of collecting it are those with access to significant amounts of money such as Government Agencies and large companies.

The Government gathers primary data to enable it to govern effectively. They need to be able to measure the results of their actions and to plan future policies. For this they require, and they obtain, a vast amount of data which is subsequently published in various journals. Typical of these journals are:

- *Monthly Digest of Statistics*
  Published each month by Her Majesty's Stationery Office, this journal is prepared by the Central Statistical Office (a section of the Civil Service) and the Statistical Divisions of various Government departments. The purpose of the digest is to provide a continual statistical description of the state of the country on a wide spectrum of topics ranging from the National Income Expenditure and External Trade to Industrial Production and Agriculture and Social Services. The *Annual Abstract of Statistics* contains much of the contents of the *Digest* in even greater detail.

- *Financial Statistics*
  Prepared each month by the Central Statistical Office, the statistical divisions of Government departments and the Bank of England this important publication details the Government's revenue and spending, local authority borrowing and the financial statistics of various large companies.

- *Employment Gazette*
  Prepared by the Department of Trade and Industry, this publication deals with all aspects of manpower and employment, detailing wages, hours worked and retail prices.

Many companies will gather primary data within their own organizations to assist them in their administration and planning. A few large companies will have sufficient funds to obtain primary data from outside their organization dealing with specific markets relating to their products and activities. This is clearly very important for those companies wishing to launch a new product or to modify an existing product.

Sources of secondary data

When primary data is used for purposes other than those for which it has been gathered it becomes a source of secondary data. For example, the following table displays the result of gathering primary data. It has been taken from the *Monthly Digest of Statistics* and represents only a very small part of a table dealing with the UK import trade:

United Kingdom Imports (European Community £millions)

Year	£million
1989	63,827
1990	65,984
1991	61,328
1992	65,609
1993	75,475
1994	83,457

This table has been constructed from information taken from a variety of sources for the purpose of displaying how much the UK has spent importing goods and services from the other countries in the European Union. From this data it can be seen that as the UK went into recession during 1991 the imports decreased. From 1992 onwards the value of imports has steadily increased. If we were to use this data as an indicator that the UK recession is becoming a memory of the past then we would be using this data as secondary data. Whilst this inference might be a reasonable one to make it may not be quite so reasonable to further infer that because we were now spending more on imports we had more money and therefore the country was becoming more financially viable. To make this inference we should have to look at other information such as the value of the country's exports and the ongoing balance of trade. The purposes for which the import data was gathered would then be quite different to the purposes for which we were using the data.

Limitations of secondary data

Secondary data is limited simply because it is second-hand. When the original primary data was collected it was done so for a specific purpose. For example, if a survey were instituted across a collection of specific geographic regions by a Finance House to determine in each area the size of the average mortgage held by a householder compared with the current market value of the property against which the mortgage was held then restrictions would necessarily be placed on the survey. Firstly, the locations to include in a given geographical region would be determined by the convenience of the Finance House. Secondly, because the Finance House would only wish to interview mortgagees they would eliminate from their enquiries all those people who rented their accommodation. The data so gathered would constitute primary data because it was collected first-hand and one element of the information so gleaned would be an average house price for each region. If at some later date a newspaper was searching for data on house prices and they came across the results of the survey they might be tempted to use it as secondary data to prove a point regarding regional house prices. If the newspaper was unaware that it only covered houses against which a mortgage was held and, furthermore, the householder was the mortgagee then the data could very well be used as a misrepresentation of the actual state of affairs. There are many people who own houses and do not have a mortgage against them and the prices of all these houses have been left out of the original survey; indeed who is to know whether their inclusion would or would not significantly affect the newspaper's conclusions – certainly the newspaper does not know.

11.3   GATHERING DATA

People form an ideal source of data. Whether you are asking them questions of fact or opinion the process is the same: you must ask questions and the art of constructing a good questionnaire is one that must be learnt.

EXAMPLE 11.3.1

Describe the use of a questionnaire as a means of gathering primary data and illustrate your answer with reference to the Population Census.

Solution 11.3.1

Questionnaire   There are two basic types of questionnaire, the postal and the non-postal. The advantage of a postal questionnaire is that it can be cheaply distributed to a large number of people. The disadvantages are that there is usually a poor level of response and it is not easy to explain any questions in the event of a query. On the other hand, a non-postal questionnaire, delivered door-to-door, may have a higher response rate but the cost of distribution is far higher. For this reason the distribution would be limited to fewer people. Every questionnaire should possess the following:

- *Object and authority*
  This describes what the enquiry is trying to establish and why it is attempting to establish it along with who is trying to establish it.

- *Instructions*
  These detail how to complete the questionnaire, when to complete it and how the completed questionnaire is to be returned.

- *Details of the respondent*
  If the questionnaire requires the details of the respondent then only those details relevant to the enquiry should be requested.

- *The body of the enquiry*
  The questions that form the main body of the enquiry should be well set apart from the remainder of the questionnaire. The questions should be clearly and concisely stated and be capable of being precisely answered: for example, questions whose answers can be given as yes or no, by selecting one from a pre-coded answer list or by requesting answers on a rating scale. This does not mean that open-ended questions cannot be asked but it must be borne in mind that answers to open-ended questions do need to be interpreted, a task that may render the responses of little value due to a subjective interpretation.

The Population Census   The Population Census is a Government questionnaire distributed to all householders every ten years. Though the idea of a Census is very old – the Babylonians were taking them 4,000 years ago – the first British Census was not held until 1801. The purpose of the Census is to provide information on social, economic and population conditions to allow the Government to plan future policy. It is completed by every householder in the country on one specified evening. Because of the widespread distribution the handling of the Census is very expensive and time consuming. It requires an elaborate organisation to distribute it with upwards of 100,000 enumeration districts and a number of years to analyse it. To ensure a complete enumeration it is compulsory to fill it in. To enable this the questionnaire is preceded by a Census Act that makes it a criminal offence not to comply with the requirements.

The questionnaire is in three parts dealing with:

Housing
People present on Census night
People usually present but absent on Census night.

By taking such a 'snapshot' view of the country's population it is possible to measure population movement both within the country and without and to predict the size of the population in the future with a reasonable degree of accuracy.

EXERCISES 11.3

1   Find the flaws in each of the following questions and amend them so that they could be sensibly answered on a questionnaire:

(a) Do you like dogs and cats?

(b) How much PAYE do you pay each week?

(c) How much alcohol do you consume in a week?

(d) Do you eat healthy food?

(e) What time do you go to bed?

(f) How many colds have you had in the past five years?

(g) How good are you at statistics?

(h) Do you think that Scotland should have a devolved assembly or do you think it should be a totally separate country?

(j) With the collapse of the Soviet Union do you not think we should foster closer ties with Russia?

2 Which method would you use to obtain precise answers on a questionnaire to each of the following questions (you may have to re-phrase the question)?

(a) How many doors do you have in your home?

(b) Do you catch a bus to work?

(c) How many hours did you work last week?

(d) Do you like sweets?

(e) What is your opinion of the present Prime Minister?

(f) How do you rate your golfing skills?

11.4 STATISTICAL SURVEYS

Having decided that you need to gather data first hand there are a number of considerations that must be borne in mind. Not least of these is cost which can be a very crucial factor in determining the type of survey to be conducted if you wish to question a large number of people.

EXAMPLE 11.4.1

Describe different types of statistical survey methods of gathering primary data with particular reference to:

(a) Interviews   **(b)** Diaries

Solution 11.4.1

Statistical surveys   Statistical surveys are fact finding exercises that are carried out by various means such as interviews, questionnaires or diaries. The type of statistical survey employed depends upon the purposes for which the data is being gathered:

- *Pilot survey*
  A pilot survey is a small-scale replica of the eventual full-scale survey. It provides basic information such as the effectiveness of the questions on a questionnaire. It is a small investigative survey that establishes the procedures and the analysis prior to the issuing of the questionnaire in the full blown survey.

- *Panel survey*
  In a panel survey a particular group – called a panel – is asked a series of questions on different occasions so that the changing reactions and awareness of individuals can be monitored. They can be used to test the effectiveness of an advertising campaign by asking questions before and after the campaign. In this way their reactions can be accurately measured.

- *Longitudinal survey*
  This is the same as a panel survey but the monitoring of the group continues over an extended period of time. For example, a selection of children can be continually inspected to monitor their growth patterns over the entire period of their childhood. In this way conclusions can be obtained regarding child growth patterns within the entire population.

- *Market research survey*
  A Company will use the Market Research survey to discover who uses their product and why they use it in preference to a competing product. Market Research Surveys monitor buying habits; test reaction to packaging; collect opinions. They are usually executed by paid interviewers and some companies exist purely to perform Market Research for other companies. It is an expensive operation.

- *Public opinion polls*
  A Public Opinion Poll is a survey that obtains the opinions of members of the public on one or more issues. A more detailed discussion of Public Opinion Polls is given in the next chapter.

Non-response   Non-response must always be borne in mind when considering the results of a survey. There is really very little that can be done to remedy non-response but awareness of non-response is necessary because it is a source of error. It is possible for a badly handled survey to generate a non-response amongst the very people that it was aimed at. In every human situation the person observed is affected by the person observing – even observing by asking questions. For example, a Systems Analyst studying the working habits of a company's labour force may find a level of resentment against his presence. This resentment could then affect the analyst's observations to such an extent that the ultimate conclusions may be at best suspect and at worst invalid.

Surveys can be conducted by interview, either direct or indirect, by questionnaire or by use of a diary.

(a) *Interviews*
Collecting data by means of an interview permits a respondent to be asked questions on a person-to-person basis. Interviews are either direct or indirect. In the direct interview the questioner and the respondent face each other and the success or otherwise of the interview will depend upon the skill and the personality of the interviewer. The interviewer must posses an ability to manage people, an ability to listen, an ability to put the respondent at ease and an ability to persuade the respondent to answer the questions. To some people these skills come naturally, others have to acquire them through formal training courses.

An interviewer must be lively and give the impression of interest in the answers to the questions even if the respondent is the hundredth person they have interviewed that day. The interviewer must possess tact and must neither offend nor generate hostility in the person being interviewed. Otherwise the answers will reflect that immediate hostility rather than the considered opinion. The interviewer's feeling about the questions must not be allowed to colour the respondent's feelings thereby affecting the answers. The phrasing of questions must be accurate and the answers must be accurately acquired and accurately recorded.

A typical indirect interview would be conducted by telephone where the interviewer and the person being interviewed are remote from one another. In this situation the interviewer must establish his or her skills without the benefit of eye contact. Because of this additional skills are required. The interviewer's manner must be pleasing and cheerful even in the face of hostility. At all times the interviewer must be polite. The interviewer should ensure that he or she speaks clearly and distinctly. The questions should be particularly short, as should the entire interview, otherwise the respondent may lose interest.

(b) *Diary*
A diary is a record of all the events that happen to a group of people in relation to some specific facet of life: for example, the Family Expenditure Survey and the Viewing Diary in the USA. In the Family Expenditure Survey a number of families each keep a diary of their expenditure over a given period. In the Viewing Diary a selection of households record their television viewing. This is of assistance to the various television companies when planning their future programmes. In the USA a large number of the television programmes are sponsored by specific advertisers. In order to convince the advertisers that there will be sufficient viewers to see their commercials the television companies use the results of the Viewing Diaries.

The advantage of a diary is that a complete record of a group of families can be obtained thereby allowing very accurate data to be obtained. The disadvantage of a diary is that only the more aware people are likely to keep the diary fully maintained. Since the diary is supposed to record all events pertinent to an enquiry it will inevitably be biased towards these more aware individuals.

EXERCISES 11.4

1 Describe how you would set about finding answers to the following questions. You must pose a sensible question, construct a questionnaire and then decide who is to complete it and how it is to be returned:

(a) What is the average number of newspapers sold by 10 newsagents?

(b) What is the average fare paid on a specific bus route over a week?

(c) What is the most popular stock item sold in a local clothes shop during a particular month?

(d) How many people own an umbrella?

2 You have just been elected to the Student Council with a brief to execute a statistical survey to provide information about the personal finances of the student body in your institution. The information that you collect will be used in conjunction with similar data provided by other Colleges to bring the plight of student poverty to the attention of Central Government. To be taken seriously the statistical survey must be conducted in the most impartial manner possible.

(a) Construct a questionnaire that will:

   (i)   ask questions that are pertinent to the information you require

   (ii) cover all aspects of student finances yet be as brief as possible

   (iii) contain responses that are easily and quickly analysed

(b) There are 15,000 students in your College and your time is limited. Describe how you are going to select those students who are going to be given the questionnaire.

(c) How will you encourage students selected to fill in the questionnaire and how will you cater for non-response?

(d) How do you think being a poor student yourself would affect your judgement in posing the questions?

11.5 ORGANIZING NUMERICAL DATA

Before data can be analysed to extract the information that it contains it is necessary to organize it in a form suitable for analysis. The simplest method of sorting numerical data is to rank it in numerical order, either ascending or descending.

EXAMPLE 11.5.1

(a) Organize the following numerical data by first ranking in ascending order and then counting the data frequencies:

10	12	11	13	14	15	15	15	14	10
13	12	10	13	12	15	14	11	11	12
14	10	11	15	14	13	14	11	12	15

(b) Organize the following numerical data by ranking in ascending order, oganizing into groups and then counting the data group frequencies:

10	12	21	43	34	15	45	25	44	40
33	42	20	43	32	45	44	31	41	42
44	40	11	45	44	13	24	41	42	45

253

Solution 11.5.1(a)

When numerical data has been obtained it must be edited into a useful format for further analysis. If the further analysis requires finding the number of times a data value appears in the list of data then *ranking* in *ascending order* provides a useful format to achieve this. This numerical data is ranked in ascending order as follows:

10	10	10	10	11	11	11	11	11
12	12	12	12	12	13	13	13	13
14	14	14	14	14	14	15	15	15
15	15	15						

By ranking the data in this way we can now easily count the number of times a particular datum appears in the list. That is we count the data frequencies:

Frequencies

10	10	10	10			4
11	11	11	11	11		5
12	12	12	12	12		5
13	13	13	13			4
14	14	14	14	14	14	6
15	15	15	15	15	15	6

Total 30

Notice the total at the bottom. The frequencies must add up to the total number of data items; this provides a check that the counting has been done correctly.

Solution 11.5.1(b)

When numerical data has values over a wide range it is often not appropriate to count the frequencies of the actual data values because many individual values may only appear once and many intermediate values may not appear at all. In such a situation the data is organized into groups and the number of data items in each group is then counted to give the *group frequencies*. First, as before, the numerical data is ranked in ascending order as follows:

10	11	12	13	15	20	21	24	25	31
32	33	34	40	40	41	41	42	42	42
43	43	44	44	44	44	45	45	45	45

The data groups are designated to be:

10–19, 20–29, 30–39, 40–49

The choice of groups is dependent upon the data, there is no absolute rule. The guiding principle is to keep the number of groups to a reasonable size and to a reasonable number.

Having ranked the data and defined the groups it is a simple matter to count the group frequencies.

Groups									*Group frequencies*
10–19	10	11	12	13	15				5
20–29	20	21	24	25					4
30–39	31	32	33	34					4
40–49	40	40	41	41	42	42	42	43	43
	44	44	44	44	45	45	45	45	17

Total 30

EXERCISES 11.5

1 Organize the following numerical data by first ranking in ascending order and then counting the data frequencies:

5	0	6	0	7	3	8	10	6
8	3	10	10	3	0	6	10	3
6	3	5	7	6	4	9	0	5
0	8	10	6	5	9	7	3	9
0	6	5	4	10	3	8	5	10
8	4	3	5	8	3	10		

2 Organize the following numerical data by ranking in ascending order, organizing into groups and then counting the data group frequencies:

2.32	43.56	23.37	3.77	56.74	27.83	4.75
40.31	22.77	62.39	33.67	51.76	35.54	30.01
63.44	47.59	88.23	59.19	27.34	92.36	74.52
21.94	3.44	29.95	36.57	61.45	43.67	69.91
49.32	32.76	76.98	33.31	47.88	84.57	39.54
57.80	30.18	1.03	39.92	77.34	50.34	27.56
49.69	71.04	20.11	105.66	59.91	28.17	

11.6 TABULATING DATA

Numerical data can best be displayed by arranging it in tables; regular arrays of rows and columns.

EXAMPLE 11.6.1
Describe how tables can be used to display data, indicating those features which add clarity and quality to the display.

Solution 11.6.1
Tables are used for storing data. For every type of table there are a number of rules to be followed when constructing them.

Columnar layout The entries in a table have to be easily located and accurately read. For these reasons the entries are placed in well-defined *rows* and *columns*. This is called a *columnar layout*. The following diagram illustrates this feature.

	Column 1	Column 2	Column 3
Row 1	0.45	0.01	11
Row 2	1.33	1.10	134
Row 3	5.88	6.44	912

Notice how the entries are placed. The decimal points are all under each other and the whole numbers in the third column are *right justified* – that is they all have the respective units, tens, hundreds and so on under each other.

Spacing and partitions As shown in the previous diagram the rows and columns are partitioned with vertical and horizontal lines. This produces a table whose entries are easily located. Also there is sufficient space in each *cell* to hold the entry without appearing cramped. This allows the data to be easily read. Notice also that the numbers are separated from the words by heavy lines. The words are called the row and column *labels* and they are separated from the body of the table by this means.

Column and row labels It must be clear what the entries in the table refer to. This is achieved by putting a description at the head of each row and column. The following table records the annual profits analysed over two-monthly intervals at a local DIY store.

Year	Jan/Feb	Mar/Apr	May/Jun	Jul/Aug	Sep/Oct	Nov/Dec
1995	234.67	322.76	455.89	934.66	872.56	788.23
1996	344.78	377.68	591.64	994.67	903.71	845.93

Notice how the columns have been labelled with abbreviations for the months of the year. This is permissible because these abbreviations are common knowledge. If abbreviations are used that are not commonly understood then a *key* must be given to explain them. This table in this example is particularly straightforward. It becomes a little more awkward when there are *multiple* rows or columns.

Multiple rows or columns Some tables have a group of columns or rows under a single label. The following table records the number of completed sales and sales enquiries connected to three salespersons over two weeks.

	Andrew		Belinda		Caradoc	
	Sales	Enquiries	Sales	Enquiries	Sales	Enquiries
Week 1	24	123	36	156	34	163
Week 2	27	135	23	104	28	174

Arrangement of data   The data should be stored in the table in a logical order. For instance, the following rearrangement of a previous table would be very confusing.

Year	Mar/Apr	Nov/Dec	Jul/Aug	May/Jun	Sep/Oct	Jan/Feb
1995	322.76	788.23	934.66	455.89	872.56	234.67
1996	377.68	845.93	994.67	591.64	903.71	344.78

Space for calculated data   Many times, after data has been entered into a table, some preliminary calculations, called *summary statistics*, have to be entered. For example, a particular column may require a total of all its entries to be calculated. The result of such a calculation is best embodied within the table so sufficient space should be allotted to it. The following table records the enrolment of students into specified areas of study at a university.

	Business studies	Engineering	Science	Total
1993	234	348	264	846
1994	321	305	258	884
1995	456	286	268	1010
1996	508	252	232	1082
Total	1609	1191	1022	3822

The number in the bottom right-hand corner is called the *grand total* and is a check that all the earlier additions are correct. It is obtained by adding all the totals above it. This should then be the same as the sum of all the totals to the left of the grand total.

Headers and footers   Every table needs to have a *header* that contains a *title*. The title should be concise yet not so brief that it does not convey the essence of what the table contains.

Many tables need a *footer* underneath them. This footer should contain:

- *Description*
  The description of the contents of the table should always be included in the footer if the title is not adequate.

257

- *Explanation*

Sometimes certain data need to be accompanied by an explanation. This is done in the footer. For example,

Sales record £'000

Quarter	1	2	3
Anne	4	5	8
Barry	3	5	7
Colin	—	4	0*
Doreen	—	8	6

* Colin left during the second quarter.

Keys A *key* is a list of explanations of abbreviations or symbols used in the table. The following table records the uses of stationery pads by a company during the month of September.

Stationery pads	A	B	C	D
Quantity used (doz.)	3	5	8	15

Key: A: A4
B: A3
C: A5
D: Shorthand notebooks

Sources There are occasions when the title and the description of the data do not adequately explain where the data was obtained. This is especially so if the data was obtained from a source of primary data. In a situation such as this the source of the data should be given in the footer.

EXERCISES 11.6

1 The audience figures for each performance during a five week run of *She Stops to Conker* in a theatre with a seating capacity of 721 were as follows:

Week	Mon	Tue	Wed	Thur	Fri	Sat
1	453	346	562	244	478	654
2	407	206	675	377	573	559
3	491	177	582	285	581	692
4	357	372	693	336	604	586
5	507	405	529	304	628	634

Construct a suitable annotated table for these figures and include totals and capacity percentages for columns and rows with a grand total at the end.

2   You have been asked by the Sales Director to prepare a table describing the sales of those items for which you and your team are responsible for selling. The Sales Director wishes to see every item listed along with the individual sales *for each week of the month of March*. She also wishes to see totals of each item sold in the month along with the sub-totals of each week. The items that you are responsible for are:

Pens
   Black, Blue and Red
Pencils
Pads of paper
   A4 Narrow lines, A4 Wide lines and Shorthand notepads
Computer discs
   $3\frac{1}{2}$ inch and $5\frac{1}{4}$ inch
Computer print-out
   Plain A4 and Plain quarto

Construct a table in readiness for the data to be entered showing clearly the divisions between items and the locations of the appropriate totals.

12

AVERAGES AND THE SPREAD OF DATA

When you have completed this chapter you will be able to:

- calculate any one of a number of averages of a collection of data
- calculate measures of spread of a collection of data
- calculate various fractiles for a collection of data

12.1 AVERAGES

If someone said to you that the average age of their class was 18 years you would have in your minds eye a group of people where an 18 year old would in some respect represent the entire class – the 18 year old would be *typical* of the membership of the class. This is the role of the average – to act as a representative of the group. It is one of the simplest statistics to think of and certainly the simplest statistic to use as a representative of a collection of data. There is, however, a complication: there is more than one average.

EXAMPLE 12.1.1

Distinguish between the mean, the median and the mode for the following data:

5, 7, 8, 8, 9, 9, 9, 9, 9, 11, 11, 12, 12, 15, 16

Solution 12.1.1

The simplest single statistic that can be used to describe the typical value of a collection of numerical data is the *average*. There is more than one measure of average and which one to use depends upon the type of information required.

Median Perhaps the simplest average is the *median*. If all the numerical data is ranked in size ranging from the smallest to the largest then the median is the *middle datum*. In this case the data as presented is already ranked and the median, the middle datum, is a 9. If there is an even number of data values then there is no middle datum. In this case the median is the number that is halfway between the middle data. For example, the median of the four numbers:

1, 2, 3, 4

is 2.5 – being the number halfway between 2 and 3. *Notice* that the median need not be one of the data values.

Mode When numerical data contains repeated values the mode is that datum that is most often repeated. In this case the mode is again 9 since there more 9s than any other data value.

Means Whereas the median and the mode are largely qualitative descriptors of data the means are quantitative descriptors.

- *Arithmetic mean*
  The arithmetic mean is found by adding up all the data values and dividing by the number of data values added. In this case there are 15 data values and they add up to 150. Hence the arithmetic mean is:

  $$150 \div 15 = 10$$

  Notice that 10 is not one of the data values. It is not necessary that a mean be one of the data values.

- *Geometric mean*
  The geometric mean is found by multiplying all the data values together and finding the nth root of the product of all *n* values. In this case the product of the 15 data values is:

  $$5.5312 \times 10^{14}$$

  and the 15th root of this number is:

  $$(5.5312 \times 10^{14})^{1/15} = 9.61$$

  to two decimal places. The geometric mean is used rather than the arithmetic mean when the data describes rates of change; the geometric mean gives the correct average rate of change whereas the arithmetic mean does not.

- *Harmonic mean*
  The harmonic mean is found by adding all the reciprocals of the data values, dividing by the number of reciprocals added and then taking the reciprocal of the result. In this case the harmonic mean is:

  $$1/\{[1/5 + 1/7 + 1/8 + 1/8 + 1/9 + 1/9 + 1/9 + 1/9 + 1/9 + 1/11 + 1/11 + 1/12 + 1/12 + 1/15 + 1/16]/15\} = 9.22 \text{ to 2 decimal places}$$

  When calculating speeds over equal distances the harmonic mean is the average to use to obtain a correct measure for the average speed.

EXERCISE 12.1

1 Find the median, the arithmetic mean, the geometric mean and the harmonic mean of each of the following collection of numbers:

(a) 1, 2, 4, 8, 16, 32, 64, 128, 256

(b) −7, −5, −3, −1, 1, 3, 5, 7

(c) 11, 15, 16, 21, 31, 54, 17, 9, 36, 5, 8, 11, 27, 3, 2

(d) −7, 9, −2, 14, −5, 31, −17, 8, −19, 6, −1, 15, −14, 27

12.2 THE SPREAD OF DATA

Consider the two sets of data:

10, 20, 30, 40, 50   and   28, 29, 30, 31, 32

They both have the same arithmetic mean of 30. We have said that the average represents the whole of the data and here we have the same value of 30 representing two quite different collections of data. But how do the two collections of data differ? They differ by the extent to which the data values are *spread* about the mean. In the first collection the data is widely spread about the mean whereas in the second collection they are more narrowly concentrated around the mean. Clearly we require a statistic that represents the spread about the mean to enable us to distinguish these two sets of data from one another.

EXAMPLE 12.2.1

Distinguish between the range, the mean absolute deviation, the variance and the standard deviation for the following data:

5, 7, 8, 8, 9, 9, 9, 9, 9, 11, 11, 12, 12, 15, 16

Solution 12.2.1

Reducing a collection of numerical data to its average may give us a statistic that represents the data but until that number is used comparatively against an equivalent statistic derived from a different collection of data it is of little value. However, two sets of data can be very clearly different yet both have the same arithmetic mean. Clearly we need a second statistic to describe that difference. We consider the idea of how the data is spread about the mean and we have a number of measures of data-spread.

Range   The range of a set of numerical data is the difference between the largest value and the smallest. For the data given the smallest value is 5 and the largest value is 16 so that the range is

16 − 5 = 11

Whilst this measure of spread indicates the extent of the spread it does not give any indication of how evenly or unevenly the data is spread.

Mean deviation   The difference between a datum value and the arithmetic mean of all the data is called the *deviation from the mean* of that datum. Because the mean represents some central location in the data there will be data with negative deviations as well as data with positive deviations. If we were to add up all the deviations the negatives would cancel the positives to result in zero as we see for the data given (where the values of f are the frequencies of individual data):

Datum x	f	fx	(x − m)	f(x − m)
5	1	5	−5	−5
7	1	7	−3	−3
8	2	16	−2	−4
9	5	45	−1	−5
11	2	22	1	2
12	2	24	2	4
15	1	15	5	5
16	1	16	6	6
Total	15	150		0

Mean $m = 10$ *Mean deviation* $= 0/15 = 0$

Consequently, the mean deviation of all the data is zero for any set of numerical data making it a worthless measure of spread. However, the idea of the deviation of a single datum does have merit as we see in the following two measures of spread.

Mean absolute deviation (MAD) The difficulty encountered with data deviations summing to zero because of the cancelling effect of negatives with positives can be eliminated *if we take the absolute value of the deviations*. Each datum then has an associated positive absolute deviation and the arithmetic mean of these absolute deviations becomes a good measure of spread. For the data given we find the mean absolute deviation as follows:

Datum x	f	fx	$\lvert x − m \rvert$	$f\lvert x − m \rvert$
5	1	5	5	5
7	1	7	3	3
8	2	16	2	4
9	5	45	1	5
11	2	22	1	2
12	2	24	2	4
15	1	15	5	5
16	1	16	6	6
Total	15	150		34

Mean $m = 10$
Mean absolute deviation (MAD) $= 34/15 = 2.27$ to 2 d.p.

Whilst this measure of spread does not indicate the extent of the spread, that is the range, it does give a good indication of the bunching effect of data about the mean. A small value of MAD indicates a tight bunching of data values about the mean and a larger value of MAD indicates less bunching.

Variance The mean absolute deviation is a perfectly reasonable measure of the spread of data. However, it does have a disadvantage. Whilst it is easily calculated

263

by applying the rules of arithmetic it is not easily manipulated as a mathematical entity in an algebraic context. An alternative measure of the spread of data about the mean is the variance, denoted by s^2, which is amenable both to arithmetic calculation and to mathematical manipulation within an algebraic context. The variance attacks the same problem of converting the negative deviations into positive deviations only this time by *squaring each deviation*. The average of all the squared deviations is called the variance. For the data given the variance is calculated as follows:

Datum x	f	fx	$(x-m)^2$	$f(x-m)$
5	1	5	25	25
7	1	7	9	9
8	2	16	4	8
9	5	45	1	5
11	2	22	1	2
12	2	24	4	8
15	1	15	25	25
16	1	16	36	36
Total	15	150		118

Mean $m = 10$ Variance $s^2 = 118/15 = 7.87$ to 2 d.p.

Standard deviation The variance, despite being mathematically viable, still has a drawback in that it is measured in the *square of the units of the data*. The ideal measure of spread that is arithmetically straighforward, algebraically manipulable and is in the units of the data is the square root s of the variance. This measure of spread is called the *standard deviation*. For the data given the standard deviation is

Standard deviation $s = \sqrt{7.87} = 2.80$ to 2 d.p.

EXAMPLE 12.2.2

Alex, Leslie and Chris sat their school examinations at the end of the school year. The results that they obtained were as follows:

	Alex	Leslie	Chris
Art	72	60	37
Chemistry	43	55	35
English	62	67	41
French	57	57	35
General Studies	46	52	34
Geography	64	64	41
History	82	70	43
Mathematics	53	53	22
Physics	61	62	40

(a) What are the median and mean of each student's marks?
(b) How are the students' marks spread about their respective means?
(c) Comment on the relative merits of the three sets of marks.

Solution 12.2.2(a)

When confronted with a collection of numerical data it is not usually possible to gain an overall impression just by looking at the entire collection of numbers. The reason being that there are just too many numbers to take in all at once. This is where statistics comes in – by reducing a collection of numerical data to a smaller collection of numbers that summarize the original collection. The simplest statistic of all is the *average* of which there are a number of instances. Two such instances are the *median* and the *arithmetic mean*.

The median is the middle datum and can be found by ranking the numerical data in ascending order of size. If there is an even number of data numbers then there is no middle datum in which case the median is the mean of the two data in the middle of the ranking.

The arithmetic mean, or *mean* for short, is obtained by adding up all the numbers and dividing the result by the number of numbers.

The means of the three sets of data are, to the nearest whole number, as follows:

	Alex	Leslie	Chris
Art	72	60	37
Chemistry	43	55	35
English	62	67	41
French	57	57	35
General Studies	46	52	34
Geography	64	64	41
History	82	70	43
Mathematics	53	53	22
Physics	61	62	40
Total	540	540	328
Average (= Total/9)	60	60	36.4

The medians are found by inspection after ranking the marks, here ranked in ascending order:

Alex:	43	46	53	57	**61**	62	64	72	82
Leslie:	52	53	55	57	**60**	62	64	67	70
Chris:	22	34	35	35	**37**	40	41	41	43

The medians are found to be the respective middle data:

Alex: 61   Leslie: 60   Chris: 37

Solution 12.2.2(b)

The *deviation* of a datum from the mean is defined as the difference between the mean and the datum value. Every datum has such a deviation and so we can find

265

the *average deviation* and use that as a statistic to describe the spread of the data about the mean.

To find the average deviation we shall proceed as follows. We construct the table of values and assign the individual numbers to a variable x. The mean value is the denoted by the symbol m:

Alex	x	$x - m$
Art	72	−12
Chemistry	43	17
English	62	−2
French	57	3
General Studies	46	14
Geography	64	−4
History	82	−22
Mathematics	53	7
Physics	61	−1
Mean $m = 60$	Total	0

If we now add up all these deviations we obtain the result 0. This is not surprising as the average acts as a balancing value between positive and negative deviations. Clearly, the average deviation is going to be no use as a statistic because it is always zero.

The problem lies in the negative values cancelling out all the positive values and we can overcome this by considering the magnitude of each deviation – we call it the *absolute value* and the absolute value of a number x is denoted by the symbol $|x|$. We find the *mean absolute deviation* (MAD) as follows:

Alex	x	$|x - m|$
Art	72	12
Chemistry	43	17
English	62	2
French	57	3
General Studies	46	14
Geography	64	4
History	82	22
Mathematics	53	7
Physics	61	1
Mean $m = 60$	Total	82

Mean absolute deviation (MAD) $= 82/9 = 9.11$ to 2 d.p.

This is a perfectly respectable statistic that measures the spread or *dispersion* about the mean of the data. It does, however, suffer from the drawback that it is not easy to handle mathematically. Fortunately, there is an alternative statistic called the *standard deviation*.

We overcame the problem of a zero total for the individual deviations from the mean by taking the absolute value of the deviation. We can also overcome the existence of negative deviations by squaring each deviation. The average of all the squared deviations is called the *variance* of the data:

Alex	x	$x - m$	$(x - m)^2$
Art	72	−12	144
Chemistry	43	17	289
English	62	−2	4
French	57	3	9
General Studies	46	14	196
Geography	64	−4	16
History	82	−22	484
Mathematics	53	7	49
Physics	61	−1	1
Mean $m = 60$		Total	1192

Variance $s^2 = 1192 \div 9 = 132.44$ to 2 d.p.

Again, this is a perfectly respectable statistic that measures the spread or *dispersion* about the mean of the data. It does, however, suffer from the drawback that it is measured in square units of the data. A more appropriate measure, which is given in the same units as that of the data, is the *square root of the variance*, called the *standard deviation:*

Standard deviation $s = \sqrt{132.44} = 11.51$ to 2 d.p.

In the same way we can derive the standard deviations for the other two sets of data. The complete derivations yield:

- *Alex*
  Average = 60   Standard deviation = 11.51
- *Leslie*
  Average = 60   Standard deviation = 5.93
- *Chris*
  Average = 36.4   Standard deviation = 5.93

Solution 12.2.2(c)

From these statistics we can see that Alex and Leslie both had the same average mark of 60% but Leslie was more consistent than Alex because Leslie's marks are less spread about the mean. On the other hand, Chris and Leslie are equally consistent, having the same standard deviation, but Chris has a significantly lower average mark than Leslie.

EXERCISES 12.2

1 Find the mean absolute deviation of each of the following set of numbers:

(a) 1, 3, 5, 7, 9, 11, 13, 15

(b) −4, −2, 0, 2, 4, 8, 16

(c) 23, 56, 18, 9, 42, 22, 19, 4, 31, 11, 7, 2, 49, 53

2 Find the variance and standard deviation of each of the following set of numbers:

(a) 0, 1, 4, 5, 8, 9, 16, 17, 32, 33

(b) −20, −15, −10, −5, 0, 5, 10, 15, 20

(c) 9, 64, 37, 25, 41, 38, 23, 17, 2, 19, 23, 67, 46, 51

3 The audience figures for each performance during a five week run of *She Stops to Conker* in a theatre with a seating capacity of 721 were as follows:

Week	Mon	Tue	Wed	Thu	Fri	Sat
1	453	346	562	244	478	654
2	407	206	675	377	573	559
3	491	177	582	285	581	692
4	357	372	693	336	604	586
5	507	405	529	304	628	634

(a) Find the mean audience

(b) Find the mean absolute deviation and the standard deviation of the audience figures

(c) What percentage of the seating was occupied

(i) each week (ii) over the entire run

4 The five minutes past noon train runs every weekday. For the past three weeks its time of departure has been recorded in the form of hrs:mins:secs as:

0:05:50	0:05:00	0:05:03	0:05:10	0:05:25
0:05:00	0:05:50	0:05:59	0:06:16	0:07:10
0:05:30	0:06:55	0:06:01	0:05:05	0:06:01

(a) Calculate the average time of departure and the standard deviation of the distribution of departure times.

(b) The train is considered as late in departing if it leaves one minute after it is due to leave. How many standard deviations is this?

(c) If the train is considered as late departing if its departure time is 0.5 standard deviations later than its average departure time, how many times was the train late during the three recorded weeks?

12.3 FRACTILES

We have seen how to calculate the arithmetic mean and the standard deviation for a single set of data. By themselves, these two statistics are only really meaningful when we are comparing one collection of data with another. However, there are many times when we are called upon to consider just one collection of data without having a second collection with which to compare it. For example, the marks attained by a group of students will have an arithmetic mean and a standard deviation but these two statistics will not tell us how the marks are spread about the full range of possible marks. If, for instance, half of the student's marks were below 40% then we could conclude that either the entire group of students did not work sufficiently well or that the examination paper was too hard. Similarly if half of the students' marks were above 70% then we might conclude that the examination was too easy. Clearly, we need to be able to generate statistics that describe the spread of a single collection of data within the full range of the data values.

EXAMPLE 12.3.1

SoftSolutions is a large organization providing software systems to the commercial sector. They have a very large sales force and maintain a company policy of promoting to middle management only from within their own sales force. Whenever a situation becomes vacant in middle management they inform their entire sales force and invite applications to sit their Management Aptitude Test. This test was devised by a company called Aptitudes Ltd who claim that they are able to select the most appropriate people from amongst any particular group that sit the test. The conditions of the test are that all those candidates whose score is on or above the third quartile of scores are to be interviewed. The successful candidate is to be selected from amongst those interviewed. Aptitudes Ltd claim that the individual so selected for the post will be found to have attained a score on the test on or above the 95th percentile and that the second choice candidate would be found to have attained a score on or above the 9th decile.

In a recent test 40 people from the sales force sat the middle management aptitude test. Each candidate was given a number and the scores in order of ascending candidate number were:

Candidate:	1	2	3	4	5	6	7	8	9
Score:	50	62	69	87	76	64	53	43	34

Candidate:	10	11	12	13	14	15	16	17	18
Score:	53	59	62	63	67	95	89	82	73

Candidate:	19	20	21	22	23	24	25	26	27
Score:	42	62	46	58	47	62	86	67	76

Candidate:	28	29	30	31	32	33	34	35	36
Score:	62	93	64	46	61	68	78	69	75

Candidate:	37	38	39	40
Score:	66	53	57	96

(a) Rank the scores in ascending order.

(b) Find the median and the 3rd quartile scores.

(c) Comment on the spread of the data.

(d) Who are selected for interview?

(e) After the interview candidate number 15 was selected to fill the advertised post and candidate number 16 was the runner up, test Aptitude Ltd's claim regarding the effectiveness of their test.

Explanation We have already seen how the mean and the standard deviation can be derived from a collection of statistics and how they can be used to represent a collection of data in terms of a centre point for the data and the spread of the data about that centre point respectively. By comparing means and standard deviations of multiple collections of data we can sensibly discuss the relative merits of one collection of data with another collection. If, however, we only have one collection of data then the mean and standard deviation of the collection, though representative of the data, merely replace the data with two alternative numbers. For example, if we find that the rate of inflation (the average price rise) is currently 3% per year we have no real means of knowing whether this is good or bad until we compare it with past rates of inflation of 17% as were experienced in the 1970s.

We need to be able to discuss meaningfully the spread of data within a single collection of data and this is where **fractiles** come in. They enable us to describe a single collection of data in terms of its internal grouping – comparing one grouping with another. We have already met one fractile – the median. The median is that statistic which divides the ranked data into halves with all the data in the first half being less than the median and all the data in the other half greater than the median.

This principle can be extended. The **quartiles** divide the ranked data into quarters, the **deciles** divide it into tenths and the **percentiles** divide it into hundredths. For example, the following ranked data:

1, 2, 3, 4, 4, 5, 6, 7, 7, 8, 9, 9

can be divided into two equally populated groups as:

1, 2, 3, 4, 4, 5   6, 7, 7, 8, 9, 9

and into four equally populated groups as:

1, 2, 3   4, 4, 5   6, 7, 7   8, 9, 9

From the first split we can see that the median M is 5.5:

1, 2, 3, 4, 4, 5   **5.5**   6, 7, 7, 8, 9, 9

and from the second grouping we can see that the first, second and third quartiles are $Q_1 = 3.5$, $Q_2 = 5.5$ and $Q_3 = 7.5$ respectively:

1, 2, 3   **3.5**   4, 4, 5   **5.5**   6, 7, 7   **7.5**   8, 9, 9

Notice that the second quartile is identical to the median, i.e. $Q_2 = M$, and remember that statistics derived from data are not necessarily equal to any of the data values.

For larger collections of data, deciles and percentiles can be derived in a similar manner.

Solution 12.3.1(a)

The original data is ranked in order of increasing candidate number. It is required to rank the data in ascending order of score as follows (the *Number* represents the location of a ranked score in the list):

Number	1	2	3	4	5	6	7	8	9
Score	**34**	**42**	**43**	**46**	**46**	**47**	**50**	**53**	**53**
Candidate	9	19	8	21	31	23	1	7	38

Number	10	11	12	13	14	15	16	17	18
Score	**53**	**57**	**58**	**59**	**61**	**62**	**62**	**62**	**62**
Candidate	10	39	22	11	32	2	28	20	12

Number	19	20	21	22	23	24	25	26	27
Score	**62**	**63**	**64**	**64**	**66**	**67**	**67**	**68**	**69**
Candidate	24	13	6	30	37	26	14	33	3

Number	28	29	30	31	32	33	34	35	36
Score	**69**	**73**	**75**	**76**	**76**	**78**	**82**	**86**	**87**
Candidate	35	18	36	5	27	34	17	25	4

Number	37	38	39	40
Score	**89**	**93**	**95**	**96**
Candidate	16	29	15	40

Solution 12.3.1(b)

The median is that score that divides the complete collection of scores into equally populated halves: half of the scores being less than the median and the other half being greater than the median. Because there is an even number of data there is no middle datum. Consequently, the median is taken to be the *average of the two middle data*, that is the average of the 20th and the 21st data values:

20th data value = 63   21st data value = 64

Median $M = (63 + 64) \div 2 = 63.5$

Notice that the median M, just like the mean, need not necessarily be one of the data values. There are three quartiles and they divide the data into four equally populated parts. Because there are 40 data items the quartiles divide the data into four groups of 10 data items each. Again, because the number of data items is divisible by 4 we have to resort to an averaging procedure. Consequently:

- the first quartile Q_1 is the average of the 10th and 11th data items
- the second quartile Q_2 is the average of the 20th and 21st data items – notice that this is identical to the median, $Q_2 = M$
- the third quartile Q_3 is the average of the 30th and 31st data items

Therefore:

$Q_3 = (75 + 76) \div 2 = 75.5$

Solution 12.3.1(c)

The first quartile Q_1 is the average of the 10th and 11th data items:

$$Q_1 = (53 + 57) \div 2 = 55$$

The *interquartile* range is a further statistic used to describe the spread of data and is defined as *half the difference between the 1st and 3rd quartile values*. That is:

$$(Q_3 - Q_1) \div 2 = (75.5 - 55) \div 2 = 10.25$$

This means that on average the boundaries of the two middle quarters of the data are each separated by 10.25 points. Furthermore, 50% of the candidates have scores lying between 55 and 75.5, a range of 20.5 scores. The complete range of scores is the difference between the largest and the smallest which is

$$96 - 34 = 62$$

Consequently 50% of the candidates are separated by approximately 30% of the range of scores indicating a tendency for the scores to bunch around the median of 63.5.

Solution 12.3.1(d)

Those selected for interview are those candidates with a score of 75.5 or more. These are candidates numbered:

4, 5, 15, 16, 17, 25, 27, 29, 34, 40

Solution 12.3.1(e)

To find the median and the upper and lower quartiles is a relatively simple procedure involving counting down the list of ranked scores. This is because 40 is straightforwardly divided by 4 to produce a whole number. The same can be said for the deciles which divide the data into ten equal parts. However, the same cannot be said for percentiles which divide the data into one hundred equal parts. To find the percentiles we shall resort to a graphical method known as the *cumulative frequency chart*. We divide the scores into groups of 10 ranging from the first group of scores being those between 20 and 30 to the last group of scores being those between 90 and 100:

Score group	Frequencey	Score	Cumulative frequency
21 to 30	0	$\leqslant 30$	0
31 to 40	1	$\leqslant 40$	1
41 to 50	6	$\leqslant 50$	7
51 to 60	6	$\leqslant 60$	13
61 to 70	15	$\leqslant 70$	28
71 to 80	5	$\leqslant 80$	33
81 to 90	4	$\leqslant 90$	37
91 to 100	3	$\leqslant 100$	40

In this table the first column lists the groups of scores and the second column lists the frequencies of those groups. The third column lists the *cumulative groups* and the fourth column lists the frequencies of the cumulative groups – the *cumulative frequencies*.

If we plot the cumulative frequency against the top value of the cumulative group scores we obtain the *cumulative frequency graph* whose characteristic shape is referred to as an *ogive* (Figure 12.3.1).

If, on this graph, we draw a horizontal line from the frequency value 20 to the ogive and then draw a vertical line from where the horizontal line meets the ogive to the horizontal axis we see that the vertical line meets the horizontal axis at 63.5 – the median value of the data (Figure 12.3.2).

Clearly, half the population of scores have values below this median and half above. The same principle applies for determining the quartiles (Figure 12.3.3).

In the same way we can graphically determine the deciles and the percentiles (Figure 12.3.4).

From this figure we can see that the score corresponding to the 95th percentile is 93.1 and that the score corresponding to the 9th decile is 88. The candidates who scored on or above the 95th percentile were those numbered:

15 and 40

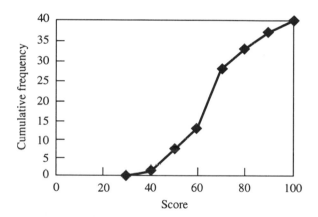

Figure 12.3.1

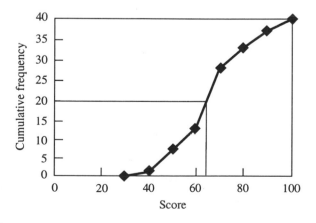

Figure 12.3.2

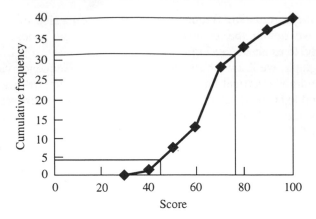

Figure 12.3.3

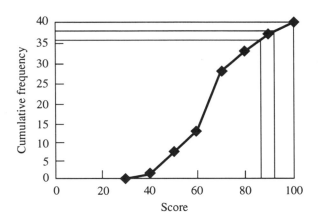

Figure 12.3.4

who scored 95 and 96 respectively (refer to the original Candidate/Score data) and the candidates who scored on or above the 9th decile were those numbered:

15, 16, 29 and 40

who scored 95, 89, 93 and 96 respectively.

Since the successful candidate was candidate number 15 and the runner up was candidate number 16 it is seen that Aptitudes' claim has been borne out.

EXERCISES 12.3

1 Find the first and third quartiles and inter-quartile range of each of the following collections of numbers:

(a) 11, 15, 16, 21, 31, 54, 17, 9, 36, 5, 8, 11, 27, 3, 1

(b) 23, 56, 18, 9, 42, 22, 19, 4, 31, 11, 7, 2, 49, 53

(c) 9, 64, 37, 25, 41, 38, 23, 17, 2, 19, 23, 46, 51

2 The following table contains the numbers of days lost per week due to employee absence for each week of the past year:

5	0	6	0	7	3	8	10	6
8	3	10	10	3	0	6	10	3
6	3	5	7	6	4	9	0	5
0	8	10	6	5	9	7	3	9
0	6	5	4	10	3	8	5	10
8	4	3	5	8	3	10		

(a) Calculate the median and mode for this data.

(b) Construct a frequency table and calculate:

(i)   the total number of days lost over the year

(ii) the mean number of days lost per week

(iii) the variance and standard deviation for this frequency distribution.

(c) Construct a cumulative frequency table and draw the cumulative frequency graph (the ogive).

(d) What is the value of:

(i)   the first quartile

(ii) the third quartile

(iii) the inter-quartile range.

3 The following data records the till receipts at one supermarket checkout during one half-shift:

2.32	43.56	23.37	3.77	56.74	27.83	4.75
40.31	22.77	62.39	33.67	51.76	35.54	30.01
63.44	47.59	88.23	59.19	27.34	92.36	74.52
21.94	3.44	29.95	36.57	61.45	43.67	69.91
49.32	32.76	76.98	33.31	47.88	84.57	39.54
57.80	30.18	1.03	39.92	77.34	50.34	27.56
49.69	71.04	20.11	105.66	59.91	28.17	

(a) Record the group frequencies for this data for the groups:

   $0-20$, $21-40$, $41-60$, $61-80$, $81-100$, $101-120$

(b) Complete the group frequency table and compute the mean till receipt and the standard deviation.

(c) Construct a histogram with equal intervals for this data,

(d) What is the median till receipt?

(e) Construct the cumulative frequency table and draw the cumulative frequency graph.

(f) Find:

   (i)   the upper quartile till receipt

   (ii) the 8th decile till receipt

   (iii) the 95th percentile till receipt.

(g) If the half-shift lasts four hours find the hourly receipt rate and the hourly transaction rate.

13

INDEX NUMBERS

When you have completed this chapter you will be able to:

- calculate a price relative
- construct a simple index and a weighted aggregative index
- construct Laspeyre and Paasche indexes
- construct a chain base index

13.1 KEEPING TRACK OF CHANGES

As time progresses, prices rise and the value of money goes down; this is known as inflation. But how best to measure it? Measuring price changes in absolute terms is not always appropriate if we are concerned about the effects of those price changes. For example, if the price of a loaf of bread rises by 10p this is surely far more important to the average household than if the price of a washing machine rises by 10p. The former has an immediate effect on the family budget whereas the latter is practically irrelevant. The best way to measure price changes is to use a *relative* measure and this is where index numbers come in.

EXAMPLE 13.1.1

(a) The average selling prices of the imported Skada XTS 6 saloon car for the three years 1994 to 1996 are listed as follows:

Year	Price
1994	£10,000
1995	£10,750
1996	£11,800

where the increases in price are a consequence of inflation and market demand for a car that is enjoying increased popularity. Using this data:

(i) describe what is meant by an *index number*, a *base year* and a *price relative*

(ii) calculate the expected price in 1996 of the super luxe model Skada XTV 8 if it costs £15,000 in 1994 stating any assumptions you might make.

(b) The following table contains the average amount spent per week on petrol and the amount spent per year on car maintenance (car tax, servicing and insurance) for the three years 1994 to 1996:

Year	Petrol/w	Maintenance/y
1994	25.00	525.00
1995	26.50	555.00
1996	28.50	660.00

The car is to be used by a salesman but is owned by a company where the terms of the salesman's contract is that the salesman pays 90% of the petrol costs but only 10% of the maintenance costs. Using this data:

(i) discuss the meaning of a weighted aggregative index

(ii) calculate a weighted aggregative index for the years 1995 and 1996 that is relevant to the salesman and a similar index that is relevant to the company.

Explanation   Change can be measured either in absolute terms or in relative terms. If my favourite monthly magazine increased its cover price by 10p from £2.50 to £2.60 I would not feel too harshly done by. If, however, my daily newspaper were to increase its price by 10p from 25p to 35p then I would feel that the price rise was rather excessive. This despite that each item only increased in price by the same amount – 10p. What is important here is not the amount by which each item rose in price but the *relative* increase in price. A 10p rise on the price of £2.50 represents a

$(10/250) \times 100 = 4\%$ price rise

whereas a 10p rise on the price 25p represents a

$(10/25) \times 100 = 40\%$ price rise – a ten-fold difference in relative effect

By considering relative prices rather than absolute price changes we can see the level of difference in the change. This is the purpose of *index numbers* – they enable changes in data values to be compared with each other in percentage terms rather than in absolute terms.

Solution 13.1.1(a(i))
An **index number** is a statistic that shows the average change in a quantity over a given period of time. Here the change in the price of the imported Skada XTS 6 for three successive years is given in the following table as:

Year	Price
1994	£10,000
1995	£10,750
1996	£11,800

By dividing the 1995 price by the 1994 price we obtain:

$10{,}750 \div 10{,}000 = 1.075$

That is, the 1995 price is 0.075 times greater than the 1994 price. Such a proportion is best expressed as a percentage so we multiply by 100. That is

$(10,750 \div 10,000) \times 100 = 107.5$

This tells us that the 1995 price is 7.5% greater than the 1994 price. Repeating this for the following year:

$(11,800 \div 10,000) \times 100 = 118$

we see that the 1996 price is 18% greater than the 1984 price. These percentages are called index numbers or price relatives. We extend the table as follows:

Year	Price	Index
1994	£10,000	100.0
1995	£10,750	107.5
1996	£11,800	118.0

Notice that the first index is 100. That is:

$(10,000 \div 10,000) \times 100 = 100$

The year 1994 is called the *base year*. It is the year upon which the subsequent indexes are *based*. By looking at the indexes we have a more absolute impression of how the price of this car has changed over the three years.

Solution 13.1.1(a(ii))
Using these percentages we can compute the expected price in 1996 of the super luxe model Skada XTV 8 if it costs £15,000 in 1994. That is

$£15,000 \times 1.18 = £17,700$ in 1996

This does, of course, assume that the proportionate increase in the price of the two cars is the same. When the price change of a single commodity is expressed by means of an index number in this way then the index is referred to as a **price relative.** What is of more interest is the *weighted aggregate index* of a number of commodities.

Solution 13.1.1(b)
Many times it is desired to reduce the price change of a number of different items to a single index number. Such is the case with the *Retail Prices Index.*

The problem of reducing a number of different items to a single index lies in the relative merits of each item. Consider the case of just two items, petrol and car maintenance. Ordinarily, an individual could buy a quantity of petrol every week but car maintenance bills may be paid just once per year. As a result, if we were considering our budget then a rise in the price of petrol would be immediately felt but a rise in the price of car maintenance would only be experienced when the car maintenance bills came in. The increased prices for these two items for the three successive years is recorded in the following table:

Year	Petrol/w	Maintenance/y
1994	25.00	525.00
1995	26.50	555.00
1996	28.50	660.00

The costs experienced by the salesman are different from those experienced by the company. The salesman pays 90% of the petrol costs but only 10% of the maintenance cost. Consequently, the following table represents the costs for the salesman:

Year	Petrol/w	Maintenance/y
1994	22.50	52.50
1995	23.85	55.50
1996	25.65	66.00

and the following table represents the costs for the company:

Year	Petrol/w	Maintenance/y
1994	2.50	472.50
1995	2.65	499.50
1996	2.85	594.00

We shall further assume petrol to be more important to us than car maintenance in the ratio 52 to 1. In other words we buy petrol 52 times per year but maintenance costs are assumed to be paid just once per year. However, the relative importance of petrol to maintenance to the salesman differs from that to the company. Because the salesman only pays 90% of petrol costs and 10% of maintenance cost we multiply the prices by the *weights* of $52 \times 0.9 = 46.8$ and $1 \times 0.1 = 0.1$ respectively and so construct our **weighted aggregative index** for the salesman as:

Year	Petrol	Petrol ×46.8	Maint. ×0.1	Sum	Index
1994	25.00	1170.0	52.50	1222.5	100.0
1995	26.50	1240.2	55.50	1295.7	$106.0 = (1295.7 \div 1222.5) \times 100$
1996	28.50	1333.8	66.00	1399.8	$114.5 = (1399.8 \div 1222.5) \times 100$

and for the company the weights are $52 \times 0.1 = 5.2$ for petrol and 1×0.9 for maintenance costs giving the weighted aggregative index for the company as:

Year	Petrol	Petrol ×5.2	Maint. ×0.9	Sum	Index
1994	25.00	130.0	472.50	602.5	100.0
1995	26.50	137.8	499.50	637.3	$105.8 = (637.3 \div 602.5) \times 100$
1996	28.50	148.2	594.00	742.2	$123.2 = (742.2 \div 602.5) \times 100$

The essence of the weighted aggregate index is that it reflects the price changes with respect to a particular purchasing pattern. The purchasing pattern is taken account of by means of the *weights*. As we see, the index numbers are different from the first set. To the salesman paying a greater proportion of the cost of the petrol than the maintenance the index increased by 6.0 and 8.5 points in successive years. To the company the index increased by 5.8 and 17.4 points during the same successive years. This raises a very important point about indexes. *We must always be aware of the reason for calculating them and to whom or to what purchasing pattern they apply.*

1 What is a price relative and how can it be used to create a series of index numbers?

2 What is a weighted aggregative index and why is it used?

3 (a) The average selling prices of the MicroHard Super486 personal computer for the three years 1994 to 1996 are listed as follows:

Year	Price
1994	£1250
1995	£1050
1996	£875

where the decreases in price are a consequence of market demand for a commodity whose latest version is rapidly superceded by newer, faster models. Using this data:

(i) describe what is meant by an *index number*, a *base year* and a *price relative*

(ii) calculate the expected price in 1996 of the Intro Multi-Media super luxe model Rapido 486STX if it sells for £1945 in 1994. State any assumptions you might make.

(b) The following table contains the cost of a representative cross-section of vegetables and meat in an average week as priced in a typical supermarket for the three years 1994 to 1996:

Year	Vegetables	Meats
1994	15.40	25.35
1995	16.85	27.08
1996	17.50	29.53

If a family of four had three vegetarian members the changes in price of the vegetables would outweigh the changes in the price of meats in the ratio of 3:1 whereas to a family of four with just one member who was a vegetarian the changes in price of the vegetables would be outweighed by the changes in price of the meats in the ratio 1:3. Using this data:

(i) discuss the meaning of a weighted aggregative index

(ii) calculate a weighted aggregative index for the years 1995 and 1996 that is relevant to the family with three vegetarians and a similar index that is relevant to the family with one vegetarian.

13.2 THE LASPEYRE AND PAASCHE INDEXES

The purpose of using index numbers as relative measures of price changes is to enable like to be compared with like – we compare the relative price change of one commodity with the relative price change of another commodity. However, as soon as we start to extend these ideas to collections of commodities where we consider the average price change of the collection we encounter further difficulties of comparing like with like. Because purchasing patterns change in time we run the risk of comparing relative price changes of different purchase patterns. In essence we must resolve the issue of whether we reflect a continuing purchasing pattern by comparing the cost of the same collection of items at two different times or we reflect a changing purchase pattern by comparing this year's purchasing pattern at last year's and this year's prices.

EXAMPLE 13.2.1

Each year the Computer Services section of Bruddersford University purchases a number of hardware and software units and accompanying manuals. Over the last two years their purchasing pattern has been as follows:

Item	Quantity last year	Unit price last year	Quantity this year	Unit price this year
Hardware units	100	1025	150	1135
Software units	50	400	47	525
Manuals	80	28	95	34

Construct both the Laspeyre and Paasche indexes for this purchasing pattern and contrast the relative merits of the two indexes.

Solution 13.2.1

Laspeyre Index The Laspeyre Index compares the cost of buying base year quantities at current year prices with the cost of buying base year quantities at base year prices. In other words, if we bought a shopping basket of goods last year the Laspeyre Index will compare its cost now with its cost last year.

The following table records the quantities of hardware units, software units and manuals purchased against the prices paid for them last year and this year:

Item	Quantity last year	Unit price last year	Unit price this year
Hardware units	100	1025	1135
Software units	50	400	525
Manuals	80	28	34

We use the quantities as weights since that is the best way to reflect their relative importance. The following table shows how the Laspeyre Index is evaluated. Q denotes the quantity. P_1 and P_2 denote the prices per unit last year and this year respectively.

Item	Q	P_1	$Q \times P_1$	P_2	$Q \times P_2$
Hardware units	100	1025	102500	1135	113500
Software units	50	400	20000	525	26250
Manuals	80	28	2240	34	2720
Totals			124740		142470

Laspeyre Index $= (142470 \div 124740) \times 100 = 114.2$

Paasche Index   The Paasche Index compares the cost of buying current year quantities at current year prices with the cost of buying current year quantities at base year prices. In other words, if we bought a shopping basket of goods *this* year the Paasche Index will compare its cost now with the cost it would have been last year. We shall use the same data as before to construct the Paasche Index for our items with this year's quantities used instead of last year's.

Item	Quantity this year	Unit price last year	Unit price this year
Hardware units	150	1025	1135
Software units	47	400	525
Manuals	95	28	34

Again we use the quantities as weights since that is the best way to reflect their relative importance. The following table shows how the Paasche Index is evaluated:

Item	Q	P_1	$Q \times P_1$	P_2	$Q \times P_2$
Hardware units	150	1025	153750	1135	170250
Software units	47	400	18800	525	24675
Manuals	95	28	2660	34	3230
Totals			175210		198155

Paasche Index = $(198155 \div 175210) \times 100 = 113.1$

Laspeyre and Paasche contrasted

The Paasche Index requires the quantities to be measured each year and this can be a costly exercise. Also, since the denominator in the index changes each year we can only compare one year's Paasche Index with the base year. The Paasche Index does, however, keep abreast of current purchasing patterns as it continually updates the items in the shopping basket.

In contrast the Laspeyre index only requires a record of current prices. Also, since the denominator in the index remains the same then each year's index can be compared with any other year's index. This makes the Laspeyre Index the more popular of the two despite the fact that this index does not take into account any change in the purchasing pattern. The contents of the shopping basket remain the same as the base year.

EXERCISES 13.2

1   Distinguish between the Laspeyre index and the Paasche Index and describe the relative merits and drawbacks of each.
2   The Faxihal Corporation maintains a central warehouse from which they distribute packs of promotional literature, packs of stationery and packs of administrative forms to its different branches throughout the country. The

following table contains the information relating to quantities distributed this year and last year and their respective prices:

Item	Quantity last year	Unit price last year	Quantity this year	Unit price this year
Promotional Lit	564	3.25	638	3.79
Stationery	829	5.40	974	5.30
Admin Packs	437	2.74	537	3.04

Construct both the Laspeyre and Paasche indexes for this purchasing pattern and contrast the relative merits of the two indexes.

13.3 THE CHAIN BASE INDEX

So far we have considered indexes that describe price changes between one year and the next relative to a fixed base year. After a number of years this historical reference to a distant past year can lose relevance. As *Monty Python* would say:

In my day I could go to the pictures, buy ten cigarettes, have a chinese meal and still have change out of 50p.

It may be true but it is hardly relevant. This is where the concept of a chain base index comes in; it permits a sequence of price changes to be compared to any one of a number of past years' prices and, in particular, to the previous year's prices.

EXAMPLE 13.3.1

At a local garage the price of 4-star petrol was recorded on the morning of January 1st for 7 successive years. These prices are recorded in the following table:

Year	Price
1	34p
2	36p
3	41p
4	52p
5	58p
6	63p
7	66p

Use these prices to construct a chain base index.

Solution 13.3.1

Chain base index A chain base index is constructed by moving the base year on a year at a time so that each index is measured relative to the previous year. The chain base index constructed from the table recording the price of a litre of 4 star petrol on January 1st of each of 7 successive years is:

	Price	Index
Year 0	34p	100
Year 1	36p	$(36 \div 34) \times 100 = 105.9$
Year 2	41p	$(41 \div 36) \times 100 = 113.9$
Year 3	52p	$(52 \div 41) \times 100 = 126.8$
Year 4	58p	$(58 \div 52) \times 100 = 111.5$
Year 5	63p	$(63 \div 58) \times 100 = 108.6$
Year 6	66p	$(66 \div 63) \times 100 = 104.8$

The chain base index shows how the rate of change is changing as well as the extent of the change over the previous year. For example, over the second year the price per litre index *increased* by

$$([113.9 - 105.9] \div 113.9) \times 100 = 7\%$$

Over the sixth year the index *decreased* by:

$$([108.6 - 104.8] \div 108.6) \times 100 = 3.5\%$$

EXAMPLE 13.3.2

Describe the main points of creating an index and illustrate these points with reference to the Retail Prices Index.

Solution 13.3.2

The creation of an index   When creating an index we must consider the purpose for which it will be used and the choice of base year.

The purpose for which it will be used
Every index is constructed using a collection of specific commodities. The price of each commodity is multiplied by a specific weight that rates its relative importance within the collection. For these reasons the index should only be used where both the chosen commodities and their associated weights are appropriate. For example, an index constructed from the prices of petrol and car maintenance costs would change for different choices of relative weights. For a salesman paying 90% of the petrol costs it would be more appropriate to heavily weight the cost of petrol. For the company employing the salesman the car maintenance costs would carry the heavier weighting. As a result an index appropriate to a salesman would be an inappropriate index for the company and vice versa. Because of this the people who are going to use the index must be borne in mind. Having identified the people then the appropriate commodities and associated weights must be used.

Choice of base year
The last point to consider is when to start the index. The base year should be a *normal* year when no abnormal changes have occurred. If a year of abnormal

change is chosen as the base year then further years of minor change will hardly show at all. This will give misleading conclusions of the true situation. Finally, the base year must not be chosen to be too far in the past. Too early a base year could make current changes irrelevant in comparison.

The Retail Prices Index   The General Index of Retail Prices otherwise known as the Retail Prices Index measures the change in the cost of living. The index is compiled for the Government and published each month in the *Monthly Digest of Statistics*. Since it measures the monthly change in the cost of living it is widely used as a measure of inflation.

The index is constructed from the prices of what is called a *representative basket of goods*. This basket of goods contains items that are bought each month by a typical household. The items and the quantities bought each month are listed in the Family Expenditure Survey. The Family Expenditure Survey is a continuing enquiry conducted by the Department of Employment. It investigates the general characteristics of households, their incomes and their expenditures. From this information the representative basket of goods is divided into the following groups:

- *Food and catering*
  The food referred to consists of various staples such as bread, dairy produce, meats and vegetables. The catering refers to meals bought in restaurants, canteens and take-away outlets. This section covers 22% of the basket of goods.

- *Alcohol and tobacco*
  This group covers beers, wines and spirits and all tobacco products. It accounts for 11% of the basket of goods.

- *Housing and household expenditure*
  Housing refers to such items as rents, mortgages, rates and other costs typical of maintaining a house. The household expenditure refers to household consumables, appliances and furniture. This section accounts for 32% of the basket of goods.

- *Personal expenditure*
  Personal expenditure covers clothing and personal services. This accounts for 11% of the basket of goods.

- *Travel and leisure*
  This group consists of holiday costs, entertainment, sports goods, car costs, petrol and a number of other items. It accounts for 13% of the basket of goods.

In the representative basket of goods there are 1000 items and each item has associated with it an index or price relative. Also associated with each item is a weight that rates the relative importance of that item in the basket of goods. Each item index is multiplied by its weight to produce a single *weighted index*. All these weighted indexes are then added and the result divided by 1000. This yields the *Retail Prices Index*. Consequently, the Retail Prices Index is an average of weighted price relatives. The base month of the index is January 1987 following various revisions in items and weights. Before the revision the base month was January 1974 and by January 1987 the index stood at nearly 400.

The Retail Prices Index has been criticized for not being truly representative of all households. For example, a single poor pensioner will not buy the same basket of goods as a high income earner. Not only would the items differ but so would their relative importance. In recognition of this each of these two groups have their own index separate from the General Index of Retail Prices. Furthermore, the items and their weights in the basket of goods are continually revised to ensure that it remains as representative as possible.

EXERCISES 13.3

1   When would it be desirable to use a chain base index rather than a simple index with a fixed base year?

2   The average house price on the 1st March in a specific region of the country was recorded for 7 successive years. These prices are recorded in the following table:

Year	Price (£000s)
1990	66.50
1991	63.25
1992	58.90
1993	52.85
1994	49.90
1995	49.00
1996	48.75

Use these prices to construct a chain base index.

3   The following table contains information taken from the UK Balance of Payments: summary contained within Economic Trends, Annual Supplement 1995 published by the Government Statistical Service:

	Visible trade	Invisible trade	External trade	Balance
1985	−3345	5583	−3720	1482
1986	−9559	8688	−3115	3986
1987	−11582	6599	6710	−1727
1988	−21480	4863	10975	5642
1989	−24683	2171	19636	2876
1990	−18809	−226	18193	842
1991	−10264	2108	8619	−443
1992	−13104	3273	3369	6462
1993	−13209	2898	8313	1998

The amounts are all in £m.

(a) Create a price relative index using 1985 as base year for all four sets of amounts

(b) Create a chain base index using 1989 as base year for all four sets of amounts

14

VARIABILITY

When you have completed this chapter you will be able to:

- plot ordered pairs of data on a scattergraph
- draw the line of best fit both by eye and by formulae
- derive the equation expressing the relationship between two linearly related variables
- interpolate and extrapolate data from a regression line
- calculate the standard error of estimate for a regression line
- calculate the coefficients of correlation

14.1 RELATED DATA

If two sets of data are related to each other then they will vary in unison. For example, if you were to take temperature readings of the outside air at recorded time intervals between 8:00 am and 11:00 am on a warm summer morning you would probably find that as the time increased so did the temperature – the time data and the temperature data increase in unison because they are related to each other. In such a situation you might also wish to *predict* the temperature at noon in which case you would need to know the exact relationship between time and temperature and this exact relationship would be in the form of a mathematical equation involving the variables time and temperature.

The simplest mathematical equation that represents a relationship between the two variables x and y is the equation of a straight line where the relationship is said to be *linear* and is expressed in an equation of the form:

$$y = ax + b$$

Here the symbol a stands for the value of the *gradient*, or *slope*, of the line and b stands for the y-value where the line crosses the y-axis; the value of y when $x = 0$. In a perfect world, plotting respective pairs of linearly related data on a scattergraph would produce points through which a straight line could be drawn as in Figure 14.1.2.

By inspecting this line we can generate its equation and thereby generate further data pairs from the equation – which was the purpose of the exercise in the first place. However, it is not a perfect world and data can often be corrupt; it may have been measured incorrectly or it may have been influenced by factors outside the control of the individual who has gathered it. In the event, when linearly related data pairs are plotted they will more than likely not lie on a straight line, as shown in Figure 14.1.3.

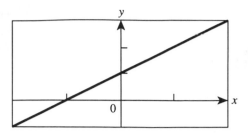

Figure 14.1.1

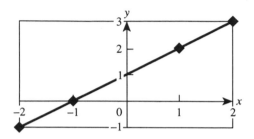

Figure 14.1.2

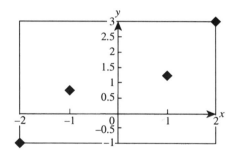

Figure 14.1.3

We still, however, need to know the equation of the straight line which best fits the data – we need to fit a straight line to the data. We can do this in one of two ways. We can draw a straight line that best fits the data by eye. This method, however, is not accurate. Alternatively, we can use a mathematical method called the Method of Least Squares which permits us to calculate the gradient and vertical intercept of the straight line that best fits the data. This line we call the **regression line** because implicit in the analysis of the data is the assumption that the data is erroneous and that it should have been on the regression line. In effect we drop the data back to the regression line – the word *regress* means to fall back.

EXAMPLE 14.1.1

SpeedAuto Ltd produce car components for the car enthusiast. In particular they produce the famous Rev-o-Tach which serves as a combined tachometer and rev counter, recording the car's speed in miles per hour and recording the engine revolution rate in revolutions per minute. Because their equipment is purchased by enthusiasts all their products have to be of high quality and, in the case of the Rev-o-Tach, very accurate. To ensure accuracy, every new Rev-o-Tach is tested on a test-bed against a standard, perfect model by recording readings from the Rev-o-Tach being tested and the standard model at 20 mph, 40 mph, 60 mph and 80 mph. The following table contains the readings from a typical test:

Revolutions (rpm)	1000	1800	2600	3400
Standard Model (mph)	20	40	60	80
Tested Model (mph)	20	38	62	80

(a) Plot the scattergraph of speed (mph) against revolutions (rpm) for:

(i) the standard model
(ii) the tested model

(b) Draw a line of best fit by eye of the data through each of the scattergraphs in part **(a)** and find the equation of each line.

Solution 14.1.1(a(i))

The data permits the following ordered pairs to be created where in each ordered pair the first number represents the speed in miles per hour (mph) as recorded by the standard model and the second number represents the corresponding tachometer reading in revolutions per minute (rpm):

(20, 1000),   (40, 1800),   (60, 2600),   (80, 3400)

These ordered pairs of numbers can be plotted on a scattergraph as in Figure 14.1.4.

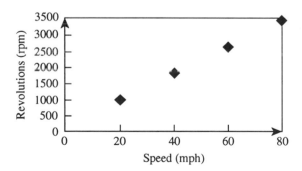

Figure 14.1.4

Solution 14.1.1 (a(ii))

For the tested model the equivalent data pairs are:

(20, 1000),   (38, 1800),   (62, 2600),   (80, 3400)

Again, these ordered pairs of numbers can be plotted on a scattergraph as in Figure 14.1.5.

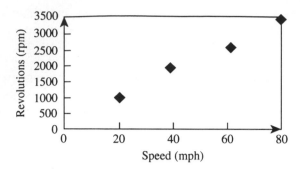

Figure 14.1.5

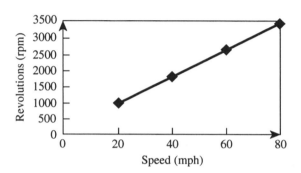

Figure 14.1.6

Solution 14.1.1(b(i))

The straight line of best fit can be drawn by eye by joining up all four points with a straight line (Figure 14.1.6).

The equation of the line is of the form:

$$r = as + b$$

where r and s are variables representing the corresponding revolutions and speed respectively. The constants a and b represent the gradient of the line and the vertical axis intercept point respectively. We can use the coordinates of any pair of points to solve this equation for a and b. For example, using the first two:

$$(20, 1000), \quad (40, 1800)$$

we can substitute values for r and s to obtain:

$$1000 = 20a + b$$
$$1800 = 40a + b$$

Subtracting the first equation from the second we see that:

$$800 = 20a \quad \text{so that} \quad a = 40$$

Substituting this value for a into the second equation yields:

$$1000 = (20 \times 40) + b$$

That is $\quad b = 200$

This gives the final form for the equation of the straight line as:

$$r = 40s + 200$$

Solution 14.1.1(b(ii))

The straight line of best fit cannot be drawn by joining up all four points with a straight line because they do not lie on a straight line. However, a line can be drawn by eye that best approximates to the data. This is the line joining the first and last point (Figure 14.1.7)

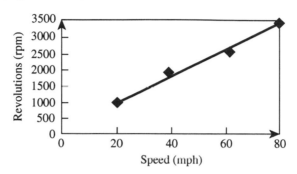

Figure 14.1.7

The equation of the line is of the form:

$$r = as + b$$

where r and s are variables representing the corresponding revolutions and speed respectively. The constants a and b represent the gradient of the line and the vertical axis intercept point respectively. We can use the coordinates of any pair of points to solve this equation for a and b. For example, using the first and the last:

$$(20, 1000), \quad (80, 3400)$$

we can substitute values for r and s to obtain:

$$1000 = 20a + b$$
$$3400 = 80a + b$$

Subtracting the first equation from the second we see that:

$$2400 = 60a \quad \text{so that} \quad a = 40$$

Substituting this value for a into the second equation yields:

$$1000 = (20 \times 40) + b$$

That is $b = 200$

This gives the final form for the equation of the straight line as:

$$r = 40s + 200 \qquad \text{the same equation as before}$$

EXAMPLE 14.1.2

Betta Toys make toy assembly kits out of plastic. A new kit, recently introduced into the market, was proving very popular and so they decided to increase production. They were concerned that the fixed production costs remain the same and that the variable production costs only increase linearly with production quantity. Below is a table of production quantity against total production costs (in £00) for the first 12 days of production.

Quantity	30	50	80	150	160	200	210	240	300	310	370	510
Total costs	9	13	19	25	27	31	33	34	40	40	49	60

(a) Plot a scattergraph of this data with the quantity plotted on the horizontal axis.

(b) Calculate the regression line and draw it on the scattergraph.

(c) From the regression line determine:

(i) the fixed production costs

(ii) the unit production cost on days 1, 6 and 12.

Explanation We are already familiar with the concept of a relationship between two variables being expressed in the form of an equation. For example, the equation:

$$y = 3x - 4$$

expresses the *linear* relationship between the two variables x and y where x is referred to as the *independent variable* and y as the *dependent variable* (the value of y depends upon the independently chosen value of x). Furthermore, by plotting on a graph pairs of numbers generated by this equation it is possible to create a pictorial representation of the relationship between the two variables. In the above example, if we plot pairs of numbers generated by the equation we obtain a collection of points that lie on a *straight line* (we call this equation an *equation of a straight line*). The line has gradient 3 and it intercepts the vertical y-axis at the point $x = 0$ and $y = -4$ (Figure 14.1.8). The straight line, obtained by joining the plotted points together, illustrates the linear relationship between the two variables x and y.

Many times we will have two sets of data whose corresponding values are assumed to be those of two linearly related variables. However, we may be faced

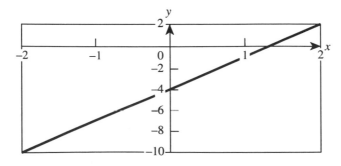

Figure 14.1.8

by two problems. Firstly, we do not know the equation that describes the relationship and secondly, when the pairs of corresponding numbers are plotted on a scattergraph, they do not lie on a straight line. There may be many reasons for this. The data values may have been obtained from an experiment and, as a consequence of the limitations of the experiment or the inaccuracy of the readings, they contain errors. What we are required to do in this case is to find the equation of the straight line to which they correspond. The straight line in Figure 14.1.9 is the line that the points are assumed to come from – the line to which the points would fall back to if they contained no errors. This line is called the *regression* line.

Solution 14.1.2(a)

The scattergraph of the following data:

Quantity	30	50	80	150	160	200	210	240	300	310	370	510
Total costs	9	13	19	25	27	31	33	34	40	40	49	60

is shown in Figure 14.1.10.

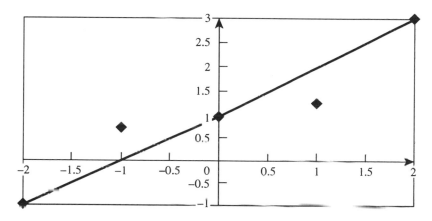

Figure 14.1.9

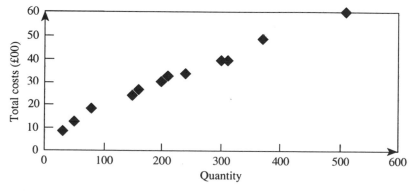

Figure 14.1.10

295

Solution 14.1.2(b)

The equation of the straight line of best fit can be obtained by using the method of least squares. It is not appropriate to discuss this method in detail here, instead we shall merely display the results of the method.

Let the equation:

$$y = ax + b$$

represent the line of best fit – the regression line – for a collection of data pairs:

$$(x_i, y_i)$$

where i takes on whole number values from 1 to n and where n represents the total number of data pairs. The method of least squares tells us that the two parameters a and b can be obtained from the following formulae:

$$a = \frac{n \, \Sigma \, yx - (\Sigma \, x)(\Sigma \, y)}{n \, \Sigma \, (x^2) - (\Sigma \, x)^2}$$

$$b = \frac{\Sigma \, y - a \, \Sigma \, x}{n}$$

where, for example, Σy represents the sum of all the y_i values from y_1 to y_n. In our example, let x (the horizontally plotted independent variable) represent the Quantity and y (the vertically plotted dependent variable) represent the Total cost. The data table can then be written as:

i	1	2	3	4	5	6	7	8	9	10	11	12
x_i	30	50	80	150	160	200	210	240	300	310	370	510
y_i	9	13	19	25	27	31	33	34	40	40	49	60

Because we need to find the sum of the x-values, the sum of the y-values and the sum of the xy-products we construct the following table:

i	x_i	y_i	x_i^2	$y_i x_i$
1	30	9	900	270
2	50	13	2500	650
3	80	19	6400	1520
4	150	25	22500	3750
5	160	27	25600	4320
6	200	31	40000	6200
7	210	33	44100	6930
8	240	34	57600	8160
9	300	40	90000	12000
10	310	40	96100	12400
11	370	49	136900	18130
12	510	60	260100	30600
Totals	2610	380	782700	104930

Applying these totals to the formulae where $n = 12$ we find that:

$a = [n\ \Sigma\ yx - (\Sigma\ x)(\Sigma\ y)]/[n\ \Sigma\ (x^2) - (\Sigma\ x)^2]$
$= [12 \times 104930) - (2610 \times 380)]/[(12 \times 782700) - (2610 \times 2610)]$
$= 267360/2580300$
$= 0.103616\ldots$
$= 0.10$ to 2 d.p.

so that

$b = [\Sigma\ y - a\ \Sigma\ x]/n$
$= [380 - (0.10 \times 2610)]/12$
$= 9.91666\ldots$
$= 9.92$ to 2 d.p.

The equation

$y = 0.10x + 9.92$

is now plotted to yield the straight line as shown in Figure 14.1.11.

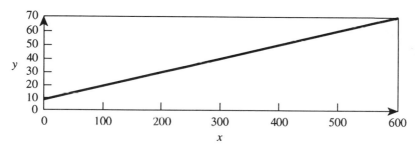

Figure 14.1.11

Solution 14.1.2(c(i))
The fixed production costs are the total costs when the production level is zero. This is found by substituting $x = 0$ into the equation of the regression line to yield:

$y = 9.92$

giving the fixed production costs as £992.00

Solution 14.1.2(c(ii))
The unit production cost on:

- day 1 is found by substituting $x = 30$ into the equation and dividing the resulting y-value by 30 to yield:

  $(9.92 + 0.10 \times 30)/30 = 0.43066$ (£43.07)

- day 6 is found by substituting $x = 200$ into the equation and dividing the resulting y-value by 200 to yield:

  $(9.92 + 0.10 \times 200)/200 = 0.1496$ (£14.96)

- day 12 is found by substituting $x = 510$ into the equation and dividing the resulting y-value by 510 to yield:

$(9.92 + 0.10 \times 510)/510 = 0.11945$ (£11.95)

EXERCISES 14.1

1 Plot the following data on a scattergraph and draw by eye the line of best fit:

x	2	4	8	10	12	14	16
y	9	20	46	55	71	81	93

From the graph:

(a) Find the value of y corresponding to:

(i) $x = 9$ (ii) $x = 18$ (iii) $x = 0$

(b) Find the value of x corresponding to:

(i) $y = 60$ (ii) $y = 100$ (iii) $y = 0$

2 Given the equation of the straight line:

$y = 10 - 5x$

(a) Construct a table of x and y values for $-5 \leqslant x \leqslant 5$

(b) Plot the data in the table of (a) on a scattergraph and draw the straight line

(c) Find from the graph the value of y corresponding to:

(i) $x = 7$ (ii) $x = -6$

(d) Find from the graph the value of x corresponding to:

(i) $y = 30$ (ii) $y = -20$

(e) Check your answers to (c) and (d) by using the equation of the straight line.

14.2 CORRELATION

When we derived the regression line for two sets of data we made the tacit assumption that the two sets of data were in fact linearly related. It is entirely possible, however, that they are not so related and that the regression line was derived by blindly applying the data to the formulae. We need to know how accurate our assumption of a linear relationship is and for this we devise a measure of *correlation*. If two sets of data are *perfectly linearly correlated* then plotting them on a scattergraph will produce points that lie on a straight line. If two sets of data have no correlation at all then their plot on the scattergraph will produce a randomly distributed set of points (Figure 14.2.1).

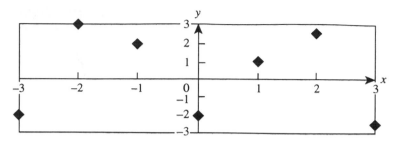

Figure 14.2.1

EXAMPLE 14.2.1

For the regression line found in Example 14.1.1 find the standard error of estimate in the straight line representing the tested model. Repeat for the data from a second tested model and compare the standard error of estimates.

Revolutions (rpm)	1000	1800	2600	3400
Standard Model (mph)	20	40	60	80
Tested Model 2 (mph)	20	39	61	80

Solution 14.2.1

The *standard error of estimate* is a measure of the scatter of the actual points plotted away from the regression line. It is given by:

$$s_{rs} = [\Sigma \{(r - r_{est})^2/n\}]^{1/2}$$

where r is the actual value of the revolutions and r_{est} is the corresponding value from the regression line. From the diagram we can see that

$$[\Sigma\{(r - r_{est})^2/n\}]^{1/2} = \sqrt{\{[(0^2) + (-2^2) + (2^2) + (0^2)]/4\}}$$
$$= \sqrt{(8/4)} = \sqrt{2} = 1.414 \text{ to 3 d.p.}$$

For small samples of data a better estimate of the standard error is given by:

$$s'_{rs} = s_{rs}\sqrt{[n/(n-2)]}$$

and in this case we find:

$$s'_{rs} = \sqrt{2}\sqrt{[4/(4-2)]} = 2$$

For the second tested model the regression line is the same but the standard error of estimate is given as:

$$[\Sigma\{(r - r_{est})^2/n\}]^{1/2} = \sqrt{\{[(0^2) + (-1^2) + (1^2) + (0^2)]/4\}}$$
$$= \sqrt{(2/4)} = \sqrt{0.5} = 0.707 \text{ to 3 d.p.}$$

For small samples of data a better estimate of the standard error is given by:

$$s'_{rs} = s_{rs}\sqrt{[n/(n-2)]}$$

and in this case we find:

$$s'_{rs} = \sqrt{0.5}\sqrt{[4/(4-2)]} = 1$$

Clearly the smaller the standard error of the estimate the better the fit and the more confident one can be that indeed there is a linear correlation between the two sets of data. Notice that by itself the standard error of estimate does not tell us very much without the experience of equivalent measures for other data.

Coefficients of correlation

We need a better way of determining how well our data fits a linear regression line so that we can form a judgement without requiring multiple sets of data. We do this by devising the *product-moment correlation coefficient r* that is an absolute measure of correlation. The value of r lies between 0 and 1 where a value of 1 signifies perfect correlation and a value of 0 signifies no correlation at all.

EXAMPLE 14.2.2

To test the effectiveness of a new drug 12 patients were examined before the drug was administered and given an initial score x, depending upon the severity of the various symptoms. After taking the drug they were examined again and given a final score y. A decrease in score represented an improvement. The scores for the 12 patients are given in the table:

Patient	1	2	3	4	5	6	7	8	9	10	11	12
Score x	60	25	9	13	40	33	31	34	40	27	19	49
Score y	51	15	3	5	30	21	20	24	31	16	8	37

(a) Plot the data on a scatter diagram.

(b) Calculate the correlation coefficient and test for its significance stating any necessary assumptions.

(c) Calculate the regression line and add it to your graph.

Solution 14.2.2(a)
From the above table it is required to form ordered pairs of numbers from the x- and y-scores respectively. We shall plot the x-scores along the horizontal axis and the y-scores along the vertical. Having decided this we can now form the collection of 12 ordered pairs from the table:

$$\text{(60, 51),} \quad \text{(25, 15),} \quad \text{(9, 3),} \quad \text{(13, 5),} \quad \text{(40, 30),} \quad \text{(33, 21)}$$
$$\text{(31, 20),} \quad \text{(34, 24),} \quad \text{(40, 31),} \quad \text{(27, 16),} \quad \text{(19, 8),} \quad \text{(49, 37)}$$

These ordered pairs can now be plotted to give the scattergraph shown in Figure 14.2.2.

Solution 14.2.2(b)
The word *correlation* means the interdependence of variable quantities and the *correlation coefficient* between two sets of variable values is a measure of how interdependent those two variables are. The question is dealing with the correlation between measurements taken before and after the administration of a drug. From the scattergraph it can be seen that for each patient the measurement

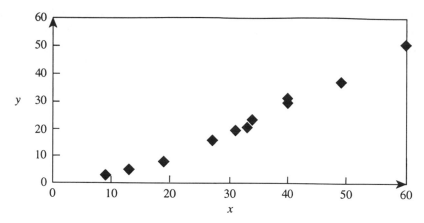

Figure 14.2.2

after resulted in a lower number than the measurement before, indicating that in each case an improvement was effected. The question arises as to whether or not there is an overall link between the size of the measurement before and the size of the measurement after the administration of the drug. The correlation coefficient r is defined as:

$$r = s_{xy}/\sqrt{(s_{xx} \times s_{yy})}$$

where

s_{xy} = covariance between the values of the two variables x and y
s_{xx} = variance of the values of the variable x
s_{yy} = variance of the values of the variable y.

The word *variance* is used to denote a spread of data about the mean value. For example, the data values of the variable x:

x 2, 4, 6, 8, 10

has a mean m, where

$$m = (2 + 4 + 6 + 8 + 10)/5 = 6$$

The data is spread about the mean value 6 – it ranges from 2 to 10 – and the *variance* is a measure of this spread. To quantify this spread we first notice that we can tabulate the *deviations* from the mean as follows:

x	$x - m$
2	−4
4	−2
6	0
8	2
10	4

Notice that if we add up all these deviations from the mean we obtain 0 – there is as much data less the mean as there is greater. The problem lies in the negative values so we get rid of them by taking the *magnitude* of the deviations. If we take the magnitude of these deviations and then add them all up we no longer obtain 0 but 12:

x	$x - m$	$\lvert x - m \rvert$
2	−4	4
4	−2	2
6	0	0
8	2	2
10	4	4
		12

If we now divide this total by the total number of data items 5 we obtain the *mean absolute deviation* $12/5 = 2.4$. This is a good measure of the spread of the data but it suffers from a cumbersome applicability when dealing with spread more mathematically. Another way of getting rid of the negative signs in the deviations is to square them:

x	$x - m$	$(x - m)^2$
2	−4	16
4	−2	4
6	0	0
8	2	4
10	4	16
		40

If we now divide this total by the total number of data items 5 we obtain the *variance* $40/5 = 8.0$. This is a better measure for the spread of the data because it is more easily handled mathematically. It does suffer from the problem of being in the square of the units of the data and to avoid this the standard measure of spread of data is taken to be the square root of the variance. This measure we call the *standard deviation*. The symbol we use for the variance is:

$$s^2 \quad \text{or} \quad s_{xx}$$

the latter being used when more than one variable is being discussed as in this problem.

If two variables vary together in perfect co-ordination they are said to be perfectly correlated. They do not have to have the same values and hence the same mean but their deviations about their respective means must match. For example, if a deviation from the mean of 4 units in the first variable is matched by a deviation of −3 in the second variable then a deviation from the mean of +4 in the first variable will be matched by a corresponding deviation of −3 in the second variable. A measure of this coordination is given by the covariance of the two variables:

$$s_{xy} = \Sigma \, (x - m_x)(y - m_y)$$

where m_x and m_y are the mean values of x and y respectively. The purpose of the correlation coefficient is to convey a sense of the correlation between one pair of variables with the correlation between a second pair. For this reason, the covariance is not sufficient. We need a quantity whose values range from -1 to $+1$ and for this reason we use the covariance normalized by dividing by the product of the standard deviations of each of the two variables:

$$r = s_{xy}/\sqrt{(s_{xx} \times s_{yy})}$$

Score x	60	25	9	13	40	33	31	34	40	27	19	49
Score y	51	15	3	5	30	21	20	24	31	16	8	37

We tabulate the data as follows:

x	$x - m_x$	$(x - m_x)^2$	y	$y - m_y$	$(y - m_y)^2$	$(x - m_x)(y - m_y)$
60	28.33	802.78	51	29.25	855.56	828.75
25	-6.67	44.44	15	-6.75	45.56	45.00
9	-22.67	513.78	3	-18.75	351.56	425.00
13	-18.67	348.44	5	-16.75	280.56	312.67
40	8.33	69.44	30	8.25	68.06	68.75
33	1.33	1.78	21	-0.75	0.56	-1.00
31	-0.67	0.44	20	-1.75	3.06	1.17
34	2.33	5.44	24	2.25	5.06	5.25
40	8.33	69.44	31	9.25	85.56	77.08
27	-4.67	21.78	16	-5.75	33.06	26.83
19	-12.67	160.44	8	-13.75	189.06	174.17
49	17.33	300.44	37	15.25	232.56	264.33
380		2338.67	261		2150.25	2228.00

$$m_x = 31.67 \qquad s_{xx} = 194.89 \qquad m_y = 21.75 \qquad s_{yy} = 179.19 \qquad s_{xy} = 185.67$$

Hence

$$r = s_{xy}/\sqrt{(s_{xx} \times s_{yy})}$$

$$= 0.994 \text{ to 3 d.p.}$$

Solution 14.2.2(c)

Let the equation

$$y = ax + b$$

represent the line of best fit – the *regression* line – for the collection of data pairs:

$$(x_i, y_i)$$

where i takes on whole number values from 1 to n and where n represents the total number of data pairs. The method of least squares tells us that the two parameters a and b can be obtained from the following formulae:

$$a = [n \Sigma \, yx - (\Sigma \, x)(\Sigma y)]/[n \Sigma \, (x^2) - (\Sigma \, x)^2]$$

$$b = [\Sigma \, y - a \Sigma \, x]/n$$

Consequently we need to consider the following tabulation:

x	y	xy	x^2
60	51	3060	3600
25	15	375	625
9	3	27	81
13	5	65	169
40	30	1200	1600
33	21	693	1089
31	20	620	961
34	24	816	1156
40	31	1240	1600
27	16	432	729
19	8	152	361
49	37	1813	2401
380	261	10493	14372

$a = [n \Sigma\, yx - (\Sigma\, x)(\Sigma\, y)]/[n \Sigma\, (x^2) - (\Sigma\, x)^2]$
$= [12 \times 10493) - (380 \times 261)]/[(12 \times 14372) - (380 \times 380)]$
$= 0.953$ to 3 d.p.

$b = [\Sigma\, y - a \Sigma\, x]/n$
$= [261 - (0.9531 \times 380)]/12$
$= -8.418$ to 3 d.p.

If we plot the data on a scattergraph and on the same graph plot the regression line (Figure 14.2.3) we can see the closeness of fit of the data to the regression line indicating the close correlation between the two sets of data.

Rank correlation

A further measure of correlation which is available when the attributes measured are non-numerical or when the numerical data has insufficient precision is the

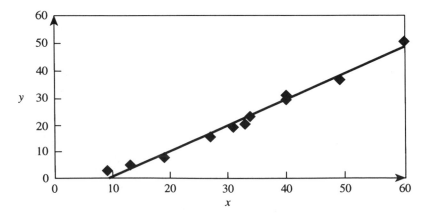

Figure 14.2.3

Spearman rank correlation coefficient which measures the correlation in the respective ranking of two collections of data.

EXAMPLE 14.2.3

Kitchen Brite Co Ltd organized a survey of its past customers to determine, amongst other things, colour preferences for kitchen cookers and utensils. On the questionnaire that they issued one question requested the respondent to rank a list of seven colours in order of preference from 1 to 7. They surveyed 2400 households and on the questionnaire they also requested to know the sex of the respondent because they wished to know whether male colour preferences matched those of female colour preferences. Of the 1913 replies they received 1423 had been filled in by a female and the remainder by a male. The results of their survey was as follows where the numbers in the table refer to the number of respondents who chose that particular colour as their favourite:

	Female	*Male*
Red	104	54
Orange	37	5
Yellow	227	83
Green	494	95
Blue	353	102
Black	86	72
White	122	79

Solution 14.2.3

The following table shows the ranking of the choice of colour for males and females:

	Female	*Male*	d	d^2
Red	5	6	1	1
Orange	7	7	0	0
Yellow	3	3	0	0
Green	1	2	1	1
Blue	2	1	−1	1
Black	6	5	−1	1
White	4	4	0	0
			Total	4

Correlation coefficient = r_s

$$= 1 - [6 \, \Sigma \, d^2 / n(n^2 - 1)]$$
$$= 1 - [(6 \times 4) \div (7 \times 48)]$$
$$= 1 - 1/14$$
$$= 0.929 \text{ to 3 d.p.}$$

Here we see that there is a high degree of correlation between male and female colour preferences.

1 To test the effect of a recent advertising campaign, 11 shoppers were questioned before the campaign and given an initial score (X), depending upon how well known a series of products were. After the advertising campaign they were questioned again and given a final score (Y). An increase in score represented an increase in product awareness. The scores for the 12 shoppers are given in the following table:

Shopper	1	2	3	4	5	6	7	8	9	10	11
Score X	5	2	3	11	35	27	33	29	38	22	17
Score Y	6	3	8	15	38	29	37	35	30	26	21

(a) Plot the data on a scattergraph.

(b) Calculate the correlation coefficient and test for its significance, stating any necessary assumptions.

(c) Calculate the regression line and add it to your graph.

(d) Calculate the standard error of the estimate.

(e) What would be your prediction of the final score of a shopper with an initial score of 25?

2 The Supplies Officer of a local authority is reviewing his policy for the replacement of photocopiers. For the 10 photocopiers in use within the local authority, the number of breakdowns during the past year has been recorded.

Photocopier	A	B	C	D	E	F	G	H	I	J
No of breakdowns	11	9	13	10	18	13	15	8	16	10
Age (in years)	6	4	6	2	9	4	8	1	7	3

The Supplies Officer wishes to determine how the number of breakdowns depends upon the age of the photocopier.

(a) Plot a scatter diagram of the above data.

(b) Calculate the coefficient of correlation between the two variables.

(c) Advise the computer manager on the number of breakdowns he might expect from a 5 year old photocopier.

14.3 GOODNESS OF FIT

We have been concerned that when we derived the regression line we were not blindly applying the data to the formulae and we have used correlation as a measure of the extent to which two sets of data are related. An alternative measure of the extent to which two sets of data are related is the χ^2 *goodness of fit* measure. If a collection of events occur with an accompanying set of observed frequencies O_i, each one of which can be compared to an expected frequency E_i then we define the *chi-squared goodness of fit* measure as:

$$\chi^2 = \Sigma \left[(O_i - E_i)^2 / E_i^2 \right]$$

If χ^2 is close to zero then we can say that the fit of the data to the theoretical expectation is very close. The greater χ^2 becomes, the less well the data fits the theoretical expectation.

EXAMPLE 14.3.1

Find the χ^2 goodness of fit measure for the regression line found in Example 14.1.2 that dealt with Betta Toys who make toy assembly kits out of plastic. A new kit, recently introduced into the market, was proving very popular and so they decided to increase production. They were concerned that the fixed production costs remain the same and that the variable production costs only increase linearly with production quantity. Below is a table of production quantity against total production costs (in £00) for the first 12 days of production.

Quantity	30	50	80	150	160	200	210	240	300	310	370	510
Total costs	9	13	19	25	27	31	33	34	40	40	49	60

After analysis of this data it was found that the regression line was given by the equation:

$$y = 0.10x + 9.92$$

where the variable x refers to quantity and the variable y refers to the corresponding total cost.

Solution 14.3.1

In the table the total costs are the *observed* values that correspond to given values of the quantity. Using the equation of the regression line it is now possible to extend the table to include the *expected* total costs as predicted by the regression line:

Total costs

Quantity	Observed (O_i)	Expected (E_i)	Difference^2 $(O_i - E_i)^2$	$(O_i - E_i)^2/E_i^2$
30	9	12.92	15.37	0.092
50	13	14.92	3.69	0.017
80	19	17.92	1.17	0.004
150	25	24.92	0.01	0.000
160	27	25.92	1.17	0.002
200	31	29.92	1.17	0.001
210	33	30.92	4.33	0.005
240	34	33.92	0.01	0.000
300	40	39.92	0.01	0.000
310	40	40.92	0.85	0.001
370	49	46.92	4.33	0.002
510	60	60.92	0.85	0.000

Total $\chi^2 = 0.124$

$$\chi^2 = \Sigma \left[(O_i - E_i)^2/E_i^2 \right] = 0.124$$

The small value of χ^2 indicates that the regression line is a reasonable fit to the data.

EXERCISES 14.3

1 The sales director of a DIY chain of stores would like to investigate the relationship between the floor area of its stores and their annual sales in the previous year. He has collected the information in the following table from a random sample of 12 of their stores.

Sales area (x)	9	7	15	13	14	7	11	14	10	25	12.5	15
Annual sales (y)	118	116	165	157	165	130	138	132	150	220	170	180

(the area is measured in 000s m² and the sales in £00,000s)

(a) Plot a scatter diagram for the above data.

(b) Calculate the value of the correlation coefficient (r) and test the hypothesis that a linear relationship exists between annual sales and sales area.

(c) With reference to your scatter diagram, do you have any reservations about your answer to part (b)?

(d) Calculate the equation of the regression line suitable for predicting the annual sales given floor area. Plot the line on the scatter diagram and interpret the gradient of this line.

(e) Calculate the goodness of fit.

(f) Use the equation found in part (d) to predict the annual sales for a store whose floor area is 16,000 m².

2 A company that manufactures ball-point pens has a cost function of the form:

$$T = T_0 + kx^2$$

where T_0 represent the fixed costs, k is a constant value linked to the production method used and x is the quantity of pens (in thousands) manufactured. During 1996 the total costs of the company were recorded as follows (where pens are recorded in thousands and costs are recorded in £000s)

Month	Jan	Feb	Mar	Apr	May	Jun	Jul	Aug	Sep	Oct	Nov	Dec
No of pens (x)	5.5	4.2	6.4	3.3	7.2	8.6	9.2	3.9	6.8	8.3	5.9	8.2
Total cost (T)	80.1	80.4	58.0	90.1	47.2	27.0	17.4	82.8	53.8	33.1	63.2	32.8

(a) Plot a scattergraph of this data plotting x^2 horizontally and T vertically.

(b) Draw a line of best fit by eye on the scattergraph.

(c) Calculate the regression line:

$$T = T_0 + kx^2$$

and obtain the values of T_0 and k.

(d) Demonstrate that the point with coordinates (p, q) where p is the mean value of x^2 and q is the mean value of T lie on the regression line.

(e) Calculate the total costs when 6000 pens are manufactured.

(f) Calculate the goodness of fit.

15

TIME SERIES

When you have completed this chapter you will be able to:

- identify time-series data and distinguish between the meanings of short-term variation and long-term tendency
- distinguish between the meanings of seasonal, cyclical and residual variation in time-series data
- construct a trend line for time-series data using the method of moving averages
- obtain the seasonal factors and from them the average seasonal factors
- understand the meaning of de-seasonalizing time-series data
- seasonalize data obtained from predictions made from de-seasonalized time-series data.

15.1 THE SHORT TERM VERSUS THE LONG TERM

Anyone who has been employed in a British coastal resort will have experienced the hive of activity of the summer months followed by the eerie quietness of the winter. As a short-term prospect for employment over a single year it does not bode well because the low pay in the winter months may militate against the good pay of the summer months. However, over the longer term of many years the overall annual pay may improve despite the highs of the summers and the lows of the winters. Situations such as this demonstrate the need to be able to analyse seasonal fluctuations in data to find out how the data is behaving in the longer term.

EXAMPLE 15.1.1

Joe was responsible for purchasing imported cold-reduced steel coils for SteelStock Ltd., a large steel stockholder with branches in all the UK major cities. For the past three years trade had been improving and all financial and market indicators seemed to suggest that this state of affairs would continue, at least into the near future. Last January Joe was was faced with a problem. He was offered a large consignment of 12 gauge cold-reduced steel coil from a supplier in Rotterdam provided that he paid for it in January but took delivery in April. Ordinarily Joe would not have taken any notice of such an offer but this time the price of the steel was incredibly low. Unfortunately, the consignment was large enough at 2000 tonnes to cover at least three months of 12 gauge cold-reduced steel sales. This was his problem. Should he buy the 2000 tonnes of steel and thereby dramatically *increase* the company's profits? But what if the steel did not all sell in the three months? The cost of storing the steel was so high that if he did not sell it all in three months the company would incur extra storage costs and thereby dramatically *decrease* the profits.

Explanation   A **time series** is the name given to data that is collected during a period of time. Typically, the data consists of the value of some quantity and the time at which it was collected. The time can be given in hours, days, months or even years – it all depends upon the nature of the problem. For example, the following table records the number of newspapers sold by a newsagent during the first six months of the year.

Month	Jan	Feb	Mar	Apr	May	Jun
Quantity	1250	1450	1500	1200	1500	1350

This record is a typical time series.

With data in this form it is natural to plot a graph of time against takings. We plot the time horizontally and the other variable vertically. Figure 15.1.1 is the graph of the time series recorded in the table.

Notice that the data consists of 6 ordered pairs, each consisting of a number and a month. These 6 ordered pairs are plotted as points and then each point is joined to its neighbour by a straight line to form a jagged-line graph. Jagged-line graphs are typical of time series.

Uses of time series   The purpose of collecting time series data is to enable us to *predict* future events. A fast-food outlet may notice that each week the number of apple turnovers that is being sold is decreasing. By a careful analysis of quantity sold over a period of time the manager may be able to predict how many apple

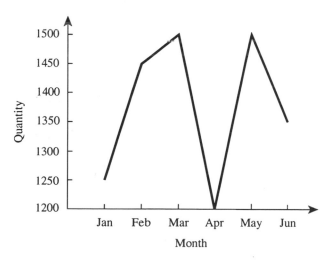

Figure 15.1.1

turnovers she will expect to sell next month. She will then be able to make sure that she does not buy in more apple turnovers than she can sell. When the quantity of apple turnovers sold decreases steadily each week it is fairly safe to predict that next week the quantity sold will decrease again. However, in most real-life situations the problems are more involved. For example, the following table records the number of cars sold by a county-wide group of car showrooms over the period of two years:

Cars sold	Year 1	Year 2
January	53	55
February	12	25
March	28	41
April	48	55
May	62	71
June	74	80
July	105	128
August	146	173
September	120	131
October	98	105
November	75	82
December	61	60

A graph of this data is given in Figure 15.1.2. It can be seen that the graph of this time series varies with troughs and peaks. Indeed the troughs and peaks occur quite regularly but at the same time there is a steady tendency for the graph to rise. Here we must distinguish between two properties of times series, namely the *short-term variation* and the *long-term tendency*.

The short-term variation The short-term variation is the rise and fall of the graph over periods of time that are short compared with the total time scale of the graph This short-term variation is displayed as a series of troughs and peaks. The

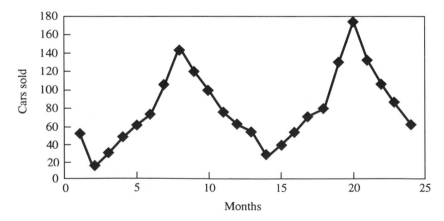

Figure 15.1.2

causes of short-term variations can be separated into three categories of seasonal, cyclical and residual fluctuations

- *Seasonal fluctuations*
  Data can vary regularly due to seasonal influences. For example, more cars are bought in August when the number plates change their prefix letter than at any other time of the year. Such variations in the data that occur regularly are called *seasonal fluctuations*. But be careful about the name *season*. It does not necessarily refer to the annual seasons. If we find regular fluctuations of a commodity over the short-term period of a week then these fluctuations are still called *seasonal*. The essential feature of a seasonal fluctuation is that it is *regular*.

- *Cyclical fluctuations*
  Data can vary because certain influences are felt at certain times in a semi-regular manner. Business activity is affected by boom and slump and these two effects occur with regularity but not at specified, regular time intervals. This sort of up-and-down variation that is not regular in time is called a *cyclical fluctuation*.

- *Residual fluctuations*
  Any variation in the data that is neither seasonal nor cyclic is called *residual*. Such fluctuations can be caused by catastrophic events such as fire or flood. They can also be caused by more predictable but still random events such as labour disputes or extreme weather conditions.

We shall only consider in detail the seasonal fluctuations.

The long-term tendency   We saw in the last illustration that the sale of cars had a regular variation over the short term. We also saw that over the two year period there was a tendency for the sales to *increase*. This *long-term tendency* is called the **trend**. In our example the trend is for the sales to increase. However, just by looking at the data or the graph it is impossible to quantify this trend. The trend is mixed up with the seasonal variations. In order to quantify the trend we must separate it from the seasonal variations. We do this by using the method of moving averages.

Solution 15.1.1
Before Joe could make a decision he had to have some idea of how much steel he could be expected to need during next April, May and June. To enable him to make this prediction he had to make a record of the steel sold for each three month (quarterly) period for the past three years. Below is a table that contains this record.

Steel sales	Year 1	Year 2	Year 3
1st Qrtr	1240	1460	1680
2nd Qrtr	1020	1300	1670
3rd Qrtr	830	1050	1440
4th Qrtr	1150	1320	1800

313

From this table Joe produced the graph shown in Figure 15.1.3. As can be seen from the graph the sales do appear to have an upward trend which confirms Joe's experiences concerning improving trade over the past three years. However, this trend is mixed up with a seasonal fluctuation that repeats itself every year. In order to even out these seasonal fluctuations Joe has three options, he can either:

draw a trend line of best fit by eye
draw a trend line using regression
draw a trend line using the method of moving averages.

Drawing a trend line of best fit by eye
This option was rejected because the line would be have to be curved and would produce predictions that were not accurate enough.

Drawing a trend line using regression
Joe could have managed this if the line had been straight. Unfortunately his mathematics was inadequate to cope with curved regression lines and so this option was ruled out.

Drawing a trend line using the method of moving averages
This is the option that Joe selected. The principle of using the method of moving averages is that the seasonal fluctuations are evened out over one short-term period at a time. This short-term period is the time over which the data falls from a maximum to a minimum and then rises back to a maximum. From the data collected by Joe it can be seen that this period is a year. As a consequence Joe found the moving average for successive yearly or four-quarterly periods. This is done in the following table.

Moving averages and seasonal variations

Qtr	Weight	4 Quarter total	Moving average	Centred average	Variations
Q1	1240				
Q2	1020				
		4240	1060		
Q3	830			1088	−258
		4460	1115		
Q4	1150			1150	0
		4740	1185		
Q1	1460			1213	247
		4960	1240		
Q2	1300			1262	38
		5130	1283		
Q3	1050			1311	−261
		5350	1338		
Q4	1320			1384	−64
		5720	1430		
Q1	1680			1479	201
		6110	1528		
Q2	1670			1588	82
		6590	1648		
Q3	1440				
Q4	1800				

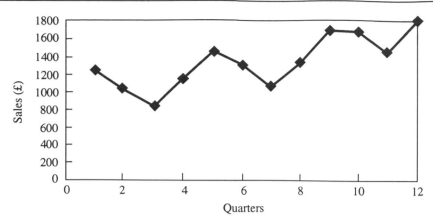

Figure 15.1.3

As we see this table consists of six columns. The first two columns contain the data collected by Joe, namely the quarter and the amount of steel sold during that quarter. The third column contains the sum of steel sold during four successive quarters – notice that the number is located in the middle of the period to which it refers. For example, the steel sold in the first year is 4240 tonnes and this quantity is located between the second and third quarters – in the middle of the year to which it refers. The next number below this is the sum of the steel sold during the last three quarters of the first year and the first quarter of the second year. The remainder of this column is obtained in the same manner, by subtracting the first quarter's steel sales in the previous sum and adding the next quarter's steel sales. The numbers in this column are the *moving totals* for consecutive four-quarter periods. The 4th column contains the *moving averages* for consecutive four-quarter periods. Each number in this column is equal to the adjacent number in the previous column divided by 4. These averages represent the average quarterly steel sales during a year – in this way the seasonal fluctuations have been averaged out.

From the spacings in the table we see that the moving averages are centred *between two quarters*. In other words the moving averages do not correspond in time to the times that the steel sales refer. Because of this we *centre* the moving averages to make them so correspond. The fifth column is the *average of the two nearest moving averages* in the fourth column. These centred moving averages are now positioned directly opposite a particular quarter's steel sales. This now allows us to complete the sixth column which contains the difference between the quarterly steel sales and the corresponding moving average for that quarter. If we had not centred the moving averages as we did then these numbers could not have been obtained.

The numbers in the fifth column represents the trend and this can now be plotted on a graph as shown in Figure 15.1.4.

Seasonal factors   The *trend* is the time series data with the *seasonal fluctuations* averaged out. In obtaining the trend as we have done we have *de-seasonalized* the original data. The variations in column six of the table represent the seasonal

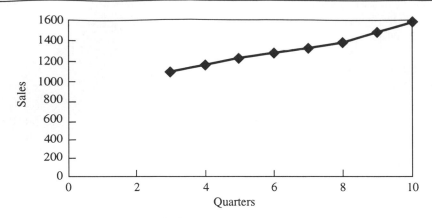

Figure 15.1.4

factors that de-seasonalize the original data. For example, the low steel sales of 830 tonnes in quarter 3 of the first year are de-seasonalized by subtracting it from the variation −258 tonnes in column 6 (effectively adding +258) to obtain 1088 tonnes. The high steel sales of 1680 tonnes in quarter 1 of the third year is de-seasonalized by subtracting the variation 201 tonnes to obtain 1479 tonnes. This is the effect of de-seasonalizing − low steel sales in one quarter are balanced against high steel sales in another quarter by subtracting the appropriate *seasonal factors*.

This principle will now allow us to de-seasonalize any future data. Each quarter in a year has a seasonal factor associated with it. This factor can then be subtracted from any future quarters usage, thereby de-seasonalizing it. Unfortunately, looking at the seasonal factors in column six we see that they are all different, so which ones should we use? What we really require are just four seasonal factors that can be applied during the appropriate quarter in any year. We achieve this by averaging the variations in column six.

In the following table the variations are given against the appropriate year and quarter.

Seasonal factors

	Qtr 1	*Qtr 2*	*Qtr 3*	*Qtr 4*	
Year 1	—	—	−258	0	
Year 2	247	38	−261	−64	
Year 3	201	82	—	—	
Total	448	120	−519	−64	
Average	224	60	−260	−32	(sum = −8)
Adjustment	+2	+2	+2	+2	(subtract −8/4 = −2)
Factors	**226**	**62**	**−258**	**−30**	

The *Total* row consists of the sum of the variations above and the Average row contains their average − the sum of the variations divided by the number of variations in the sum. These are the four unadjusted seasonal factors.

If the average seasonal fluctuations are added together their sum equals −8 (the number in brackets at the end of the Average row). We require seasonal factors that add up to zero so that over a complete year they cancel each other out. If the seasonal factors do not add up to zero their non-zero sum would be added to the trend. This would mean that they were not purely seasonal factors but contained additive factors as well. To achieve a zero sum we add +8 in four equal parts of +2 to each quarter's average. This gives the final row of adjusted seasonal *Factors* whose sum is zero. Notice that to take the seasonal effect out of the quarterly data we must *subtract* the seasonal factors − this is the process of *de-seasonalizing the data*.

Predictions   Joe could now use both the trend line and the seasonal factors to predict his anticipated steel sales during next April, May and June. If we refer to the original table we can see that in column five the trend falls short of the data by *two* quarters. By using the seasonal factors for these quarters we can de-seasonalize them.

In the 3rd quarter of year 3 the steel sales amounted to 1440 tonnes. The 3rd quarter seasonal factor is −258 tonnes which we subtract from the actual steel sales in order to de-seasonalize it. The same applies to the following quarter's 1800 tonnes of steel sales. This must be de-seasonalized by *subtracting* −30 tonnes. Thus,

$$1440 - (-258) = 1440 + 258$$
$$= 1698 \quad \text{(3rd quarter)}$$

and

$$1800 - (-30) = 1800 + 30$$
$$= 1830 \quad \text{(4th quarter)}$$

The complete trend is now plotted on the graph shown in Figure 15.1.5. We see that for the last two years the trend line more or less follows a smooth curve. We now project this curve by two quarters where the extension follows naturally from what has gone before (Figure 15.1.6)

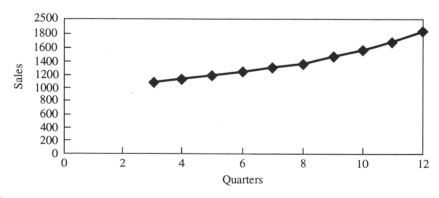

Figure 15.1.5

317

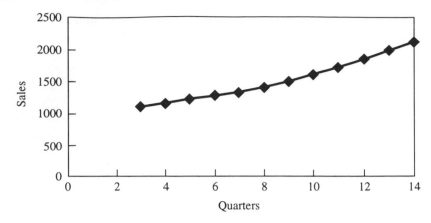

Figure 15.1.6

The projection represents the *prediction* of future steel sales over the next two quarters. This prediction is made against past sales and the reasonable expectation that the pattern in the graph will continue.

Reading off the second predicted quarters usage we see that 2100 tonnes of steel sales are expected to be sold during that 2nd quarter. Now we must remember that this number comes from the trend line which is a plot of de-seasonalized data. To obtain the predicted *actual* steel sales for the 2nd quarter we must *seasonalize* it by the seasonal factor for that quarter. This means that we must *add* the seasonal factor of 62 tonnes:

$$2100 + 62 = 2160 \text{ tonnes}$$

Since Joe had been offered 2000 tonnes of steel he accepted the offer and looked forward to a substantial increase in profits during that quarter.

Caution Using time series to make predictions in this way requires the exercise of caution. There are two assumptions that have been made that we must be aware of, namely the continuance of the trend pattern and that no residual or cyclical fluctuations are expected:

- **Continuance of the trend pattern**
  We are assuming that future behaviour will follow the same pattern as past behaviour. In many situations this can be a reasonable assumption but there is a limit to how far into the future we can go.

- **No residual or cyclical fluctuations expected**
  We are assuming that influences other than seasonal influences will not occur during the period of our prediction. This assumption must be made with careful consideration of future possibilities. For example, if the weather is likely to affect the figures then abnormal weather could seriously upset the prediction. Always remember Murphy's Law – *If it can go wrong then it more than likely will.* When making this second assumption always try to foresee any event whose occurrence could seriously affect the prediction.

EXERCISES 15.1

1 With regards to time series data distinguish between:

(a) short-term variation and long-term tendency

(b) seasonal, cyclical and residual variation.

2 What is meant by:

(a) de-seasonalizing time-series data

(b) seasonalizing data obtained from predictions made from de-seasonalized time-series data

3 The quarterly sales (£0000) of a Departmental Store have been monitored for the past 5 years with the following information being produced:

Total quarterly sales (£0000)

Year	Q_1	Q_2	Q_3	Q_4
1992	70	83	95	70
1993	66	76	87	61
1994	57	69	79	47
1995	45	60	75	47
1996	40	51	63	38

(a) Plot the given data as a time series leaving room for your forecasts for 1997.

(b) Construct the time series table of moving averages (this would be given in an examination with just a few numbers to fill in).

(c) Plot the trend line on the same graph

(d) Calculate the seasonal averages for each of the quarters.

(e) Find the de-seasonalized data for the last two quarters of 1996.

(f) Extend the trend line and use it to forecast the sales of the Departmental Store for each of the first two quarters of 1997, describing clearly the method used. State your forecasts.

4 The table below shows the number of passengers per quarter (in thousands) who flew with the Wings Charter Airline during the years 1993-1995 and the first quarter of 1996:

Year	Q_1	Q_2	Q_3	Q_4
1993	44	92	156	68
1994	60	112	180	80
1995	64	124	200	104
1996	76			

(a) Plot the given data as a time series.

(b) Construct the time series table of moving averages.

(c) Plot the trend line on the same graph.

(d) Estimate the average annual increase in the number of passengers over the period given.

(e) Calculate figures for the seasonal variation and hence de-seasonalize the data in the table above.

(f) Find the de-seasonalized data for the last quarter of 1995, and the first quarter of 1996.

5 The quarterly index numbers of the retail price of a particular commodity are recorded for four years as:

Year	Q_1	Q_2	Q_3	Q_4
1993	295	283	266	265
1994	257	284	251	261
1995	255	254	255	258
1996	255	260	249	261

Calculate the trend and the four seasonal fluctuations.

6 The following table shows the number of houses sold by a firm of estate agents:

Year	Q_1	Q_2	Q_3	Q_4
1994	135	198	182	156
1995	112	181	158	131
1996	80	164	143	107

(a) Use the method of moving averages to find the trend.

(b) Use the additive model to find the seasonal averages.

(c) Use the results from (a) and (b) to predict the sales in the first quarter of 1997.

16

SETS AND RANDOM EXPERIMENTS

When you have completed this chapter you will be able to:

- define a random experiment and its result and list its outcomes
- distinguish between an outcome, an event and the sample space of a random experiment.
- distinguish between elements and subsets of a set, the empty set and the universal set
- manipulate sets using the operations of union, intersection and complement
- understand the meaning of the cardinality of a set
- construct outcome trees for a random experiment
- combine outcomes into events and to illustrate these events using Venn diagrams

16.1 INFERENTIAL STATISTICS

Successful marketing depends upon the quality and reliability of the product being sold and to ensure quality and reliability a company must continually test its product. If, however, a company is producing large quantities of a particular item the costs involved in testing every single item may very well exceed the profit that it makes from selling them. Fortunately this problem can be overcome by taking samples of a production run and, from a knowledge of the properties of the samples, properties of the entire production run can be inferred. This is the domain of that aspect of statistics known as *inferential statistics*. Crucial to the study of inferential statistics is a knowledge of sets, random experiments and probability.

EXAMPLE 16.1.1

A potato crisp factory buys potatoes in large batches. Their crisp production line requires each potato to be of a certain minimum size and this is made clear to the potato merchant when the potatoes are purchased. The company will tolerate 5% of their purchase to be undersized but above that they require compensation from the merchant. As part of their quality control system the potatoes are sorted by rolling them over a filter-grid; the small potatoes fall through the grid and the large potatoes pass over the grid. For every batch of potatoes sorted in this way the quality control department weighs the collection of small potatoes filtered out to check that they are less than or equal to 5% of the batch; if they are less than or equal to 5% of the batch they decide to pass the batch, otherwise they fail it. By considering the process of weighing and sorting and the process of passing or failing the batch as two separate experiments:

(a) Define each process as a random experiment.

(b) Distinguish between the results of each random experiment and the outcomes of each random experiment.

(c) Define a random variable and list its values for each experiment.

(d) Describe the sample space of each random experiment.

(e) What conditions are imposed on the outcomes of each random experiment.

(f) Distinguish between a continuous and a discrete random variable.

Explanation An **experiment** is any action or sequence of actions that are performed to find the value of some unknown quantity. The unknown quantity whose value we are trying to find is called the *result* of the experiment and its value, found from an experiment, is called an *outcome* of the result. By the very nature of an experiment, an outcome is unknown before the experiment is performed; a result can be anticipated but its actual value – the outcome – is unknown until the experiment is completed. Any experiment that has a result with more than one possible outcome is referred to as a **random experiment** and the complete list of possible outcomes is called the **sample space** of the experiment. The only requirement that is made of the outcomes of a random experiment is that they be *mutually exclusive*, that is that only one of the possible outcomes can actually occur when the experiment is performed – *the result can only have one value*.

Solution 16.1.1(a)

The process of sorting and weighing the small potatoes is an experiment as is the process of comparing the weight of the collection of small potatoes to the weight of the batch. The sequence of actions in the first experiment consists in sorting the small potatoes from the larger potatoes and weighing the small potatoes; the value of the unknown quantity found being the weight of the small potatoes. The sequence of actions in the second experiment consists in comparing two weights with each other, the value of the unknown quantity found being the decision to accept or reject the batch of potatoes based upon the comparative weight of the small potatoes in relation to the total weight of all the potatoes in the batch.

Consider the first experiment of sorting and weighing potatoes. Before the sorted potatoes are weighed it is not known how heavy they are. It is, however, known that they will have a weight – the experiment will produce a result. Because the result can have more than one value ranging from the smallest to the largest value on the weighing scale the experiment is a random experiment.

The experiment of comparing the weight of the small potatoes to the entire batch potatoes and deciding on the fitness of the batch is also a random experiment because the result can have one of two values – Pass or Fail.

Solution 16.1.1(b)

The result of the first experiment is the weight of the small potatoes. The outcomes are the many possible values of the weight. The result of the second experiment is a decision. The outcomes are the decision Pass and Fail.

Solution 16.1.1(c)

A random variable represents the result of a random experiment. The values of the random variable are the outcomes of the experiment. In the case of the first experiment the random variable is the weight W of the small potatoes and the values of that variable are the possible values of the weight. In the case of the second experiment the random variable is the decision D and the values of that variable are the possible values of the decision – namely, Pass and Fail.

Solution 16.1.1(d)

The sample space consists of the list of the outcomes. In the case of the first experiment the sample space consists of each possible weight of the small potatoes. Symbolically, we can write the sample space S as:

$S = \{W$ where W is the weight of the small potatoes$\}$

In the case of the second experiment the sample space consists of just two outcomes – namely, Pass and Fail. Here

$S = \{$Pass, Fail$\}$

Solution 16.1.1(e)

The outcomes must be mutually exclusive, that is only one of them can occur. In the case of the first experiment the small potatoes will have a weight whose value is just one of the many listed in the sample space. In the case of the second experiment the decision will have just one value – namely, Pass or Fail.

Solution 16.1.1(f)

A continuous random variable is one whose values come from a continuous scale of values whereas a discrete variable is one whose values come from a scale of values consisting of isolated points. In the case of the first experiment the random variable is continuous because the weight of the small potatoes will have a value taken from a continuous scale of weights ranging from the smallest to the largest weight on the weighing scale. In the case of the second experiment the random variable is discrete because the decision will have a value taken from just the two distinct values – namely, Pass and Fail.

EXAMPLE 16.1.2

In the office of an insurance agency there are 23 clerks amongst a total of 32 employees. Of the 23 clerks 15 have typing skills and 13 have filing skills. The telephone rings and an employee answers it. Considering the answering of the telephone by one of the employees as a random experiment where the outcome is the identity of the employee:

(a) Construct the sample space and give its cardinality.
(b) Describe the two subsets of the sample space that are distinguished by the skills of their members but are not mutually exclusive.
(c) In terms of the two subsets of **(b)** define the three events:
    (i) $E1$: the person answering the telephone possesses both skills
    (ii) $E2$: the person answering the telephone possesses only one of the two skills
    (iii) $E3$: the person answering the telephone possesses neither of the skills
(d) How many people possess:
    (i)   both skills
    (ii) only one of the two skills
    (iii) neither of the skills
(e) How many employees can either file or not type
(f) What is the difference between an outcome and an event.

Explanation   A **set** is a collection of objects such as a set of tools or a set of numbers or a set of outcomes of the result from a random experiment. The notation used to denote a set consists of a pair of curly brackets { ... } where the individual objects that comprise the set are described inside the brackets. For example, the set consisting of the whole numbers 1 to 5 can be written as:

$$\{1, 2, 3, 4, 5\}$$

where the contents are listed individually. Alternatively, the set could be written as:

$$\{x : x \text{ is a whole number and } 1 \leqslant x \leqslant 5\}$$

This is read as:

> *The set of x values, where the value of x is a whole number and x is greater than or equal to one and less than or equal to five.*

The colon (:) stands for the word *where*. In this description of the set the contents are *prescribed* by describing the properties that they hold in common. Notice that sets:

$$\{1, 1, 2, 2, 2, 3, 4, 5\} \quad \text{and} \quad \{1, 2, 3, 4, 5\}$$

are the same set; sets do not contain repeated elements.

    Many times it is more convenient to refer to a set without continually describing its contents in which case we use capital letters as identifiers. For example:

$$A = \{\text{Head, Tail}\}$$

Here the set consisting of the possible outcomes from tossing a coin has been called set A and can now be referred to in future by simply using the letter A.

The individual objects that are contained within a set are called **elements** of the set and the symbol $\in$ is used to denote membership of a set. For example, if:

$$A = [a, b, c\} \quad \text{and} \quad B = \{c, d, e\}$$

then $a \in A$ and $d \in B$. That is, *a is an element of set A and b is an element of set B*. Note that $a \notin B$ and $d \notin A$: the slash through the symbol negates the symbol so that $\notin$ means *not a member*. Hence, *a is not an element of B* and *d is not an element of A*.

Set notation is used to describe the sample space of possible outcomes of the result of a random experiment. For example, if a random experiment were performed to select a coloured ball from a bag containing red, blue, yellow and green balls then the sample space (denoted by set S) of this experiment would be:

$$S = \{\text{Red, Blue, Yellow, Green}\}$$

Here the result of the experiment is a ball drawn from the bag and its possible values are its possible colours – the four possible outcomes.

Solution 16.1.2(a)

The sample space of the random experiment of answering the telephone is:

$$S = \{x : x \text{ is an employee of the insurance office}\}$$

Explanation Additional sets can be formed by using the elements of a given set. For example, given the set:

$$A = \{a, b, c\}$$

then by just using the elements of set A the following additional sets could be formed:

$$\{a\}, \{b\}, \{c\}, \{a, b\}, \{a, c\}, \{b, c\}$$

Each of these sets is called a **subset** of A and the notation used to denote a subset is $\subseteq$ or $\supseteq$. For example:

$$\{a, b\} \subseteq \{a, b, c\} \quad \text{or, alternatively} \quad \{a, b, c\} \supseteq \{a, b\}$$

The set $\{a, b\}$ is a subset of the set $\{a, b, c\}$.

If two sets A and B are such that:

$$A \subseteq B \quad \text{and} \quad B \subseteq A \quad \text{then} \quad A = B$$

Two sets are equal if they both contain the same elements.

If $A \subseteq B$ and $A \neq B$ then A is called a *proper subset* of B and the symbol to denote a proper subset is $\subset$ or $\supset$. That is

$$\{a, b\} \subset \{a, b, c\} \quad \text{or} \quad \{a, b, c\} \supset \{a, b\}$$

The empty set The empty set is defined as the set that contains no elements at all and is denoted by:

$$\{\} \quad \text{or, more commonly, by} \quad \varnothing$$

The empty set may seem to be an odd set to define but it is necessary to complete the rules which govern the manipulation of sets. The empty set is unique and every set has the *empty set* as a subset.

Any pair of subsets that have no elements in common are said to be *mutually exclusive subsets* so that:

$\{a\}$, $\{b\}$ and $\{c\}$ are all mutually exclusive as are $\{a\}$ and $\{b, c\}$

because they have no elements in common. However, sets

$\{a\}$ and $\{a, b\}$ are not mutually exclusive

because they both contain the element a.

The universal set The universal set – denoted by U – is the set that contains all the elements under discussion. For example, if

$A = \{x : x$ is a person with blue eyes$\}$ and $B = \{x : x$ is a person with green eyes$\}$

then the universal set could be:

$U = \{x : x$ is a person with blue or green eyes$\}$

Notice the words 'could be'. The universal set is not unique. In the past example the universal set could have been defined as:

$U = \{x : x$ is a person$\}$

The definition of a universal set depends upon the context of the problem. The overriding factor is that all the sets that are going to be discussed *must be subsets of the universal set*. For a random experiment the universal set is the sample space:

$U = S$

Solution 16.1.2(b)
The two subsets of the sample space that are distinguished by the skills of their members we shall call A and B where:

$A = \{a : a \in S$ and a has typing skills$\}$

$B = \{b : b \in S$ and b has filing skills$\}$

We can demonstrate this situation graphically using a Venn diagram (Figure 16.1.1). Here the rectangle is taken to represent the universal set – the sample space – and the circles are each taken to represent the sets A and B respectively. Notice that sets A and B overlap because there are employees who can both type and file. Remember that there are 15 typing clerks and 13 filing clerks but only 23 clerks in total so some clerks must be able to perform both tasks. That region of the sample space that consists of the overlap of the two sets is called:

the **intersection** of the two sets A and B

and is written as:

$A \cap B$

Clearly, if $x \in A \cap B$ then x is a clerk who can *both type and file*.

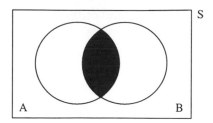

Figure 16.1.1
Intersection $A \cap B$

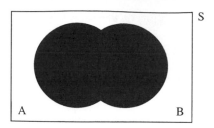

Figure 16.1.2
Union $A \cup B$

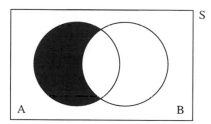

Figure 16.1.3
$A \cap B'$

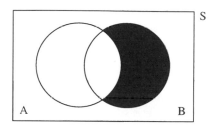

Figure 16.1.4
$B \cap A'$

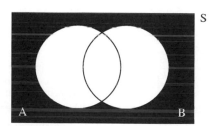

Figure 16.1.5
$A' \cap B'$

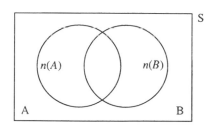

Figure 16.1.6
$n(A \cup B) = n(A) + n(B) - n(A \cap B)$

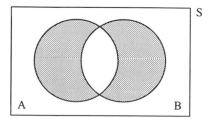

Figure 16.1.7
$n(A) + n(B) - 2n(A \cap B)$

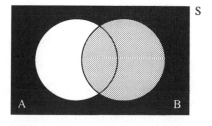

Figure 16.1.8
$n(B \cup A') = n(A') + n(A \cap B)$

That region of the sample space that consists of the totality of the two sets is called:

the **union** of the two sets A and B

and is written as:

$A \cup B$

Clearly, if $x \in A \cup B$ then a is a clerk who can *either type or file*. This *or* is an *inclusive or* because it permits the situation where an element of the union can both type and file as can be seen from Figure 16.1.2.

Explanation   Whilst the result of a random experiment will be a single outcome we may not be interested in the specific outcome but whether the outcome lies within a range of possible outcomes. For example, if we roll a six-sided die we may be interested to know not the actual value but whether the value showing on the uppermost face is less than 4. Here the range of possible outcomes is:

1, 2 or 3

Events   To cater for ranges of possible outcomes we define an event. An *event* is a subset of the sample space. In the example just considered we would define event E as:

$E = \{1, 2, 3\}$

An *event* is a subset of the sample space and different events may or may not be mutually exclusive. An event containing a single outcome is called a *simple event*. For example, for the random experiment of tossing a coin, the sample space is:

$\{H, T\}$

and the collection of mutually exclusive subsets:

$\{H\}$ and $\{T\}$

are the only two possible simple events associated with the random experiment. All random experiments have a unique collection of simple events; however, they are not always the only events that can be defined. In the random experiment of throwing a die we could define the events:

$E1$ an even number
$E2$ a number less than four

These events are then described by the following sets:

$E1 = \{2, 4, 6\}$ and $E2 = \{1, 2, 3\}$

which are not mutually exclusive because the number 2 is common to both.

Solution 16.1.2(c(i))

The event $E1$ is the set of those people who possess both skills. A person who possesses typing skills is an element of set A and a person who possesses filing skills is an element of set B. Consequently, a person who possesses both skills is an element of both set A and set B – the intersection of set A and set B:

$E1 = A \cap B$

Solution 16.1.2(c(ii))

The event $E2$ is the set of those people who possess only one of the two skills. A person who possesses only typing skills is an element of set A but not an element of set B, i.e. an element of the intersection of A with the complement of B, namely $A \cap B'$ (Figure 16.1.3). (The complement B' of B contains those elements in S but not in B.)

A person who possesses only filing skills is an element of set B but not an element of set A, i.e. an element of the intersection of B with the complement of A, namely $B \cap A'$ (Figure 16.1.4).

A person who possesses only one of the two skills is an element of the union of these two sets:

$$E2 = (A \cap B') \cup (B \cap A')$$

Solution 16.1.2(c(iii))

The event $E3$ is the set of those people who possess neither of the skills. A person who does not possess typing skills is an element of the complement of A and a person who does not possess filing skills is an element of the complement of B. A person who possesses neither of these two skills is member of the intersection of these two complements (Figure 16.1.5):

$$E3 = A' \cap B'$$

Explanation   The number of elements in a set – the set **cardinality** – can be discussed by appeal to the Venn diagram in Figure 16.1.6.

Here we see that if we use the notation:

$$n(A)$$

to denote the number of elements in a set then:

$$n(A \cup B) = n(A) + n(B) - n(A \cap B)$$

The reason the number in the intersection is subtracted is because in adding the number in A to the number in B we add the number in the intersection twice. Also

$$n(S) = n(A) + n(A')$$

because the union of a set and its complement is the entire sample space.

Solution 16.1.2(d(i))

If an employee possesses both skills then the employee is an element of the intersection of A and B where:

$$n(A \cup B) = n(A) + n(B) - n(A \cap B)$$

We are given that:

$$n(A \cup B) = 23$$
$$n(A) = 15$$
$$n(B) = 13$$

Consequently:

$$23 = 15 + 13 - n(A \cap B)$$

$n(A \cap B) = 15 + 13 - 23 = 5$, the number of clerks who can both type and file.

Solution 16.1.2(d(ii))

If an employee only possesses one of the two skills then the employee is a member of the shaded region in the Venn diagram of Figure 16.1.7.

From the Figure we can see that the number possessing only the typing skill is:

$$n(A) - n(A \cap B) = 15 - 5 = 10$$

and the number possessing only the filling skill is:

$$n(B) - n(A \cap B) = 13 - 5 = 8$$

so that 18 possess only one of the two skills.

Solution 16.1.2(d(iii))

If an employee possesses neither of the skills then the employee is a member of the shaded region in the Venn diagram of Figure 16.1.5. From the Figure we can see that the number possessing neither skill is:

$$
\begin{aligned}
n(A' \cap B') &= n(A') + n(B') - n(A' \cup B') \\
&= (32 - 15) + (32 - 13) - (32 - 5) \\
&= 17 + 19 - 27 \\
&= 9
\end{aligned}
$$

Solution 16.1.2(e)

The number of employees who can either file or not type is given by (Figure 16.1.8):

$$
\begin{aligned}
n(B \cup A') &= n(A') + n(A \cap B) \\
&= (32 - 15) + 5 \\
&= 22
\end{aligned}
$$

Solution 16.1.2(f)

The difference between an outcome and an event is that an event is a set and an outcome is an element of an event.

EXAMPLE 16.1.3

The Quality Control Division of a large corporation manufacturing kitchen and bathroom units is responsible for making regular inspections of all equipment and manufactured items. In this way they maintain a level of control over the quality of the corporation's output prior to it being despatched to the various sales outlets. Part of the manufacturing process involves fitting strips of plastic sheet to the edges of blocks of chipboard using a fast drying adhesive. There are two machines responsible for performing this task, Machine A and Machine B, and a daily inspection is made by the Quality Control Division. This inspection is executed by randomly selecting a finished product from each machine and noting whether it is perfect or defective. Describe the following events in terms of the outcomes of two sequential random experiments:

(a) *E*1: a defect found from Machine B
(b) *E*2: two defects
(c) *E*3: at least one perfect product
(d) *E*4: a defect found from Machine B or at least one perfect product
(e) *E*5: a perfect product found from Machine A and a defect found from Machine B
(f) *E*6: no defect found from Machine B.

Illustrate your answers using a Venn diagrams.

Solution 16.1.3

When two or more random experiments are performed one after the other, the final outcomes of the sequence of experiments will consist of combinations of the outcomes of the individual experiments. Here, the two random experiments consist of:

(i) Selecting a product from Machine A
(ii) Selecting a product from Machine B.

We shall denote the sample space of the first by:

$$\{AP, AD\}$$

where *A* stands for the selection of Machine A and where *P* and *D* stand for perfect and defective product respectively. Similarly we denote the sample space of the second by:

$$\{BP, BD\}$$

where *B* stands for the selection of Machine B.

We can describe this sequence of experiments by using an outcome tree, as shown in Figure 16.1.9.

Experiment 1, represented by the square containing the number 1, is performed first and the two possible outcomes of its result are represented by the two branches labelled *AP* and *AD* respectively. Experiment 2, represented by the square containing the number 2, is then performed and the two possible outcomes of its result are represented by the two branches labelled *BP* and *BD* respectively. Notice that there are two sets of two branches for experiment 2 because of the two possible outcomes from experiment 1.

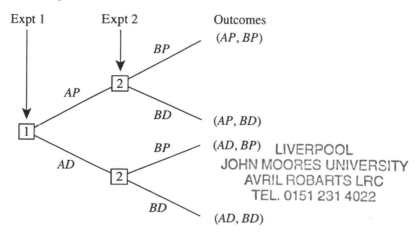

Figure 16.1.9

331

Each experiment has two possible outcomes so the sequence of two experiments has four possible combined outcomes and each combined outcome is represented by a specific route through the tree. For example, if the first experiment produced an outcome AP and the second an outcome BD then the final, combined outcome is (AP, BD) represented by the appropriate route through the tree. Each route is labelled with the two combined outcomes along that route.

From the outcome tree it can be seen that the sample space of the random experiment consisting of these two experiments performed in sequence is:

$$\{(AP, BP), (AP, BD), (AD, BP), (AD, BD)\}$$

Combining outcomes into events From this sample space we can construct events as follows.

Solution 16.1.3(a)

$$E1 = \{(AP, BD), (AD, BD)\}$$

Solution 16.1.3(b)

$$E2 = \{(AD, BD)\}$$

Solution 16.1.3(c)

$$E3 = \{(AP, BP), (AP, BD), (AD, BP)\}$$

Solution 16.1.3(d)

Here $E4$ consists of all the elements of $E1$ and all the elements of $E3$ – with no repetition. We say that $E4$ is the *union* of $E1$ and $E3$ and symbolically write this as:

$$
\begin{aligned}
E4 &= E1 \cup E3 \\
&= \{(AP, BD), (AD, BD)\} \cup \{(AP, BP), (AP, BD), (AD, BP)\} \\
&= \{(AP, BD), (AP, BP), (AD, BP), (AD, BD)\}
\end{aligned}
$$

Solution 16.1.3(e)

$E5$: a perfect product found from Machine A *and* a defect found from Machine B.

Here $E5$ consists of that element of $E1$ that is also in $E3$. We say that $E5$ is the intersection of $E1$ and $E3$ and symbolically write this as:

$$
\begin{aligned}
E5 &= \{(AP, BD)\} \\
&= E1 \cap E3
\end{aligned}
$$

Solution 16.1.3(f)

$E6$ (no defect found from Machine B) $= \{(AP, BP), (AD, BP)\}$

Here $E6$ consists of all the elements of the sample space that are *not* elements of $E1$. We say that $E6$ is the **complement** of $E1$ and symbolically write this as:

$$E6 = E1'$$

where the symbol $'$ stands for the complement of the set $E1$.

Sample space

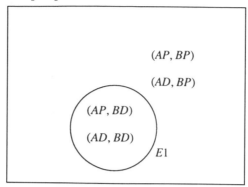

Figure 16.1.10

Venn diagrams In the Venn diagram of Figure 16.1.10 the sample space:

$$\{(AP, BP), (AP, BD), (AD, BP), (AD, BD)\}$$

is represented by the rectangle and the event $E1$ is represented by the circle. The three diagrams of Figure 16.1.11 represent

$$E4 = E1 \cup E3, \ E5 = E1 \cap E3 \text{ and } E6 = E1'$$

$$E4 = E1 \cup E3 = \{(AP, BD), (AP, BP), (AD, BP), (AD, BD)\}$$

The *union* of $E1$ and $E3$ consists of all the elements of $E1$ and $E3$ combined together. Notice that the element (AD, BD) is common to both but when the union is listed it is not repeated.

$$E5 = E1 \cap E3 = \{(AD, BD)\}$$

The *intersection* of $E1$ and $E3$ consists of the element that is in both $E1$ and $E3$.

$$E6 = E1' = \{(AP, BP), (AD, BP)\}$$

The *complement* of $E1$ consists of those elements of the sample space that are not in $E1$. In this case we have not represented $E6$ by a circle in order to stress the fact that $E6$ contains those elements of the sample space *not in $E1$*.

EXAMPLE 16.1.4

In an Engineering Shop there are 58 employees. Of the 58 employees 54 are fully trained and capable of using a lathe to machine helical gears. Using such a lathe requires calculating the settings prior to assembling the rig on the lathe, adjusting and setting the rig on the lathe and then supervising the gear cutting once the rig has been assembled. Of the 54 employees:

26 are capable of calculating the settings
30 are capable of adjusting and setting the rig
25 are capable of supervising the gear cutting
11 are capable of both calculating the settings and then adjusting and setting the rig

Sample space

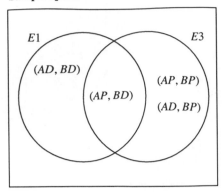

Notice: $E1 \cup E3$ = sample space

Sample space

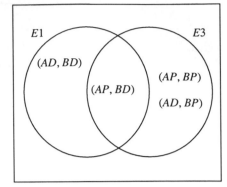

Notice: $E1 \cap E3 = \{(AD, BD)\}$

Sample space

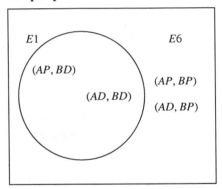

Notice: $E6 = E1' = \{(AP, BP), (AD, BP)\}$

Figure 16.1.11

9 are capable of both calculating the settings and supervising the gear cutting
12 are capable of adjusting and setting the rig and supervising the gear cutting

How many employees are capable of performing all three tasks?

Solution 16.1.4

Use the following set identifiers for brevity:

A = {employees capable of calculating the settings}
B = {employees capable of adjusting and setting the rig}
C = {employees capable of supervising the gear cutting}

The information that we are given can be rewritten in terms of set cardinality as follows:

$$n(A) = 26 \qquad n(A \cap B) = 11$$
$$n(B) = 30 \qquad n(A \cap C) = 9$$
$$n(C) = 25 \qquad n(B \cap C) = 12$$

plus the information that there are 54 qualified employees:

$$n(A \cup B \cup C) = 54$$

We are are required to find:

$$n(A \cap B \cap C)$$

From the properties of set cardinality:

$$n(A \cup B \cup C) = n(A) + n(B) + n(C) - n(A \cap B) - n(A \cap C) - n(B \cap C) \\ + n(A \cap B \cap C)$$

In terms of the specific cardinalities of sets A, B and C this is:

$$54 = 26 + 30 + 25 - 11 - 9 - 12 + n(A \cap B \cap C)$$

that is:

$$54 = 49 + n(A \cap B \cap C)$$

so that:

$$n(A \cap B \cap C) = 5$$

There are 5 employees who are capable of managing all three tasks.

EXERCISES 16.1

1   In each of the following random experiments define a random variable and determine whether the random variable is continuous or discrete:

(i)   Weighing portions of cheese

(ii) Counting the number of sheep in a pen

(iii) Determining the number of days lost per year due to illness

(iv) Recording the actual arrival time of a bus that is due to arrive on the hour every hour

(v)   Measuring the lengths of metre rules manufactured by an unreliable machine

(vi) Measuring the number of grains of sugar in a kilo.

2   A random experiment has a result whose value is one of the three outcomes: a, b or c. Construct the sample space of this experiment and write down all possible events.

3   Given the three sets:

$$A = \{-2, -1, 0, 1, 2\}, \, B = \{0, 1, 2\}, \, C = \{-3, -2, -1, 0\}$$

and the universal set:

$$S = \{-3, -2, -1, 0, 1, 2, 3\}$$

find:

(i) $A \cap B$ (iii) $A \cap (B \cup C)$ (v) $(A \cap B) \cup (A \cap C)$

(ii) $A \cup B$ (iv) $A \cup (B \cap C)$ (vi) $A' \cap B'$

4   A coin is tossed and then a coloured ball is drawn from a bag containing one red, one blue and one white ball. Construct the outcome tree for this sequence of random experiments. What are the simple events associated with this sequence of experiments?

5   ScrewLoose Ltd manufacture items of hardware such as screws, nuts, bolts and washers for the wholesale trade. One machine that they use to produce bolts is getting rather old and producing the occasional defective unit. However, the cost of replacement is rather high and to avoid the expense of replacement ScrewLoose have decided to continue using the machine whilst closely monitoring its output. This monitoring consists of selecting a sample of the day's production run and testing it for quality. If the sample they have collected contains more than 1 % of defective items the entire days production run is rejected. Otherwise, the production run is accepted; the company being willing to counter complaints with a policy of the immediate replacement of any defective goods found by their customers. By considering the process of sampling and testing and the process of passing or failing the batch as two separate experiments:

(a) Define each process as a random experiment.

(b) Distinguish between the results of each random experiment and the outcomes of each random experiment.

(c) Define a random variable and list its values for each experiment.

(d) Describe the sample space of each random experiment.

(e) What conditions are imposed on the outcomes of each random experiment?

(f) Construct an outcome tree for the sequences of experiments.

(g) Distinguish between a continuous and a discrete random variable.

6   In the office of a computer software agency there are 7 technicians amongst a total of 13 employees. Of the 7 technicians 5 have software installation skills and 4 have software user training skills. The first person in the office on any working day is responsible for filling the large automatic kettle with water in readiness for a continuous supply of fresh tea and coffee for the rest of the agency employees. Considering the arrival of the first employee as a random experiment where the outcome is the identity of the employee:

(a) Construct the sample space and give its cardinality.

(b) Describe the two subsets of the sample space that are distinguished by the skills of their members but are not mutually exclusive.

(c) How many people possess:

(i) both skills?

(ii) only one of the two skills?

(iii) neither of the skills?

(d) How many employees can either install software or not user train?

(e) Define three events:

(i) *E*1: the first person in the office possesses both skills

(ii) *E*2: the first person in the office possesses only one of the two skills

(iii) *E*3: the first person in the office possesses neither of the skills.

(f) Define the event *E*4: the first person in the office can either install software or not user train.

(g) What is the fundamental difference between an outcome and an event?

7 The following data shows the results of a market investigation on the frequency of usage of a particular product in the different regions of the country. It is based upon a random sample of 550 customers.

Region	Not at all	Once	More than once
North	20	40	60
Midlands	60	35	35
South	100	60	20
Scotland and Wales	35	45	40

By considering the selection of a person as coming from a particular region and ascertaining that person's usage as a sequence of two random experiments:

(a) Find the cardinality of each of the following events:

(i) *E*1: does use the product

(ii) *E*2: lives in the North

(iii) *E*3: does not live in the South or the Midlands.

(b) Describe each of the following events and give their cardinality:

(i) $E4 = E1 \cup E2$

(ii) $E5 = E1' \cap E3$

(iii) $E6 = E1' \cap (E3 \cup E2)$

8 In a bakery there are 20 employees of whom 11 are trained to mix ingredients, 11 are trained to supervise the baking ovens and 11 are trained to check the quality of the finished product. In addition, 4 are trained to both mix the ingredients and supervise the ovens, 5 are trained to mix the ingredients and check the quality of the finished product and 6 are trained to supervise the baking ovens and check the quality of the finished product. How many are trained for all three tasks?

17

EVENTS AND PROBABILITIES

When you have completed this chapter you will be able to:

- assign probabilities to simple events using either statistical regularity or *a priori* methods
- assign probabilities to events compounded by AND, OR and/or NOT
- determine whether two events are mutually exclusive or not
- calculate probabilities associated with sequences of random experiments, taking into account the dependence of events whenever it is evident

17.1 PROBABILITIES

If a sample of 10 items is to be extracted from a production run of 1000 for the purposes of testing the quality of the production run as a whole we need to be confident that the sample of 10 is a small *representation* of the entire 1000. To ensure this we need to discuss issues of *chance* – what are the chances that 1 defect in the sample of 10 means that there are 100 defects in the run of 1000? *Probability* is our means of measuring chance and to consider the chance outcomes to a random experiment in a meaningful way we need to be able to associate probabilities with events.

EXAMPLE 17.1.1

In a simple lottery a ball is drawn at random from a bag that contains 2 green, 3 yellow and 5 pink balls – 10 balls in total. After 1000 draws it has been recorded that the colours were drawn with the following frequencies:

Colour	Frequency
Green	220
Yellow	310
Pink	470

(a) Construct the relative frequencies of the three outcomes.

(b) Explain why this lottery is a random experiment and construct the three simple events whose union is the sample space of the random experiment.

(c) Describe how probabilities can be assigned to these events using the notion of *statistical regularity*.

(d) Assign probabilities to the events in **(b)** using the notion of *a priori* and discuss the relative merits of the two methods of assigning probabilities. With each method determine the probabilities that the ball drawn is:

(i) not green

(ii) either green or yellow

(iii) neither yellow nor pink.

Solution 17.1.1(a)

The relative frequency of an outcome is the frequency of the outcome divided by the total number of trials – in this case 1000. Hence the relative frequency table is given as:

Colour	Frequency	Relative frequency
Green	220	$220/1000 = 0.22$
Yellow	310	$310/1000 = 0.31$
Pink	470	$470/1000 = 0.47$
		$Total = 1.00$

Notice that each relative frequency is less than unity and the sum of all the relative frequencies is unity.

Solution 17.1.1(b)

The lottery is a random experiment because it has more than one possible outcome, the drawing of a green, yellow or a pink ball. The three simple events are:

$E1$: {green ball}
$E2$: {yellow ball}
$E3$: {pink ball}

Explanation   In the motor car construction industry robots are used to perform tasks that were originally performed by human operators. This is possible because the tasks can be precisely defined: two pieces of metal are aligned and clamped into a specified position, the robotic arm descends to a given location on the metal and places a weld in a precisely defined spot. Nothing is left to chance. The Oxford Dictionary defines chance as the *absence of design or discoverable cause* and in the case of a robotic welding rig design is omnipresent and based upon known causes. The behaviour of a tossed coin on the other hand is a perfect example of the absence of a discoverable cause. If we flip a coin it will spin, rise in the air and fall to the ground; this much we do know. However, whether it will land head up or tail up we do not know because we do not possess sufficient information to discover the cause.

There are many such instances where we know that any one of a collection of outcomes will occur but because we do not possess sufficient information we are unable to predict ahead of time which outcome of the collection actually will occur: a horse race, a lottery and a card drawn from a deck in a game of poker.

Such is the area of the random experiment, we know that one of the outcomes will occur but we just do not know which one.

Because the outcome of a random experiment is important we need to create a *measure of the chance of a particular outcome occurring* and this is where probability comes in.

Consider the random experiment of tossing a coin that has a head on both sides – a double-headed coin. If you toss this coin then it is *certain* to fall heads up. The event $\{H\}$ is a certain event and we shall define the probability of a certain event to be unity:

$$\Pr(\{H\}) = \Pr(\text{certainty}) = 1$$

Similarly, it is *impossible* for it to fall tails up – the event $\{T\}$ is an impossible event. We define the probability of an impossible event as zero:

$$\Pr(\{T\}) = \Pr(\text{impossibility}) = 0$$

If the double-headed coin is now replaced by a normal coin possessing a tail as well as a head then the event $\{H\}$ is no longer *certain* and the event $\{T\}$ is no longer *impossible*. In each case their probabilities lie between zero and unity:

$$0 < \Pr(\{H\}) < 1 \quad \text{and} \quad 0 < \Pr(\{T\}) < 1$$

Assigning correct numbers to these probabilities is not simple but what we do say is that because when a normal coin is tossed it is certain to show either a head or a tail then the two probabilities add up to the probability of certainty, that is unity:

$$\Pr(\{H\}) + \Pr(\{T\}) = \Pr(\text{certainty}) = 1$$

Assigning probabilities   Because the actual outcome from a random experiment that occurs when the experiment is performed does so according to the rules of chance we can assign probabilities to outcomes or, more precisely, we can assign probabilities to events.

Probabilities can be assigned to events either *a priori* – beforehand – or by *statistical regularity* – afterwards. For example, if we make the assumption that a coin is fair then we have tacitly assigned probabilities beforehand because the notion of fairness means that there is an equal chance of the tossed coin falling down heads as there is of it falling down tails. That is:

$$\Pr(\{H\}) + \Pr(\{T\}) = 1 \quad \text{and} \quad \Pr(\{H\}) = \Pr(\{T\})$$

so that $\Pr(\{H\}) = 1/2 = 0.50$

and $\Pr(\{T\}) = 1/2 = 0.50$

If, instead of assuming the coin to be fair, we tossed it 1000 times and found that we ended up with 510 heads and 490 tails then we would say that, based on statistical regularity, the probabilities were defined as:

$$\frac{\text{Number of times a simple event occurs in a sequence of trials}}{\text{Total number of trials}}$$

Consequently,

| probability of a head | $\Pr(\{H\}) = 510/1000 = 0.51$ |
| probability of a tail | $\Pr(\{T\}) = 490/1000 = 0.49$ |

Remember that the probabilities must add up to 1.

Solution 17.1.1(c)

Using the notion of statistical regularity we can assign probabilities to the three simple events by using the relative frequencies obtained from 1000 trials. Hence:

$$\Pr(\{\text{green ball}\}) = 0.22$$
$$\Pr(\{\text{yellow ball}\}) = 0.31$$
$$\Pr(\{\text{pink ball}\}) = 0.47$$

Notice that all the probabilities lie between zero and unity and they all add up to unity as they must.

Solution 17.1.1(d)

The only way that probabilities can be assigned *a priori* is by devising some notion of fairness and this we do by assuming that each ball in the bag has an equal probability of being drawn. This means that the probability of drawing any particular ball is then:

$$\Pr(\{\text{any particular ball}\}) = 1/10 = 0.1$$

Because there are:

2 green balls   3 yellow balls   5 pink balls

the probabilities are thus:

$$\Pr(\{\text{green ball}\}) = 2 \times 0.1 = 0.2$$
$$\Pr(\{\text{yellow ball}\}) = 3 \times 0.1 = 0.3$$
$$\Pr(\{\text{pink ball}\}) = 5 \times 0.1 = 0.5$$

Notice the similarity to the other probabilities assigned using statistical regularity, namely 0.22, 0.31 and 0.47 respectively.

The advantage of using statistical regularity to assign probabilities lies in the fact that they are derived from actually performing the experiment. The disadvantage is that by executing a few more trials of the experiment the probabilities are more than likely to change. For instance, if 10 more trials were executed and the frequencies became:

Colour	Frequency
Green	225
Yellow	313
Pink	472

then the probabilities would become:

$$Pr(\{green\ ball\}) = 0.223$$
$$Pr(\{yellow\ ball\}) = 0.310$$
$$Pr(\{pink\ ball\}) = 0.467$$

each to three decimal places. Consequently, the assigned probabilities depend upon when the trials cease.

The advantage of assigning probabilities *a priori* is that by using the notion of fairness each simple event has the same probability. This makes the assigning of probabilities to any compound event simply achieved by counting the number of outcomes to each event. The disadvantage lies in the assumption itself – the experiment may not be 'fair' at all and some bias towards one or a selection of outcomes may exist that may not evidence itself without a series of trials being performed.

Solution 17.1.1(e(i))

The ball drawn is not green.

A priori: there are 7 balls that are not green so $Pr(\{not\ green\ ball\}) = 7/10 = 0.7$

Statistical regularity: we know that the ball drawn will either be green or it will not be green. Therefore:

$$Pr(\{green\ ball\}) + Pr(\{not\ green\ ball\}) = 1$$

so that:

$$Pr(\{not\ green\ ball\}) = 1 - Pr(\{green\ ball\})$$
$$= 1 - 0.22$$
$$= 0.78$$

Solution 17.1.1(e(ii))

The ball drawn is either green or yellow.

A priori: there are 5 balls that are either green or yellow so:

$$Pr(\{green\ ball\ or\ yellow\ ball\}) = 5/10 = 0.5$$

Statistical regularity: we know that the ball drawn will either be pink or it will not be pink. Therefore:

$$Pr(\{pink\ ball\}) + Pr(\{not\ pink\ ball\}) = 1$$

so that:

$$Pr(\{not\ pink\ ball\}) = Pr(\{green\ ball\ or\ yellow\ ball\})$$
$$= 1 - Pr(\{pink\ ball\})$$
$$= 1 - 0.47$$
$$= 0.53$$

Solution 17.1.1(e(iii))

If the ball drawn is neither yellow nor pink then it must be green so that:

A priori: $Pr(\{green\ ball\}) = 0.2$ *Statistical regularity:* $Pr(\{green\ ball\}) = 0.22$

1 A loaded six-sided die was thrown 1200 times and the frequency with which certain numbers came up was as follows:

1	2	3	4	5	6
100	300	400	300	50	50

(a) What is the probability that on the next roll of the die the number that will come up is:

(i) 2   (ii) less than 3   (iii) 4 or 5   (iv) an odd number

(b) What would these probabilities have been had the die not been loaded but had been fair?

2 A company created an age profile of its workforce. The number of employees in specific age groups were found to be as follows:

<20	20–29	30–39	40–49	50–59	60>
355	910	430	250	108	14

(a) What is the probability that an employee, selected at random is aged:

(i) between 30 and 39   (ii) less than 40   (iii) more than 29

(b) What is the probability that an employee, selected at random is as old as or older than:

(i)   the average age

(ii) one standard deviation more than the average age

(iii) one standard deviation either side of the average age

if the average age of those under 20 is 19.70 and the average age of those over 60 is 63.00 and all calculations are taken to two decimal places at most.

3 Dyestampers Co Ltd produce components for the automotive trade that are cut out of 12 gauge cold-reduced sheet steel. One component, intended for a rotary unit, must have a weight of 10 grammes with a maximum tolerance of ±0.2 grammes. From a recent production run of this component the following results were obtained:

Weight	9.7	9.8	9.9	10.0	10.1	10.2	10.3
Number	10	50	785	666	949	0	10

(a) What is the probability that a component, selected at random, weighs:

(i)   more than 9.8 gm and less than 10.2 gm

(ii) less than 10.0 gm

(iii) more than 9.9 gm

(b) What is the probability that a component, selected at random, weighs more than:

  (i)   the average weight

  (ii) two standard deviations more than the average weight

  (iii) one standard deviation either side of the average weight

if all calculations are taken to one decimal places at most.

17.2 ASSIGNING PROBABILITIES TO COMPOUND EVENTS

Compound events

A compound event associated with a random experiment is a subset of the sample space and as such can be generated from the collection of simple events by using the operations of union, intersection and complementation.

EXAMPLE 17.2.1

The staff in a local University are identified as either academic or administrative staff and the following table lists the male and female academic and administrative staff:

	Academic	Administrative
Male	396	151
Female	245	208

If an individual member of staff is selected at random from the personnel list what is the probability that that person is:

(a) A male academic OR a female administrator

(b) Either female OR an academic

(c) NOT a male administrator.

Solution 17.2.1

Let $E1$ and $E2$ be two events associated with a random experiment. These two events can be connected via the set operation of *union* to form the event $E3$:

$$E3 = E1 \cup E2$$

Event $E3$ can be described in English as:

  event $E1$ OR event $E2$

In other words:

  either **event $E1$ occurs** *or* **event $E2$ occurs or** *both* **occur**

This is an *inclusive or* because it permits both events to occur simultaneously.

  The probability of $E3$ occurring depends upon whether $E1$ and $E2$ are or are not *mutually exclusive* events.

Mutually exclusive events

If events $E1$ and $E2$ are mutually exclusive they contain no outcomes in common (Figure 17.1.1). In this case the probability of the union of $E1$ and $E2$ is equal to the sum of each probability:

$$\Pr(E1 \cup E2) = \Pr(E1) + \Pr(E2)$$

Solution 17.2.1(a)

There is a total of 1000 staff in the university of which 396 are male academics and 208 are female administrators. If we define the events:

$E1$: a male academic
$E2$: a female administrator
$E3$: a male academic OR a female administrator

we can define their associated probabilities:

$$\Pr(E1) = 396/1000 = 0.396$$
$$\Pr(E2) = 208/1000 = 0.208$$

and, because $E1$ and $E2$ are mutually exclusive events, we can add their probabilities:

$$\Pr(E1 \cup E2) = \Pr(E1) + \Pr(E2) = 0.396 + 0.208 = 0.604$$

Sample space

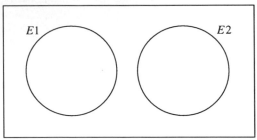

Figure 17.1.1 Mutually exclusive events

Sample space

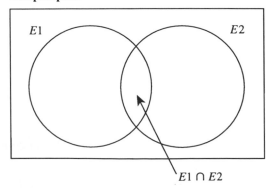

Figure 17.2.1 Non-mutually exclusive events

Non-mutually exclusive events If events $E1$ and $E2$ do have outcomes in common then they are not mutually exclusive (Figure 17.2.1).

In this case the probability of their union is equal to the sum of the probabilities minus the probability of their intersection:

$$\Pr(E1 \cup E2) = \Pr(E1) + \Pr(E2) - \Pr(E1 \cap E2)$$

This latter equation also holds true when the events are mutually exclusive because the intersection of two mutually exclusive events is the empty set and the probability of the empty set is zero.

Solution 17.2.1(b)

The events:

E4: is female
E5: is an academic

with associated probabilities:

$\Pr(E4) = 0.453$
$\Pr(E5) = 0.641$

are not mutually exclusive because it is possible to be a female academic. Consequently:

$$\Pr(E4 \cup E5) = \Pr(E4) + \Pr(E5) - \Pr(E4 \cap E5)$$

and

$$\Pr(E4 \cap E5) = 0.245$$

Therefore

$$\Pr(E4 \cup E5) = 0.453 + 0.641 - 0.245 = 0.849$$

Solution 17.2.1(c)

Because there are 151 male administrators out of a total staff complement of 1000 there are 849 staff members who are NOT male administrators. Consequently, defining the event:

E6: a male administrator

we see that:

$$\Pr(E6) = 0.151 \quad \text{and} \quad \Pr(E6') = 1 - 0.151 = 0.849$$

EXAMPLE 17.2.2

In a factory, items pass through two processes, namely cleaning and painting. The probability that an item has a cleaning fault is 0.2 and the probability that an item has a painting fault is 0.3. Cleaning and painting faults occur independently of one another. Calculate the probability that a selected item

(a) has a cleaning fault or a painting fault or both

(b) has both cleaning and painting faults

(c) has neither cleaning nor painting faults

(d) has a cleaning fault but does not have a painting fault.

Solution 17.2.2

Two random experiments are performed in sequence. Let $E1$ be an event associated with a first random experiment and $E2$ be an event associated with a second random experiment. These two events can be connected via the set operation of *intersection* to form the event $E3$:

$$E3 = E1 \cap E2$$

Event $E3$ can be described in English as:

event $E1$ *and* event $E2$

In other words:

both event $E1$ occurs *and* event $E2$ occurs

We are already familiar with the idea of a sequence of random experiments and the outcome tree that results from it. Now, instead of dealing with outcomes we are dealing with events and their associated probabilities and as a result the outcome tree becomes a probability tree. A probability tree is completely analogous to an outcome tree where, instead of outcomes listed against the branches of the tree, the probabilities of events are given. The probabilities of combined events are then products of probabilities as shown in the tree in Figure 17.2.2.

Applying the idea of a probability tree to this problem we first define the random experiments and the associated events that are involved.

Cleaning and painting are *independent* of each other. Let

Cleaning be experiment 1 with sample space {cleaning fault, no cleaning fault}
Painting be experiment 2 with sample space {painting fault, no painting fault}

In experiment 1, we are given:

$$\Pr(\{\text{cleaning fault}\}) = 0.2$$

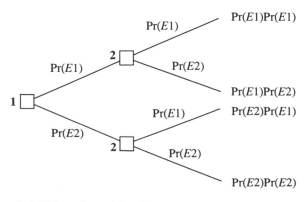

Figure 17.2.2 Probabilities of combined events

hence

$$Pr(\{no\ cleaning\ fault\}) = 0.8$$

since any item either does or does not have a cleaning fault and the sum of the probabilities must equal 1. In experiment 2 we are given:

$$Pr(\{painting\ fault\}) = 0.3$$

hence

$$Pr(\{no\ painting\ fault\}) = 0.7$$

Solution 17.2.2(a)

$$Pr(\{cleaning\ fault\}\ and\ \{painting\ fault\})$$
$$= Pr(\{cleaning\ fault\})Pr(\{painting\ fault\})$$
$$= (0.2)(0.3)$$
$$= 0.06$$

Solution 17.2.2(b)

$$Pr(\{no\ cleaning\ fault\}\ and\ \{no\ painting\ fault\})$$
$$= Pr(\{no\ cleaning\ fault\})Pr(\{no\ painting\ fault\})$$
$$= (0.8)(0.7)$$
$$= 0.56$$

Solution 17.2.2(c)

$$Pr(\{cleaning\ fault\}\ and\ \{no\ painting\ fault\})$$
$$= Pr(\{cleaning\ fault\})Pr(\{no\ painting\ fault\})$$
$$= (0.2)(0.78)$$
$$= 0.14$$

Refer to Figure 17.2.3.

The probability of $E3$ occurring depends upon whether $E1$ and $E2$ are *dependent* or *independent* events.

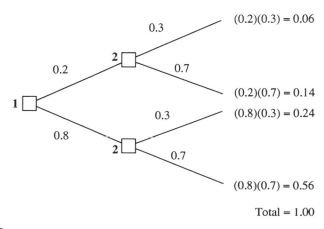

Figure 17.2.3

EXAMPLE 17.2.3

Four men and six women have been shortlisted for two posts that are available in a company's accounts department. If each person has an equal chance of being selected for either post what is the probability that:

(a) the first post is filled by a woman and the second post is filled by a man

(b) each post is filled by a woman

(c) the second post is filled by a man.

Solution 17.2.3

If two random experiments are performed in sequence, one after the other, then it may be possible for the outcome of the first experiment to affect the outcome of the second. If this is the case the outcomes are dependent upon each other and the probabilities change after the first experiment has been performed.

Here the two random experiments are the processes involved in selecting a person to fill each of the two vacant posts. For each post there are two associated simple events, namely:

$E1$: selection of a man
$E2$: selection of a woman

Because the number of candidates available to fill the second post will be one less than the number available to fill the first post the two experiments are dependent upon each other. Indeed, the probability tree for this sequence of experiments is shown in Figure 17.2.5.

Solution 17.2.3(a)

The first post can be filled by a woman in 6 ways out of a total of 10 possible selections. Having filled the first post with a woman there are still 4 ways a man can be chosen to fill the second post out of a total of 9 possible selections.

$$\Pr(E2 \cap E1) = \Pr(E2)\Pr(E1) = (6/10)(4/9) = 24/90$$

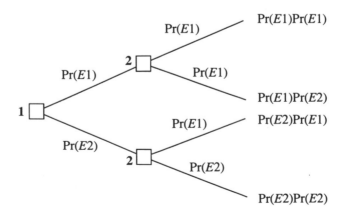

Figure 17.2.4

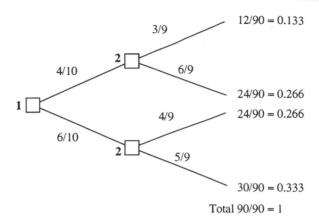

Figure 17.2.5

Solution 17.2.3(b)

$$\Pr(E2 \cap E2) = \Pr(E2)\Pr(E2) = (6/10)(5/9) = 30/90$$

Solution 17.2.3(c)

$$\Pr([E1 \cap E1] \cup [E2 \cap E1]) = \Pr(E1)\Pr(E1) + \Pr(E2)\Pr(E1)$$
$$= (4/10)(3/9) + (6/10)(4/9)$$
$$= (12 + 24)/90 = 36/90$$

EXERCISES 17.2

1 During the last year two employees, Alan and Barbara, were recorded as being off sick for 10 days and 6 days respectively, where for 3 days they were both at work simultaneously. If the working year has 235 days and a particular working day from last year was selected at random what is the probability that:

(a) Either Alan or Barbara was off work

(b) Barbara and Alan were both off work

(c) Alan was not off work

2 If a random experiment has a number of outcomes and four events are defined with associated probabilities as:

$$\Pr(E1) = 0.1, \Pr(E2) = 0.5, \Pr(E3) = 0.6, \Pr(E4) = 0.9$$

which events may be mutually exclusive and which cannot be mutually exclusive? Explain why using a Venn diagram.

3 A bag contains four balls numbered 1 to 4. A ball is drawn at random followed by the draw of a second ball. What is the probability that the numbers on the two balls add up to:

(a) 4   (b) an odd number   (c) a number less than 6

351

if the second ball is selected:

(i) after replacing the first ball drawn

(ii) without replacing the first ball drawn.

4 The following data shows the results of a market investigation on the frequency of usage of a particular product in the different regions of the country. It is based upon a random sample of 550 customers.

Region	Not at all	Once	More than once
North	20	40	60
Midlands	60	35	35
South	100	60	20
Scotland and Wales	35	45	40

(a) What is the probability that a customer selected at random

(i)   does not use the product

(ii) lives in the North and does not use the product

(iii) does not use the product if they live in the South or the Midlands.

(b) If no-one in the sample used the product more than twice a week what is the expected number of times per week that a person in the North would use the product?

5 Munchkin plc manufactures sweets and chocolate. It is a very popular brand and operates its production 24 hours a day on three eight-hour shifts. The first shift is from seven in the morning to three in the afternoon, the second shift then begins and ends at eleven in the evening when the third shift starts. Munchkin is a caring employer and does not like to force people to work during hours that are not desired. Accordingly, they employ people at a time that accords with their preferences. Of its 90 employees 15 have expressed a preference for the first shift, 13 have expressed a preference for the second shift and 14 have expressed a preference for the third shift. 22 employees are willing to work either the first or second shift, 28 are willing to work either the first or third shift and 22 are willing to work either the second or third shift. If an employee is selected at random from the workforce what is the probability that the employee is rostered for:

(a) the first shift

(b) the first or the second shift

(c) any one of the three shifts.

6 An office lottery is organized each week amongst the 10 members of the typing pool. 5 red counters, 2 blue counters and 3 green counters are placed in a bag. Of the 5 red counters 2 of them have the number 1 and 3 have the number 2 printed on them. Of the blue counters 1 is numbered 1 and 1 is numbered 2. Of the green counters 1 is numbered 1 and 2 are numbered 2. The counters are shaken in the bag and one counter is selected as that week's winner. Construct a probability tree of this random experiment and determine the counter or counters that is or are

(a) most likely   (b) least likely

to produce a winner.

18

PROBABILITY DISTRIBUTIONS

When you have completed this chapter you will be able to:

- identify a random variable for a random experiment and construct a probability distribution
- use the idea of expectation to derive the mean and variance of a probability distribution
- recognise a Bernoulli trial and manipulate a binomial probability distribution
- use expectation to derive the mean and variance of a binomial probability distribution
- recognise the need for and use a Poisson probability distribution

18.1   SIMPLE EVENTS AND THEIR PROBABILITIES

Every simple event of a random experiment has a related probability and the complete collection of probabilities associated with a particular random experiment is called a **probability distribution**. Probability distributions share common properties (such as possessing a mean and a standard deviation) as well as having distinct properties related to their individual nature (such as being discrete or continuous).

EXAMPLE 18.1.1

A bag contains 4 red beads, 3 blue beads, 2 yellow beads and 1 green bead. A bead is drawn from the bag and its colour noted. If each bead has an equal chance of being drawn:

(a) By defining the notion of a *random variable,* code the simple events of this random experiment and construct a probability distribution.

(b) Using the concept of expectation find the mean and variance of the probability distribution.

Solution 18.1.1(a)

Every random experiment gives rise to a collection of mutually exclusive simple events, each with an associated probability of that event occurring. This collection of probabilities is called the *probability distribution* of the random experiment and we have seen how a probability distribution can be divined either from a relative frequency distribution using the notion of statistical regularity or from *a priori* considerations.

Divining the probability distribution using statistical regularity is reasonably straightforward – the random experiment is repeated a number of times sufficient to do the job. Divining the probability distribution from *a priori* considerations is not always quite so straightforward. The process can, however, be greatly assisted when a formalised method is available but to create such a formalised method requires the notion of a *random variable*.

Every random experiment has a result and associated with that result is a set of possible simple events. Because all the simple events are mutually exclusive it is possible to code each simple event with its own unique number. Here, the random experiment of selecting a bead gives rise to the four simple events {R}, {B}, {Y} and {G}, representing the selection of a red, blue, yellow or green bead respectively. These events can be coded as:

{R} coded as 1
{B} coded as 2
{Y} coded as 3
{G} coded as 4

Next, the result of the random experiment, namely that *a bead will be drawn*, will be represented by the variable x where 1, 2, 3 and 4 are the only allowed values of the variable. If the selection is *fair* then:

$$\Pr(\{R\}) = \Pr(x = 1) = \Pr(1) = 4/10 = 0.4$$

$$\Pr(\{B\}) = \Pr(x = 2) = \Pr(2) = 3/10 = 0.3$$

$$\Pr(\{Y\}) = \Pr(x = 3) = \Pr(3) = 2/10 = 0.2$$

$$\Pr(\{G\}) = \Pr(x = 4) = \Pr(4) = 1/10 = 0.1$$

Notice that the coding of the simple events is not unique, we could have coded as:

{R} coded as −2
{B} coded as −1
{Y} coded as +1
{G} coded as +2

in which case:

$$\Pr(\{R\}) = \Pr(x = -2) = \Pr(-2) = 4/10 = 0.4$$

$$\Pr(\{B\}) = \Pr(x = -1) = \Pr(-1) = 3/10 = 0.3$$

$$\Pr(\{Y\}) = \Pr(x = 1) = \Pr(1) = 2/10 = 0.2$$

$$\Pr(\{G\}) = \Pr(x = 2) = \Pr(2) = 1/10 = 0.1$$

By coding in this manner a relationship is defined between the values of the variable x and their associated probabilities. This relationship is expressed as a *probability distribution* and because the variable x is associated with the result of a random experiment it is referred to as a **random variable**.

Solution 18.1.1(b)

Every permitted value of a random variable x associated with a random experiment has a probability $\Pr(x)$ of being realised.

In complete analogy to defining the average values of a collection of data as the sum of the products of the various datum values with their relative frequencies so we can define an *average* value of a random variable as the sum of the products of its values with their respective probabilities:

$$\mu = \Sigma \; x \Pr(x)$$

(the symbol μ is lower-case Greek letter m, pronounced 'myou'). Here, the *average* random variable value, μ, is called the **expectation** of x – denoted by $E(x)$. That is:

$$\mu = E(x) \quad \text{the expectation of } x \text{ or the mean value of } x$$

Note that the use of the word expectation can be misleading. It does not mean that the most likely value to be expected is μ because the most likely value to be expected is that with the highest probability. For example, in the case of the random experiment of a fair selection of a bead the expectation is given as:

$$\begin{aligned}
E(x) &= 1.\Pr(1) + 2.\Pr(2) + 3.\Pr(3) + 4.\Pr(4) \\
&= 1(0.4) + 2(0.3) + 3(0.2) + 4(0.1) \\
&= 2
\end{aligned}$$

In a similar manner, the variance σ^2 of the random variable is given as:

$$\begin{aligned}
\sigma^2 &= E([x-\mu]^2) \\
&= \Sigma \; (x-\mu)^2 \Pr(x)
\end{aligned}$$

In the previous example of the selection of a bead

$$\begin{aligned}
\sigma^2 &= \Sigma \; (x-\mu)^2 \Pr(x) \\
&= (1-2)^2(0.4) + (2-2)^2(0.3) + (3-2)^2(0.2) + (4-2)^2(0.1) \\
&= 1 \\
&= E([x-\mu]^2)
\end{aligned}$$

The symbol used for the variance of a random variable is σ^2, where σ is a lower-case Greek letter s, pronounced 'sigma'. Notice that σ is the standard deviation of the random variable.

EXERCISES 18.1

1 Twenty-eight discs, each one a colour of the rainbow

1 red, 2 orange, 3 yellow, 4 green, 5 blue, 6 indigo, 7 violet

are placed in a bag. A disc is drawn from the bag and each disc has an equal probability of being selected. If, for this random experiment, a random variable c is defined and given a set of whole number values ranging from 1 for red to 7 for violet a probability distribution is created.

(a) Write down the probabilities associated with each value of the probability distribution.

(b) What is the mean of this distribution and to what colour does it correspond?

(c) What is the standard deviation of this probability distribution and what range of colours does it define?

(d) If now 7 red, 6 orange, 5 yellow, 4 green, 3 blue, 2 indigo and 1 violet discs were placed in another bag and the experiment repeated how would your answers to (a), (b) and (c) differ?

2 A company created an age profile of its workforce. The number of employees in specific age groups were found to be as follows:

<20	20–29	30–39	40–49	50–59	60⩾
355	910	430	250	108	14

If a random experiment consisted of selecting an employee at random and had an associated random variable x with values assigned as follows:

$x = 1$ if age of employee <20
$x = 2$ if $20 \leqslant$ age of employee <30
$x = 3$ if $30 \leqslant$ age of employee <40
$x = 4$ if $40 \leqslant$ age of employee <50
$x = 5$ if $50 \leqslant$ age of employee <60
$x = 6$ if age of employee $\geqslant 60$

(a) Construct a probability distribution for this random experiment.

(b) What is the probability that:

(i) $1 < x \leqslant 3$ (ii) $x < 5$ (iii) $x \geqslant 3$

(c) Find:

(i) the mean value of x
(ii) the standard deviation of the probability distribution.

3 Dyestampers Co Ltd produce components for the automotive trade that are cut out of 12 gauge cold-reduced sheet steel. One component, intended for a rotary unit, must have a weight of 10 grammes with a maximum tolerance of ± 0.2 grammes. From a recent production run of this component the following results were obtained:

Weight	9.7	9.8	9.9	10.0	10.1	10.2	10.3
Number	10	50	785	666	949	0	10

If a random experiment consisted of selecting an employee at random and had an associated random variable x with values assigned as follows:

$x = 1$ if weight $= 9.7$
$x = 2$ if weight $= 9.8$
$x = 3$ if weight $= 9.9$
$x = 4$ if weight $= 10.0$
$x = 5$ if weight $= 10.1$
$x = 6$ if weight $= 10.2$
$x = 7$ if weight $= 10.3$

(a) Construct a probability distribution for this random experiment.

(b) What is the probability that:

   (i) $2 \leqslant x < 5$ (ii) $x \leqslant 4$ (iii) $x > 3$

(c) Find:

   (i) the mean value of x

   (ii) the standard deviation of the probability distribution.

18.2 THE BINOMIAL PROBABILITY DISTRIBUTION

The binomial probability distribution occurs whenever the performance of a random experiment will result in one of only two possible outcomes.

EXAMPLE 18.2.1

(a) Describe what is meant by a Bernoulli trial and demonstrate how it is used to construct a binomial probability distribution.

(b) On any day, the probability of a bus arriving at a certain bus stop within a 2 minute wait is 0.4. What is the probability that:

(i) there will only be two days out of five when you will have to wait for longer than 2 minutes

(ii) you will have to wait more than 2 minutes for every one of the five days

(iii) you will have to wait more than two minutes for no more than 3 days out of the five.

Solution 18.2.1(a)

A **Bernoulli trial** is any random experiment whose result gives rise to only two possible simple events which we shall call {*success*} with probability p and {*failure*} with probability q:

$$\Pr(\{success\}) = p \quad \text{and} \quad \Pr(\{failure\}) = q$$

where, naturally:

$$p + q = 1$$

A typical Bernoulli trial is the tossing of a coin where a head could be considered as success and a tail as failure. The actual connotations of success and failure are unimportant. What is important is that the random experiment has *only two possible outcomes*.

    In what follows we shall be concerned not with just a single Bernoulli trial but rather with a succession of such trials where each successive trial is independent of the previous trials. Here the Bernoulli trial consists in waiting at a bus stop. Success (S) is achieved in the trial if a bus arrives within two minutes. If a bus does not arrive within two minutes the outcome of the trial is Fail (F). Consider the five successive days when you wait at the bus stop – the fivefold repetition of a single random experiment where the result of each repetition is independent of the result of its predecessor. One such sequence of outcomes could be:

S, S, F, F, F

Here there are 2 successes and 3 failures – on Monday and Tuesday a bus arrived within 2 minutes but on Wednesday, Thursday and Friday it took longer than 2 minutes for a bus to arrive.

The event associated with this outcome is:

$E = \{S\} \cap \{S\} \cap \{F\} \cap \{F\} \cap \{F\}$

If we assume the Bernoulli trial to have a probability of success as p and the probability of failure as q then the probability of event E is:

$p.p.q.q.q = p^2 q^3$

The combination of two successes and three failures given here is not unique. For example, the following is another such sequence:

S, F, F, S, F

and this has the same probability as the other sequence, namely:

$p.q.q.p.q = p^2 q^3$

The next question to ask is:

How many such combinations of 2 successes and 3 failures are possible?

Assume that we have five fixed locations into each of which we can place either a p or a q:

☐   ☐   ☐   ☐   ☐

We can place the first p in any one of 5 locations leaving 4 yet to be filled. For each choice of location for the first p there are 4 locations to place the second p. Consequently we can locate the 2 p's in

$5 \times 4 = 20$

different ways – or at least *almost* different ways. In fact there are only half as many different arrangements of the 2 p's amongst the five locations because each of the different arrangements is duplicated by simply switching the first p with the second p to produce an identical arrangement. Once the 2 p's have been arranged amongst the five locations the 3 q's fill the remaining gaps. In conclusion, there are:

$$\frac{5 \times 4}{2} = 10$$

different arrangements of 2 p's and 3 q's. We can write this as:

$$\frac{5 \times 4 \times 3 \times 2 \times 1}{2 \times 1 \times 3 \times 2 \times 1}$$

We have a shorthand notation for successively decreasing products such as these. We write this as:

$$\frac{5!}{2!3!} \quad \text{or} \quad \frac{5!}{2!(5-2)!}$$

where

$$5! = 5 \times 4 \times 3 \times 2 \times 1$$
$$2! = 2 \times 1$$
$$3! = 3 \times 2 \times 1$$

and where the 5! is referred to as 5-**factorial**.

As a consequence there are 10 different combinations of 2 successes and 3 failures, each combination having the same probability:

$$p^2 q^3$$

This gives the probability of having two successes in five trials as:

$$10p^2 q^3$$

This probability we shall denote by the symbol $\Pr(2:5)$. In general, we can say that the probability of 2 *successes in 5 Bernoulli trials* is:

$$\Pr(2:5) = {}^5C_2 p^2 q^{5-2} = 10p^2 q^3$$

where the symbol ${}^5C_2$ refers to the ratio of factorials:

$${}^5C_2 = \frac{5!}{2!(5-2)!}$$

the number of combinations of 2 identical items amongst 5 locations. This result can be generalized to the probability of r successes in n trials, $\Pr(r:n)$. The result is given in the form:

$$\Pr(r:n) = {}^nC_r p^r q^{n-r}$$

where

$${}^nC_r = n!/[(n-r)!r!]$$

Notice that here the random variable is r which can take on $n+1$ values $0, 1, 2, \ldots, n$.

Solution 18.2.1 (b(i))

On any day, the probability of a bus arriving at a certain bus stop within a 2 minute wait is 0.4. Waiting at this bus stop constitutes a Bernoulli trial where *success* will be that a bus arrives within a 2 minute wait and *failure* is that a bus does not arrive within a 2 minute wait. Clearly:

$$\Pr(\{\text{success}\}) = p = 0.4$$

$$\Pr(\{\text{failure}\}) = q = 1 - p = 0.6$$

The probability that there will only be 2 days out of 5 when you will have to wait for longer than 2 minutes is the probability of 2 failures out of 5 Bernoulli trials which is the same as 3 successes out of 5 trials. This is then given by:

$$\Pr(3:5) = {}^5C_3 p^3 q^2$$
$$= [5!/(3!2!)](0.4)^3(0.6)^2$$
$$= 10(0.064)(0.36)$$
$$= 0.2304$$

Solution 18.2.1(b(ii))

The probability that you will have to wait more than 2 minutes for every one of the 5 days is the probability of 5 failures out of 5 Bernoulli trials which is the same as 0 successes out of 5 trials. This is then given by:

$$\Pr(0:5) = {}^5C_0 p^0 q^5$$
$$= [5!/(0!5!)](0.4)^0(0.6)^5$$
$$= 1(1)(0.07776)$$
$$= 0.07776 \qquad \text{(Notice we define } 0! = 1.\text{)}$$

Solution 18.2.1(b(iii))

The probability that you will have to wait more than 2 minutes for no more than 3 days out of the 5 is the probability of no more than 3 failures out of 5 Bernoulli trials which is the same as:

2 successes out of 5 trials OR
3 successes out of 5 trials OR
4 successes out of 5 trials OR
5 successes out of 5 trials.

This is then given by:

$$\Pr(\geqslant 2:5) = \Pr(2:5) + \Pr(3:5) + \Pr(4:5) + \Pr(5:5)$$
$$= {}^5C_2 p^2 q^3 + {}^5C_3 p^3 q^2 + {}^5C_4 p^4 q^1 + {}^5C_5 p^5 q^0$$
$$= [5!/(2!3!)](0.4)^2(0.6)^3 + [5!/(3!2!)](0.4)^3(0.6)^2$$
$$+ [5!/(4!1!)](0.4)^4(0.6)^1 + [5!/(5!0!)](0.4)^5(0.6)^0$$
$$= 10(0.16)(0.216) + 10(0.064)(0.36) + 5(0.0256)(0.6)$$
$$+ 1(0.01024)(1)$$
$$= 0.66304$$

EXAMPLE 18.2.2

A certain public examination has a consistent past record of a 25% failure rate. For a group of 6 people sitting the examination this year

(a) Construct the probability distribution of 0, 1, 2, 3, 4, 5 and all 6 of the group pass the examination.

(b) Use the notion of *expectation* to find the mean and standard deviation of this probability distribution.

(c) Draw the bar graph of this probability distribution.

(d) From the bar graph of this probability distribution construct the histogram that represents the piecewise continuous extension of the binomial probability distribution.

(e) Indicate the location of the mean and the standard deviation of the probability distribution on the histogram.

Solution 18.2.2(a)

The sitting of the examination is taken to be a Bernoulli trial where success means passing the examination with probability:

$$p = 0.75$$

and failure means failing the examination with probability:

$$q = 0.25$$

When 6 people sit the examination then their respective successes and failures form a binomial probability distribution where the probability of 0 people passing the examination is:

$$\Pr(0:6) = {}^6C_0 p^0 q^6$$
$$= {}^6C_0 (0.75)^0 (0.25)^6$$
$$= [6!/(0!6!)](0.75)^0 (0.25)^6$$
$$= 0.00024 \text{ to 5 decimal places}$$

The probability of 1 person passing the examination is:

$$\Pr(1:6) = {}^6C_1 p^1 q^5$$
$$= {}^6C_1 (0.75)^1 (0.25)^5$$
$$= 0.00439 \text{ to 5 decimal places}$$

The probability of 2 people passing the examination is:

$$\Pr(2:6) = {}^6C_2 (0.75)^2 (0.25)^4$$
$$= 0.03296 \text{ to 5 decimal places}$$

The probability of 3 people passing the examination is:

$$\Pr(3:6) = {}^6C_3 (0.75)^3 (0.25)^3$$
$$= 0.13184 \text{ to 5 decimal places}$$

The probability of 4 people passing the examination is:

$$\Pr(4:6) = {}^6C_4 (0.75)^4 (0.25)^2$$
$$= 0.29663 \text{ to 5 decimal places}$$

The probability of 5 people passing the examination is:

$$\Pr(5:6) = {}^6C_5 (0.75)^5 (0.25)^1$$
$$= 0.35596 \text{ to 5 decimal places}$$

The probability of all 6 people passing the examination is:

$$\Pr(6:6) = {}^6C_6 (0.75)^6 (0.25)^0$$
$$= 0.17798 \text{ to 5 decimal places}$$

Solution 18.2.2(b)

The mean μ of this probability distribution is given by the expectation of the random variable x as:

$$\begin{aligned}
\mu &= E(x) \\
&= \Sigma\ x\ \Pr(x:6) \\
&= 0\ \Pr(0:6) + 1\ \Pr(1:6) + 2\ \Pr(2:6) + 3\ \Pr(3:6) \\
&\quad + 4\ \Pr(4:6) + 5\ \Pr(5:6) + 6\ \Pr(60:6) \\
&= 0(0.00024) + 1(0.00439) + 2(0.03296) + 3(0.13184) \\
&\quad + 4(0.29663) + 5(0.35596) + 6(0.17798) \\
&= 4.50003 \\
&= 4.50\ \text{to 2 decimal places}
\end{aligned}$$

Notice that $4.5 = 6(0.75)$ where 6 is the number (n) of Bernoulli trials and 0.75 is the probability (p) of {success}. This result then confirms the expectation $E(x)$ of the binomial probability distribution consisting of n Bernoulli trial as:

$$\mu = np$$

Similarly the variance σ^2 of this probability distribution is given by the expectation of the random variable x as:

$$\begin{aligned}
\sigma^2 &= E([x - \mu]^2) \\
&= \Sigma\ [x - \mu]^2\ \Pr(x:6) \\
&= [0 - 4.50003]^2\ \Pr(0:6) + [1 - 4.50003]^2\ \Pr(1:6) \\
&\quad + [2 - 4.50003]^2\ \Pr(2:6) \\
&\quad + [3 - 4.50003]^2\ \Pr(3:6) + [4 - 4.50003]^2\ \Pr(4:6) \\
&\quad + [5 - 4.50003]^2\ \Pr(5:6) + [6 - 4.50003]^2\ \Pr(60:6) \\
&= 20.25027(0.00024) + 12.25021(0.00439) + 6.25015(0.03296) \\
&\quad + 2.25009(0.13184) + 0.25003(0.29663) \\
&\quad + 0.24997(0.35596) + 2.24991(0.17798) \\
&= 1.12488\ \text{to 5 decimal places}
\end{aligned}$$

Hence, the standard deviation σ is given as the square root of the variance as:

$$\begin{aligned}
\sigma &= 1.06060\ \text{to 5 decimal places} \\
&= 1.06\ \text{to 2 decimal places}
\end{aligned}$$

Notice that to three decimal places the variance is $1.125 = 6(0.75)(0.25)$ where 6 is the number (n) of Bernoulli trials, 0.75 is the probability (p) of {success} and 0.25 is the probability (q) of {failure}. This result then confirms the expectation $E([x - \mu]^2)$ of the binomial probability distribution consisting of n Bernoulli trial as:

$$\sigma^2 = npq$$

Solution 18.2.2(c)

The bar graph of this probability distribution is obtained by plotting the points:

$$(x,\ \Pr(x:\ 6))$$

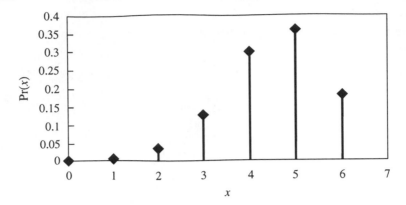

Figure 18.2.1

for each value of x. We construct the following table to make this more clear, restricting the probabilities to 3 decimal places:

x	0	1	2	3	4	5	6
$\Pr(x:6)$	0.000	0.004	0.033	0.132	0.297	0.356	0.178

The graph is shown in Figure 18.2.1. The actual plot of this binomial probability distribution consists of just the seven points in the plane; the vertical bars are drawn in to give a visual aid to the location of the points. Notice that the probabilities are *equal to the lengths of the bars* – hence the sum of the lengths of the bars is 1.

Solution 18.2.2(d)
The graph of the binomial probability distribution is a graph of *discrete points* – each plotted point is isolated from any other plotted point because each point relates to a value of the discrete random variable x. However, we can convert this discrete graph into a *piecewise continuous* graph by constructing the *histogram* of Figure 18.2.2.

In the histogram each discrete point has been replaced by a straight line extending between the mid-points of two adjacent values of the random variable x. This is what is meant by piecewise continuous; the horizontal straight lines are each continuous except at their ends where they are discontinuous. One good reason for constructing this histogram is to give a more striking visual display of how the probabilities are spread across the probability distribution.

What has happened here is that each discrete value of the random variable x has been replaced by a continuous set of values ranging from mid-way between adjacent x-values. In doing so, the original identification of the probability associated with a given value of x being the height of the respective bar has been changed. Now the probability associated with a given value of x has become the probability that the value of x lies between the mid-points of adjacent x-values and is identified as the magnitude of the area of the appropriate rectangle. Hence the total area beneath the graph of the binomial distribution is 1.

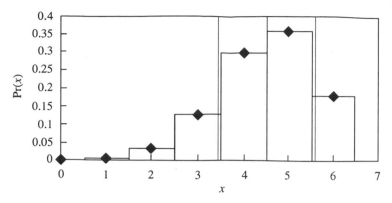

Figure 18.2.2

Solution 18.2.2(e)

The mean of the probability distribution is:

$$\mu = 4.50$$

and is indicated by the vertical straight line through the point $x = 4.50$. The straight line is there, again, for visual impact only. The standard deviation of the probability distribution is:

$$\sigma = 1.06$$

and this is represented by the vertical lines through $x = 3.44$ and 5.56 respectively, each having a horizontal distance of 1.06 from the mean. Again, the vertical lines are only drawn to give the eye a clear indication of how the probabilities are spread about the mean.

EXERCISES 18.2

1 (a) ChukkaLob make squash balls from blocks of latex. The blocks are annealed by heating and rolling and then chopped into segments ready for producing the individual balls. It is a very dirty process that makes heavy demands on the health of the personnel operating the machinery with the consequence that during any one day 5% of the workforce are likely to be off work. What is the probability that on any one day, out of a workforce of 25:

    (i)   5 are off work
    (ii) less than 3 are off work
    (iii) 3 or more are off work

   (b) What is the mean and standard deviation of this probability distribution?

2 (a) A company makes small plastic toys for the Christmas cracker trade. Whilst the toys do not have to be perfect they do have to pass a number of quality criteria before they are sold to the cracker manufacturer. If it is found that 15% of all the toys produced by the company are defective what is the probability that out of 5 toys selected at random

(i) 2   (ii) 0   (iii) at most 3

toys will be found to be defective?

(b) If a new process reduced the defective rate by 50% find the:

(i) mean   (ii) standard deviation

of the distribution of defective toys as a consequence of using the new process.

18.3   EXPECTATION FOR A BINOMIAL DISTRIBUTION

EXAMPLE 18.3.1

Beever plc is a mining consortium that owns a large number of mines throughout the world. At each site a target is defined of the amount of material mined and at the end of each week they fax the head office to inform them as to whether or not they have managed to attain their target. As a first stage in their management control Beever plc collect this information and use it to decide if the consortium overall is maintaining its target. There are 137 sites, each of which is expected to attain its weekly target 44 times a year in order to permit the consortium as a whole to attain its target. What is the average number of mines that are required to attain their target each week to enable the consortium as a whole to attain its target and what is the standard deviation?

Solution 18.3.1

The attainment of a target by an individual mine is a Bernoulli trial. For a single Bernoulli trial there are two simple events, namely {success} and {failure}. Define a random variable r for this trial where $r = 0$ if the target is not met (failure) and $r = 1$ it the target is met (success). The probabilities of these two events are:

$Pr(0) = q$, the probability of {failure}

which occurs when the random variable $r = 0$, and

$Pr(1) = p$, the probability of {success}

which occurs when the random variable $r = 1$. Consequently, the expectation of r for a single Bernoulli trial is:

$$E(r) = \mu = \Sigma\ r\ Pr(r) = 0.q + 1.p = p$$

Similarly, the variance σ^2 is $E((r - \mu)^2)$ where:

$$
\begin{aligned}
E((r - \mu)^2) &= \Sigma\ (r - \mu)^2\ Pr(r) \\
&= (0 - p)^2 q + (1 - p)^2 p \\
&= p^2 q + q^2 p \\
&= pq(p + q) \\
&= pq
\end{aligned}
$$

The mean μ of a single Bernoulli trial is p and the variance σ^2 is pq. Because a binomial distribution is derived from a sequence of n Bernoulli trials we can see that the mean of a binomial distribution is given as:

$$\mu = np$$

and the variance as:

$$\sigma^2 = npq$$

What is the average number of mines that are required to attain their target each week to enable the consortium as a whole to attain its target and what is the standard deviation.?

The target attainment of all 137 mines can be represented as a binomial distribution with:

$$n = 137, p = 44/52 \text{ and } q = 8/52$$

The mean μ is given as:

$$\mu = np = 137 \times 44/52 = 115.9 \text{ to 1 dec.pl.}$$

Consequently, the average number of mines required to attain their target each week is 116. The variance is:

$$\sigma^2 = npq = 137 \times 44/52 \times 8/52 = 17.8 \text{ to 1 dec. pl.}$$

giving a standard deviation of $\sigma = 4.2$ to 1 dec. pl.

EXERCISES 18.3

1 It has been found from past experience that new recruits to the army, when introduced to the shooting gallery have, on average, a 20% success rate of hitting the target. What is the probability that in 5 shots a new recruit will hit the target:

(a) twice

(b) at least twice

(c) at most three times

What assumptions are you making in your answers?

2 Marso manufactures electric light bulbs and have devised a package that considerably reduces the risk of damage to the bulb. If the probability of a light bulb being broken between its sale and despatch by Marso to the supermarket and its eventual purchase by a customer is 0.01 what is the probability that in a batch of 5 light bulbs:

(a) none are broken

(b) 2 at most are broken

(c) at least 3 are broken.

18.4 RARE EVENTS AND THE POISSON DISTRIBUTION

EXAMPLE 18.4.1

(a) The probability of selecting a defective item from an assembly line is 0.015. Using a binomial probability distribution, find the probability of finding, from a sample of 10 items selected off the assembly line:

(i) one tenth of the items are defective

(ii) one fifth of the items are defective.

(b) If the sample size is increased from 10 to 100 use a Poisson probability distribution to find the probabilities of part (a).

(c) Check your answers of part (a) using a binomial probability distribution against your answers of part (a) using a Poisson probability distribution.

Solution 18.4.1(a(i))

A **rare event** is one whose probability is very small. What is meant by *small* will be discussed later; for now we simply state that a probability $p = 0.015$ is sufficiently small to indicate a *rare* event. The process of selecting a defective item from an assembly line is a Bernoulli trial with a probability of success, $p = 0.015$ and a probability of failure $q = 1 - p = 0.985$. Consequently, the probabilities associated with the selection of 10 items from this assembly line form a binomial probability distribution with the probability of finding n defective items amongst the 10 selected being given as:

$$\Pr(n : 10) = {}^{10}C_n (0.001)^n (0.999)^{10-n}$$

One tenth of the ten items is 1 item so the probability of finding 1 item that is defective from amongst the 10 selected is:

$$\Pr(1 : 10) = {}^{10}C_1 (0.015)^1 (0.985)^{10-1}$$
$$= 10(0.015)(0.985)^9$$
$$= 0.1309 \text{ to four decimal places}$$

Solution 18.4.1(a(ii))

One fifth of the ten items is 2 items so the probability of finding 2 items that are defective from amongst the 10 selected is:

$$\Pr(2 : 10) = {}^{10}C_2 (0.015)^2 (0.985)^{10-2}$$
$$= 45(0.015)^2 (0.985)^8$$
$$= 0.0089 \text{ to four decimal places}$$

Solution 18.4.1(b(i))

When we increase the sample size the manipulation of the binomial distribution may become very difficult as can be seen from the following:

One tenth of the items from the sample of size 100 is 10 items so the probability of finding 10 items that are defective from amongst the 100 selected is:

$$\Pr(10 : 100) = {}^{100}C_{10} (0.015)^{10} (0.985)^{100-10}$$

To evaluate this probability would take a computational power beyond even the most ambitious hand calculator – it would have to be able to evaluate 100!.

Fortunately, for rare events it is found that the Poisson probability distribution is a reasonable approximation to the binomial probability distribution and much easier to evaluate. The Poisson probability distribution is given as:

$$\Pr(x) = \frac{\lambda^x e^{-\lambda}}{x!}$$

where $\lambda = np$, the mean of the binomial probability distribution. To maintain a reasonable approximation to the binomial distribution we must ensure that $\lambda < 2$.

In our problem of a sample size of 100 with a probability of selecting a defective $p = 0.015$ we see that:

$$n = 100, \; p = 0.015 \quad \text{so that} \quad \lambda = (100)(0.015) = 1.5 < 2$$

Solution 18.4.1(b(ii))

One tenth of the hundred items is 10 items so the probability of finding 10 items that are defective from amongst the 100 selected is given to a good approximation by the Poisson distribution as:

$$\begin{aligned}
\Pr(10) &= \lambda^{10} e^{-\lambda}/10! \\
&= (1.5)^{10} e^{-1.5}/10! \\
&= 3.56 \times 10^{-6}
\end{aligned}$$

Solution 18.4.1(b(iii))

One fifth of the hundred items is 20 items so the probability of finding 20 items that are defective from amongst the 100 selected is given to a good approximation by the Poisson distribution as:

$$\begin{aligned}
\Pr(20) &= \lambda^{20} e^{-\lambda}/20! \\
&= (1.5)^{20} e^{-1.5}/20! \\
&= 3.05 \times 10^{-16}
\end{aligned}$$

Solution 18.4.1(c(i))

Repeating the working of part **(a)** using the Poisson probability distribution we see that for a probability of selecting a defective as $p = 0.015$ and the sample size $n = 10$ then:

$$n = 10, \; p = 0.015 \quad \text{so that} \quad \lambda = (10)(0.015) = 0.15 < 2$$

The probability of finding 1 item that is defective from amongst the 10 selected is given to a good approximation by the Poisson distribution as:

$$\begin{aligned}
\Pr(1) &= \lambda^1 e^{-\lambda}/1! \\
&= (0.15)^1 e^{-0.15}/1! \\
&= 0.1291 \text{ to four decimal places}
\end{aligned}$$

This compares favorably to the exact value of 0.1309 found by using the binomial probability distribution.

Solution 18.4.1(c(ii))

The probability of finding 2 items that are defective from amongst the 10 selected is given to a good approximation by the Poisson distribution as:

$$Pr(2) = \lambda^2 e^{-\lambda}/2!$$
$$= (0.15)^2 e^{-0.15}/2!$$
$$= 0.0097 \text{ to four decimal places}$$

as compared to the exact value of 0.0089 found by using the binomial probability distribution.

EXERCISES 18.4

1 The arrival of customers during randomly chosen 10-minute intervals at a drive-in facility specializing in photo development and film sales has been found to have the distribution given in the following table. Does this distribution appear to follow the Poisson distribution?

No of arrivals	0	1	2	3	4	5
Probability	0.15	0.25	0.24	0.20	0.10	0.06

2 It is known that the injection of a serum to counter the latest flu virus causes an adverse reaction in 1 patient in 100,000. In a national immunization campaign 30,000 people were injected with the serum. What is the probability that:

(a) no-one

(b) at least two people

(c) more than 2 people

suffered an adverse reaction?

3 A local company employs 150 people and operates on three eight-hour shifts a day. A rearranged shift rota resulted in one percent of all employees arriving late for work on any given day. Using the Poisson distribution find the probability that on any given day:

(a) no-one was late for work

(b) 3 people were late for work

(c) more than 2 but less than 6 people were late for work.

19

THE NORMAL PROBABILITY DISTRIBUTION

When you have completed this chapter you will be able to:

- distinguish between a discrete and a continuous probability distribution
- recognize the normal probability distribution
- relate areas beneath a normal distribution to equivalent areas beneath a standard normal distribution

19.1 CONTINUOUS PROBABILITY DISTRIBUTIONS

The binomial and the Poisson probability distributions are example of *discrete* probability distributions – they give the probabilities associated with the values of a discrete random variable x.

Whilst many random experiments such as tossing coins or rolling dies can be described using a discrete random variable, many others cannot. For example, if the random experiment involved measuring the height of a person the result of the experiment would be a measured height. This result would then have to be described using a *continuous* variable because height is a continuous quantity – no individual can grow from 1 m to 2 m in height without attaining a continuous scale of heights in between. It does not matter that the recorded measure might be restricted to a given number of decimal places so that in reality the recorded measure would be discrete; the value of the result itself must be considered as being available on a continuous scale of values.

For a continuous random variable to have with it associated probabilities the probability distribution itself must necessarily be continuous. The most useful and most common of these continuous probability distributions is the **normal** or **Gaussian probability distribution** whose graph is characterized by the bell-shaped curve of Figure 19.1.1 where x represents the random variable and $\Pr(x)$ the continuous probability distribution.

In the case of a discrete probability distribution each value of the random variable has an associated probability and the sum of all such probabilities is unity. For a continuous probability distribution we cannot associate a probability to a given value of the random variable because there is an infinity of such values and hence there would be an infinity of associated probabilities whose sum would exceed unity. Instead we associate probabilities to *ranges of values* of the random variable where the probabilities are equal to the area beneath the graph of the probability distribution within that range. For example, in the graph (Figure

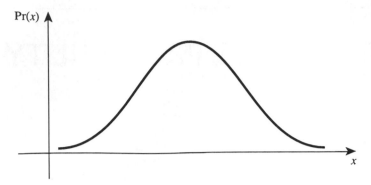

Figure 19.1.1

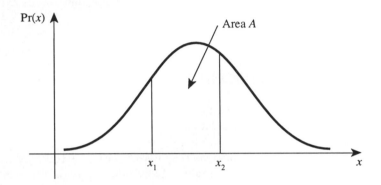

Figure 19.1.2

19.1.2) of the normal probability distribution of the random variable x the probability that x is found to have a value less than x_2 but greater than x_1 is equal to the area A:

$$\Pr(x_1 < x < x_2) = A$$

Notice that this probability is the same as:

$$\Pr(x_1 \leqslant x < x_2), \Pr(x_1 < x \leqslant x_2) \text{ and } \Pr(x_1 \leqslant x \leqslant x_2) = A$$

The addition of single points at the ends of the range does not affect the probability.

EXAMPLE 19.1.1

The Barminster Bank is reviewing its service charges and interest paying policies on current accounts. The bank has found that the current account balance at the end of a day's trading can, to a good approximation, be said to be normally distributed with a mean of £580 and a standard deviation of £147.

(a) What percentage of current account customers carry end-of-day balances in excess of £800?

(b) What percentage of current account customers carry end-of-day balances between £300 and £700?

(c) The bank is considering paying interest to customers carrying end-of-day balances in excess of a certain amount. If the bank does not want to pay interest to more than 5% of its customers, what is the minimum end-of-day balance it should be willing to pay interest on?

(d) The bank intends to impose service charges on those current account customers whose end-of-day balance falls below £400. What percentage of customers will pay service charges?

(e) If five current account customers are selected at random, what is the probability that at least two of them will pay service charges?

Explanation   When the bank claims that the *end-of-day balance is approximately normally distributed* it means that if the proportion of customers (the customer *relative frequency*) with a given bank balance is plotted against the value of the given bank balance for all possible bank balances and then all the plotted points are joined up to form a continuous curve, the resulting graph will be very similar to the bell-shaped *Normal* curve (Figure 19.1.3).

Here the end-of-day current account balances are symbolized by the variable b and the respective customer frequencies by f. This curve is symmetrical about a vertical line drawn through the peak of the curve as shown in Figure 19.1.4.

Where this vertical line crosses the horizontal axis of bank balances is called the mean of the normal distribution – it is the average current account balance at the end of that trading day. Here we see that this value is £580.

If you look closely at the normal curve in Figure 19.1.3 you will see that it is symmetrical to the left and the right of the maximum peak and that as it rises from the left-hand side it is *concave* – it bends inwards so that the slope of the curve increases as the curve rises. Eventually, the curve becomes *convex* – it bends outwards so that the slope decreases as the curve rises until the curve reaches the maximum. The same effect is observed in reverse to the right of the maximum peak. The point on the curve to the right of the maximum where it changes from being convex to concave is called a *turning point* and the horizontal distance of

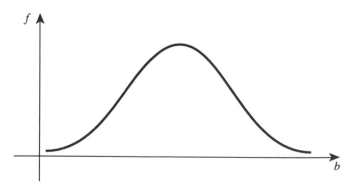

Figure 19.1.3

373

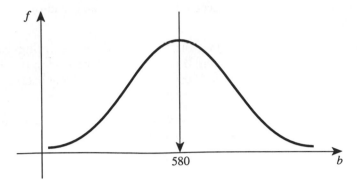

Figure 19.1.4

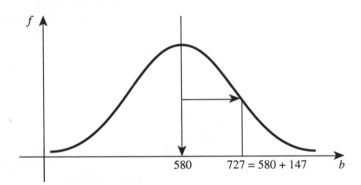

Figure 19.1.5

that turning point from the vertical line of symmetry is used as a measure of how much the curve is spread about the mean. Different sets of data have different spreads about the mean.

The distance between the turning point from the vertical line of symmetry is called the *standard deviation* and in the case of the end-of-day balances of the bank's current accounts this has been found to be £147.

Finally, the area beneath the normal curve is equal to the total number of customers – the sum of all the relative frequencies of bank customers that have current accounts.

Solution 19.1.1(a)
Because the total area under the bell-shaped curve is equal to the total number of customers, the area to the left of the mean – £580 – is equal to half the total number of customers. In fact it is equal to the number of current account holders whose end-of-day account balance is *less than* £580. By the same reasoning if we mark the balance £800 on the horizontal axis and draw a vertical line through this point to cross the curve, the area beneath the curve and to the right of this line will equal the number of customers whose current account balance has an end-of-day balance greater than £800. This is then where the answer to the question is going

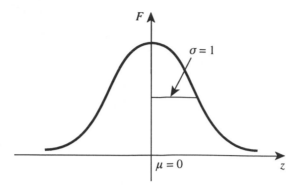

Figure 19.1.6

to come from. Unfortunately, we do not have any simple method available to measure this area. Fortunately, however, we can make use of what is known as the *standard normal distribution* which has a mean value of 0, a standard deviation of 1 and a total area beneath the curve of 1 (Figure 19.1.6).

The proportionate areas beneath this standard normal distribution are tabulated in Standard Normal Tables (see Appendix) as demonstrated in Figure 19.1.7.

In this table the numbers give the area, to three significant figures, beneath the standard normal curve to the right of the central line of symmetry and to the left of a specified z-value on the horizontal axis as indicated by the small diagram at the top of the table. For example, the area beneath the standard normal curve to the right of the central line of symmetry and to the left of the z-value:

$z = 0.56$

is found from the table (p. 413) by looking down the left-hand column to the z-value:

$z = 0.5$

and then looking across to the column headed 6 to read the area in question as:

0.212

This means that:

$0.212 \times 100 = 21.2\%$

of the area beneath the entire standard normal curve lies between the central line of symmetry and the z-value of 0.56.

By linking the normal distribution curve obtained by plotting the customer frequencies against their end-of-day current account balance to the standard normal distribution we can extend this facility to determine proportional areas of the standard normal distribution to find proportional areas of the normal distribution. To do this we must first amend the plotted graph by plotting *relative customer frequencies* rather than actual frequencies against the average current account balance. The relative customer frequency is found by dividing the customer frequency by the total number of customers. The resulting graph looks identical in shape to the original. The only difference is that instead of having customer frequencies plotted up the vertical axis it now has relative customer

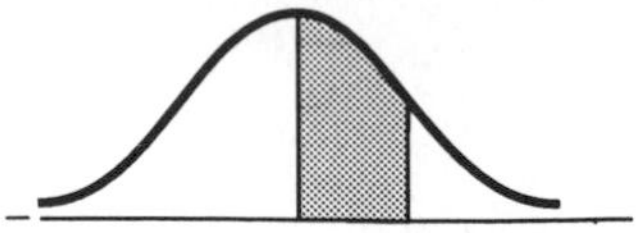

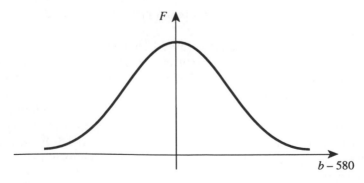

Area beneath the standard normal curve

z	0	1	2	3	4	5	6	7	8	9
0.0	0.000	0.004	0.008	0.012	0.016	0.020	0.024	0.028	0.032	0.036
0.1	0.040	0.044	0.048	0.052	0.056	0.060	0.064	0.068	0.071	0.075
0.2	0.080	0.083	0.087	0.091	0.095	0.099	0.103	0.106	0.110	0.114
0.3	0.118	0.122	0.126	0.129	0.133	0.137	0.141	0.144	0.148	0.152
0.4	0.155	0.159	0.163	0.166	0.177	0.174	0.177	0.181	0.184	0.188
0.5	0.192	0.195	0.199	0.202	0.205	0.209	0.212	0.216	0.219	0.222
0.6	0.226	0.229	0.232	0.236	0.239	0.242	0.245	0.249	0.252	0.255
0.7	0.258	0.261	0.264	0.267	0.270	0.273	0.276	0.279	0.282	0.285

Figure 19.1.7

frequencies $F = f/T$ where T is the total number of customers. This means that the total area beneath the graph is now equal not to the total number of customers but to unity and this is the link with the standard normal curve.

To establish the quantitative link between this curve and the standard normal curve we next shift the curve so that its central line of symmetry coincides with the vertical axis (Figure 19.1.8).

This involves changing the variable of the horizontal average account balances to the same balances minus the mean balance of £580. The new variable on the horizontal axis is then:

$$b - 580$$

and the mean of the shifted distribution is zero as it is for the standard normal distribution. The area under the shifted curve is still unity.

Next we recognize that the standard deviation for the standard normal distribution is unity whereas the standard deviation for this shifted distribution is still £147. To finalize the quantitative link between the standard normal distribution and the bank balances distribution we squeeze the curve until its standard deviation is unity – at all times preserving the area beneath the curve as

F

$b - 580$

Figure 19.1.8

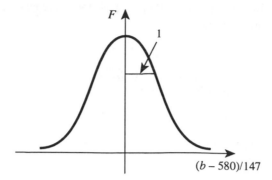

$(b - 580)/147$

Figure 19.1.9

unity. Now we have transformed the average current account balances curve into the standard normal distribution as in Figure 19.1.9.

As before, this squeezing can be achieved by changing the variable on the horizontal axis; this time it is done by dividing the variable $b - 580$ by the standard deviation 147 to form the z-variable:

$$z = (b - 580)/147$$

This is the equation that links the standard normal distribution whose proportional areas we know with the average current account balances normal distribution whose proportional areas we do not know.

We first transform the b-value of 800 into its equivalent z-value using the equation:

$$z = (800 - 580)/147$$
$$= 1.49659 \ldots$$
$$= 1.50 \text{ to 2 decimal places}$$

Next we look up the proportional area from our table of areas beneath the standard normal distribution and we find that the area to the right of the central line of symmetry and to the left of the z-value 1.50 is:

0.433

Since the total area to the right of the central line of symmetry is half of the total area beneath the curve, namely:

0.5

we can deduce that the area beneath the standard normal curve and to the right of the z-value 1.50 is:

$$0.500 - 0.433 = 0.067$$

This means that:

$$0.067 \times 100 = 6.7\%$$

of the area beneath the standard normal curve is to the right of the z-value 1.5. By

377

the same reasoning, the area beneath the original normal curve and to the right of the b-value £800 is the same, namely:

6.7%

And thus we have answered the question: 6.7% of the bank's customers have average account balances in excess of £800.

Solution 19.1.1(b)

To answer this question we need to know the z-values that are equivalent to these two b-values.

$$z_1 = (300 - 580)/147$$
$$= -1.91 \quad \text{to 2 decimal places}$$

and

$$z_2 = (700 - 580)/147$$
$$= 0.82 \quad \text{to 2 decimal places}$$

The question now transforms to one of finding the area beneath the standard normal distribution between these two z-values (see Figure 19.1.10).
   The area between the central line of symmetry at $z = 0$ and the z-value 0.82 is:

0.294

The area between the z-value -1.91 and the central line of symmetry is the same as the area between the central line of symmetry and the z-value $+1.91$ which is:

0.472

The sum of these two areas then gives us the area under the standard normal curve between the two z-values $z_1 = -1.91$ and $z_2 = 0.82$, namely:

0.294 + 0.472 = 0.766

Hence:

$0.766 \times 100 = 76.6\%$

of the area lies between these two z-values which is the same as the area beneath the original normal curve between the values £300 and £700. Consequently:

76.6%

of customers have average daily account balances between £300 and £700.

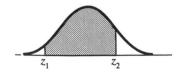

Figure 19.1.10

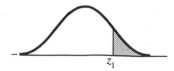

Figure 19.1 11

Solution 19.1.1(c)

The answer to this question is the b-value which has 5% of the area under the original normal curve to the right of it; representing the average daily account balance which is exceeded by only 5% of its customers.

First we need to know the z-value which has 5% of the area beneath the standard normal curve to the right of it (Figure 19.1.11).

This means that 45% of the area beneath the standard normal curve is between the central line of symmetry and the z-value we seek. The actual area corresponding to 45% of the total area is:

$$45 \div 100 = 0.45$$

By looking at the table of areas we see that this area corresponds to a z-value of:

$$z = 1.64$$

Using the equation that links b-values to z-values we see that:

$$1.64 = (b - 580)/147$$

Multiplying both sides by 147 we find that:

$$1.64 \times 147 = b - 580$$

and adding 580 to both sides yields the corresponding b-value:

$$(1.64 \times 147) + 580 = b = 821 \qquad \text{to the nearest whole number}$$

Consequently, if the bank pays interest to those customers whose average daily account balance is £821 or above then it will only be paying interest to 5% of its customers.

Solution 19.1.1(d)

Again, to answer this question we need to know the proportionate area beneath the original normal curve to the left of the b-value of 400. We find this by considering the z-value that corresponds to a b-value of 400. This is:

$$z = (400 - 580)/147$$
$$= -1.22 \quad \text{to 2 decimal places}$$

Using the standard normal tables we see that the area beneath the curve to the left of this value is equal to the area to the right of the z-value of 1.22. That is,

$$= 0.500 - 0.389 = 0.111$$

That is 11.1% of the area beneath the standard normal curve lies to the left of $z = -1.21$ and, equivalently, for the original normal curve, to the left of $b = 400$. Consequently, 11.1 % of the banks customers will pay service charges.

Solution 19.1.1(e)

Since 11.1% of the customers pay service charges the probability that a single current account customer, selected at random, pays service charges is:

$$11.1 \div 100 = 0.111$$

Because a current account holder either pays service charges or does not pay service charges, the probability that the same customer does not pay service charges is:

$$1.000 - 0.111 = 0.889$$

If 5 current account customers are selected at random the probabilities of them paying or not paying service charges follows a binomial probability distribution. This means that:

the probability that none of the five customers will pay service charges is:

$$(0.889)^5 = 0.5553$$

the probability that one of the five customers will pay service charges is:

$$5(0.889)^4(0.111) = 0.3467$$

The probability that at most one of the five customers will pay service charges is given by the sum of these two probabilities:

$$0.5553 + 0.3467 = 0.902$$

Consequently, the probability that at least two of the current account customers pay service charges is:

$$1.000 - 0.902 = 0.098$$

EXERCISES 19.1

1 Find the areas beneath the standard normal probability distribution corresponding to the following z-values:

(a) $0 < z \leqslant 1.45$ (e) $z \leqslant -2.54$

(b) $-0.36 \leqslant z < 0$ (f) $z \leqslant 2.19$

(c) $-2.10 < z < 1.07$ (g) $z > -1.67$

(d) $z > 0.78$

2 The probability associated with a continuous random variable x is normally distributed with a mean value of 123 and a standard deviation of 14.5. A value of x is selected at random.

(a) What is the probability that:

(i) $x > 123$ (ii) $x \geqslant 136$ (iii) $x < 95$
(iv) $x \leqslant 95$ (v) $100 < x < 130$

(b) Why can the probability that $x = 123$ not be given?

3 The Barminster Bank is reviewing its service charges and interest paying policies on current accounts. The bank has found that the average daily balance is normally distributed with a mean of £580 and a standard deviation of £140.

(a) What percentage of current account customers carry average balances in excess of £800?

(b) What percentage of current account customers carry average daily balances between £300 and £700?

(c) The bank is considering paying interest to customers carrying average daily balances in excess of a certain amount. If the bank does not want to pay interest to more than 5% of its customers, what is the minimum average daily balance it should be willing to pay interest on?

(d) The bank intends to impose service charges on those current account customers whose average daily balance falls below £400. What percentage of customers will pay service charges?

(e) If five current account customers are selected at random, what is the probability that at least two of them will pay service charges?

4 A mail order company has weekly sales that are normally distributed about a mean of £125 with a standard deviation of £21. They have decided that as an attempt to boost sales they will offer to post their products to their customers free provided they place a single order over a stated amount of money. They are unsure of at what point they should continue to charge postage but feel that no more than 5% of their customers should be charged.

(a) What percentage of customers place orders with a value less than £50?

(b) What percentage of their customers place orders with a value between £75 and £145?

(c) 5% of their customers place orders below what value?

5 Traffic density on a motorway was measured in vehicles per minute passing beneath a certain bridge. The survey lasted 24 hours and the mean density was found to be 87 vehicles per minute with a standard deviation of 6 vehicles per minute. Assuming the traffic density to be normally distributed:

(a) What is the probability of counting the number of vehicles passing under the bridge in a randomly selected minute and finding the traffic density was:

(i) less than 90 vehicles per minute

    (ii)   more than 70 vehicles per minute

    (iii) between 85 and 100 vehicles per minute

(b) How many minutes in the 24 hours have a traffic density of:

    (i)   less than 90 vehicles per minute

    (ii)   more than 70 vehicles per minute

    (iii) between 85 and 100 vehicles per minute.

6 The Personnel Officer of ACA Ltd has been asked to investigate the cost of giving extra holiday as a reward for long service to its 3000 employees. Upon investigation of service records, the length of service per employee is found to be approximately normally distributed with a mean of 4.6 years and a standard deviation of 1.7 years.

(a) What is the probability that an employee chosen at random has worked for the company for longer than 6 years?

(b) How many employees have worked for between 3 and 5 years

(c) What length of service has been exceeded by 10% of the employees?

(d) One policy that has been suggested is to give 1 extra day's holiday for each completed year over 5 years with a maximum of 4 extra days. What is the expected number of extra days holiday per employee under this policy?

20

SAMPLING AND ESTIMATION

When you have completed this chapter you will be able to:

- distinguish between the effects of sampling with and sampling without replacement and to distinguish between a finite and an infinite population
- determine the mean and the standard deviation of a population from the mean and standard deviation of a sampling distribution of a statistic.
- recognize when the sampling distribution of a statistic is approximately normal
- calculate confidence intervals for appropriate statistics

20.1 SAMPLING

When a market research company wishes to canvas opinions about certain products or to discover purchasing habits of sections of the population they select samples of people from appropriate locations and question them. From the results of their statistical survey they can then deduce the opinions and the purchasing habits of the population at large. Of course, the best way to find out would be to question the entire population but that is not possible, it being too expensive and too time consuming a task. For a market research company to succeed its results and subsequent advice must be accurate and to attain accuracy correct procedures must be followed when taking samples from a population to ensure that the characteristics of the samples taken do in fact reflect the characteristics of the population—the samples must be *representative* of the population. To ensure this the samples must be chosen from the population at random; every member of the population must have the same chance of being selected for a sample. One way that this can be achieved is to allocate each member of the population a unique number and then select numbers at random using a computer or tables of random numbers specially designed for the purpose.

In a typical sampling exercise many samples are selected from a single population. For each sample selected an appropriate statistic can be measured such as the sample mean or the sample standard variation. At the end of the sampling exercise a collection of sample statistics will have been obtained; it is called a *sampling distribution of the statistic* and from that distribution it is possible to infer appropriate population statistics. How the sampling distribution of the statistic relates to the appropriate population statistic depends upon how the sampling was performed and how large the population is. However, if the sample sizes are large enough (greater than 30) then the sampling distribution of the statistic can be demonstrated to be approximately a normal distribution; this despite the type of distribution of the population from which the samples are drawn.

Sampling can be performed by selecting members of the population with or without replacement. If, after a member of the population has been selected for inclusion in a sample, that member is returned to the population thereby permitting it to be re-selected for the same sample then we refer to this as *sampling with replacement*. Otherwise, sampling is *without replacement*. The population from which samples are drawn is considered to be either finite or infinite depending upon whether there is or is not a limit to the size of the samples that can be selected. Selecting 6 names from a population of 10 names is sampling from a finite population if it is performed without replacement but if it is performed with replacement then it can be considered as sampling from an infinite population because there is no limit to the size of the sample that can be drawn. Sampling from a population which is very large can also be considered as sampling from an infinite population even when sampling without replacement.

20.2 SAMPLING DISTRIBUTION OF MEANS

Let a population have a mean value of μ and a standard deviation of σ and let *all possible* samples of size n be drawn from it at random with replacement (infinite population). If the mean values of each sample are noted a *sampling distribution of means* is created. The outcome is that the individual sample mean values in the sampling distribution of means are normally distributed about a mean value m and with a standard deviation s where:

$m = \mu$ the population mean

and

$$s = \frac{\sigma}{\sqrt{n}}$$

where σ is the population standard deviation.

If the sampling is performed without replacement from a finite population of size n_p where $n_p > n$ then the mean is the same but:

$$s = \frac{\sigma\sqrt{(n_p - n)}}{\sqrt{[n(n_p - 1)]}}$$

It should be emphasised that these consequences depend crucially on *all possible samples* of size n being drawn.

EXAMPLE 20.2.1

A bakery has recently installed an automatic dough mixer and portioner to speed up its production of bread buns. Each bun is supposed to weigh 125 gm and the distribution of bun weights is required to have a standard deviation no more than

2.5 gm to ensure the consistency of production. As a check on the success of the installation, a production run of 1250 bread buns in 25 batches of 50 was tested for consistency by randomly selecting two buns from each batch. Each bun in the sample was weighed and the mean weight of the two buns recorded. The sampling distribution of mean weights had a mean of 125 gm with a standard deviation of 1.5 gm.

(a) Do these results confirm or deny the consistency of the production if the sampling is done:

    (i)   with replacement?

    (ii) without replacement?

(b) By comparing the results of **(a)** what can be said about the two sampling methods?

Solution 20.2.1(a(i))
Whilst the statistical connection between a sampling distribution and the population requires every possible sample to be taken, here only 25 samples have been taken. This is considered to be sufficient for the purposes of the problem.

With replacement
The mean m of the sampling distribution of means is equal to the population mean μ and because:

$$m = 125 \text{ gm} \qquad \text{this is in agreement with the population mean } \mu = 125 \text{ gm.}$$

The standard deviation s of the sampling distribution of means is related to the standard deviation of the population σ by the equation:

$$s = \sigma/\sqrt{n}$$

where n is the sample size and sampling is performed *with replacement*. From the production run we can deduce that:

$$s = 1.5 = \sigma/\sqrt{2}$$

so that

$$\sigma = 1.5 \times \sqrt{2} = 2.12 \text{ to 2 dec. pl.}$$

Because $2.12 < 2.5$ it is deduced that the automatic dough mixer and portioner had been successfully installed and was producing bread buns within the consistency limits laid down.

Solution 20.2.1(a(ii))

Without replacement
When sampling is performed *without replacement* the standard deviation s of the sampling distribution of means is related to the standard deviation of the population σ by the equation:

$$s = \frac{\sigma\sqrt{(n_p - n)}}{\sqrt{[n(n_p - 1)]}}$$

where n is the sample size and n_p is the population size. From the production run:

$$s = 1.5 = \frac{\sigma\sqrt{(1250-2)}}{\sqrt{[2(1250-1)]}}$$

so that

$$\sigma = 1.5 \times \sqrt{2498} \div \sqrt{1248} = 2.12 \text{ to dec. pl.}$$

Because $2.12 < 2.5$ it is deduced that the automatic dough mixer and portioner had been successfully installed and was producing bread buns within the consistency limits laid down.

Solution 20.2.1(b)

Sampling with replacement is sampling from an infinite population because there is no restriction on either the size or the number of different samples that can be taken from the population. Sampling without replacement is sampling from a finite population. Because the results from both sampling methods are the same (at least to 2 decimal places) we can deduce that sampling without replacement is akin to sampling from an infinite population when the samples sizes are small and the population is large.

EXERCISES 20.2

1 A population consists of the six numbers 1, 2, 4, 6, 8, 9 and samples of 2 numbers are selected from it.

(a) Find the mean μ and standard deviation σ of the population

(b) Write down all possible different samples taken from the population with replacement and obtain the sampling distribution of their means.

(c) Confirm the fact that the sampling distribution of means has a mean m and standard deviation s where:

$m = \mu$ and $s = \sigma/\sqrt{n}$ where $n = 2$, the sample size.

(d) Repeat (b) but this time sample without replacement.

(e) Confirm the fact that the sampling distribution of means has a mean m and standard deviation s where:

$$m = \mu \quad \text{and} \quad s = \frac{\sigma\sqrt{(n_p - n)}}{\sqrt{[n(n_p - 1)]}}$$

where $n = 2$, the sample size, and $n_p = 6$, the population size.

2 The average petrol consumption of that popular family car the Rovolva 1.2 is advertised as 35 mpg with a standard deviation of 3.5 mpg. The Advertising Standards Authority commissioned a check on this claim where it found that from a sample of 8 cars taken from a limited production run of 25 cars the average petrol consumption was 35 mpg, as the maker claimed, with a standard deviation of 1.2 mpg. Do these results bear out the manufacturer's claim in their entirety if sampling of the 8 cars from the 25 was done:

(i) with replacement? (ii) without replacement?

3 If a population of data possesses a mean μ with a standard deviation σ what size of sample must be chosen if the sample standard deviation is to be 10% of the population standard deviation, assuming that sampling is done:

(i) with replacement? (ii) without replacement?

from a population of size 10.

20.3 SAMPLING DISTRIBUTION OF PROPORTIONS

Let samples of size n be drawn from an infinite, binomially distributed population where p is the probability of {success} and $q = 1 - p$ is the probability of {failure}. If, for each sample, the proportion P of successes is noted a *sampling distribution of proportions* is obtained. This sampling distribution is, for $n > 30$, approximately normally distributed with mean m and standard deviation s where:

$$m = p \quad \text{and} \quad s = \sqrt{[pq/n]}$$

EXAMPLE 20.3.1

The shipping line O & P have been operating cruises around the South Atlantic and Caribbean for a great many years. One of their smaller liners, the *Ranioa* has recently undergone a re-fit during which time the medical service provision was updated to cater, not only for minor injuries and severe seasickness but also for more serious medical complaints. Because of space limitations this has resulted in less provision being made for severe seasickness. Working on past experiences the company normally caters for 5% of the passengers suffering from severe seasickness at any one time with a worst case during exceptionally heavy weather of 8%. During the re-fit new stabilizers were fitted to the ship which, it was anticipated, would significantly reduce the incidence of severe seasickness. Accordingly the new medical provision for severe seasickness was reduced to a normal incidence of 2.5% with a worst case of 5%.

(a) Assuming that the new stabilizers do reduce the incidence of severe seasickness what is the probability that out of a passenger complement of 500

(i) 8% or more suffer from severe seasickness

(ii) 2.5% or less suffer from severe seasickness

(b) Assuming that the new stabilizers do not reduce the incidence of severe seasickness what is the probability that out of a passenger complement of 500

(i) 8% or more suffer from severe seasickness

(ii) 5% or less suffer from severe seasickness

Explain your reasoning and interpret your results.

Solution 20.3.1 (a(i))

Each cruise with a passenger complement of 500 is considered as a sample taken from an infinite population that consists of all the passengers that have been taken on all the cruises since recording of this data began. The statement that a given percentage (proportion) suffers from severe seasickness refers to the totality of past experience and, therefore, relates to the population.

If the new stabilizers do reduce the incidence of seasickness the company claims that the sampling distribution of proportions of those who suffer from seasickness has a mean:

$$m = p = 0.025$$

and hence, a standard deviation of:

$$s = \sqrt{[pq/n]} = \sqrt{[(0.025)(0.975)/500]} = 0.007 \text{ to 3 dec. pl.}$$

This is telling us that the sampling distribution of proportions, which is normally distributed, has a mean value of 0.025 and a standard deviation of 0.007.

To find the probability that on a given cruise 8% or more suffer from severe seasickness we need to find the standard normal probability distribution z-value that corresponds to the normal distribution value of 8%. However, because the population of proportions is a discrete binomial distribution we must first use the correction for the conversion of a discrete variable to the continuous variable of the normal distribution:

$$1/2n = 1/1000 = 0.001$$

yielding a corrected proportion on a continuous scale of:

$$0.08 - 0.001 = 0.079$$

This is the corrected proportion for the normal distribution of the sampling distribution of proportions. This must now be converted to the z-value of the standard normal distribution as:

$$z = (0.079 - 0.025)/0.007$$
$$= 7.71 \text{ to 2 dec. pl.}$$

Consequently, the required probability is equal to that area under the standard normal curve to the right of $z = 7.71$ which is effectively 0. This means that it is highly unlikely that more than 8% of the passengers will suffer from severe seasickness if the new stabilzers are as effective as claimed.

Solution 20.3.1(a(ii))

To find the probability that on a given cruise 2.5% or less suffer from seasickness we need to find the standard normal probability distribution z-value that corresponds to the normal distribution value of 2.5%. Again, we must use the correction for the conversion of a discrete variable to the continuous variable of the normal distribution:

$$1/2n = 1/1000 = 0.001$$

yielding a corrected proportion on a continuous scale of:

$$0.025 + 0.001 = 0.026$$

Notice that this time the correction is added because we are considering proportions less that 5%.

This corrected proportion for the normal distribution of the sampling distribution of proportions must now be converted to the z-value of the standard normal distribution as:

$z = (0.026 - 0.025)/0.007$
$\quad = 0.14$ to 2 dec. pl.

Consequently, the required probability is equal to that area under the standard normal curve to the left of $z = 0.14$ which is $0.5 + 0.056 = 0.556$. This means that there is just over a 55% chance of less than 2.5% of the passengers suffering from severe seasickness if the new stabilizers are as effective as claimed and the re-fit of the ship can cope with a problem of this magnitude.

Solution 20.3.1(b(i))

If the previous calculations are repeated for $p = 0.05$, which is the proportion of those suffering from seasickness if the new stabilizers have no additional effect over the previous stabilizers, it is found that:

$m = p = 0.05$ and $s = \sqrt{[pq/n]} = \sqrt{(0.05)(0.95)/500} = 0.010$ to 3 dec. pl.

The continuity correction of 0.001 is applied to yield a corrected normal distribution value of:

$0.08 - 0.001 = 0.079$

which converts to the z-value of the standard normal distribution as:

$z = (0.079 - 0.05)/0.010$
$\quad = 2.9$

Consequently, the required probability is equal to that area under the standard normal curve to the right of $z = 2.9$ which is $0.5 - 0.498 = 0.002$. This means that there is only a 0.2% chance of more than 8% of the passengers likely to suffer from severe seasickness. Because the probability is so low it is anticipated that weather conditions would be so bad for this to happen that the ship's company would be able to make emergency measures available.

Solution 20.3.1(b(ii))

The continuity correction of 0.001 is applied to yield a corrected normal distribution value of:

$0.05 + 0.001 = 0.051$

which converts to the to the z-value of the standard normal distribution as:

$z = (0.051 - 0.05)/0.010$
$\quad = 0.1$

Consequently, the required probability is equal to that area under the standard normal curve to the left of $z = 0.10$ which is $0.5 + 0.040 = 0.540$. This means that there is just over an evens chance that 5% of the passengers would suffer from severe seasickness but the re-fit has been designed to cope with just this situation.

EXERCISES 20.3

1 A mathematics course that had been running for many years has produced, over the time it has been running, a first time pass rate of 65% of the students. Recently the lecturer attended a professional development course where she was introduced to a number of computer aided learning modules that would greatly assist her in delivering her course. The following year the course was redesigned to permit the course delivery to include the use of computer aided learning and at the end of the year the number of students who passed the course first time was 59 out of a class size of 85.

(a) Find the mean and standard deviation of the sampling distribution of proportions before the introduction of computer aided learning. What was the probability that out of a class of 85 the number of students who would have passed the course first time is:

(i) 59 or less   (ii) 45 or more

(b) If the introduction of computer aided learning has improved the first time pass rate what is the probability that out of a class of 85 the number of students who will pass the course first time is:

(i) 59 or less   (ii) 45 or more

2 Acme Motors manufacture electric motors. They find that on average 10% of their motors require new bushes after 200 hours of use and 5% require new bushes after only 150 hours of use. By introducing a tighter specification in their manufacture whereby they increase the amount of copper in each bush to 75% they find, after testing, that they can reduce the bush replacement rate to 7% after 200 hours and 3% after 150 hours.

(a) Assuming that the Acme's testing was valid and that the new bushes do reduce the bush replacement rate, what is the probability that out of 100 electric motors:

(i)   10% or less will require new bushes after 200 hours of use

(ii) 5% or more will require new bushes after 150 hours of use

(b) Assuming that the Acme's testing was invalid and that the new bushes do not reduce the bush replacement rate, what is the probability that out of 100 electric motors:

(i)   10% or less will require new bushes after 200 hours of use

(ii) 5% or more will require new bushes after 150 hours of use

3 A company finds that 3% of all the invoices that it sends to its debtors contain a mistake. What is the probability that out of a sample of 250 such invoices:

(a) 10 or more will contain a mistake

(b) 8 or less will contain a mistake

(c) a number between 7 and 11 will contain a mistake

20.4 SAMPLING DISTRIBUTION OF SUMS AND DIFFERENCES

In a highly competitive marketplace where the quantity of goods sold is in direct proportion to the quality and reliability of the goods for sale it is necessary that a company maintains a watchful eye on its competitors' products. Part of the brief given to the quality control department will be to test the comparative quality of the company's product with that of its competitors. In doing so it will be necessary to sample from different populations and compare differences in relevant statistics.

Let all possible samples of size n_1 be taken from population 1 and a particular statistic measured for each sample thereby producing a sampling distribution of that statistic with mean m_1 and standard deviation s_1. Next, let all possible samples of size n_2 be taken from population 2 and the same statistic measured for each sample thereby producing a sampling distribution of that statistic with mean m_2 and standard deviation s_2. From these two sampling procedures it is now possible to compare the results from all possible pairings of samples from the two sets of samples and compute the sum or difference in the measured statistic thereby creating a *sampling distribution of sums* or *differences* in the statistic. If this last sampling distribution has a mean $m_\pm$ and a standard deviation $s_\pm$ then, provided the two sampling procedures from the two populations were independent of each other, the mean of the sampling distribution of sums is:

$$m_+ = m_1 + m_2$$

and the mean of the sampling distribution of differences is:

$$m_- = m_1 - m_2$$

Furthermore, the standard deviation in the sampling distribution of sums or differences is:

$$s_\pm = \sqrt{\{s_1^2 + s_2^2\}}$$

Again, these distributions are approximately normally distributed.

In particular, if the measured statistic in each sample was the mean value then:

$$m_+ = \mu_1 + \mu_2 \quad \text{and} \quad m_- = \mu_1 - \mu_2$$

where μ_1 is the mean of population 1 and μ_2 is the mean of population 2 and:

$$s_\pm = \sqrt{\{\sigma_1^2/n_1 + \sigma_2^2/n_2\}}$$

where σ_1 is the standard deviation of population 1 and σ_2 is the standard deviation of population 2 and where n_1 and n_2 refer to the respective sample sizes.

EXAMPLE 20.4.1

A consumer survey magazine published the results of a comparative survey that it had performed on floppy discs manufactured by the two companies DiscSave and SuperDisc. Their reported findings claimed that they had tested samples of each company's discs by saving and retrieving a given file automatically until the disc failed. They then recorded the number of disc transactions up to failure with the following results:

- DiscSave floppy discs had a mean usage life of 10,000 transactions with a standard deviation of 12 transactions.
- SuperDisc floppy discs had a mean usage life of 9,990 transactions with a standard deviation of 10 transactions.

Accordingly they recommended DiscSave as a better buy than SuperDisc. SuperDisc reacted to this adverse publicity by conducting their own trials after which they claimed that the consumer magazine were being unfair and that the chances of DiscSave discs being capable of more than 11 transactions more than SuperDisc discs were less than 1 in a thousand and that this minor difference was more than compensated for by the lower price they charged.

If SuperDisc tested 550 discs of each brand what is the probability that DiscSave floppy discs will last for:

(a) 12 or more transactions than SuperDisc's product.
(b) 10 or more transactions than SuperDisc's product.
(c) 0 or less transactions than SuperDisc's product.

How fair was SuperDisc's response to the criticism?

Solution 20.4.1(a)

Let the discs produced by DiscSave form population 1 and the discs produced by SuperDisc form population 2 so that, according to the consumer report:

$$\mu_1 = 10,000 \quad \text{and} \quad \sigma_1 = 12$$

and

$$\mu_2 = 9,990 \quad \text{and} \quad \sigma_2 = 10$$

When SuperDisc tested the consumer magazine's findings they took a sample from each population of size 550 so that:

$$n_1 = n_2 = 550$$

The sampling distribution of differences in the means has a mean value m_- where:

$$m_- = \mu_1 - \mu_2 = 10,000 - 9,990 = 10$$

and a standard deviation s_- where:

$$s_- = \sqrt{(\sigma_1^2/n_1 + \sigma_2^2/n_2)} = \sqrt{(12^2/550 + 10^2/550)} = 0.67 \text{ to 2 dec. pl.}$$

SuperDisc considered the probability that DiscSave discs last for more than 11 transactions more than SuperDisc discs. More than 11 transactions means 12 transactions or more. To find the probability of finding a difference of 12 or more transactions in the two samples chosen by SuperDisc we need to recognize that the sampling distribution of differences is normally distributed. Accordingly, we need to find the standard normal variable equivalent to a difference of 12 transactions. It is given in the usual way as:

$$z = [12 - 10]/0.67 = 2.98$$

From the tables of the standard normal distribution we find that the probability of obtaining a difference of 12 or more transactions is, therefore, $0.500 - 0.499 = 0.001$. One transaction in a thousand.

Solution 20.4.1(b)

For a difference of 10 or more in the means the standardized variable for the differences in the means is:

$$z = [10 - 10]/0.67 = 0$$

so that the probability of finding a difference in the samples of 10 or more transactions is 0.5 or one chance in two.

Solution 20.4.1(c)

For a difference of 0 or less in the means the standardized variable for the differences in the means is:

$$z = [0 - 10]/0.67 = -14.9$$

so that the probability of finding a difference in the samples of 0 or less transactions is practically zero – virtually impossible.

When SuperDisc claimed that the consumer report was unfair and produced the figure of 1 in a thousand for a difference of more than 11 transactions they were merely confirming the consistency in the quality of the two products as indicated by the small standard deviations. Had the standard deviations been larger the equivalent z-value would have been less and the consequent probability greater. They were also being dishonest to their customers by using a quantity description of *more than 11* – intimating just one more than claimed by the consumer report – they were in fact saying 12 or more transactions which is really 2 transactions greater than the 10 originally published. Furthermore, from parts (b) and (c) it is clear that the consumer report's findings were indeed fair and that the differences in reliability were real and not spurious.

EXERCISES 20.4

1 Hammerjones Valves produce heavy duty equipment for the oil industry. A machine that they use for lapping flat steel surfaces has been in operation without service for some time and is producing defects in 10% of all its lapped units. Taking two separate samples of 25 units each what is the probability of finding a difference in the two samples of:

(a) 2 or more defects

(b) 3 or less defects

(c) What is the probability of finding, taking both samples collectively

  (i) 4 or more defects   (ii) 6 or less defects

2 Two national biscuit manufacturers have both simultaneously developed a new chocolate biscuit with nuts. Crawobs new biscuit is called Choconut and

393

Jacfords is called Nutochoc. In a market research survey it was found that 65% preferred the Choconut to the Nutochoc. What is the probability, from two samples of 100, of finding a difference in preferences of:

(a) 15 or more people preferring the Nutochoc to the Choconut

(b) 23 or more preferring the Choconut to the Nutochoc.

3 Sugar is packed in 1 kilo bags with a standard deviation of 25 grammes. What is the probability that two samples of 500 bags will differ in weight by:

(a) more than 9 kilos

(b) less than 12 kilos

4 Population A has a mean of 100 and a standard deviation of 10 and population B has a mean of 120 with a standard deviation of 15. If samples of 25 units from population A and B are taken what is the probability of finding:

(a) a difference in the sample means of more than 10

(b) a difference in the sample means of less than 15

(c) a sum of the sample means of more than 210

(d) a sum of the sample means of less than 225

20.5 ESTIMATION OF POPULATION STATISTICS

We have seen that when we take all possible samples from a population and measure some particular statistic in each sample (such as, for example, the mean or the standard deviation) we obtain a sampling distribution of that statistic. Furthermore, we have also seen that the mean of the sampling distribution of that statistic is equal to the mean of the same statistic over the whole population. This equality would immediately open a door to a method of determining the mean of the population statistic if it were not for the fact that with large populations it would be easier to measure the population itself rather than measure every possible sample.

Consider the situation where we have a population of numerical values whose mean μ and standard deviation σ we do not know but wish to know. How do we set about finding their values? First of all, consider what we do know.

We know that we can take a single sample of size n and measure its mean M and standard deviation S. We also know that if we take all possible samples of size n from the population and measure their means we shall obtain a sampling distribution of means that itself has a mean m and a standard deviation s where:

$$m = \mu \text{ the population mean}$$

and

$$s = \sigma/\sqrt{n} \text{ where } \sigma \text{ is the population standard deviation}$$

We also know that for $n > 30$ the sampling distribution is approximately normally distributed. Now, what do we know about the normal distribution? We know that if a collection of data is normally distributed then a plot of relative frequencies against data values will produce the familar bell-shaped curve of the normal distribution.

From the mathematical knowledge of this curve we known that approximately 68.3% of all the plotted data values lie within one standard deviation either side of the mean (just consider the z-value of 1 – the standard deviation of the standard normal distribution – and see what comes from the table), 95.5% lie within two standard deviations either side of the mean and 99.7% lie within three standard deviations either side of the mean (Figure 20.5.1).

As a consequence of this we deduce that when we take a single sample and measure its mean M (where 68.3% of *all possible* samples lie within one standard deviation of the mean) we can be 68.3% confident that M will lie within an interval that is one sampling distribution standard deviation s either side of the sampling distribution mean m. That is

$$m - s < M \quad \text{and} \quad M < m + s$$

We can rearrange these inequalities.

$$m - s < M \text{ is the same as } m < M + s$$

and

$$M < m + s \text{ is the same as } M - s < m$$

We can now write these latter two inequalities as:

$$M - s < m < M + s$$

They tell us that the mean of the sampling distribution m is within one standard deviation s of the sampling distribution of the single sample mean M. Now, the

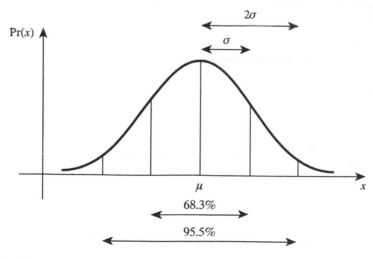

Figure 20.5.1

395

sampling distribution has a mean m that is equal to the population mean μ and the sampling distribution standard deviation s is related to the population standard deviation by:

$$s = \sigma/\sqrt{n}$$

Hence we can say:

$$M - \sigma/\sqrt{n} < \mu < M + \sigma/\sqrt{n}$$

Finally, we need to relate σ, the population standard deviation, which we do not know to something we do know. It can be shown (though not here) that S, the single sample standard deviation is a good estimate for a sample size greater than 30 to the population standard deviation σ. Consequently, we can replace the population standard deviation σ with the single sample standard deviation S to give:

$$M - S/\sqrt{n} < \mu < M + S/\sqrt{n}$$

This pair of inequalities represents the 68.3% confidence interval for the population mean μ. Other inequalities represent different levels of confidence, for example:

$M - 2S/\sqrt{n} < \mu < M + 2S/\sqrt{n}$ is the 95.5% confidence interval

$M - 3S/\sqrt{n} < \mu < M + 3S/\sqrt{n}$ is the 99.7% confidence interval

$M - 1.96S/\sqrt{n} < \mu < M + 1.96S\sqrt{n}$

is the 95% confidence interval because 95% of the plotted data in a normal distribution lies within 1.96 standard deviations of the mean.

EXAMPLE 20.5.1

A confectioner packs 500 gm of candy into boxes. If a sample of 50 boxes are weighed and their weights had a mean value of 500 gm and a standard deviation of 10 gm.

(a) Quantify the

(i) 95.5% (ii) 99%

confidence intervals for the mean weight of all boxes and interpret your results.

(b) If the sample size had been 100 boxes how would this have affected the results?

(c) How large a sample would have to be taken to ensure that the mean value of the total production lay within the interval 500 gm ± 5 gm with 95% confidence?

Solution 20.5.1(a(i))
The 95.5% confidence limits are:

$$M - 2S/\sqrt{n} < \mu < M + 2S/\sqrt{n}$$

where $M = 500$ is the sample mean, $S = 10$ is the sample standard deviation and

$n = 50$ is the sample size. Consequently the 95.5% confidence interval is:

$$500 - (2 \times 10/\sqrt{50}) < \mu < 500 + (2 \times 10/\sqrt{50})$$

That is:

$$500 - 2.83 < \mu < 500 + 2.83$$

This confidence interval is stating that we can be 95.5% confident that the average weight of all the boxes of candy lies within 500 ± 2.83 gm. Alternatively, we can interpret it by saying that 95.5% of all the boxes produced have a mean weight that lies within the range 500 ± 2.83 gm.

Solution 20.5.1(a(ii))

To find the 99% critical values consider the table of areas beneath the standard normal distribution. We see that 49.5% of the area lies between the mean at $z = 0$ and somewhere between $z = 2.57$ and 2.60. The actual value to 2 decimal places is 2.58. This means that 99% of the area under the standard normal distribution lies between $z = -2.58$ and $z = 2.58$ so that 99% of the area under any normal distribution lies within 2.58 standard deviations of the mean. The 99% confidence limits are thus:

$$M - 2.58S/\sqrt{n} < \mu < M + 2.58S/\sqrt{n}$$

Substituting values gives:

$$500 - (2.58 \times 10/\sqrt{50}) < \mu < 500 + (2.58 \times 10/\sqrt{50})$$

That is:

$$500 - 3.65 < \mu < 500 + 3.65$$

This confidence interval is stating that we can be 99% confident that the average weight of all the boxes of candy lies within 500 ± 3.65 gm. Alternatively, 99% of all the boxes produced have a mean weight that lies within the range 500 ± 3.65 gm. Notice that the confidence interval widens to accommodate an increased level of confidence.

Solution 20.5.1(b(i))

The 95.5% confidence limits are:

$$M - 2S/\sqrt{n} < \mu < M + 2S/\sqrt{n}$$

If $M = 500$ is the sample mean, $S = 10$ is the sample standard deviation and $n = 100$ is the sample size, the 95.5% confidence interval is:

$$500 - (2 \times 10/\sqrt{100}) < \mu < 500 + (2 \times 10/\sqrt{100})$$

That is:

$$500 - 2.0 < \mu < 500 + 2.0$$

Solution 20.5.1(b(ii))

The 99% confidence limits are:

$$M - 2.58S/\sqrt{n} < \mu < M + 2.58S/\sqrt{n}$$

Substituting values gives:

$$500 - (2.58 \times 10/\sqrt{100}) < \mu < 500 + (2.58 \times 10/\sqrt{100})$$

That is:

$$500 - 2.58 < \mu < 500 + 2.58$$

Clearly, for a given confidence interval the level of confidence increases if the sample size increases so making the determination of μ more precise.

Solution 20.5.1(c)

The 95% confidence limits are:

$$M - 1.96S/\sqrt{n} < \mu < M + 1.96S/\sqrt{n}$$

To ensure that this limit is:

$$500 - 5 < \mu < 500 + 5$$

we require that $1.96S/\sqrt{n} = 5$ where $S = 10$. This means that

$$\sqrt{n} = 1.96 \times 10/5 \quad \text{so that } n = 15.36$$

Clearly, a sample of size 16 would suffice.

EXERCISES 20.5

1 A sample of size 36, taken from a population, has a mean $M = 15$ and a standard deviation $S = 3$.

(a) Find the confidence interval corresponding to the confidence level:

(i) 68.3% (ii) 90% (iii) 95.5% (iv) 98%

(b) Find the confidence interval and confidence level corresponding to the critical values:

(i) 0.68 (ii) 1.28 (iii) 1.96 (iv) 2.58

(c) Describe exactly what is meant by each confidence interval found in (a) and (b).

2 A company employs a large number of experienced typists and it wishes to examine their performance. It selects a random sample of 10 typists and finds that the average number of words typed per minute measured over a normal working day were as follows:

50, 57, 55, 75, 60, 46, 53, 65, 52, 67

(a) If the population standard deviation can be taken as 6 words per minute calculate a 95% confidence interval for the population mean typing speed. Explain carefully what the interval indicates.

(b) The firm is considering taking over another company which also employs a large number of experienced typists. It measures the average number of words typed per minute over a normal working day for a random sample of 9 typists from this company, and the results were as follows:

58, 63, 62, 76, 52, 60, 79, 71, 64

(c) Test the firm's suspicion that the typists from the other company, whose population standard deviation of typing speeds can also be taken as 6 words per minute, type faster, on average, than those which the firm currently employs.

(d) Comment critically upon the way the firm has tested its suspicion in (b) above.

3 Jones plc is a company retailing fashionwear for men and women throughout a nationwide chain of 20 high street stores in England and Wales and is considering introducing its own credit card. As part of a feasibility study, Jones conducted a survey of a random sample of its customers at its Oxford Street store in London. From a sample of 80 customers, 32 indicated that they would apply for such a credit card if it should become available. These 32 people were then asked to anticipate how much they would borrow on a credit card. For the 32 replies, the mean amount was £450 with a standard deviation of £150.

(a) Explain what is meant by the term 'random sample'.

(b) Find a 95% confidence interval for the percentage of all customers who would apply for such a credit card.

(c) Find a 95% confidence interval for the mean amount of anticipated loans in the credit card.

(d) It was believed that the mean amount borrowed on such a credit card might differ for male and female customers. In order to test this hypothesis, random samples were selected of male and female customers, who had indicated that they would apply for such a card. The results are listed below:

Men	Women
$n = 12$	$n = 20$
$\bar{x} = 425$	$\bar{x} = 460$
$s = 187$	$s = 115$

Does the data support this hypothesis?

4 A survey of tickets in use by adults on selected British Rail express trains one Thursday before the Great Strike revealed the following pattern of passenger journeys on the Manchester, Huddersfield, Leeds route:

| | Number of passengers | |
| | From | |
To	Manchester	Huddersfield	Leeds
Manchester		361 (26)	422 (43)
Huddersfield	376		483 (17)
Leeds	925	844	

The numbers in brackets are the rail mileages between these stations

(a) Calculate the mean distance travelled per adult passenger.

(b) If the standard deviation of distance travelled per adult passenger is 11.63 miles find the standard error of the mean and hence a 95% confidence interval for the population mean.

(c) Explain what this confidence interval measures, the assumptions underlying its calculation and the nature of the population.

(d) If the mean 2nd class fare on British Rail is 6p per passenger mile, first class fares are 50% higher than 2nd class fares and one fifth of the above passenger mileage was first class, calculate a 95% confidence interval for the mean fare per adult passenger-journey. Comment on the assumptions underlying this analysis.

21

HYPOTHESIS TESTING

When you have completed this chapter you will be able to:

- formulate a null hypothesis and an accompanying alternative hypothesis
- understand the role of significance levels
- conduct one- and two-sided hypothesis tests
- distinguish between and compute the values of Type I and Type II errors

21.1 HYPOTHESES

Business decisions very often have to be made upon the basis of evidence from a single sample extracted from a larger population. To facilitate this it is common practice to make assumptions about the population, assumptions which may or may not be true. An assumption, referred to as an *hypothesis*, is always given in the form of a statement about the statistical nature of the population. Then if, on the evidence from a single sample taken from the population, it is found that the results obtained from the sample would have been unlikely to occur if the hypothesis were true, we would be inclined to reject the hypothesis.

21.2 ONE-SIDED HYPOTHESIS TESTS

EXAMPLE 21.2.1

Albatross Ltd sell packs of assorted remaindered books to retail booksellers. The promotional literature is sent out to 2000 booksellers each month and from this alone they manage to sell an average of 100 packs of books each week; their weekly sales being normally distributed with a standard deviation of 10 packs per week. Recently, they invested in some printing equipment that enables them to print their own promotional literature. Apart from the cash investment made they find that they can now save a significant sum of money by not paying someone else to print the material. However, they do require an extra employee to assist with the printing and this additional weekly cost would cut into their saving. They estimate that an increase in sales of just 10 packets each week would provide them with sufficient extra income to cover the additional costs of the new employee. To attain this end they increased the size of their customer database and now send out promotional literature to 2350 booksellers and decided to test for increased sales in three weeks time. In the third week after increasing their database they found that they sold 120 packs of books.

Has the new database resulted in a genuine increase in their sales or is the observed increase just due to normal market fluctuations?

How different would their conclusions be had they sold 110 packs of books?

Solution 21.2.1

We have seen how information about a population can be obtained by taking samples from the population and inferring results from the samples to the population. Now we wish to take a single sample and test it against some pre-determined statement or *hypothesis* about the population. In other words, the nature of hypothesis testing is to test whether or not a claim about the population can be verified by sampling. To answer the question concerning Albatross' sales we first make a hypothesis that in fact:

The extended database has not resulted in an increase in sales and that their sales are still normally distributed around a mean weekly sales of 100 packs of books and a standard deviation of 10 packs of books.

Because we are dealing with a continuous probability distribution we cannot evaluate the probability of a specific value; we can only evaluate the probability of a *range* of values. What we do, therefore, is calculate the probability of selling 120 packs of books *or more* under the stated hypothesis.

Under the hypothesis the weekly sales are still normally distributed with the same mean of 100 packs of books and a standard deviation of 10 packs of books. The z-value of the third week's sales of 120 packs of books is, therefore:

$$z = (120 - 100)/(10) = 2$$

From the tables of the standard normal distribution the area under the curve between $z = 0$ and $z = 2$ is 0.477. Consequently, the area under the curve to the right of $z = 2$ is:

$$0.500 - 0.477 = 0.023 \qquad \text{(Figure 21.2.1)}$$

This means that the probability of obtaining a z-score of 2 or more is 0.023. That is, there is only a 2.3% chance of selling 120 or more packs of books under the hypothesis that the population mean is 100 (Figure 21.2.2).

If, instead of the third week's sale of 120 packs of books, Albatross had only sold 110 packs of books then the appropriate z-score would have been:

$$z = (100 - 100)/(10) = 1$$

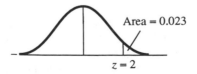

Area = 0.023

$z = 2$

Figure 21.2.1

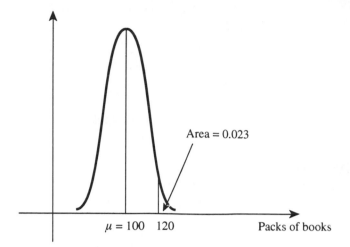

Figure 21.2.2

From the tables of the standard normal distribution the area under the curve between $z = 0$ and $z = 1$ is 0.341. Consequently, the area under the curve to the right of $z = 1$ is:

$$0.500 - 0.341 = 0.159 \qquad \text{(Figure 21.2.3)}$$

This means that the probability of obtaining a z-score of 1 or more is 0.159. That is, there is a 15.9% chance of obtaining a weekly sale of 110 packs of books or greater under the hypothesis that the population mean is 100.

The question to answer now is whether the findings from the samples do or do not support the hypothesis; are the findings significant enough to enable us to accept or reject the hypothesis. To do this we have to make a decision. For example, if we decide to accept the hypothesis if the probability of obtaining the sales of 120 or greater is more than 0.05 then our conclusion would be to reject the hypothesis from the findings of the first sample of 120 packs of books and to accept it from the findings of the second sample of books (Figure 21.2.4).

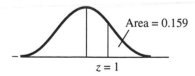

Figure 21.2.3

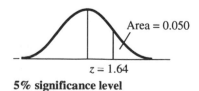

Figure 21.2.4

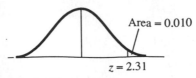

Figure 21.2.5

If, on the other hand, we decide to accept the hypothesis if the probability of obtaining the sample mean of 120 or greater is more than 0.01 then we would accept the hypothesis from the results of either sample (Figure 21.2.5).

This is the essence of hypothesis testing. We first set up what is called a *significance level* and then test the sample against that significance level. In our example above we considered the effects of two significance levels, namely 5% (0.05) and 1% (0.01).

In any hypothesis test we deal with two hypotheses, the null and alternative hypotheses. The **null hypothesis** (labelled H_0) is the hypothesis that we test and the **alternative hypothesis** (labelled H_1) is the hypothesis we accept if we reject (nullify) the null hypothesis. In the example concerning Albatross the null hypothesis H_0 was:

The mean weekly sales had not increased

and the alternative hypothesis H_1 was:

The mean weekly sales had increased

EXERCISES 21.2

1 A large supermarket group wishes to investigate the mean household income in the neighbourhood of a site A, which it is considering for development. It also wishes to compare it to the mean household income of a site B, where it has an existing store. Random samples of households in the neighborhoods of the two sites produced the following results:

Household income	Site A	Site B
Mean	£15,700	£14,500
Standard deviation	£700	£850
Sample size	16	24

(a) Explain the terms 'null hypothesis' and 'significance level' which are used in hypothesis testing

(b) Test at the 5% level of significance the hypothesis that the mean household income in the neighbourhood of site A is greater than that in the neighbourhood of site B

(c) Explain the term 'confidence interval'

(d) Calculate the 95% confidence intervals for the mean household incomes in the neighborhoods of site A and site B

(e) Consider your results for parts (a) and (d). Are these results consistent? Support your conclusion.

2 A golfer finds that over a large number of games his average score is 92 with a standard deviation of 5. He buys a new set of golf clubs and on his first game with his new clubs he goes round in 84. He claims that the new clubs have improved his game. Is his claim true:

(a) at the 5% level of significance

(b) at the 1% level of significance

3 The sales of a commodity have been steady at 100 units per week with a standard deviation of 11 units per week. Immediately after an extensive advertising campaign the following week's sales were 120. Has the campaign been successful:

(a) at the 5% level of significance

(b) at the 1% level of significance

21.3 TWO-SIDED HYPOTHESIS TESTS

The hypothesis test considered earlier was an example of a one-sided test – it only considered one side of the standard normal distribution. In a two-sided test the significance level is shared between the two end regions of the standard normal distribution. Figure 21.3.1 demonstrates a two-sided test at a 5% significance level and Figure 21.3.2 a 1% significance level.

The distinction between a one- and a two-sided hypothesis test lies in the nature of the alternative hypothesis. If the null hypothesis sets a hypothesized mean and the alternative hypothesis claims the new mean to be greater than this mean or, alternatively, less than this mean then the test to apply will be one-sided. If, however, the alternative hypothesis merely states that the new mean is different without saying it is either larger or smaller then a two-sided test is to be used.

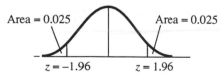

Area = 0.025   Area = 0.025

$z = -1.96$ $z = 1.96$

5% two-sided significance level

Figure 21.3.1

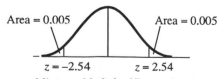

Area = 0.005   Area = 0.005

$z = -2.54$ $z = 2.54$

1% two-sided significance level

Figure 21.3.2

EXAMPLE 21.3.1

A manufacturer of wire consistently produces filament with an average diameter of 2.5 mm and a standard deviation of 0.25 mm. Due to a labour dispute the machinery used in the manufacture missed a crucial service. The works manager selected two filaments at random and measured their diameters as 3.01 mm and 2.35 mm respectively. Has the consistency of the manufacturing process changed at the 5% level of significance?

(a) if each measured filament was considered as a sample of size 1

(b) if both measured filaments were considered as a single sample of size 2

Solution 21.3.1(a)

Take the null hypothesis H_0 as:

The mean filament diameter has not changed

and the alternative hypothesis H_1 as:

The mean filament diameter has changed

At the 5% significance level, under the null hypothesis, 95% of the sample means lie on either side of the mean of 2.5 mm. That is, 47.5% lie to the right and 47.5% lie to the left. This means that if the z-value of the sample diameter lies between ± 1.96 then the null hypothesis should be accepted.

The z-value for a diameter of 3.01 mm is:

$$z = (3.01 - 2.50)/0.25 = 2.04$$

with an accompanying probability of 0.021 of producing this diameter size under the null hypothesis.

The z-value for a diameter of 2.35 mm is:

$$z = (2.35 - 2.50)/0.25 = -0.6$$

with an accompanying probability of 0.274 of producing this diameter size under the null hypothesis.

Clearly, the first sample would indicate that the hypothesis should be rejected at the 5% level or even at the 1% level as it is quite unlikely that such a diameter would have occurred under the hypothesis that the machine is performing as it should. The second sample, on the other hand, has a probability of occurring of 0.274 which indicates that the null hypothesis should be accepted at the 5% level of significance or even at the 25% level of significance.

Solution 21.3.1(b)

If the two filaments of diameters 3.01 mm and 2.35 mm are to be regarded as a sample of size 2 with mean:

$$(3.01 + 2.35)/2 = 2.68$$

then the z-value is:

$$z = (2.68 - 2.50)/(0.25/\sqrt{2})$$
$$= 1.02 \text{ to 2 dec. pl.}$$

which has an associated probability of 0.346. Notice the divisor $0.25/\sqrt{2}$, the $\sqrt{2}$ refers to the fact that the sample size was 2.

Here we see that we would accept the null hypothesis at the 1% level but reject it at the 5% level.

EXERCISES 21.3

1 Many shoppers have expressed unhappiness about the practice adopted by supermarkets to stop putting prices on individual items. A random sample of supermarket shoppers was selected and each was classified according to age and whether or not they felt the need for item pricing. The results are given in the following table:

	Age				
	<30	30–39	40–49	50–59	>60
Number wanting item pricing	127	118	77	61	41
Number who do not mind	23	23	5	2	8

(a) Test the hypothesis that the need for item pricing is independent of age. Use the 5% level of significance.

(b) What is the probability that a shopper selected at random is in the age group:

(i) 50–59 and wants item pricing?

(ii) <30 and does not want item pricing?

(c) Test the claim that over 80% of all supermarket shoppers in the <30 age group want item pricing.

2 A salmon farmer culls his stock of hen salmon every year in order to harvest the roe. The average weight of the culled salmon has been 22.5 lb with a standard deviation of 1.5 lb for the past ten years. This year a pollutant entered the water and the farmer feels that his fish have been affected. He selects a fish at random and finds that it weighs 20.4 lb. At what level of significance can the farmer state that:

(a) his fish have been affected

(b) his fish have not been affected

(c) his fish have been affected adversely

(d) his fish have not been adversely affected

3 Prior to a Party Political Broadcast it was found that 43% of the electorate favoured the Umbra party as opposed to the Penumbra party. After the

broadcast a sample of 246 people were interviewed and it was found that 125 people favoured the Umbra party as opposed to the Penumbra party. Has the broadcast had any significant effect at:

(a) the 5% level   (b) the 1% level

21.4 ERRORS

The Example 21.3.1 highlights a problem with hypothesis testing. There is no guarantee that the hypothesis is true or false so it is possible, having set a level of significance, to reject a true hypothesis or to accept a false hypothesis. Rejecting a true hypothesis by concluding that it is false is referred to as a Type I error. Accepting a false hypothesis by concluding that it is true is referred to as a Type II error.

EXAMPLE 21.4.1

Extending Example 21.3.1, find the Type I and II errors if, after missing its crucial service, the wire filament machine was actually producing wire filament with a mean diameter of 2.95 mm with a standard deviation of 0.35 mm.

Solution 21.4.1
It was decided to reject the null hypothesis at the 5% level. The critical z-values at this level of significance are $z = \pm 1.96$. The diameter of filament that gives a z-value of 1.96 is d where:

$$1.96 = (d - 2.5)/0.25$$

That is $d = 2.99$ mm

and a z-value of -1.96 is:

$$-1.96 = (d - 2.5)/0.25$$

That is $d = 2.01$ mm

In Figure 21.4.1 the probability of rejecting the null hypothesis when it should be accepted is represented by the combined area α formed by the sum of $\alpha/2$ from each end of the tail of the distribution with mean 2.5 mm. This gives us the magnitude of a Type I error and is equal to 0.05, that is 5% of the total area.

The Type II error (the error in accepting a false null hypothesis as being true) is represented by the area β enclosed between the diameters 2.01 and 2.99 beneath

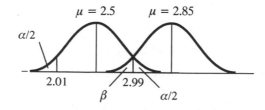

Figure 21.4.1

408

the right-hand distribution with mean 2.85 mm and standard deviation 0.35 mm. To evaluate this area we need to find the respective z-values of $d = 2.01$ and $d = 2.99$ for the distribution with mean 2.85 mm and standard deviation 0.35. These are:

$$z_1 = (2.01 - 2.85)/0.35 = -2.4$$

and

$$z_2 = (2.99 - 2.85)/0.35 = 0.4$$

The area beneath the standard normal distribution between the z-values -2.4 and 0.4 is $0.492 + 0.155 = 0.647$.

EXERCISES 21.4

1 Calculate the Type I and Type II errors in Question 2 Exercises 21.2 by comparing with the golfer's possible improved average score due to the new clubs of 90 with a standard deviation of 4.

2 Calculate the Type I and Type II errors in Question 2 Exercises 21.3 by comparing with the possible change in the average weight of the culled salmon to 21.2 lb with a standard deviation of 1.5 lb.

3 Calculate the Type I and Type II errors in Question 3 Exercises 21.2 by comparing with the possible improved sales due to the advertising campaign resulting in a new average sales of 115 units per week with a standard deviation of 10 units per week.

4 Calculate the Type I and Type II errors in Question 3 Exercises 21.3 by comparing with the popularity of the Umbra party having possibly increased to 45%.

5 Which of the two errors Type I or Type II is the more serious?

APPENDIX 1

USING THE STANDARD NORMAL TABLES

Areas beneath the standard normal distribution

The total area beneath the standard normal distribution is unity. Partial areas beneath the standard normal distribution have been calculated and are contained in the Statistical Table at the end of this Appendix, a section of which is reproduced here:

Area beneath the standard normal curve

z	0	1	2	3	4	5	6	7	8	9
0.0	0.000	0.004	0.008	0.012	0.016	0.020	0.024	0.028	0.032	0.036
0.1	0.040	0.044	0.048	0.052	0.056	0.060	0.064	0.068	0.071	0.075
0.2	0.080	0.083	0.087	0.091	0.095	0.099	0.103	0.106	0.110	0.114
0.3	0.118	0.122	0.126	0.129	0.133	0.137	0.141	0.144	0.148	0.152
0.4	0.155	0.159	0.163	**0.166**	0.177	0.174	0.177	0.181	0.184	0.188
0.5	0.192	0.195	0.199	0.202	0.205	0.209	0.212	0.216	0.219	0.222
0.6	0.226	0.229	0.232	0.236	0.239	0.242	0.245	0.249	0.252	0.255
0.7	0.258	0.261	0.264	0.267	0.270	0.273	0.276	0.279	0.282	0.285

The values of the horizontal variable z, to one decimal place, are ranged down the first column on the left and the second decimal places are ranged across the first row at the top. The numbers in the body of the table give the area beneath the curve and between the $z = 0$ and the appropriate z-value as indicated by shading in the small diagram at the top of the table.

For example, selecting the z value **0.4** in the first column on the left and moving across to the column headed **3** locates the highlighted number:

0.166

This tells you that the area beneath the standard normal curve between:

$z = 0$ and $z = 0.43$ is, to three decimal places, equal to 0.166.

Using the tables

Looking closely at the table and the shading in the small figure above the table you will see that the numbers only give areas to the right of $z = 0$. By the symmetry of the normal curve, areas to the left of $z = 0$ are the same as equivalent areas to the right so these can be easily read from the table. There are a number of cases of areas between two z values z_1 and z_2 that we should consider, remembering at all times that:

The area beneath the whole curve = 1 so that the area
beneath the left and right hand halves both equal 0.5.

Case 1 $z_1 = -1.5$ and $z_2 = 0$

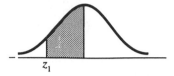

Areas to the left of $z = 0$ match areas to the right. Consequently:

the area between $z = -1.5$ and $z = 0$

equals

the area between $z = 0$ and $z = +1.5$

that is: 0.433

Case 2 $z_1 = 1$ and $z_2 = \infty$

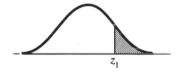

From the table, the area between $z = 0$ and $z = 1$ is given as 0.341. From the symmetry of the curve the area between $z = 0$ and $z = \infty$ is half the total area. Thus the area between $z = 1$ and $z = \infty$ is:

(the area between $z = 0$ and $z = \infty$) − (the area between $z = 0$ and $z = 1$)

equals

the area between $z = 1$ and $z = \infty$

that is: $0.500 - 0.341 = 0.159$

Case 3 $z_1 = -\infty$ and $z_2 = -1.5$

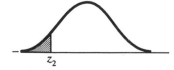

Again, this is the same area as the area between $z = +1.5$ and $z = +\infty$ which is:

$0.500 - 0.433 = 0.067$

Case 4 $z_1 = -\infty$ and $z_2 = 1$

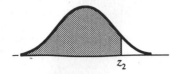

The area between $z = -\infty$ and $z = 0$ is half of the total area and the area between $z = 0$ and $z = 1$ is 0.341. As a result:

(the area between $z = -\infty$ and $z = 0$) + (the area between $z = 0$ and $z = 1$)

equals

the area between $z = -\infty$ and $z = 1$

that is: $0.500 + 0.341 = 0.841$

Case 5 $z_1 = -1.5$ and $z_2 = \infty$

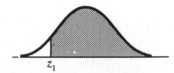

By the symmetry of the curve this area is the same as the area between $z = 0$ and $z = +1.5$ plus half the area beneath the curve:

$0.433 + 0.500 = 0.933$

Case 6 $z_1 = -1.5$ and $z_2 = 1$

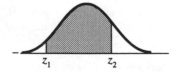

The area between $z = -1.5$ and $z = 0$ is 0.433. The area between $z = 0$ and $z = 1$ is 0.341. Consequently, the area between $z = -1.5$ and $z = 1$ is:

$0.433 + 0.341 = 0.774$

Case 7 $z_1 = 1$ and $z_2 = 1.5$

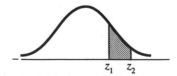

The area between $z = 0$ and $z = 1.5$ is 0.433. The area between $z = 0$ and 1 is 0.341. As a result, the area between $z = 1$ and $z = 1.5$ is:

$0.433 - 0.341 = 0.092$

Area beneath the standard normal curve

z	0	1	2	3	4	5	6	7	8	9
0.0	0.000	0.004	0.008	0.012	0.016	0.020	0.024	0.028	0.032	0.036
0.1	0.040	0.044	0.048	0.052	0.056	0.060	0.064	0.068	0.071	0.075
0.2	0.080	0.083	0.087	0.091	0.095	0.099	0.103	0.106	0.110	0.114
0.3	0.118	0.122	0.126	0.129	0.133	0.137	0.141	0.144	0.148	0.152
0.4	0.155	0.159	0.163	0.166	0.177	0.174	0.177	0.181	0.184	0.188
0.5	0.192	0.195	0.199	0.202	0.205	0.209	0.212	0.216	0.219	0.222
0.6	0.226	0.229	0.232	0.236	0.239	0.242	0.245	0.249	0.252	0.255
0.7	0.258	0.261	0.264	0.267	0.270	0.273	0.276	0.279	0.282	0.285
0.8	0.288	0.291	0.294	0.297	0.300	0.302	0.305	0.308	0.311	0.313
0.9	0.316	0.319	0.321	0.324	0.326	0.329	0.332	0.334	0.337	0.339
1.0	0.341	0.344	0.346	0.349	0.351	0.353	0.355	0.358	0.360	0.362
1.1	0.364	0.367	0.369	0.371	0.372	0.375	0.377	0.379	0.381	0.383
1.2	0.385	0.387	0.389	0.391	0.393	0.394	0.396	0.398	0.400	0.402
1.3	0.403	0.405	0.407	0.408	0.410	0.412	0.413	0.415	0.416	0.418
1.4	0.420	0.421	0.422	0.424	0.425	0.427	0.428	0.429	0.431	0.432
1.5	0.433	0.435	0.436	0.437	0.438	0.439	0.441	0.442	0.443	0.444
1.6	0.445	0.446	0.447	0.448	0.450	0.451	0.452	0.453	0.454	0.455
1.7	0.455	0.456	0.457	0.458	0.459	0.460	0.461	0.462	0.463	0.463
1.8	0.464	0.465	0.466	0.466	0.467	0.468	0.469	0.469	0.470	0.471
1.9	0.471	0.472	0.473	0.473	0.474	0.474	0.475	0.476	0.476	0.477
2.0	0.477	0.478	0.478	0.479	0.479	0.480	0.480	0.481	0.481	0.482
2.1	0.482	0.483	0.483	0.483	0.484	0.484	0.485	0.485	0.485	0.486
2.2	0.486	0.486	0.487	0.487	0.488	0.488	0.488	0.488	0.489	0.489
2.3	0.489	0.490	0.490	0.490	0.490	0.491	0.491	0.491	0.491	0.492
2.4	0.492	0.492	0.492	0.493	0.493	0.493	0.493	0.493	0.493	0.494
2.5	0.494	0.494	0.494	0.494	0.495	0.495	0.494	0.495	0.495	0.495
2.6	0.495	0.496	0.496	0.496	0.496	0.496	0.496	0.496	0.496	0.496
2.7	0.497	0.497	0.497	0.497	0.497	0.497	0.497	0.497	0.497	0.497
2.8	0.497	0.498	0.498	0.498	0.498	0.498	0.498	0.498	0.498	0.498
2.9	0.498	0.498	0.498	0.498	0.498	0.498	0.499	0.499	0.499	0.499
3.0	0.499	0.499	0.499	0.499	0.499	0.499	0.499	0.499	0.499	0.499
3.1	0.499	0.499	0.499	0.499	0.499	0.499	0.499	0.499	0.499	0.499
3.2	0.499	0.499	0.499	0.499	0.499	0.499	0.499			

APPENDIX 2

SOLUTIONS TO EXERCISES

Chapter 1

Exercises 1.1

1 (a) Equation has solution $x = 3/2$.
(b) Equation has solutions $x = 13.6$ and $x = 51.4$.

Exercises 1.2

1 (a) $y = 20 - 3x$ (b) $y = 4x - 5$

2 (a)(i) $p = 300 - 3x$ (ii) $p = 225 - 9x$
(b)(i) $y = 1.5x - 12$ (ii) $y = -1.75x - 18$

3 (a) $y = 3x + 4$ (b) $y = -4x - 18$

Exercises 1.3

1 (a) a^8 (b) a^8 (c) a^2 (d) b (e) a^7 (f) $b^{5/2}$
(g) $a^{1/2}$ (h) b^{12} (i) a^4 (j) a^{10} (k) $a^4 b^3$ (l) $a^2 b^7$

2 (a) 2   (b) 1/8   (c) 4   (d) 1/3   (e) 8   (f) 4
(g) 2   (h) 8   (i) 216   (j) 25

3 (a) 64   (b) 6.1917   (c) 5.1962   (d) 91634.9293
(e) 0.6389   (f) 0.0001   (g) 2.8284

4 (a) $2y - x + y^2 + 3$ (b) $14a - 3b - ab + 2$
(c) $2a - 11b + 6ab$ (d) $6b^2 - 3a - 6a^2$
(e) $4b^3 - 2a^2 - ab + 4a^3$ (f) Cannot be simplified
(g) $4a^3 b - 4a^2 - 4ab^3$

5 (a) $24x + 16y$ (b) $12c - 15a$ (c) $18ac - 8ab - 10bc$
(d) $x^3 - 3x^2 + 8x$ (e) $6x^5 - 10x^3$ (f) $2a^2 b^6 - 3a^2 b^4$
(g) $5a^3 b^4 + 2a^2 b^4$ (h) $8a^2 - 18b^2$
(i) $66xy + 36x^2 - 30x + 24y^2 - 15y$ (j) $6x^6 - 5x^4 - 6x^2$
(k) $6a^5 + 9a^3 b^2 - 4a^2 b^4 - 6b^6$
(l) $2x^3 y - 4x^4 y + 6x^3 + 12x^2 y + 9x^2 - 8y + 4xy - 6$

6 (a) 2   (b) 3   (c) 4   (d) 1/3   (e) 4   (f) 1
(g) -2   (h) -6   (i) 1/2   (j) 1/3   (k) 4   (l) 4

Exercises 1.4

1 (a) $5x(4 - x)$ (b) $3x^3(2 - 3x^2)$ (c) $a^2 b^2(b - a^2 c)$
(d) $ab^2 c^3(b^2 + c^2)$ (e) $2(2a + d)(2b - 3c)$
(f) $2(2a + d^2)(3b - 2c^2)$

2 (a) $(x + 3)(x - 1)$ (b) $(x - 6)(x - 2)$ (c) $(x + 3)(x + 8)$
(d) $(x - 8)(x + 5)$ (e) $(x - 1)(x - 7)$

3   (a) $3(x+2)^2$ (b) $(3x-2)(x-4)$ (c) $(2x-1)(x+2)$
(d) $2(3x+2)(2x-5)$ (e) $(9x+4)(x+1)$ (f) $(2x-1)^2$

Exercises 1.5

1   (a) $x=30$ (b) $x=-2$ (c) $x=6$ (d) $x=3/2$
(e) $x=-20/13$

2   (a) $x=9/13$ (b) $x=13/8$ (c) $x=-4$ (d) $x=1/9$

3   (a)(i) $x=-3$ or -8 (ii) $x=-6$ or 3 (iii) $x=5/3$ or -3
(b)(i) $x=4$ or -2 (ii) $x=4$ or 5 (iii) $x=1/3$ or -1
(c)(i) $x=0.88$ or 5.12 (ii) $x=-2.93$ or 0.43
(iii) $x=-1.29$ or -0.31 (iv) $x=-1.08$ or 0.58

4   (a) 0.79 (b) 7.60 (c) 1.16 (d) 1.26 (e) 1.36

Exercises 1.6

1   (a) $x=-6$, $y=4$ (b) $a=4$, $b=8$ (c) $x=3$, $y=-2$

2   (a) $x=1$, $y=2$, $z=1$ (b) $x=4$, $y=-4$, $z=-5$ (c) $a=5$, $b=2$, $c=0$

3   (a)(i) $p=300-3x$ (ii) $p=225-9x$
(b)(i) $y=1.5x-12$ (ii) $y=-1.75x-18$

4   (a) For A, $T=10x+2000$ and for B, $T=20x+1400$.
(b) B is cheaper up to 60 units/week, A is cheaper above 60 units/week.

5   (b) $S=4t^2+500$

6   (a) $T=0.5x^2+60x+2800$ (b) $T=1.6x^2+160x+10000$

7 $x=382-2p^2$

Exercises 1.7

1 $a-2.5$, $b=10.0$ (plot n against s^7)

2 $a=0.20$, $b=0.92$ (plot y against x^3)

3 $a=30,000$, $b=2000$ (plot V against $1/d$)

4   (a) Plot y against x^3 (b) Plot y against $1/x^2$ (c) Plot y^2 against x

Chapter 2

Exercises 2.1

1   (a) Maximise $\qquad\qquad G=7x+4y$
Subject to the constraints:
$$4y\leqslant 900$$
$$4x+3y\leqslant 1200$$
$$8x+2y\leqslant 1600$$
$$x\geqslant 0,\ y\geqslant 0$$

(b) 150 units of P and 200 units of Q per day. Profit $=£1850$ per day.
(c) Reduce time in A, so that profit $=£1793.75$ per day (for 156.25 units of P and 175 units of Q per day).

2 (a) 200 ovens and 60 dishwashers per week. Profit = £23,200 per week.
(b) Increase time in B. Profit = £24,800 per week.

3 40 overcoats, 75 jackets per week. Profit = £1690 per week.

4 (a) 750 'Super' and 300 'Supreme' mattresses per month. Profit = £69,000 per month.
(b) 600 'Super' and 400 'Supreme' mattresses per month. Profit = £68,000 per month.
(c) 20 hours per month.

5 (a) 180 model S and 160 model T tractors per month. Profit = £1,110,000 per month.
(b) An extra 4500 litres of ZB-90 are required. 60 model S and 300 model T tractors should be produced next month.

6 (a) 30 of the 2-day and 10 of the 4-day courses per year. Annual profit = £500.
(b) Profit for a 2-day course can increase by £33.33.

Exercises 2.2

1 60 hours for plant A and 10 hours for plant B. Cost = £85,000.

2 84 gms of meat, 147.8 gms of mixed vegetables per can. Cost per can = 14.2 pence.

3 (a) 30 spread jars and no paste jars per pack. Cost = £3 per pack.
(b) 20 spread jars and 10 paste jars per pack. Extra cost = 50 pence per pack.

4 48 loaves and 98 pints of milk per day. (Actual amounts required are 47.2 loaves and 97.9 pints of milk.)

5 300 gallons of X and 150 gallons of Y per week. Cost = £10,500 per week.

6 Initially, the proportions are A: 1/8, B: 3/5, C: 11/40. Cost = £47.30 per ton. When costs change, cost = £49 per ton (where proportions are A: 9/10, B: 0, C: 1/10).

Chapter 3

Exercises 3.1

1 (a) Maximise
Subject to the constraints:

$R = 60x + 75y$
$4x + 3y \leqslant 360$
$2x + y \leqslant 160$
$2x + 3y \leqslant 300$
$2x \leqslant 140$
$x \geqslant 0, y \geqslant 0$

(b) The initial tableau is

x	y	s_1	s_2	s_3	s_4	R	Quantity
4	3	1	0	0	0	0	360
2	1	0	1	0	0	0	160
2	3	0	0	1	0	0	300
2	0	0	0	0	1	0	140
-60	-75	0	0	0	0	1	0

The initial feasible solution is $x = 0, y = 0, s_1 = 360, s_2 = 160, s_3 = 300, s_4 = 140, f = 0$

(c) The subsequent tableaux are

x	y	s_1	s_2	s_3	s_4	f	Quantity
2	0	1	0	-1	0	0	60
4/3	0	0	1	$-1/3$	0	0	60
2/3	1	0	0	1/3	0	0	100
2	0	0	0	0	1	0	140
-10	0	0	0	25	0	1	7500

x	y	s_1	s_2	s_3	s_4	f	Quantity
1	0	1/2	0	$-1/2$	0	0	30
0	0	$-2/3$	1	1/3	0	0	20
0	1	$-1/3$	0	2/3	0	0	80
0	0	-1	0	1	1	0	80
0	0	5	0	20	0	1	7800

Optimum solution is $x = 30$ units of P, $y = 80$ units of Q, $R = £7800$ (where $s_1 = 0$ hours, $s_2 = 20$ hours, $s_3 = 0$ hours, $s_4 = 80$ hours). All figures are per week.
(d) Divisions B and D have spare capacity (20 hours/week and 80 hours/week, respectively).
(e) £3750 per week.

2 Optimum solution is $x = 60$ units of P, $y = 40$ units of Q, $G = £3900$ (where $s_1 = 0$ hours, $s_2 = 0$ hours, $s_3 = 60$ hours, $s_4 = 20$ hours). All figures are per week.

3 $x_1 = 0$, $x_2 = 300$, $x_3 = 50$, $s_1 = 200$, $s_2 = 800$, $s_3 = 0$, $s_4 = 0$, $f = 11,000$.

4 (a) Maximise $f = 13x + 20y + 12z$
   Subject to the constraints: $2x + 4y + 2z \leqslant 1000$
                                    $2x + 3y + 2z \leqslant 850$
                                    $x + 2y + 3z \leqslant 800$
                                    $x + y \leqslant 400$
                                    $x \geqslant 0, \ y \geqslant 0, \ z \geqslant 0$

(b) The initial tableau is

x	y	z	s_1	s_2	s_3	s_4	f	Quantity
2	4	2	1	0	0	0	0	1000
2	3	2	0	1	0	0	0	850
1	2	3	0	0	1	0	0	800
1	1	0	0	0	0	1	0	400
-13	-20	-12	0	0	0	0	1	0

(c) The optimum solution is $x = 200$ units of 'Standard', $y = 150$ units of 'Superior', $z = 0$ units of 'Supreme'. Maximum profit $= £5600$. $s_1 = 0$ kgs of wool, $s_2 = 0$ kgs of cotton, $s_3 = 300$ hours, $s_4 = 50$ units (spare demand). All figures are per week.

5 (a) £1 per unit   (b) $0 \leqslant C < £6$.

Exercises 3.2

1   (a) $x = 60$, $y = 30$, $s_1 = 0$, $s_2 = 30$, $s_3 = 0$, $s_4 = 40$, $s_5 = 0$, $f = 900$ where the constraints are assumed to be written as

$$2x + 6y + s_1 = 300$$
$$2x + 3y + s_2 = 240$$
$$y + s_3 = 30$$
$$x - s_4 + s_5 = 20 \qquad s_5 \text{ is an artificial variable}$$

(b) $x_1 = 30$, $x_2 = 25$, $x_3 = 0$, $s_1 = 0$, $s_2 = 0$, $s_3 = 15$, $s_4 = 0$, $s_5 = 5$, $s_6 = 0$, $f = 850$ (s_4, s_6 are artificial variables).

2   $x = 45$, $y = 20$, $s_1 = 10$, $s_2 = 0$, $s_2 = 0$, $s_4 = 0$, $s_5 = 0$, $s_6 = 0$, $f = 1700$ (s_2, s_4, s_6 are artificial variables).

3   Minimise $\qquad\qquad\qquad C = 10x + 10y$
    Subject to the constraints: $\qquad x + 3y \geqslant 18$
    $$2x + 4y \geqslant 28$$
    $$x \geqslant 3$$
    $$y \geqslant 0$$

The least-cost solution is $x = 3$ litres of X, $y = 5.5$ litres of Y, $C = £85$. ($s_1 = 1.5$ mgs of A, $s_2 = 0$, $s_3 = 0$, $s_4 = 0$, $s_5 = 0$, $s_6 = 0$, where s_2, s_4, s_6 are artificial variables.)

4   $x_1 = 15$, $x_2 = 0$, $x_3 = 10$, $s_1 = 0$, $s_2 = 0$, $s_3 = 0$, $s_4 = 0$, $s_5 = 60$, $f = 325$ (s_2 and s_4 are artificial variables).

Chapter 4

Exercises 4.1

1   (a) $\begin{pmatrix} 13 & -19 & 12 \\ -17 & 43 & -4 \end{pmatrix}$ (b) not defined   (c) $\begin{pmatrix} -33 & 41 & 20 \\ -21 & 32 & 5 \\ 0 & -13 & 17 \end{pmatrix}$

(b) $\begin{pmatrix} 21 & -6 \\ -7 & -5 \end{pmatrix}$ (e) not defined   (f) $\begin{pmatrix} -9 & 32 \\ 12 & 14 \\ -39 & 14 \end{pmatrix}$

(g) $\begin{pmatrix} -82 & 12 \\ 6 & -10 \end{pmatrix}$

Each side of the equation $(A + D)B = AB + DB$ is equal to the matrix $\begin{pmatrix} 28 & 11 \\ -30 & 18 \end{pmatrix}$

2   (a) $\begin{pmatrix} 24 & -6 \\ 1 & 5 \\ -3 & -6 \end{pmatrix}$ (b) not defined   (c) not defined

(d) $\begin{pmatrix} -11 & 6 & 11 \\ -22 & 12 & 22 \end{pmatrix}$ (e) $\begin{pmatrix} 27 & 36 \\ 81 & -36 \end{pmatrix}$

Each side of the equation $(AB)E = A(BE)$ is equal to the matrix

$$\begin{pmatrix} 26 & 28 \\ -17 & 35 \\ 20 & -47 \end{pmatrix}$$

3 (a) $\begin{pmatrix} 5 & 4 & 3 \\ 4 & 5 & 6 \\ 8 & 6 & 3 \end{pmatrix} \begin{pmatrix} 70 \\ 60 \\ 40 \end{pmatrix} = \begin{pmatrix} 710 \\ 820 \\ 1040 \end{pmatrix}$ grapes (kilos)   Input quantities

                                            sugar (kilos)   necessary to

                                            time (hours)   meet demand

(b) $(2 \quad 1.50 \quad 10) \begin{pmatrix} 5 & 4 & 3 \\ 4 & 5 & 6 \\ 8 & 6 & 3 \end{pmatrix} = (\quad 96 \quad 75.50 \quad 45 \quad)$

                                                    Sup.   Spec.   Ord.

                             costs per gallon of wine (£)

(c) $(2 \quad 1.50 \quad 10) \begin{pmatrix} 710 \\ 820 \\ 1040 \end{pmatrix} = (13,050)$ total cost (£) of

                                                             meeting demand

$(96 \quad 75.50 \quad 45) \begin{pmatrix} 70 \\ 60 \\ 40 \end{pmatrix} = (13,050)$

4 (a) $(40 \quad 50 \quad 30) \begin{pmatrix} 6 & 10 & 7 \\ 4 & 16 & 4 \\ 9 & 20 & 9 \end{pmatrix} = (\quad 710 \quad 1800 \quad 750 \quad)$

                                                     Seed   Fert.   Pest.

                                               (bags)   (tons)   (drums)

These are the input quantities to meet demand for the present year.

(b) $\begin{pmatrix} 6 & 10 & 7 \\ 4 & 16 & 4 \\ 9 & 20 & 9 \end{pmatrix} \begin{pmatrix} 30 & 4 \\ 20 & 10 \\ 25 & 6 \end{pmatrix} - \begin{pmatrix} 555 & 166 \\ 540 & 200 \\ 895 & 290 \end{pmatrix}$ Wheat   total

                                                       Corn   costs

                                                    Barley   (£/acre)

                                    prod.   del.

5 (a) $\begin{array}{c} \\ A \\ B \end{array} \begin{array}{ccc} X & Y & Z \\ \left(54\right. & 26 & 20 \\ \left.62\right. & 18 & \left.20\right) \end{array}$ quantities of X, Y, Z in gms/pack

(b) $(286,000 \quad 114,000 \quad 100,000)$ quantities in gms required

         X   Y   Z   to fulfill order

(c) $\begin{array}{c} A \\ B \end{array} \begin{pmatrix} 60 \\ 60 \end{pmatrix}$ costs per pack in pence

6   $AB = \begin{pmatrix} 15 & 30 & 40 \\ 20 & 0 & 30 \\ 20 & 25 & 0 \end{pmatrix} \begin{pmatrix} 4 & 3 & 6 \\ 7 & 5 & 4 \\ 3 & 8 & 3 \end{pmatrix} = \begin{array}{c} \\ P1 \\ P2 \\ P3 \end{array} \begin{array}{ccc} F1 & F2 & F3 \\ \left(390\right. & 515 & 330 \\ 170 & 300 & 210 \\ \left.255\right. & 185 & \left.220\right) \end{array}$

These are the total delivery costs (in £), if each factory supplies *all* of one type of pump to the customers. It is therefore cheapest if F3 supplies all of P1, F1 all of P2, and F2 all of P3.

Exercises 4.2

1 (a) $\begin{pmatrix} 3 & 4 \\ 2 & 5 \end{pmatrix} \begin{pmatrix} x \\ y \end{pmatrix} = \begin{pmatrix} 6 \\ 4 \end{pmatrix}$

(b) $A^{-1} = \dfrac{1}{7} \begin{pmatrix} 5 & -4 \\ -2 & 3 \end{pmatrix}$ The equations have solution $x = 2, y = 0$

2 (a) $\begin{pmatrix} -5 & 7 \\ 2 & -4 \end{pmatrix} \begin{pmatrix} x \\ y \end{pmatrix} = \begin{pmatrix} 6 \\ 12 \end{pmatrix}$

(b) $A^{-1} = \dfrac{1}{6} \begin{pmatrix} -4 & -7 \\ -2 & -5 \end{pmatrix}$ The equations have solution $x = -18, y = -12$

3 (a) $(50 \quad 40 \quad 30) \begin{pmatrix} 1 & 2 & 1 \\ 1 & 1 & 2 \\ 3 & 0 & 1 \end{pmatrix} = (180 \quad 140 \quad 160)$
$$ C1 \quad\;\; C2 \quad\; C3$$
$$ \text{tons produced}$$

(b) $(x \quad y \quad z) \begin{pmatrix} 1 & 2 & 1 \\ 1 & 1 & 2 \\ 3 & 0 & 1 \end{pmatrix} = (600 \quad 300 \quad 500)$

Therefore

$(x \quad y \quad z) = (600 \quad 300 \quad 500) \, A^{-1}$

$$= \frac{1}{8} (600 \quad 300 \quad 500) \begin{pmatrix} 1 & -2 & 3 \\ 5 & -2 & -1 \\ -3 & 6 & -1 \end{pmatrix}$$

$$= (75 \quad 150 \quad 125) \qquad \begin{array}{l} \text{hours required in} \\ \text{each factory} \end{array}$$
$$ F1 \quad\; F2 \quad\;\; F3$$

4   $BA = \dfrac{1}{3} \begin{pmatrix} 6 & 4 & -3 \\ 0 & 3 & 0 \\ 0 & 0 & 3 \end{pmatrix}$ errors in B must be in the first row

$AB = \dfrac{1}{3} \begin{pmatrix} 3 & 6 & -4 \\ 0 & 6 & -2 \\ 0 & 0 & 3 \end{pmatrix}$ errors in B must be in the second and third columns

The correct inverse is

$A^{-1} = \dfrac{1}{3} \begin{pmatrix} 5 & -7 & -1 \\ -3 & 6 & 0 \\ 1 & -2 & 1 \end{pmatrix}$ corrected values are hightlighted

The required monthly outputs of the three machines are

(200   300   100)
Econ.   Sup.   Spec.

5 $x = 4/3$, $y = -10/3$, $z = 1/3$

6 $BA = \begin{pmatrix} 1 & 0 & 0 \\ 0 & 2 & 0 \\ 0 & 0 & 3 \end{pmatrix}$ B is not the inverse of A but can be used in the same way to solve the equations

   $x = 2$, $y = 3$, $z = 5$.

7 $r = 5x + 26y - 3z$, $s = 7y - 6z$, $t = 4x - 10y$

Exercises 4.3

1 A 3/4, B 1/4

2 (a) $\begin{pmatrix} 520 \\ 380 \end{pmatrix} \begin{matrix} A \\ B \end{matrix}$ purchasers for first week $\begin{pmatrix} 568 \\ 332 \end{pmatrix} \begin{matrix} A \\ B \end{matrix}$ purchasers for second week

   (b) A 2/3, B 1/3

3 (a) $\begin{pmatrix} 1780 \\ 830 \\ 690 \end{pmatrix} \begin{matrix} X \\ Y \\ Z \end{matrix}$ purchasers for first year $\begin{pmatrix} 1624 \\ 852 \\ 824 \end{pmatrix} \begin{matrix} X \\ Y \\ Z \end{matrix}$ purchasers for second year

   (b) X 1/2, Y 1/4, Z 1/4

4 (a) $\begin{pmatrix} 1260 \\ 460 \\ 1580 \end{pmatrix} \begin{matrix} X \\ Y \\ Z \end{matrix}$ purchasers for first year $\begin{pmatrix} 1416 \\ 408 \\ 1476 \end{pmatrix} \begin{matrix} X \\ Y \\ Z \end{matrix}$ purchasers for second year

   (b) X 1/2, Y 1/10, Z 2/5

5 The steady—state equation is

$$\begin{pmatrix} 0.2 & 0.4 & 0.4 \\ 0.4 & 0.2 & 0.2 \\ 0.4 & 0.4 & 0.4 \end{pmatrix} \begin{pmatrix} x \\ y \\ z \end{pmatrix} = \begin{pmatrix} x \\ y \\ z \end{pmatrix}$$

   The proportions are X 1/3, Y 4/15, Z 2/5.

6 (a) The transition table is

		From		
		X	Y	Z
	X	0.5	0.4	0.2
To	Y	0.3	0.5	0.4
	Z	0.2	0.1	0.4

   (b) X 2/5, Y 2/5, Z 1/5.
   (c) The proportions are now Y 2/7, Z 3/14. $p = 4/35$.

Chapter 5

Exercises 5.1

1 (a) £1420 (b) £1720   The required time for (a) is 15 years.

2 (a) £2012.52 (b) £2035.06 (c) £2055.06
   For (a) and (b), 11 years and 10.5 years are required, respectively.

3 £2655.46   4 £1477.33

5 (a) £1303.12 (b) 9.9% p.a.

6 £399.28   7 £1450, 12% p.a.

Exercises 5.2

1 (a) £5096.01 (b) £2475.13 (c) 16.8% p.a.

2 (a) 5.9 years (b) 8.7% p.a.

3 416.9 hours   4 5.1 days

Exercises 5.3

1 (a) £18,444.63 (b) £14,218.51

2 (a) £867,706.86 (b) £70,547.03 p.a.

3 (a) 5 years (b) 6.5 years

4 (a) £1737.73 p.a. (b) £1726.16 p.a.

5 Increase of £74.16 per half year

6 £16,640   7 £46,000, 14 years

Chapter 6

Exercises 6.1

1 (a) A: £1089.04, B: £1230.83, C: £738.09

2 £20,641.67 (hiring), £21,813.95 (buying). Cheaper to hire.

3 (a) £11,774.69 (b) £24,822.53

4 N.P.V. of outflows is £258,489.58, £251,463.16 for first and second alternatives, respectively. Second alternative is cheapest.

5 £102,181.94   6 £19,400.44

Exercises 6.2

1 (a) £139.44 (b) 18% p.a.

2 (a) 23% p.a. (b) 23.4% p.a.

3 (a) 32% p.a. (b) 32.1% p.a.

4 (a) £20,540.16 (b) 20% p.a.

Exercises 6.3

1   (a) £800   (b) £1126.00

2   (a)(i) £400 p.a.   (ii) 23.53% p.a.
    (b) £1800 (straight-line method) and £1341.51

3   A has N.P.V. of inflows £1939.42 and B £1880.91. A is preferred.

4   (a) £8394.32   (b) 21.81% p.a.

Exercises 6.4

1   £2263.21

2   (a)(i) £1629.64 p.a., £135.80 p.m.   (ii) £13,435.14

3   £310.86   4   £13,853.84 p.a.

5   (a) £116,849.57   (b) 15th month

6   A: £637.50, B: −£334.52 (written-down value for B is £2655.81). A is better.

7   (a) £435.97 p.a.   (b) 7 years

8   10 instalments of £300, final payment of £179.70.

Chapter 7

Exercises 7.1

1   (a) $C = 30x + 9000$, $R = 60x$, $G = 30x - 9000$
    (b),(c) Break-even at 300 tons/week
    (d),(e) 500 tons/week   (f) Increase of £15/ton

2   (a)(i) 20 units/week   (ii) 25 and 45 units/week   (iii) 35 units/week
    (b) 20 units/week, £375/unit.

3   (a) 40 units/week, £7600/week   (b) 80 units/week
    (c) 10.2 and 156.4 units/week   (d) 60 and 80 units/week
    (e) $a = -1.75$, $b = 260$.

4   (a) $C = 30x + 2800$ (b) $p = 210 - 2x$, $R = 210x - 2x^2$, outputs are 15 and 90 units/week
    (d) 35 and 55 units/week. Prices are £140/unit and £100/unit, respectively.
    (e) Outputs as in (d).

5   (a) $R = 270x - 3x^2$ (b) 15 and 45 units/week
    (c) 25 and 60 units/week   (d) 50 and 54 units/week

6   $p = 140 + 12x - 0.2x^2$,   demand $= 65$ units/week   at   £75/unit. $C = 5x + 9450$,
    $R = 140x + 12x^2 - 0.2x^3$, $G = 135x + 12x^2 - 0.2x^3 - 9450$

7   5 units/week, £90.25/unit.

Exercises 7.2

1   (a) $x_s = 12p + 250$ (b) 58.80/unit, 955.6 units/week

2   (a) £25/unit, 600 units   (b)(i) $x_d = 140 - 1.5p$ (hundreds of packets)
    (b)(ii) 20 pence/packet, 11,000 packets/week

3   (a) $x_s = 0.2p^2 + 1760$ (b) £20/unit, 1840 units/week

4   (a) £10/unit, 280 units/week   (b) $a = 6$

5   (b) £15/unit, 775 units/month.

Chapter 8

Exercises 8.1

1
x	R	Δx	ΔR	$\Delta R / \Delta x$
15	525			
14.5	514.75	−0.5	−10.25	20.50
14.8	520.96	−0.2	− 4.04	−20.20
14.9	522.99	−0.1	− 2.01	20.10
14.96	524.1984	−0.04	− 0.8016	20.04

Estimate for dR/dx is £20/unit, when $x = 15$.

2   (a) $18x^2 - 3$ (b) $32x^3 - 10x^4 + 6x$
   (c) $2x^3 - 2x^5 - 6/x^4 - 6$ (d) $\frac{5}{8}x^{3/2} - \frac{2}{3}x^{-2/3} + 5$

   (e) $\dfrac{2}{3\sqrt[3]{x}} - 5$ (f) $\frac{7}{2}(\sqrt[4]{x})^3$ (g) $-\dfrac{4}{3x^2} + 20x$

3   (a) $5x^4 + 12x^3 - 12x^2$ (b) $16x^3 + 40x$ (c) $8x^7 - 8x^3$

   (d) $4x - \dfrac{9}{x^4}$ (e) $14x^{5/2} - 3 + x^{-1/2}$

4   (a) $10x$ (b) $18x^2$ (c) $-1/x^2$

5   (a) M.C. $= 4q + 100$, M.R. $= -q^2 + 34q + 1100$, M.G. $= -q^2 + 30q + 1000$
   (b) M.C. $=$ £260 per acre, M.R. $=$ £860 per acre, M.G. $=$ £600 per acre.
   Approximate increase in revenue $=$ £172.   (c) 30 acres.

6   (a)
x	C	Δx	ΔC	$\Delta C / \Delta x$
5	13300			
5.2	13320.32	0.2	20.32	101.60
5.1	13310.08	0.1	10.08	100.80
5.04	13304.0128	0.04	4.0128	100.32
5.01	13301.0008	0.01	141.0008	100.08

Estimate for dC/dx is £100/unit, when $x = 5$.
   (b) M.C. $= 16x + 20$, M.R. $= 1500 - 6x^2$
   (c) £340 per ton   (d) 12 tons/day

7   (b)(i) $dR/dx =$ £60 per unit   (ii) $dR/dx = -$£100 per unit.
   (d) M.C. $= 50$, M.G. $= 130 - 4x$
   (e) Both rates of increase are £50 per unit.   (f) $a = 3$

Exercises 8.2

1   (a) 60 units/week, £7200 per week.
   (b) 46 units/week, £2890 per week.
   (c) Reduction of £1354.90 in weekly profit (average cost minimised at 69.28 units/week).

2 (a) $p = 60 - 0.25x$
(b) At 50 units/week, maximum profit = £200 per day. At this output level, M.C. = M.R. = £35 per unit
(c) £350 per day

3 (a) 25 units/week, £3031.25 per week
(b) 15.54 units/week, £90.41 per unit.

4 40 units/week, £40 per unit.

5 (a) 67.16 units/month (b) As in (a) (c) £14,483.97 per month
(d) 33.33 units/month
(e) 10 units/month and 100 units/month (by trial and error).
(f) 10 units/month
(g) Increase in profit of £3000 per month.

6 4 thousand units per annum.

7 $C = 0.4x^2 + 20x + 850$

8 For first function, (2, 5) is a minimum point and (−1, 32) is a maximum point.
For second function, (0, −10) is a minimum point and (1.5, −6.625) is a point of inflexion.
For third function, (0, 20) is a minimum point and (−2, 36) is a maximum point.

Exercises 8.3

1 (a) $E_D = -\dfrac{10p}{500 - 10p}$ for original product $E_D = -\dfrac{0.5p^2}{400 - 0.25p^2}$ for modified product

(b)(i) $E_D = -0.25$ for original product, and $E_D = -0.13$ for modified product. The response of demand to change in price is therefore half what it was.
(ii) $E_D = -1.5$ for original product, and $E_D = -2.6$ for modified product. The response of demand to change in price is almost twice what it was.

2 (a) $E_D = -\dfrac{p}{180 - 3p}$

(b)(i) $E_D = -1/3$. Demand is inelastic and revenue will increase when the price is increased.
(ii) $E_D = -5/3$. Demand is elastic and revenue will decrease when the price is increased.
(c) $R = 60x - 0.12x^4$. At maximum revenue, $x = 5$ units, and so $p = £45$ per unit, $E_D = -1$ (unitary elasticity).

3 (a) $x_s = 0.07p + 0.2$ (thousands of tonnes)
Equilibrium occurs when price = 20 pence/kg and quantity = 1600 tonnes.

(b) $E_S = \dfrac{0.07p}{0.2 + 0.07p}$ $E_D = -\dfrac{0.02p}{2 - 0.02p}$

When $p = 20$, $E_S = 0.88$ and $E_D = -0.25$. Thus, if the price changes, the response in supply is approximately 3.5 times that of demand.

4 $x = -0.1p^2 - p + 160$ (where $a = -0.1$, $b = -1$, $c = 160$). Therefore, revenue is $R = 160p - p^2 - 0.1p^3$, and revenue is maximised at a price of £20 per unit.

425

Chapter 9

Exercises 9.1

1   (a) $\frac{1}{2}x^4 - \frac{3}{2}x^2 + 6x + K$ (b) $x^6 - \frac{1}{8}x^4 - x + K$

    (c) $\frac{1}{2}x^2 - \dfrac{10}{x} + K$ (d) $2x^2 + \frac{2}{3}x^{3/2} + K$

    (e) $\frac{2}{7}x^{7/2} - \frac{4}{5}x^{5/2} + x^{3/2} + K$ (f) $\frac{2}{5}x^5 - \frac{2}{3}x^6 + \frac{3}{2}x^2 + K$

    (g) $\frac{3}{7}x^7 + \dfrac{2}{x^2} + K$ (h) $4x^{5/2} + 2x^{3/2} + K$

    (i) 32   (j) 445/6

2    $y = x^3 - \frac{2}{3}x - \dfrac{3}{x} - 4$

3   (a) 4   (b) 4/3
    (c)(i) 17/2   (ii) 10

4   1(a) $C = 2x^2 + 20x + 10500$, $R = 380x - x^2$
    (b) 60 units/week, £300 per week.
    (c) 50 units/week.

5   Profit maximized at 20 units/week. $C = 200x + 2x^2 + 6750$, $R = 800x - 3x^2 - \frac{1}{3}x^3$.
    Maximum profit = £583.33 per week.

6   Terminate 'run' after 40 hours. Profit = £149,333.33.

7   (a)(i) 32000/3   (ii) 1225
    (b)(i) 4500   (ii) 3250/3

8   Consumers' surplus = 250, producers' surplus = 1000/3.

9   Consumers' surplus = 7000/3, producers' surplus = 2312.62.

Exercises 9.2

1   (a)(i) $\partial z/\partial x = 8x^3 + 4$, $\partial z/\partial y = -\frac{3}{2}y^2 + 12y$
    (ii) $\partial z/\partial x = 3xy^4 - 9y + 36$, $\partial z/\partial y = 6x^2y^3 + 6y - 9x$,
    (iii) $\partial z/\partial x = 2xy - y^3$, $\partial z/\partial y = x^2 - 3xy^2$
    (b) $\partial u/\partial x = 15x^2z^{1/2} - 20xy^6$, $\partial u/\partial y = -60y^5x^2 + 8y^3z^3$,
    $\partial u/\partial z = \frac{5}{2}x^3z^{-1/2} + 6y^4z^2$

2   (a) $R = 420x - 10x^2 + 650y - 2y^3$, $G = 400x - 10x^2 + 600y - 2y^3 - 1000$
    (b) 20 units/week of first product, at a price of £220 per unit; 10 units/week of second
    product, at a price of £450 per unit. Profit = £7000 per week.

3   (a) $R = 56x - \frac{1}{4}x^2 + 94y - \frac{1}{2}y^2$
    $G = 56x - \frac{1}{2}x^2 + 94y - \frac{3}{2}y^2 - 4xy - 300$
    (b) 16 units/week of first product, at a price of £52 per unit; 10 units/week of second
    product, at a price of £89 per unit. Profit = £618 per week.

4    $S = 20$ sales offices, $A = £2000$ per month. Profit = £1668 per month.

5   Stationary points are $x = 0$ units, $y = 150$ units, $C = £55,500$, and $x = 90$ units, $y = 150$
    units, $C = £19,050$.

6 Stationary points are $x = 0$ Viewmaster I models/week, $y = 50$ Viewmaster II models/week, $G = -£22,500$/week, and $x = 30$ Viewmaster I models/week, $y = 50$ Viewmaster II models/week, $G = £4500$/week.

Chapter 10

Exercises 10.1

1 100 crates/order, £13,200 p.a. (based upon $d = 800$, $f = 25$, $p = 16$, $h = 4$).

2 300 tons/order, every 6.5 weeks, at a cost of £180,200 p.a. (based upon $d = 2400$, $f = 450$, $p = 70$, $h = 24$).

3 (a) 400 tents/order, £162,000 p.a.   (b) £159,562.50

4 £162,400 p.a. (batch ordering), £134,000 p.a. (batch production).

Exercises 10.2

1 (a) 600 items/order (at 8% discount), cost = £23,523 p.a. (Alternative costs are £24,300 p.a., at non-discount, and £23,802 p.a. at 4% discount.)
(b) 60 items/order. (Costs are £24,300 p.a., £24,602 p.a. and £25,923 p.a. for non-discount, 4% discount and 8% discount cases, respectively.)

2 (a) 3000 metres/order (at 5% discount), cost = £118,200 p.a. Orders placed every 3 months. Reorder level is 2000 metres. (The alternative cost, at non-discount, is £123,000 p.a.)
(b) Discount of at least 8.25% on cost price.

3 800 items/order, cost – £15,617 p.a. (Alternative costs are £18,240 p.a., at non-discount, and £16,427.68 p.a. at 10% discount.)

Exercises 10.3

1 (a) 60 pumps/order
(b) Reorder level is 80 pumps from the following table:

Reorder level	Safety stock	Annual cost of holding safety stock	Expected shortfall per lead time	Expected annual cost of shortfalls	Additional cost of safety stock and shortfall
50	0	0	8.8	440	440
60	10	40	4.9	245	285
70	20	80	2.5	125	205
80	30	120	1.1	55	175*
90	40	160	0.4	20	180

(c) £12,415 p.a.

2 (a) 40 motors   (b) 149 motors/order

3 Order quantity is 40 tons/order, reorder level 50 tons, and cost £66,069 p.a.

Chapter 11

Exercises 11.3

1 (a) Two questions in one. Also the use of the word 'like' is subject to different interpretations.
(b) Not everyone will know that the abbreviation PAYE will stand for tax deductions Pay As You Earn.
(c) Not everyone will know how much alcohol is in a given drink. It is best to question how many glasses of wine, for example, or how many pints of beer during a specified period.
(d) Everyone eats healthy food, otherwise they would die. The word 'healthy' is being used here in a perjorative sense. The question should be phrased to find out how much fresh food is consumed as opposed to pre-prepared food at which it is assumed the question is aiming.
(e) Does everybody go to bed at the same time every day?
(f) Asking questions requiring a memory of events over an extended time in the past results in unreliable answers.
(g) What is meant by the word 'good' and to what level of statistical knowledge is the question aimed?
(h) Two questions in one coupled with the assumption that there is no alternative to the two choices given.
(i) A leading question attempting to elicit the answer yes.

2 (a) A space for the respondent to enter a single number.
(b) A list of options such as: Every Day, Occasionally, Rarely, Never.
(c) A graded scale ranging from 0 to 100 with a request to mark the number on it.
(d) Do you eat sweets: Every Day, Occasionally, Rarely, Never.
(e) Best to break the question into a collection of questions each one querying a particular facet such as the Prime Minister's effectiveness, leadership, commitment, etc., each followed by a Yes/No option.
(f) On a scale of 1 to 10.

Exercises 11.5

1
Datum	0	3	4	5	6	7	8	9	10	
Frequency	6	9	3	7	7	3	6	3	8	Total 52

2
Group	0–29.99	30.00–59.99	60.00–89.99	90.00–119.99	
Frequency	14	22	10	2	Total 48

Chapter 12

Exercises 12.1

1
	Median	A-mean	G-mean	H-mean
(a)	16	56.78	16	4.52
(b)	0	0	3.2	*
(c)	15	17.73	12.71	8.32
(d)	2.5	3.21	*	−9.89

* Not defined

Exercises 12.2

1 (a) 4   (b) 5.06 to 2 dec. pl.   (c) 15.35 to 2 dec. pl.

2 (a) 128.25 and 11.32 to 2 dec. pl.
   (b) 166.67 and 12.91 to 2 dec. pl.
   (c) 354.86 and 18.84 to 2 dec.pl.

3 (a) 477 to nearest unit
   (b) 128.42 and 147.80 to 2 dec. pl.
   (c)(i) 63%, 65%, 65%, 68%, 70%   (ii) 66%

4 (a) 00 : 05 : 45 and 39 seconds to nearest second
   (b) 1.53
   (c) 3 times

Exercises 12.3

1 (a) 8, 27, 9.5
   (b) 9, 42, 16.5
   (c) 18, 43.5, 12.75

2 (a) 6, 3
   (b)(i) 292   (ii) 5.62   (iii) 9.43, 3.07 each to 2 dec.pl.
   (d)(i) 2.5   (ii) 7.8   (iii) 2.7 each approx.

3 (b) 45.42, 23.18 to 2 dec.pl.
   (d) 42 approx.
   (f)(i) 53   (ii) 60   (iii) 95 each approx.

Chapter 13

Exercises 13.1

3 (a)(ii) £1361.50
   (b)(ii) 108, 115: 107, 116 each to 3 sig.fig.

Exercises 13.2

2 Laspeyre 104.70, Paasche 104.64

Exercises 13.3

2 100, 95.1, 93.1, 89.7, 94.4, 98.2, 99.5

Chapter 14

Exercises 14.1

1 (a)(i) 51   (ii) 109   (iii) −7
   (b)(i) 10.5   (ii) 16.8   (iii) 1.0

2 (c)(i) −25   (ii) 40
   (d)(i) −4   (ii) 6

Exercises 14.2

1 (b) 0.96
   (c) $y = 0.92x + 3.98$
   (d) 2.57 to 2 dec.pl.
   (e) 27 to 2 sig.fig.   (All calculations to 2 dec. pl. only.)

2   (b) 0.89 to 2 dec.pl.
    (c) 12

Exercises 14.3

1   (b) 0.899 to 3 dec.pl.
    (d) $y = 5.53x + 83.14$
    (e) 0.069 to 3 dec.pl.
    (f) 172 to 3 sig.fig.

2   (c) $T = 100 - 0.99x^2$
    (e) 94 to 2 sig.fig.
    (f) 0.03

Chapter 15

Exercises 15.1

3   (d) -11.08, 2.92, 16.98, -8.82 to 2 dec.pl.
    (e) 46, 47
    (f) 42, 40

4   (e) -46.08, 4.92, 70.50, -29.33 to 2 dec.pl.
    (f) 133, 122

5   (d) -3.15, 8.06, -5.77, 0.85 to 2 dec.pl.

6   (b) -47.21, 34.8, 16.87, -4.27 to 2 dec.pl.

Chapter 16

Exercises 16.1

1   (a) Continuous   (b) Discrete   (c) Discrete
    (d) Continuous   (e) Continuous   (f) Discrete

2 $\{a, b, c\}$: $\{a\}$, $\{b\}$, $\{c\}$, $\{a, b\}$, $\{a, c\}$, $\{a, b, c\}$, $\{a, b, c\}$

3   (i) B (ii) A (iii) A (iv) A (v) A (vi) A'

4 $\{H, R\}$, $\{H, B\}$, $\{H, W\}$ $\{T, R\}$, $\{T, B\}$, $\{T, W\}$

6   (c)(i) 2   (ii) 5   (iii) 6
    (d) 11

7   (a)(i) 335   (ii) 120   (iii) 240
    (b)(i) 355   (ii) 55   (iii) 55

8   2

Chapter 17

Exercises 17.1

1   (a)(i) 0.25   (ii) 1/3   (iii) 0.29166...   (iv) 0.45833...
    (b)(i) 1/6   (ii) 1/3   (iii) 1/3   (iv) 1/2

2 (a)(i) 0.208   (ii) 0.820   (iii) 0.388
(b)(i) 0.39   (ii) 0.18   (iii) 0.83

3 (a)(i) 0.972   (ii) 0.342   (iii) 0.658
(b)(i) 0.388   (ii) 0.004   (iii) 0.976

Exercises 17.2

1 (a) 13/235   (b) 3/235   (c) 225/235

2 $E_1, E_2; E_1, E_3; E_1, E_4$ can be
$E_2, E_3; E_2, E_4; E_3, E_4$ cannot be

3 (a)(i) 3/16   (ii) 1/6
(b)(i) 1/2   (ii) 2/3
(c)(i) 5/8   (ii) 2/3

4 (a)(i) 215/550   (ii) 20/550   (iii) 160/310
(b) 4/3

5 (a) 53/90
(b) 76/90
(c) 12/90

6 (a) Red 2 most likely to occur
(b) Either numbered Blue or Green 1 are least likely to occur

Chapter 18

Exercises 18.1

1 (a) $Pr(R) = 1/28$, $Pr(O) = 2/28$, $Pr(Y) = 3/28$, $Pr(G) = 4/28$, $Pr(B) = 5/28$, $Pr(I) = 6/28$, $Pr(V) = 7/28$
(b) If random variable x takes on values 1 for R, 2 for Y and so on up to 7 for V then the mean value is 5 which corresponds to Blue.
(c) Standard deviation is $\sqrt{3}$ (1.73 ...) representing a range of colours starting between yellow and green and ranging up to somewhere between indigo and violet.
(d) Mean still 5 but now corresponds to Yellow. Standard deviation still $\sqrt{3}$ but range of colours starting between red and orange and ranging to somewhere between blue and green.

2 (a) $Pr(1) = 0.172$, $Pr(2) = 0.440$, $Pr(3) = 0.208$, $Pr(4) = 0.121$, $Pr(5) = 0.052$,
$Pr(6) = 0.007$ to 3 dec.pl.
(b)(i) 0.82   (ii) 0.941   (iii) 0.388
(c)(i) 2.462   (ii) 1.110

3 (a) $Pr(1) = 0.004$, $Pr(2) = 0.020$, $Pr(3) = 0.318$, $Pr(4) = 0.270$, $Pr(5) = 0.384$,
$Pr(6) = 0$, $Pr(7) = 0.004$ to 3 dec.pl.
(b)(i) 0.608   (ii) 0.612   (iii) 0.658
(c)(i) 4.026   (ii) 0.924

Exercises 18.2

1 (a)(i) 0.006   (ii) 0.873   (iii) 0.127
(b) 1.25, 1.410

431

2   (a)(i) 0.138   (ii) 0.443   (iii) 0.998
      (b)(i) 0.375   (ii) 0.120

Exercises 18.3

1   (a) 0.205   (b) 0.262   (c) 0.993

2   (a) 0.951   (b) 0.99999   (c) 9.8506×10^{-6}

Exercises 18.4

1   Yes. If the mean of the given distribution, 2.03, is used for X then the corresponding values of the Poisson distribution are: 0.13, 0.27, 0.27, 0.18, 0.09, 0.04 which are close to the values given.

2   (a) 0.741
      (b) 0.996
      (c) 0.004

3   (a) 0.223
      (b) 0.126
      (c) 0.187

Chapter 19

Exercises 19.1

1   (a) 0.427   (b) 0.141   (c) 0.840
      (d) 0.218   (e) 0.005   (f) 0.986
      (g) 0.953

2   (a)(i) 0.5   (ii) 0.184   (iii) 0.027   (iv) 0.027   (v) 0.628

3   (a) 6%   (b) 78.2%   (c) £809.60
      (d) 9.8%   (e) 0.079

4   (a) Approximately zero   (b) 82%   (c) £159.44

5   (a)(i) 0.692   (ii) 0.998   (iii) 0.614
      (b)(i) 996.48   (ii) 1437.12   (iii) 884.16

6   (a) 0.209   (b) 1263   (c) 8.55 years

Chapter 20

Exercises 20.2

1   (a) Mean = 5, Standard deviation = 2.94 to 2 dec.pl.

2   (a) Yes
      (b) No

3   (a) 100
      (b) A sample of size 9 produces a standard deviation that is 11.11% of the population standard deviation. A sample of size 10 (the entire population) gives the population standard deviation.

Exercises 20.3

1 (a)(i) 0.832   (ii) 0.993
   (b)(i) 0.548   (ii) To the accuracy of the tables, all of them

2 (a)(i) 0.912   (ii) 0.189
   (b)(i) 0.568   (ii) 0.591

3 (a) 0.233   (b) 0.641   (c) 0.126

Exercises 20.4

1 (a) 0.174
   (b) 0.921
   (c)(i) 0.681   (ii) 0.681

2 (a) 0.692   (b) 0.337

3 (a) 0.236   (b) 0.832

4 (a) 0.997   (b) 0.982   (c) 0.997   (d) 0.082

Exercises 20.5

1 (a) (i) $14.50 < \mu < 15.50$
        (ii) $14.18 < \mu < 15.82$
        (iii) $14.00 < \mu < 16.00$
        (iv) $13.84 < \mu < 16.16$
   (b) (i) $14.66 < \mu < 15.34$, 50.4%
        (ii) $14.36 < \mu < 15.64$, 80%
        (iii) $14.02 < \mu < 15.98$, 95%
        (iv) $13.71 < \mu < 16.29$, 99%

2 (a) $54 < \mu < 61.7$

3 (b) $29\% < \mu < 51\%$ (c) $398 < \mu < 502$

4 (a) 29.21   (b) 0.199, $28.82 < \mu < 29.60$
   (d) $£1.90 < \mu < £1.95$

Chapter 21

Exercises 21.2

1 (b) Significant
   (d) A: $15,357 < \mu < 16,043$, B: $14,160 < \mu < 14,840$
   (e) Yes

2 (a) No   (b) No

3 (a) Yes   (b) No

Exercises 21.3

1 (b)(i) 0.13   (ii) 0.05

2 (a) 4%   (b) 92%   (c) 8%   (d) 92%

3 (a) Yes   (b) Yes

INDEX